Cakes And Treats For Special Occasions

Decorator's Mini Course

Products

For licensing information, see Party Theme Index (p.106)

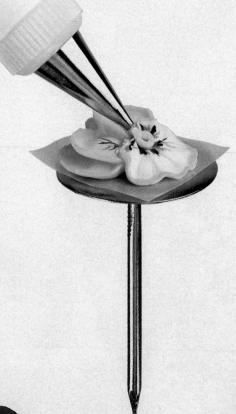

WILTON Cake Decorating!
1997 YEARBOOK

Creative Director
Richard Tracy

Cake Designer
Steve Rocco

Senior Cake Decorator
Susan Matusiak

Cake Decorators
Mary Gavenda
Corky Kagay
Nancy Suffolk Guerine
Judy Wysocki
Darcy Simenson

Editor
Jeff Shankman

Writers
Mary Enochs
Marita Seiler

Production Manager
Laura Fortin

Production Coordinator
Mary Stahulak

Cake Photography
Jeff Carter
Peter Dean Ross Photographs
Sanders Studio, Inc.

Set Designer
Jenny Nagle
Carey Thornton

Luscious Cupcakes!
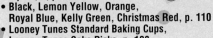
- Standard Muffin Pan, p. 165
- Tips 2, 5, p. 116-119
- Black, Lemon Yellow, Orange, Royal Blue, Kelly Green, Christmas Red, p. 110
- Looney Tunes Standard Baking Cups, Looney Tunes Cake Picks, p. 188
- Rainbow Peanut Bits Sprinkle Decorations, p. 126
- Buttercream Icing, p. 92
- Bake and cool cupcakes; ice smooth with spatula. Outline a square in center of cupcake with tip 5, fill in and smooth with finger dipped in cornstarch. Pipe tip 2 beads around square. Add sprinkles and picks.

Each serves 1.

Kookie Cookies!
- 4-Pc. Looney Tunes Cookie Cutter Set, Looney Tunes Lollipop Bags, p. 188
- No-Taste Red, Sky Blue, Orange, Violet, Lemon Yellow Icing Colors, p. 110
- Roll-Out Cookie Dough Recipe, p. 94
- Tint cookie dough, cut out cookies, bake and cool. Wrap in lollipop bags for party treats.

Each serves 1.

Looney Tunes Candy Pretzel Treats
- Looney Tunes Pretzel Candy Molds, p. 188
- Candy Melts®*- Orange, Yellow, Light Cocoa, Dark Cocoa, White, Pastel Mix, Green, Red (1 bag each needed), Decorator Brush Set, p. 120
- Disposable Decorating Bags, p. 114
- Pretzel rods

*brand confectionery coating
- Mold candy using "Painting Method" on p. 105. Fill mold, position pretzel in mold and let set until firm in refrigerator. Note: mix pink and blue melts to make gray Bugs color.

Each serves 1.

Bugs On The Run
- Bugs Bunny Pan, p. 188
- Tips 2, 3, 4, 16, 21, p. 116-117
- Black, Terra Cotta, Brown, Lemon Yellow, Violet, Christmas Red, Sky Blue, Orange Icing Colors, p. 110
- Cake Board, Fanci-Foil Wrap, p. 159
- Buttercream Icing, p. 92
- Ice sides and background areas smooth.
- Outline body and facial features with tip 4 strings. Pipe in eyes, inside ears, mouth, tongue, teeth, cuffs and pads of feet with tip 4 (smooth with finger dipped in cornstarch).
- Cover body, ears, feet, hands with tip 16 stars. Pipe tip 16 pull-out star on top of head. Add tip 2 whiskers. Pipe tip 21 bottom shell border. Edge shells with tip 3 zigzag.

Serves 12.

Starring Looney Tunes
- Star Cookie Treat Pan, p. 122
- Candy Melts*--White, Yellow, Lt. Cocoa, Dark Cocoa, Red, White, Orange (1 bag each needed), Decorator Brush Set, p. 120
- Looney Tunes Candy Molds, Looney Tunes Lollipop Bags, p. 188
- Cookie Treat Sticks, p. 122
- Cooling Rack, p. 160
- Disposable Decorating Bags, p. 114
- Mold Looney Tunes candy using "painting" method, p. 104. Refrigerate to set.
- Bake and cool cookie treat pops following recipe on pan label. Place on rack over drip pan, cover with melted candy and position Looney Tunes candy.

Each serves 1.

Looney Tunes Ideas!

Twirlin' Tweety

- 8 in. Round Pan, p. 164
- Sylvester and Tweety Mini Pan, 10 Pc. Looney Tunes Candle Holder Set, p. 188
- Tips 1, 2, 3, 7, 789, p. 116-119
- No-Taste Red, Black, Orange, Lemon Yellow, Golden Yellow, Violet, Royal Blue Icing Colors, p. 110
- Decorating Triangle, p. 160
- '97 Pattern Book (Tweety Hand Pattern), p. 108
- Cake Boards, Fanci-Foil Wrap, p. 159
- 4 in. Lollipop Sticks, p. 121
- Candy Melts®*, Yellow (1 pkg. needed), p. 120
- 56 Pc. Make Any Message Letter Press Set, p. 113
- Buttercream Icing, p. 92
- Thin candy sticks, waxed paper

*brand confectionery coating

- Using melted candy mold candy plaque Tweety head (see p. 104). Refrigerate to set and unmold. Attach lollipop stick to back of head using melted candy; let set. Using buttercream icing, outline Tweety facial features with tip 1 and pipe in using tip 3. Make a cone hat using Fanci-Foil Wrap, attach to head with dots of icing. Pipe tip 2 pull-out dot pom-pom and brim fringe. Coat candy sticks with melted candy, let set. Using cut bag, melted candy and Pattern, pipe two Tweety Hands on waxed paper. When set, peel off paper and attach candy hands to ends of coated candy sticks with dots of melted candy. Set all aside.
- Ice 2-layer cake smooth. Mark 2 3/4 in. center circle on cake top; ice in blue. Comb around circle using Decorating Triangle.
- Pipe tip 789 smooth side up band at bottom border. Using tip 2, outline and pipe in triangles on band; trim one edge with line. Edge top of band with tip 2 beads. Using individual letters from Make Any Message Letter Press Set, imprint message, outline using tip 2.
- Pipe tip 7 bead bottom border; edge beads with tip 2 strings. Add tip 3 double bead top border. Pipe tip 3 beads around circle on cake top.
- Insert Tweety head and arms into cake top. Position candles.

Serves 12.

Quick As A Bugs Bunny

- 8 in. Square Pan, p. 164
- Bugs Bunny Candle, p. 188
- Alphabet/Numerals Icing Decorations, p. 126
- Cake Board, Fanci-Foil Wrap, p. 159
- Buttercream Icing, p. 92
- Jelly rings, candy-coated chocolate dots

- Spatula ice 2-layer cake.
- Position candy-coated chocolate dots 1/2 in. from edge on cake top. Add Icing Decoration message.
- Cut jelly rings in half and place at bottom border. Attach candy-coated chocolate dots to every other ring using dots of icing. Position candle.

Serves 16.

4

Looney Tunes Brownies
- 9 x 13 in. Sheet Pan, p. 161
- Candy Melts®*- White (1 bag needed), 4 Pc. Candy Colors Set, p. 120
- Disposable Decorating Bags, p. 114
- Looney Tunes Icing Decorations, p. 188
- Brownie mix or favorite brownie recipe, favorite chocolate fudge icing recipe

*brand confectionery coating

- Bake and cool brownies. Ice with chocolate icing.
- Divide Candy Melts into four equal portions, melt and color with candy colors. Place melted candy in cut disposable bags and make drizzle design on brownies. Cut brownies; position icing decorations.

Each serves 1.

Taz Has A Surprise!
- Tasmanian Devil Cake Pan, p. 188
- Tips 1, 2, 2B, 3, 4, 6, 7, 9, 16, 21, p. 116-117
- Black, Brown, Christmas Red, Lemon Yellow, Creamy Peach, Royal Blue, Leaf Green Icing Colors, p. 110
- Cake Board, Fanci-Foil Wrap, p. 159
- Buttercream Icing, p. 92
- Sugar ice cream cone

- Ice cake sides, background and package areas smooth. Outline body, facial features and package with tip 3 strings. Pipe in tip 9 nose and eyes (smooth with finger dipped in cornstarch). Pipe in tip 7 ears and whites of eyes (smooth with finger dipped in cornstarch). Add tip 6 dot pupils. Cover face and body with tip 16 stars.
- Pipe in mouth with tip 3 and add tip 2 outline and dot whiskers. Pipe tip 2B smooth side up ribbon and bow. Add tip 3 dots. Outline and fill-in card on package with tip 3 (smooth with finger dipped in cornstarch). Write tip 1 message. Add tip 21 shell bottom border.
- **For party hat:** Carefully cut bottom 2 inches from cone. Ice smooth. Add tip 4 dots on hat and cake. Position on cake and add tip 2 pull-out fringe on hat and streamers on cake.

Serves 12.

Marvin Conquers The Cake!
- 6 in. x 3 in.; 8 in. Ovencraft™ Round Pan, p. 161
- Tips 1, 2, 8, 13, p. 116-117
- Kelly Green, Royal Blue, Golden Yellow, Lemon Yellow, Black Icing Colors, p. 110
- '97 Pattern Book (Lunar Surface Pattern), p. 108
- Marvin The Martian Candle, p. 188
- Cake Boards, Fanci-Foil Wrap, p. 159
- Buttercream Icing, p. 92

- Ice 1-layer 6 in. cake smooth. Trace Lunar Surface Pattern with toothpick. Outline pattern in black with tip 2. Fill in Golden Yellow areas of rocks with tip 1 (smooth with finger dipped in cornstarch). Cover remainder of rocks with tip 13 stars (mix Golden Yellow and Lemon Yellow). Pipe tip 13 stars in sky and tip 1 planets and dots.
- Ice 1-layer 8 in. cake: Ice smooth name area, ice rest of cake fluffy. Pipe tip 8 bead bottom border. Edge beads with tip 2 zigzags; pipe diagonal zigzags and dot over alternating beads. Print tip 2 name. Position candle.

Serves 12.

LOONEY TUNES, characters, names, and all related indicia are trademarks of Warner Bros. ©1996.

Tall For His Age!
- Partysaurus Pan, p. 168
- Tips 2, 4, 5, 9, 12, 16, 21, p. 116-119
- Kelly Green, Royal Blue, Brown, Lemon Yellow, Orange, Christmas Red Icing Colors, p. 110
- '97 Pattern Book (Giraffe Pattern), p. 108
- Cake Board, Fanci-Foil Wrap, p. 159
- Buttercream Icing, p. 92
- Candy sticks, giant red gumballs

- Ice cake smooth. Mark pattern with toothpick. Build up ears and legs with tip 12. Outline giraffe with tip 4 strings (do not outline color spots).
- Pipe in tip 5 eyes and tip 4 nostrils (smooth both with finger dipped in cornstarch).
- Cover cake with tip 16 stars Add tip 9 pull-out mane and tail. Print tip 2 name.
- Outline number with tip 2 and pipe in with tip 5. Pipe tip 21 star bottom border.
- Insert candy sticks into gumballs and position in cake for horns.

Serves 12.

THE SMASH CAKE TRADITION...
The smash cake is given to the birthday child at the first milestone celebration, to be smashed, smeared, enjoyed and eaten (remember to take lots of photos for the album!). The main cake is then enjoyed, untouched by little hands, by your guests.

Note: Some colors may stain fabrics.

A Smashing Success
- 4 Pc. Sports Ball Pan Set, p. 168
- Tips 1A, 2, 2A, 5, 16, 18, p. 116-119
- Lemon Yellow, Christmas Red, Kelly Green, Orange, Royal Blue, Brown, p. 110
- '97 Pattern Book (Smash Face Pattern), p. 108
- Buttercream Icing, p. 92
- Sugar ice cream cones

- Spatula ice half ball cake. Trace pattern with toothpick. Ice mouth area smooth; using tip 5, outline mouth and pipe dot teeth. Smooth and shape with finger dipped in cornstarch. Add tip 2 message.
- Pipe tip 1A dot eyes; add tip 5 dot pupils. Pipe tip 2A dot cheeks and nose. Shape and smooth with finger dipped in cornstarch.
- Cover ice cream cone with tip 18 stars. Position cone in cake. Add tip 16 star details and pull-out star pom-pom. Add tip 18 pull-out star fringe.

Serves 5.

Character Cupcakes
- Standard Muffin Pan, p. 165
- Tips 2F, 4, p. 116-119
- 6 Pc. Sesame Street Cookie Cutter Set, p. 189
- Brown, Copper (Lt. Skintone), Christmas Red, Pink, Black, Teal, Lemon Yellow, Royal Blue, Orange Icing Colors, p. 110
- Sesame Street Baking Cups, p. 189
- Decorator Brush Set, p. 120
- 4 in. Lollipop Sticks, p. 121
- Roll-Out Cookie Dough, p 94
- Buttercream Icing, p. 92

- Cut cookies out of dough, bake and cool. Thin icing colors with water and paint cookies. Let dry.
- Cover cupcakes with tip 2F swirls. Attach cookies to lollipop sticks using tip 4 and buttercream. Position stick in cupcake.

Each serves 1.

Elmo Takes The Cake
- Elmo Pan, p. 189
- Tips 2, 4, 7, 11, 16, 18, 21, p. 116-119
- Orange, Royal Blue, Kelly Green, Black, Lemon Yellow, Red-Red Icing Colors, p. 110
- Cake Board, Fanci-Foil Wrap, p. 159
- Flower Spikes (1 pk. needed), p. 151
- 3 Pc. Circus Balloons Set, p. 132
- Buttercream Icing, p. 92

- Ice cake background and sides smooth.
- Using tip 4, outline hat, facial features and body and cake slice; pipe in mouth (smooth with finger dipped in cornstarch). Cover Elmo, hat and cake/crumbs with tip 16 stars. Using tip 7, pipe icing on cake, fluff with tip; pipe icing on mouth. Outline hands with tip 4; cover with tip 16 stars. Pipe tip 11 dots for white eyes and nose. Using tip 4 add dot eye centers and pipe number; shape and smooth with finger dipped in cornstarch.
- Insert flower spike in cake; place balloons in spike. Add tip 4 balloon strings. Pipe tip 18 e- motion and c-motion stars for pom-pom. Pipe tip 2 name. Add tip 21 bottom star border.

Serves 12.

Her Enchanted Celebration
- Wonder Mold Kit, p. 170
- Tips 1, 3, 16, p. 116-119
- Rose Icing Color, p. 110
- Ready-To-Use Rolled Fondant (2 pks. needed), p. 112
- '97 Pattern Book (Fairy's Clothes Patterns: Bodice, Sleeve, Crown; Wand Star), p. 108
- Teen Doll Pick, p. 132
- 12 in. Round White Doilies, p. 159
- 4 in. Lollipop Sticks, p. 121
- Buttercream Icing, p. 92
- Pink tulle, approx. 72 in. long x 6 in. wide
- Prepare cake for rolled fondant (p. 92). Tint fondant and roll eight 7 in. long x ³/₄ in. diameter logs; position vertically and space evenly around side of cake to create skirt pleats; taper at top and smooth evenly.
- Cover cake with rolled fondant. Cut fondant into ¹/₂ in. wide strips and position at bottom border. Cut bodice, 2 sleeves, crown and star using patterns. Assemble crown, using dots of water to secure ends; using buttercream, pipe tip 3 beads along peaked edge, add tip 16 fleur-de-lis. Set aside and let dry. Prepare doll pick: Secure fondant bodice to doll pick using drops of water; smooth. Roll 2 marble-size pieces of fondant, place one on each shoulder, cover with sleeve pieces. Cut v-neckline. Carefully position doll pick in cake, smooth at waistline. Cover bodice, sleeves, area from waist down and band at bottom border with tip 1 cornelli lace.
- Tie tulle around waist, knot at back; loop ends and tie a bow to create wings, knot to secure. **Make wand:** Attach fondant star to lollipop stick with dots of icing. Position wand in hand and place crown on head, securing with dots of icing, if necessary.
Serves 12.

Zap! It's A Magical Day.

Rabbit Tricks
- 6 in. Round Pan, p. 161
- Nesting Bunny Cookie Cutter Set, p. 174
- Tips 2, 3, 4, 14, 44, 45, 233, p. 116-119
- Black, Pink, Golden Yellow Icing Colors, p. 110
- 10 in. Cake Boards, Fanci-Foil Wrap, p. 159
- Cookie Treat Sticks, p. 122
- Plastic Dowel Rods, p. 156
- Meringue Powder, p. 111
- Roll-Out Cookie Dough Recipe, p. 94
- Buttercream, Chocolate Buttercream, Royal Icings, p. 92
- Candystick Candles, p. 128
- Small candy dots, jelly bean, two sandwich cookies, candy coated gum
- Bake and cool bunny cookie using largest cutter and roll-out cookie dough. Using royal icing, ice ears smooth, cover bunny with tip 233 pull-out fur. Add candy eyes, nose and teeth. Outline mouth using tip 3. Let dry. Attach cookie treat stick to back of cookie with royal icing, let dry.
- Tint chocolate buttercream with black icing color. Ice 3-layer cake smooth. Cut 4 ¹/₂ in. center hole out of two 10 in. round cake boards. Cover boards with foil and ice smooth, pipe tip 45 band around edge. Position iced board on stacked cakes. Pipe tip 4 beads on inside top edge and at bottom border.
- Position bunny cookie with stick in cake top. Pipe tip 233 pull-out hair paw over hat brim edge. Cut plastic dowel rod to 5 in. and insert on angle into cake top, cover with tip 233 pull-out fur.
- Stack sandwich cookies and ice smooth for "cake". Pipe tip 2 drop strings and add tip 14 shell top and bottom borders. Attach cake to dowel rod using tip 4; cover bottom with tip 233 pull-out fur.
- Position candles in tip 14 rosettes. Pipe tip 44 message and tip 14 burst marks.
Serves 12.

Barbie™ Springtime Cupcakes

- Standard Muffin Pan, p. 165
- Tip 3, p. 116
- Lemon Yellow, Royal Blue Icing Colors, p. 110
- Barbie Standard Baking Cups, Barbie Icing Decorations, p. 187
- Decorator Brush Set, p. 120
- 6 Pc. Nesting Heart Cookie Cutter Set, p. 123
- Buttercream Icing, p. 92

- Bake and cool cupcakes. Ice cupcakes smooth with spatula. Use second smallest heart cutter to imprint heart pattern on cupcake top. Outline heart with tip 3; fill in and smooth. Pipe tip 3 beads around heart. Position icing decorations.

Each serves 1.

Barbie Doll Debut

- Beautiful Day Barbie Pan, p. 187
- Tips 1A, 2, 4, 16, 19, 127, 224, p. 116-119
- Violet, Royal Blue, Rose, Lemon Yellow, Icing Colors, p. 110
- Meringue Powder, p. 111
- Small Doves, p. 151
- Edible Glitter, p. 112
- Cake Boards, Fanci-Foil Wrap, p. 159
- Royal, Buttercream Icings, p. 92

- Using royal icing, make 60 (20 rose, 20 yellow, 20 blue) tip 224 drop flowers with tip 2 dot centers.
- Paint dove with thinned royal icing. Let dry.
- Ice cake sides smooth. Position facemaker (included with pan).
- Pipe tip 1A bands in folds of dress. Outline dress with tip 4; cover with tip 16 stars. Pipe tip 127 ruffles on sleeves. Pipe tip 2 dot necklace and medallion.
- Add tip 19 shell bottom border. Positon bird and flowers.

Serves 12.

BARBIE is a trademark owned by and used under license from Mattel, Inc. ©1995 Mattel, Inc. All Rights Reserved.

Magical Carousel Ride

- 6, 8, 12 in. Round Pans, p. 161
- Tips 3, 16, 21, 131, 352, p. 116-119
- Violet, Lemon Yellow, Rose, Teal, Kelly Green Icing Colors, p. 110
- '97 Pattern Book (Heart Pattern), p. 108
- Numeral Candle, p. 129
- 26 Pc. Happy Birthday Candle Holder Set, p. 130
- 8 Pc. Carousel Horse Separator Set, p. 132
- 9 Pc. Flower Former Set, p. 113
- Romantic Heart Base, p. 152
- Meringue Powder, p. 111
- Wooden Dowel Rods, p. 156
- 16 in. Ruffle Board, p. 159
- Royal, Buttercream Icings, p. 92

- Using royal icing and tip 131, make 230 drop flowers with tip 3 dot centers. Make extras to allow for breakage and let dry.
- Make 10 Hearts: Tape Heart Pattern to the convex side of largest flower former. Tape waxed paper over pattern. Using royal icing and tip 16, pipe zigzag heart. Let dry at least 1-2 days. Position drop flowers on dry hearts with dots of icing. Add tip 352 leaves. Let dry.
- Prepare 1-layer 6 in. and 8 in. cakes and 2-layer 12 in. cake for stacked and pillar construction (p. 96).
- **On 6 in. tier:** Pipe tip 16 shell bottom border.
- **On 8 in. tier:** Pipe tip 16 zigzag puff bottom border. Edge puffs with tip 3 zigzag.
- **On 12 in. tier:** Pipe tip 21 zigzag puff bottom border. Edge puffs with tip 16 zigzag. Pipe tip 16 shells around plate. Position hearts on cake attaching with dots of icing.
- Pipe a mound on icing on top of Romantic Heart Base with tip 16. Position candle, flowers and tip 352 leaves; position on cake. Position flowers and tip 352 leaves on top borders of 6 in. and 8 in. cakes and between puffs on 12 in. cake. Print tip 3 name. Add candles to holders and position on cake.

Serves 46.

Wishes Do Come True!

DISNEY'S
THE
HUNCHBACK
OF
NOTRE DAME

Festival Cupcakes

- Standard Muffin Pan, p. 165
- Tip 101s, p. 119
- Red, Lemon Yellow, Violet, Teal, Orange Icing Colors, p. 110
- The Hunchback of Notre Dame Standard Baking Cups, Cake Picks p. 185
- Buttercream Icing, p. 92

- Spatula ice cupcakes. Pipe tip 101s streamers and confetti. Position pick.

Each serves 1.

Enchanting Esmeralda

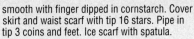

- Esmeralda Cake Pan Set, p. 185
- Tips 3, 7, 16, p. 116-119
- Teal, Golden Yellow, Violet, Brown, Black, Burgundy, Red-Red, Orange Icing Colors, p. 110
- Cake Board, Fanci-Foil Wrap, p. 159
- Buttercream Icing, p. 92

- Ice sides and background areas of cake smooth. Position Esmeralda Face Maker (included with pan). Outline skirt, bodice, waist scarf, shoes and coins with tip 3. Fill in bodice area with tip 3 and smooth with finger dipped in cornstarch. Cover skirt and waist scarf with tip 16 stars. Pipe in tip 3 coins and feet. Ice scarf with spatula.
- Pipe tip 7 ball bottom border. Add tip 16 stars and pipe tip 3 moons on sides of cake.

Serves 12.

Quatrefoil Cookies

- 4 Pc. The Hunchback of Notre Dame Cookie Cutter Set, p. 185
- Tip 3, p. 116
- Black, Teal, Golden Yellow, Burgundy, Moss Green, Orange, Brown, Copper (Lt. Skintone), Violet, Delphinium Blue Icing Colors, p. 110
- '97 Pattern Book (Quatrefoil Pattern), p. 108
- Decorator Brush Set, Candy Melting Plate, p. 120
- Clear Vanilla Extract, Meringue Powder.
- Almond Extract, Butter Flavor, p. 111
- Large Batch Roll-Out Cookie Recipe, p. 94
- Snow-White Buttercream Icing Recipe, p. 92

- Reserve half cookie recipe; tint remainder yellow for background cookies. Using pattern, trace and cut out background cookies. Thin down ½ cup of cookie dough with water for each accent color, to a consistency that will pass through tip 3. Reserve remainder of untinted dough. Using tip 3 and thinned, tinted cookie dough, outline background cookie and pipe tip 3 beads. Bake and cool as directed.
- Cut out Hunchback characters with untinted cookie dough, bake and cool.
- Pour a small amount of vanilla into candy melting plate cavity. Add a few drops of copper icing color to achieve flesh-colored stain. Use brushes to paint flesh areas of cookies (use darker color to paint facial features).
- Decorate characters with icing and tip 3: **For Esmeralda:** Pipe in swirl motion hair, string earrings. Pipe blouse and ribbon in hair (smooth with finger dipped in cornstarch). Add accent lines and zigzag trim on blouse. **For Phoebus:** Pipe in clothing and hair (smooth with finger dipped in cornstarch). **For Quasimodo:** Pipe in clothing (smooth with finger dipped in cornstarch); add pull-out hair. **For Djali:** Pipe in hooves, horns and facial features. Pipe swirl motion fur. Attach character cookies to background cookies with dots of icing.

Each serves 1.

Crowned With Candy

- The Hunchback of Notre Dame Lollipop Mold, p. 185
- Candy Melts*--White, Lt. Cocoa, Pastel Mix, p. 120
- 8 in. Lollipop Sticks, p. 121
- 4 Pc. Candy Colors Set, p. 120
- Fanci-Foil Wrap, Gold, p. 159
- Disposable Decorating Bags, p. 114
- '97 Pattern Book (Festival Crown Pattern), p. 108
- Styrofoam block, candy-coated chocolate dots, red tissue paper, red curling ribbon, glue, transparent tape

*brand confectionery coating

- Tint melted white candy using Candy Colors Set. Mold candy using layering and painting techniques (p. 104), let set. Cut lollipop sticks to various lengths and attach candy to sticks with dots of melted candy.
- Cut styrofoam into 4 in. x 3 in. high circle. Wrap in tissue paper.
- Cut two Festival Crown patterns out of Fanci-Foil Wrap. Glue back to back. Wrap around covered styrofoam and tape in place. Attach candy-coated chocolate dots to crown with melted candy.
- Cut curling ribbon and tie onto sticks; push stick ends into prepared crown.

A Proclamation For Celebration!

- Long Loaf Pan, p. 163
- Tips 3, 6, 17, 32, 789, p. 116-119
- Violet, Orange Icing Colors, p. 110
- Cake Board, Fanci-Foil Wrap, p. 159
- 10 Pc. The Hunchback of Notre Dame Candle Holder Set, p. 185
- Buttercream Icing, p. 92

- Ice cake smooth. Pipe tip 789 smooth side up band of icing around bottom of cake. Pipe tip 32 crown border with tip 3 dots. Edge top of band with tip 3 beads.
- Pipe tip 17 fleur de lis and swags on band. Add tip 6 bottom bead border. Pipe tip 6 block of icing as base for first letter of message; smooth with finger dipped in cornstarch. Print tip 3 message. Position candles.

Serves 18.

© Disney

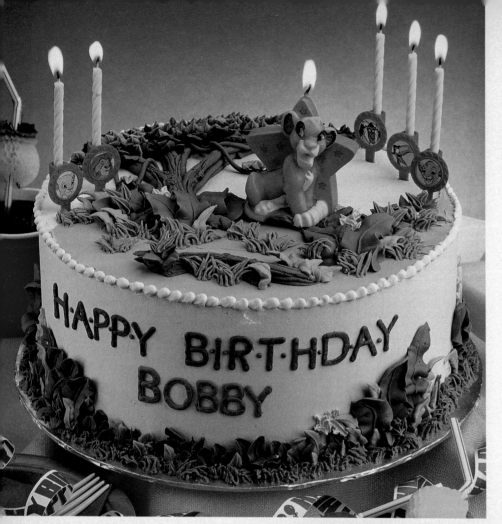

Wishes From Simba

- 10 in. Round Pan, p. 164
- Tips 2, 3, 5, 10, 14, 16, 67, 70, 233, 352, p. 116-119
- Black, Brown, Pink, Violet, Kelly Green, Royal Blue, Leaf Green Icing Colors, p. 110
- Make-Any-Message Letter Press Set, p. 113
- '97 Pattern Book (Jungle Scene Pattern), p. 108
- Cake Board, Fanci-Foil Wrap, p. 159
- Simba Candle, Lion King Candle Holder Set, p. 186
- Buttercream Icing, p. 92

- Ice 2-layer cake smooth. Lightly trace Jungle Pattern with toothpick. Ice grass area on cake top with spatula.
- Pipe several rows of tip 10 lines to build up tree trunk and log; score both with tapered spatula. Smooth area above trunk with spatula. Pipe tip 352 leaves in two different shades of green (add a small amount of black to leaf green to achieve darker shade). Add tip 5 vines and tip 352 leaves. Pipe tip 3 bead top border.
- Press message on cake sides, pipe tip 3 message with tip 2 dots. Randomly pipe tip 67, 70 and 352 leaves in 2 shades of green on grassy area, log and bottom border. Pipe tip 233 pull-out grass on bottom border and randomly on cake top. Add tip 14 and 16 pull-out flowers.
- Position candles.
Serves 24.
© Disney

Disney's Aladdin

Aladdin's Adventures

- One-Mix Book Pan, p. 168
- Tips 2, 4, 16, p. 116-119
- Golden Yellow, Royal Blue, Red-Red Icing Colors, p. 110
- 10 Pc. Aladdin Candle Holder Set, Jasmine Candle, p. 186
- Designer Pattern Press, p. 113
- Decorating Comb, p. 160
- Tube Decorating Gel - Blue, Red, p. 111
- Cake Board, Fanci-Foil Wrap, p. 159
- Buttercream Icing, p. 92

- Ice top and sides of cake smooth. Use decorating comb on cake sides. Imprint corner flourish pattern press in lower right hand corner. Pipe press design with tip 4 and overpipe with tip 2.
- On left hand page, imprint corner flourish pattern press on each corner; pipe tip 4 design and overpipe with tip 2. Pipe tip 2 bead lines to form frame centered on left page. Pipe tip 16 bottom shell and tip 2 top bead borders.
- Position candle holder, candles. Add gel dots for jewels. Pipe gel name.
Serves 12.
© Disney

A Snack In The Sunshine!
- 10 in. Round Pan, p. 164
- Tips 2, 6, 7, 225, 233, p. 116-119
- Sky Blue, Lemon Yellow, Kelly Green, Christmas Red Icing Colors, p.110
- 4 Pc. Rustic Fence Set, p. 134
- Cake Board, p. 159
- Lazy Daisy Cake Server, p. 112
- Meringue Powder, Small Angled Spatula, p. 111
- Pooh With Hunny Pot Candle, Lollipop Mold, p. 185
- Candy Melts®*- Pastel Mix (Pink, Lavender, Blue), Dark Cocoa, White, Red, Yellow, Orange, p. 120
- Buttercream, Royal Icings, p. 92

*brand confectionery coating

- Using melted Candy Melts, mold candy following package directions. Refrigerate to set.
- Using royal icing, make approximately 30 tip 225 drop flowers with tip 2 dot centers. Make extras to allow for breakage and let dry.
- Ice 2-layer cake smooth in buttercream icing.
- Using small angled spatula, ice bottom border and cake top grass areas. Add tip 233 pull-out grass. Pipe tip 6 dot and string sun, pipe tip 7 clouds; flatten and shape with finger dipped in cornstarch. Pipe tip 6 top bead border. Add tip 2 message. Position flowers.
- Attach candy to sides using dots of icing. Position fence sections on cake top. Position candle.

Serves 24.

Sunshine Cupcakes!
- Standard Muffin Pan, p. 165
- Tip 1B, p. 118
- Golden Yellow Icing Color, p. 110
- Winnie The Pooh Standard Baking Cups, 10 Pc. Winnie The Pooh Candle Holder Set, p. 185
- Buttercream Icing, p. 92

- Bake and cool cupcakes. Pipe tip 1B swirl on cupcakes. Position candles in holders.

Hunny Of A Cookie
- Winnie The Pooh Pan, p. 185
- Tip 3, p. 116
- Pooh 2 Pc. Icing Colors Set p. 185
- Black, Royal Blue, Violet Icing Colors, p. 110
- Cake Board, Fanci-Foil Wrap, p. 159
- Buttercream Icing, p. 92
- Roll-Out Cookie Dough Recipe, p. 94
- Piping Gel or honey

- Make 1/2 recipe of Roll Out Cookie Dough. Tint to Winnie the Pooh (gold) shade. Press into pan and bake 15 to 20 minutes until edges are light brown. Pop out of pan and let cool. Ice areas smooth with spatula and outline with tip 3. Pipe tip 3 dot and string facial features and printing on honey pot. Pipe tip 3 drips of icing on Pooh's finger and on top of Hunny Pot; cover drips with honey or piping gel tinted with Winnie The Pooh gold color.

Serves 12.

Birthday Fireworks

- 6 in. Round Pan, 10 in. Round Pan (3 in. deep), p. 161
- Tips 2, 4, 13, 18, p. 116-117
- Lemon Yellow, Red-Red, Royal Blue Icing Colors, p. 110
- 12 in. Separator Plates (2 needed), p. 157
- 3 in. Pillars (4 needed), p. 156
- Ready-To-Use Rolled Fondant (2 pkgs. needed), p. 112
- Meringue Powder, p. 111
- Dowel Rods, p. 151
- Florist Wire, p. 112
- Flower Spikes, p. 151
- 56-Pc. Make Any Message Letter Press Set, p. 113
- Mickey #1 Candle, p. 184
- Buttercream, Royal Icings, p. 92
- Floral tape

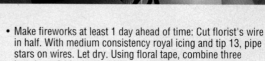

- Make fireworks at least 1 day ahead of time: Cut florist's wire in half. With medium consistency royal icing and tip 13, pipe stars on wires. Let dry. Using floral tape, combine three bunches of 14 wires each.
- Bake two 6 in. round cakes to each measure 1 ½ inches (6 in. round cakes should measure 3 inches when stacked).
- Prepare cakes for rolled fondant (p. 92) and stacked construction (p. 96).
- Pipe tip 18 rosette bottom borders; add tip 2 dot centers.
- Imprint message and print with tip 4.
- Insert flower spikes in cakes. Position sparklers in spikes, and candle.

Serves 24.

Mickey Bearing Gifts

- Mickey Mouse Cake Pan, Cookie Treat Pan, p. 184
- Tips 4, 10, 16, p. 116-117
- Cornflower Blue, Golden Yellow, Black, Copper (Lt. Skintone), Terra Cotta, Lemon Yellow, Royal Blue, Leaf Green, Pink Icing Colors, p. 110
- Cake Board, Fanci-Foil Wrap, p. 159
- 15 in. Parchment Triangles, p. 114
- Buttercream, Poured Cookie Icing, p. 92
- Ribbon

- Ice cake sides and background areas smooth. Outline Mickey with tip 4. Pipe-in eyes, nose and mouth with tip 4 (smooth with finger dipped in cornstarch). Cover Mickey with tip 16 stars. Pipe tip 10 ball bottom border.
- Bake and cool cookies using recipe on Cookie Treat Pan label (no sticks needed). Position cookies on a cooling grid and coat with Poured Cookie Icing. Let dry.
- Position cookies around cake and attach to ribbon with dots of icing.

Cake serves 12; each cookie serves 1.

Disneyland Train!

- 2-Pc. Choo Choo Train Pan Set, p. 169
- 8 ½ x 4 ½ in. Loaf Pan, p. 163
- Mickey Mouse Cookie Treat Pan, p. 184
- Tips 3, 10, 16, 18, p. 116-117
- Red-Red, Royal Blue, Kelly Green, Lemon Yellow Icing Colors, p. 110
- Cake Boards, Fanci-Foil Wrap, p. 159
- Candy Melts®*- Red, Yellow, White, Dark Cocoa, Pink, Green, p. 120

© Disney

- Mickey & Friends Candy Mold, Goofy, Minnie with Packages, Donald Duck, Pluto Candles, p. 184
- Buttercream Icing, p. 92

*brand confectionery coating

- Using melted Candy Melts, mold candy following package directions; mold a Mickey Mouse silhouette for front of train using Cookie Treat Pan. Refrigerate to set. Set aside.
- **Engine:** Cover engine with tip 16 stars. Using tip 18, add zigzag cowcatcher and spiral wheels. Add tip 10 ball wheel centers, red lights, green ball trim around engine (flatten and smooth with finger dipped in cornstarch). **Flat car:** Ice loaf cake smooth. Pipe tip 18 star top border, tip 3 bead bottom border. Using tip 18, pipe spiral wheels; add tip 10 ball centers.
- Attach candy using dots of icing. Position candles. Pipe tip 3 name.

Serves 18.

Star Attraction

- Mini Mickey Mouse Pan, p. 184
- Star Pan, p. 170
- Tips 2B, 3, 4, 5, 6, 7, 16, 18, 44, p. 116-119
- Lemon Yellow, Black, Christmas Red, Copper (Lt. Skintone), Terra Cotta Icing Colors, p. 110
- Mickey & Friends Candy Mold, p. 184
- Candy Melts,*--Pastel Mix (Pink, Lavender, Blue), White, Yellow, Red, Orange, Green, Lt. Cocoa, Dark Cocoa, p. 120
- Decorator Brush Set, Candy Melting Plate, p. 120
- 10 Pc. Mickey Mouse Candle Holder Set, p. 184
- Cake Boards, Fanci-Foil Wrap, p. 159
- Buttercream Icing, p. 92

*brand confectionery coating

- Using melted Candy Melts and "painting" method (p. 105) mold an assortment of candy; 10 candies are needed for cake, make extras to serve separately. Refrigerate until set.
- Ice 2-layer star cake smooth. Pipe smooth side tip 2B band on cake sides at top and bottom edges. Pipe tip 44 "holes" centered on each band. Pipe a vertical line of tip 3 beads between sections. Add tip 6 bead top and bottom borders.
- Position mini cake on cake board cut to fit and ice sides smooth. Outline using tip 3. Pipe tip 3 string mouth, tip 4 dot eyes. Add tip 5 bead tongue, smooth into heart shape. Cover face and ears with tip 16 stars.
- Position mini cake on star cake top, pipe tip 7 bottom bead border. Add tip 3 message, pipe tip 18 rosettes and position candle holders. Attach candy to cake sides with dots of icing.

Serves 25.

Party with Mickey!

Dazzle every celebration with fun, easy-to make Mickey Mouse treats! You'll find everything you need on p. 184 – pans, baking cups, candy molds, cookie cutters, candles, cake picks and treat bags, too.

© Disney

Start The Year In High Gear!

Gargoyles Guard The City

- 6 in., 8 in. Square Pans, p. 161
- Tips 2, 2B, 4, 45, p. 116-119
- Royal Blue, Violet, Black, Golden Yellow Icing Colors, p. 110
- '97 Pattern Book (Skyline Buildings Patterns), p. 108
- Cake Boards, Fanci-Foil Wrap, p. 159
- Color Flow Mix, p. 111
- Dowel Rods, p. 156
- Goliath Candle, 10 Pc. Gargoyles Candle Holder Set, p. 186
- Buttercream, Color Flow Icings, p. 92
- Waxed paper

- Make Color Flow panels using Color Flow Icing and Skyline Building Patterns. Royal Blue and Violet Icing Colors combined produce the color shown. You will need to make four of each size building. Outline using tip 2 then flow in (see p. 101). Make extras to allow for breakage and let dry.
- Prepare one 6 in. and three 8 in. layers for stacked construction (see p. 96): Stack and dowel rod two 8 in. layers, position on foil-covered board. Place a cake board cut to fit on top, add the remaining 8 in. and 6 in. tiers. Ice smooth.
- 6 in. tier: Cover sides with tip 45 bricks. Pipe, then overpipe tip 2B band at top border and on cake top. Add tip 4 bead bottom border.
- Edge top and sides of 8 in. stacked cakes with tip 4 beads. Position Color Flow panels and secure with dots of buttercream icing. Pipe tip 2 message. Position candle.

Serves 22.

Hot Number

- Little Fire Truck Pan, p. 168
- 10 Pc. Numbers Pan Set, p. 170
- Tips 2, 3, 4B, 5, 8, 16, 21, 32, 103, p. 116-119
- Red (No-Taste), Golden Yellow, Royal Blue, Black Icing Colors, p. 110
- Cake Boards, Fanci-Foil Wrap, p. 159
- 6 Pc. Small Derby Clowns Set, p. 132
- Buttercream Icing, p. 92
- Candy rods

- Cut and assemble cake board to fit both cakes. For fire truck: Ice sides, "cake" and background areas smooth.
- Outline truck with tip 3 strings. Pipe-in center of wheels with tip 5 (smooth with finger dipped in cornstarch). Cover tires with tip 21 stars; fire truck with tip 16 stars. Pipe tip 5 dot door handles and taillights.
- With toothpick, mark garlands on "cake". Pipe with tip 5 zigzag garland above, tip 3 zigzag garland below. Pipe tip 21 shell borders on "cake" top and base. Pipe tip 5 dots at garland points.
- Figure pipe clowns (see p. 102) using tips 2, 4B, 5, 8, 32 and 103. Pipe tip 5 string hose.
- Print tip 3 message. Pipe tip 8 bead bottom border.
- Position number cake; outline with tip 16 stars and cover with tip 16 stars. Push candy rods into "cake" and pipe tip 16 spatula striped pull out star flames on candles.

Serves 13.

Take The Loop At Full Speed!

- Long Loaf Pan, p. 164
- 6 in. Round Pans (2 needed), p. 161
- Tips 2, 4, 16, 18, 789, p. 116-119
- Golden Yellow, Christmas Red, Violet Icing Colors, p. 110
- '97 Pattern Book (Race Track Pattern), p. 108
- 2-Pc. Race Car Set (2 needed), p. 134
- 16 in. Featherweight Decorating Bag, p. 114
- Yellow Celebration Candles, p. 128
- Cake Board, Fanci-Foil Wrap, p. 159
- Meringue Powder, p. 111
- Royal, Buttercream Icings, p. 92
- Waxed paper

- To make race track (at least 2 days in advance): Stack two 6 in. round pans together and tape. Wrap race track pattern around sides of pans and secure with tape (A). Next, wrap and tape waxed paper over pattern. Use tip 789 (smooth side up) and royal icing to pipe track following line on pattern. Pipe remaining flat area of track, with tip 789 (serrated side up), two pieces each measuring 6 ½ in. long (B). Let all pieces dry at least 2 days.
- When dry, attach upside down race car with royal icing. Pipe tip 4 bead borders with royal icing.
- Ice cake smooth. Pipe tip 16 shell top border and tip 18 rosette bottom border with tip 4 center dots. Print tip 2 string and dot message. Position track on cake. Add tip 18 rosette bases for candles. Position cars and candles.

Serves 18.

A.  **B.**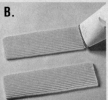

HAPPY BIRTHDAY RICHARD

HAPPY BIRTHDAY CHUCKIE

It really turns!

"Turning" Another Year Older!

Peter

SANDY

HAPPY BIRTHDAY

Dawn

Merry Clown Go-Round

- 12 in. Round Pan, p. 161
- Tips 6, 6B, 9, 21, p. 116-119
- Lemon Yellow, Red-Red, Christmas Red, Orange, Royal Blue, Kelly Green Icing Colors, p. 110
- '97 Pattern Book (Clown-Go-Round Pattern), p. 108
- 14 in. Tall Tier Plate, 6½ in. Column, Bottom Column Bolt, Glue-On Plate Legs (6 needed), Cake Corer Tube, p. 154
- 26 Pc. Alphabet Cookie Cutter Set, p. 124
- 4 Pc. Comical Clowns Set, p. 132
- 3 Pc. Decorator Brush Set, p. 120
- Ready-To-Use Rolled Fondant (3 pkgs. needed), p. 112
- Meringue Powder, p. 111
- Cake Boards, Fanci-Foil Wrap, p. 159
- Buttercream, Royal Icings, p. 92
- Large gumball, jelly beans, styrofoam

Note: To achieve shade of red shown, mix Red-Red and Christmas Red in both fondant and royal icing.

- Tint 2 packages fondant yellow. Tint ¼ of third package red; reserve ¼ white and tint remaining fondant in equal amounts of orange, green and blue.
- Roll-out and cut an 8 in. circle from white fondant. Use Cake Corer to cut hole in center for column. Using alphabet cutters, cut desired letters from red fondant. Also, roll 8 red log-shaped handles, 1½ in. long, for clown-go-round. Roll-out other fondant colors and cut circles using tips 6B, 21 and center of letter "O" as cutters.
- Cut Clown-Go-Round from two 12 in. cake circles (reverse grain for added strength), using pattern. Test to insure that Clown-Go-Round will turn freely on threads of column, trimming center hole if necessary. Cover with foil and position on column.
- Place column with Clown-Go-Round in styrofoam block for support. Figure pipe clown bodies with tip 6B and royal icing (see p. 102). Attach handles with royal icing. Add tip 21 arms and tip 9 hands handles. Let dry.

- Glue plate legs on plate. Core out center of 2-layer 12 in. cake; prepare cake for rolled fondant (p. 92). Using decorator brush and a small amount of water, attach fondant pieces to cake. Pipe tip 9 bead bottom border. Place 8 in. circle of white fondant on cake top. Pipe tip 6 beads around outer edge of center fondant circle. Pipe tip 9 beads around center opening.
- Position Clown-Go-Round; secure with column bolt. Pipe tip 6B legs with royal icing and attach jelly bean feet. Make sure feet do not touch cake. Attach center gumball knob with royal icing.

Serves 36.

Pretzel Party-Goers

- Bear and Clown Pretzel Candy Molds, p. 121
- Candy Melts®*- Brown, Orange, Yellow, Pastel Mint, Pastel Mix (1 bag each needed), p. 120
- Thin pretzel rods, curling ribbon, place cards

*brand confectionery coating

- Mold a variety of bear and clown pretzel pops using "painting" method (p. 105) and directions on mold package.
- Unmold; attach place cards and curling ribbon with dots of melted candy.

Each serves 1.

Start The Year Brightly!

- Happy Birthday Pan, p. 171
- Tip 21, p. 116-119
- Golden Yellow Icing Color, p. 110
- Candy Melts®*- White, Pastel Mix, (1 pkg. each needed), 4 Pc. Candy Colors Set, p. 120
- Cake Board, Fanci-Foil Wrap, p. 159
- Rainbow Nonpareils Sprinkle Decorations, p. 126
- Disposable Decorating Bags, p. 114
- Buttercream Icing, p. 92
- Canned ready-to-use fudge icing

- Melt candy in disposable bags; tint white candy using candy color. Cut bags and pipe letters inside of pan. Refrigerate until set, then pop out.
- Ice sides of cake smooth.
- Melt canned icing, following directions on p. 92. Place melted icing in cut bag; pipe over cake top and down sides. Immediately add sprinkle decorations. Let set.
- Pipe tip 21 bottom shell border. Position letters.

Serves 12.

She Baked Just For You

- 7 x 11 in. Pan, p. 162
- Tips 2, 4, 6, 20, 112, p. 116-119
- Pink, Royal Blue, Lemon Yellow Icing Colors, p. 110
- Honey Bear Cake Decoration, p. 132
- Cake Board, Fanci-Foil Wrap, p. 159
- Cupcakes Candles, p. 130
- Script Letter Icing Decorations, Rainbow Nonpareils Sprinkle Decorations, p. 126
- Buttercream Icing, p. 92

- For cupcake in bear's hand, pipe tip 6 yellow lines over bear's ball to create liner effect. Pipe tip 6 puffy icing swirls on top of "cupcake". Sprinkle with Rainbow Nonpareils. Set aside.
- Ice 2-layer cake smooth. Measure 1 in. from top edge of cake and pipe tip 4 yellow line. Divide cake front and back in thirds; sides in halves. Mark 1¾ in. deep from top edge down, pipe tip 4 drop strings.
- Cover top and side areas above drop strings with tip 20 stars. Add tip 4 zigzag below drop strings and dots at points. Pipe tip 112 bottom ruffle border with tip 2 dots. Position bear, candles and icing decorations message.

Serves 35.

Goal Oriented Guy

- Teddy Bear With Block Pan, p. 171
- Tips 2, 4, 5, 14, 18, 233, p. 116-119
- No-Taste Red, Royal Blue, Black, Kelly Green, Brown, Lemon Yellow Icing Colors, p. 110
- 4 Pc. Soccer Cookie Cutter Set, p. 125
- '97 Pattern Book (Soccer Bear Shirt Pattern), p. 108
- Cake Board, Fanci-Foil Wrap, p. 159
- Roll-Out Cookie Dough Recipe, p. 94
- Buttercream Icing, p. 92

- Tint dough to be used for "Goal" cookies yellow, leave remainder of dough plain. Cut out cookies, bake, cool. Outline soccer ball cookies with tip 2 and pipe in with tip 14 stars. Pipe in "Goal" letters with tip 5.
- Ice cake sides and background area smooth. Trace Soccer Bear Shirt Pattern with toothpick. Position ball cookie. Outline body and facial features with tip 4. Pipe tip 4 smooth area of ear (smooth with finger dipped in cornstarch), nose, mouth and eyes. Cover face, hands, shirt, tail, pants, legs and shoes with tip 18 stars. Build up arm and hands with tip 18 stars. Outline number "9" on jersey sleeve with tip 2; fill in with tip 14 stars.
- Add tip 233 pull-out grass on top playing field and at bottom border. Position cookies. *Serves 12.*

Sugar And Spike!

- Ballerina Bear Pan, p. 171
- 4 Pc. Sports Ball Pan Set, p. 169
- Tips 2, 4, 5, 7, 16, 18, 21, p. 116-119
- Pink, Kelly Green, Black, Copper (Lt. Skintone), Brown, Christmas Red Icing Colors p. 110
- '97 Pattern Book (Uniform, Volleyball Patterns), p. 108
- Cake Boards, Fanci-Foil Wrap, p. 159
- Buttercream Icing, p. 92

- **Volleyball:** Lightly ice half ball cake smooth. Mark Volleyball Pattern. Outline using tip 4; cover with tip 16 stars. Set aside.
- **Girl Player:** Ice cake sides and background areas smooth. Mark Uniform Pattern. Use tip 4 for the following: Outline girl, outline and pipe in mouth (pat smooth with finger dipped in cornstarch), pipe tongue and add indentation using edge of toothpick. Pipe tip 5 whites of eyes; add tip 4 dot eye centers. Pipe tip 7 ball nose.
- Pipe tip 16 star uniform, face, arms, shoes and legs. Using tip 18, add c-motion and e-motion hair with pull-out star ponytails; add tip 7 string barrettes. Pipe tip 4 string eyebrows and zigzag soles of shoes; add tip 2 string shoelaces and dot eyelets. Pipe tip 21 star bottom border.
- Position ball cake. *Serves 18.*

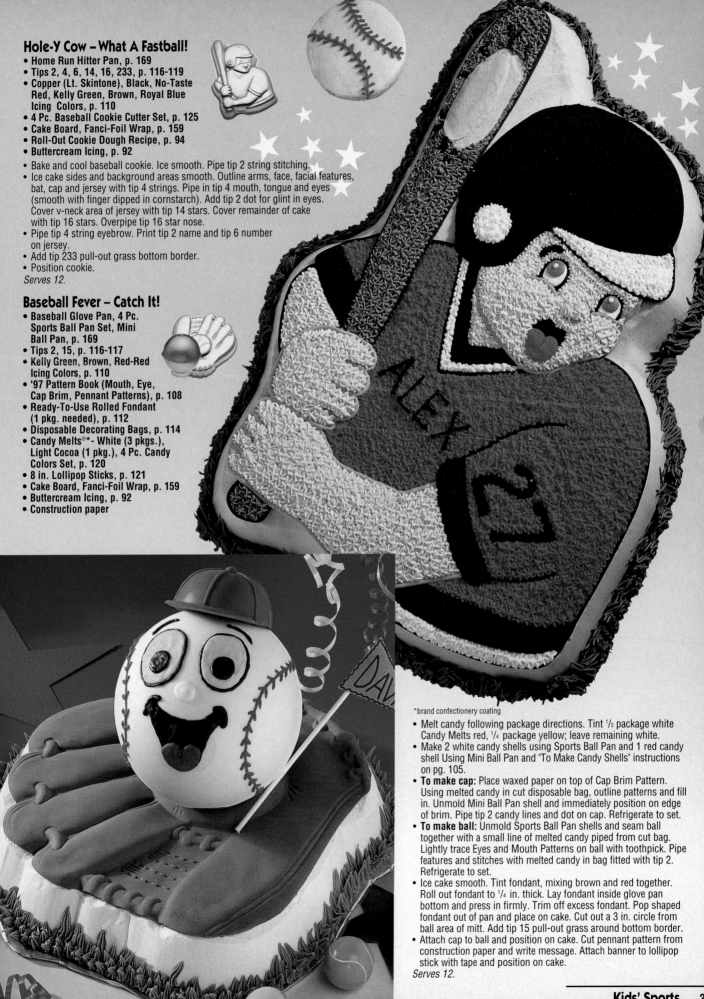

Hole-Y Cow – What A Fastball!
- Home Run Hitter Pan, p. 169
- Tips 2, 4, 6, 14, 16, 233, p. 116-119
- Copper (Lt. Skintone), Black, No-Taste Red, Kelly Green, Brown, Royal Blue Icing Colors, p. 110
- 4 Pc. Baseball Cookie Cutter Set, p. 125
- Cake Board, Fanci-Foil Wrap, p. 159
- Roll-Out Cookie Dough Recipe, p. 94
- Buttercream Icing, p. 92

- Bake and cool baseball cookie. Ice smooth. Pipe tip 2 string stitching.
- Ice cake sides and background areas smooth. Outline arms, face, facial features, bat, cap and jersey with tip 4 strings. Pipe in tip 4 mouth, tongue and eyes (smooth with finger dipped in cornstarch). Add tip 2 dot for glint in eyes. Cover v-neck area of jersey with tip 14 stars. Cover remainder of cake with tip 16 stars. Overpipe tip 16 star nose.
- Pipe tip 4 string eyebrow. Print tip 2 name and tip 6 number on jersey.
- Add tip 233 pull-out grass bottom border.
- Position cookie.
Serves 12.

Baseball Fever – Catch It!
- Baseball Glove Pan, 4 Pc. Sports Ball Pan Set, Mini Ball Pan, p. 169
- Tips 2, 15, p. 116-117
- Kelly Green, Brown, Red-Red Icing Colors, p. 110
- '97 Pattern Book (Mouth, Eye, Cap Brim, Pennant Patterns), p. 108
- Ready-To-Use Rolled Fondant (1 pkg. needed), p. 112
- Disposable Decorating Bags, p. 114
- Candy Melts®*- White (3 pkgs.), Light Cocoa (1 pkg.), 4 Pc. Candy Colors Set, p. 120
- 8 in. Lollipop Sticks, p. 121
- Cake Board, Fanci-Foil Wrap, p. 159
- Buttercream Icing, p. 92
- Construction paper

*brand confectionery coating

- Melt candy following package directions. Tint 1/2 package white Candy Melts red, 1/4 package yellow; leave remaining white.
- Make 2 white candy shells using Sports Ball Pan and 1 red candy shell Using Mini Ball Pan and "To Make Candy Shells" instructions on pg. 105.
- **To make cap:** Place waxed paper on top of Cap Brim Pattern. Using melted candy in cut disposable bag, outline patterns and fill in. Unmold Mini Ball Pan shell and immediately position on edge of brim. Pipe tip 2 candy lines and dot on cap. Refrigerate to set.
- **To make ball:** Unmold Sports Ball Pan shells and seam ball together with a small line of melted candy piped from cut bag. Lightly trace Eyes and Mouth Patterns on ball with toothpick. Pipe features and stitches with melted candy in bag fitted with tip 2. Refrigerate to set.
- Ice cake smooth. Tint fondant, mixing brown and red together. Roll out fondant to 1/4 in. thick. Lay fondant inside glove pan bottom and press in firmly. Trim off excess fondant. Pop shaped fondant out of pan and place on cake. Cut out a 3 in. circle from ball area of mitt. Add tip 15 pull-out grass around bottom border.
- Attach cap to ball and position on cake. Cut pennant pattern from construction paper and write message. Attach banner to lollipop stick with tape and position on cake.
Serves 12.

La Quinceañera

La Quinceañera Fantasia
- 7, 8, 12 in. Round Pans, p. 161, 164
- Tips 2, 3, 6, p. 116
- Rose Icing Color, p. 110
- '97 Pattern Book (Overlay Pattern), p. 108
- 7 in. Crystal-Look Pillars (1 pkg. needed), p. 152
- 7 in. Crystal-Look Plate (2 needed), 13 in. Crystal-Look Plate (1 needed), p. 157
- Crystal-Look Bowl, p. 152
- 30 Pc. Gum Paste Flowers Kit, Ready-To-Use Rolled Fondant (8 pkgs. needed), p. 112
- Decorator Brush Set, p. 120
- Cake Boards, Fanci-Foil Wrap, p. 159
- Dowel Rods, p. 156
- Cake Dividing Set, Designer Pattern Press Set, p. 113
- Fresh Flower Holders (2 pkgs. needed), p. 158
- La Quinceañera Figurine, p. 145
- Buttercream Icing, p. 92
- Fresh flowers, greenery, wood block or styrofoam

- Prepare 2-layer 7 in. and 12 in. round and four 2-layer 8 in. rounds for rolled fondant (p. 92) and pillar and stacked construction (p. 96). Cover 7 in. and 12 in. tiers in rolled fondant. For the four 8 in. tiers, tint 3 boxes of rolled fondant with ¾ teaspoon icing color; cover. Cut overlay pattern from untinted fondant, cut out flowers from overlay using the forget-me-not and apple blossom cutters (reserve flower cut-outs). Carefully position overlay on tiers. Make ruffles for overlay: Cut fondant strips 6 in. long, ¾ in. wide. Ruffle the edges following instructions in Gum Paste Kit Instruction Book. Attach fondant ruffle to edge of overlay by brushing edge with water. Let set.
- Including the reserved flower cut-outs, cut out fondant flowers to total approximately 80 forget-me-nots and 50 apple blossoms. Shape flowers using stick and foam following instructions included in kit.
- **8 in. tiers:** Pipe tip 3 beads around ruffles. Pipe tip 2 center dots on small flower openings, tip 3 center dots on large flower openings. Add tip 6 bottom bead border.
- Using Cake Dividing Set, divide 7 in. tier into 4ths, dot mark on cake side 1 in. up from bottom edge; divide 12 in. tier into 4ths, dot mark on cake side 1½ in. down from top edge.
- Imprint vine pattern press on top of 12 in. cake. Pipe vines using tip 2. Position flowers and add tip 3 dot centers and dots.
- Position flowers on sides of 12 in. and 7 in. tiers, placing a large flower on center mark, then arrange large and small flowers in drape formation. Add tip 3 dot centers and dots. Pipe tip 6 bottom bead borders.
- **At reception:** Assemble the four 8 in. cakes, place wood block in center to support 12 in. tier. Position 12 in. tier on cakes, position plate legs between each 8 in. cake. Position 7 in. cake, fresh flowers in holders and crystal-look bowl and La Quinceañera figurine.
Serves 174.

Bar and Bat Mitzvah

Celebrated Coming Of Age

- 8, 14 in. Round Pans, p. 161, 164
- Sports Ball Pan Set, p. 169
- Tips 2, 16, 17, 21, p. 116-117
- '97 Pattern Book (Star of David Pattern), p. 108
- Decorator Preferred Separator Plates (one 14 in., two 9 in. needed), p. 157
- 7 in. Grecian Pillars (1 set needed), Dowel Rods, p. 156
- Decorator Favorites Pattern Press Set, Cake Dividing Set, p. 113
- 4 in. Lollipop Sticks (1 pk. needed), p. 121
- Cake Boards, Fanci-Foil Wrap, p. 159
- Crystal-Look Bowl, Iridescent Grapes (4 pkgs. needed), p. 152
- Candlelight Cake Stand, p. 154
- Color Flow Mix, p. 111
- Buttercream, Color Flow Icings, p. 92
- Candles, fresh flowers

- Reserve ¼ cup full-strength Color Flow mixture. Make 26 stars using pattern and full-strength Color Flow Icing: outline with tip 2, then flow in with thinned color flow (p. 101). Make extras to allow for breakage and let dry. Make 13 star sticks: Sandwich a lollipop stick between 2 stars using reserved Color Flow icing. Let dry completely.
- Prepare 2-layer 14 in., 1 layer 8 in. and ½ ball cakes for pillar and stacked construction (p. 96).
- Using Cake Dividing Set, divide 14 in. tier into 12ths and ½ ball into 4ths.
- Decorate tiers. **14 in.:** Pipe embellished Fleur de lis (p. 103) on cake sides ¼ in. from top edge at division marks. Outline imprints using tip 16. Pipe tip 16 upright shell at top fleur de lis opening.

Pipe tip 16 top and tip 21 bottom shell borders. Outline plate with tip 16 e-motion. **8 in.:** Imprint Small C-Scroll along top edge of cake, outline using tip 16. Add tip 16 top and tip 17 bottom shell borders. **½ Ball:** Imprint Fleur de lis pattern press 1 ½ in. from bottom edge at division marks. Imprint Small C-Scroll pattern press at bottom border and between each fleur de lis. Outline imprints using tip 16.
- Insert star sticks, attach grapes using dots of icing. Position cake on stand, assemble tier on pillars, add candles and fresh flowers in bowl. *Serves 94.*

A Chorus Of Crooners

- Long Loaf Pan, p. 163
- Tips 2, 2D, 3, 4B, 6, 8, 18, 32, 352, p. 116-119
- Orange, Royal Blue, Kelly Green, Lemon Yellow, Christmas Red, Black Icing Colors, p. 110
- Meringue Powder, p. 111
- 56-Pc. Make-Any-Message Letter Press Set, p. 113
- Cake Board, Fanci-Foil Wrap, p. 159
- Plastic Dowel Rods (2 pkgs. needed), p. 156
- Buttercream, Royal Icings, p. 92
- Black shoestring licorice

- Make 8 candles: With royal icing, pipe tip 6 "melting wax" on top of dowel rods. Immediately insert a 3 in. length of licorice for wick. Pipe tip 18 spatula striped (see p. 93) pull-out flames on wicks. Pipe tip 2 dot and string facial features. Position into craft block and let dry.
- With royal icing, make 14 tip 2D drop flowers with tip 3 dot centers. Let dry.
- Ice top of cake smooth in yellow; sides in white. Divide long cake sides into 4ths. Pipe tip 8 zigzag garland from division points to measure 3 1/2 in. wide and 1 1/2 in. deep at lowest point. Add tip 3 zigzag on top of garland. Pipe tip 4B shell bottom border with tip 3 dots; edge shells with tip 3 zigzags. Pipe tip 32 shell top border. Position flowers and add tip 352 leaves.
- Individually imprint letters without bar. Pipe tip 3 message with tip 3 dots. Position candles at random heights and angles. Pipe tip 18 circle around base of candles.

Serves 18.

Hidden Treasures Candy "Cake"

- 6 x 3 in. Excelle Non-Stick Springform Pan, p. 162
- 8 in. Round Pan, p. 161
- Tips 1, 2, 3, 7, p. 116
- 4 Pc. Candy Colors Set, Candy Melts®*- Light Cocoa (2 pkgs. needed), White, Yellow (1 pkg. each needed), p. 120 (You will need additional colors of your choice to mold candies that will be hidden under cake)
- Disposable Decorating Bags, p. 114
- Favorite Wilton Candy Molds, p. 121
- Rainbow Nonpareils Sprinkle Decorations, p. 126
- Cake Board, p. 159
- Candy sticks, mini round candies, spice drops, waxed paper

*brand confectionery coating

- Mold a variety of your favorite Wilton candies. Let set.
- Make candy plaque "plate" approximately 3/8 in. thick (see p. 104) using 8 in. round pan and melted yellow Candy Melts. Let set.
- Mold chocolate cake candy mold from 6 in. springform pan: Melt 18 oz. of Candy Melts. Pour 12 oz. of melted candy in pan and spread to cover sides of pan. Refrigerate to set. Apply 2 to 3 more coats of chocolate, using remaining 6 oz. of candy. Refrigerate to set. Remove carefully from springform pan.
- To decorate candy cake, place on a waxed paper covered cake board. Cover top of cake with melted white Candy Melts; pipe drips with disposable bag fitted with tip 3.
- Sprinkle top with nonpareils. Use tinted melted candy in disposable bags to pipe tip 7 shell bottom border. Let set, then add tip 1 zigzag above shell border. Pipe tip 2 zigzag garland and position mini round candies. Let set.
- **To make candles:** Cut bottoms off spice drops and push candy sticks into tops. Attach to "cake" with drops of melted candy. Cut yellow spice drops and form into flame shapes; attach to candles with drops of melted candy.
- Place molded candies on candy plate; carefully cover candies with decorated "cake".

Did I Do That?
- 3-D Cuddly Bear Pan, p. 165
- 6-Cup Muffin Pan, p. 171
- Tips 2A, 7, 16, 17, p. 116-119
- Copper (Lt. Skintone), Royal Blue, Christmas Red, Brown, Black, Lemon Yellow, p. 110
- '97 Pattern Book (Cake Board Pattern), p. 108
- Cake Board, Fanci-Foil Wrap, p. 159
- Assorted Celebration Candles, p. 128
- Buttercream Icing, p. 92
- Favorite Firm-textured Pound Cake Recipe (for 6½ cups batter)

- Bake and cool cake and one muffin. Trace cake board pattern on cardboard and cover with foil wrap. Position muffin on foil-covered board. Using spatula, ice muffin "cake" smooth. Ice top fluffy. Add tip 16 shell bottom border. Set aside.
- Cut ears from cake. Pipe in eyes, nose and mouth with tip 7; add tip 7 dot pupils and bead tongue (smooth with finger dipped in cornstarch). Ice bottom of shoes smooth. Cover face and tops of shoes with tip 16 stars. Cover pants and shirt with tip 17 stars. Pipe tip 17 rosettes for curly hair look.
- Push cake board with muffin "cake" into boy cake. Pipe in tip 2A arms. Pipe tip 17 star and zigzag sleeves and hands.
- Pipe in tip 7 icing splashes on face and head. Insert candle on top of head.
Serves 13.

Birthday On Line
- 10 in. Round Pan, p. 161
- Tips 1, 2, 4, 8, 18, 301, p. 116-119
- Royal Blue, Christmas Red, Kelly Green, Lemon Yellow, Black Icing Colors, p. 110
- Cake Board, Fanci-Foil Wrap, p. 159
- Computer Candles, p. 131
- Buttercream Icing, p. 92

- Ice 2-layer cake smooth. Pipe tip 18 top shell border; edge shells with tip 2 zigzags. Pipe tip 18 zigzag puff bottom border edged with tip 2 zigzags. Pipe tip 2 dots on cake sides. Pipe tip 2 message.
- To make mice: Using stiffened buttercream and tip 8, pipe ball body; add tip 2 string tail and tip 301 ears. Pipe tip 4 pull-out hat with tip 1 trim and dot facial features.
- Position candles on cake.
Serves 24.

SOME BIRTHDAYS JUST HIT YOU LIKE THAT

ANOTHER YEAR SCURRIES BY

Nowhere To Hide

- Tombstone Pan, p. 170
- Tips 2, 3, 4, 9, 12, 14, 18, 20, 233, p. 116-119
- Kelly Green, Black, Red, Royal Blue, Lemon Yellow, Copper (Lt. Skintone), Brown Icing Colors, p. 110
- '97 Pattern Book (Spotlight Guy, Shadow), p. 108
- Cake Board, Fanci-Foil Wrap, p. 159
- Buttercream Icing, p. 92

- Ice sides and grass area of cake smooth. Lightly trace Spotlight Guy and Shadow Patterns with toothpick. Outline tombstone and "over the hill" message with tip 3. Cover background area with tip 18 stars, spotlight, shadow and "over the hill" with tip 14 stars.
- Using tips 2, 3, 4, 9 and 12, figure pipe Spotlight Guy (p. 102). Smooth with fingers dipped in cornstarch.
- Pipe tip 14 zigzags around edge of tombstone. Add tip 233 pull-out grass. Pipe tip 20 shell bottom border.
- Pipe tip 2 sweat beads around head. Print tip 2 message.

Serves 12.

Doing Hard Time

- Cute Clown Pan, p. 167
- 10 Pc. Numbers Pan Set, p. 170
- Tips 1, 3, 16, p. 116-119
- Copper (Lt. Skintone), Teal, Black, Golden Yellow Icing Colors, p. 110
- '97 Pattern Book (Prisoner Face Pattern), p. 108
- Cake Boards, Fanci-Foil Wrap, p. 159
- Buttercream Icing, p. 92
- String licorice, 36 in. long

- Position number cakes on cake boards cut to fit. Ice background areas smooth. Cover with tip 16 stars.
- Trim hat peak off clown cake. Ice background area smooth. Lightly ice face and mark Prisoner Face Pattern; outline face, eyes, arms, uniform, shoes and tag using tip 3. Fill in tip 3 eyes and tag, smooth with finger dipped in cornstarch; add tip 1 dots to eyes. Pipe tip 16 stars in alternating double rows to cover hat and uniform. Cover face, legs and hands with tip 16 stars, overpiping nose and fingers for dimension. Pipe tip 16 pull-out hair, tip 3 zigzag mouth. Using tip 16, cover shoes with stars, add zigzag around ankle. Pipe tip 1 numbers on tag.
- To make chain, bring ends of 36 in. string licorice together and tie a series of loops with double knots. After tying each loop, tighten slightly for a straight, uniform look. Attach chain to cakes with dots of icing.

Serves 14.

Getting older? Laugh it off!

Over The Hill cupcakes are festive, easy to decorate, fun to serve and sure to bring a grin to even the grouchiest getting-older birthday celebrant. Just bake cupcakes in our Standard Muffin Pan (p. 165) and Over The Hill Baking Cups (p. 127). Ice with a tip 2110 (1M) swirl and decorate with Sprinkles (p. 126) and Over The Hill Candle Holder Set (p. 130). Because at your age, you should take it easy!

Meet The Reaper!

- 10 1/2 in. Ring Mold Pan, p. 166
- 4-Pc. Over the Hill Cookie Cutter Set, p. 124
- Tips 3, 4, 8, p. 116
- Kelly Green, Rose, Lemon Yellow, Violet, Black Icing Colors, p. 110
- 8 in. Lollipop Sticks, p. 121
- 56-Pc. Make-Any-Message Letter Press Set, p. 113
- Over The Hill Mix Sprinkle Decorations, p. 126
- Cake Board, Fanci-Foil Wrap, p. 159
- Grim Reaper Cake Topper, p. 134
- Roll-Out Cookie Dough Recipe, p. 94
- Buttercream Icing, p. 92
- Curling ribbon (violet, yellow, green, red, pink), styrofoam (3 1/2 in. round, 2 1/4 in. high; 2 1/2 in. x 1 3/4 in. cube)

- Cut out cookies from tinted dough and place on sticks. To decorate cookies: Thin down cookie dough with water to a consistency that can easily be piped through tip 3. With tip 3, pipe desired string outlines and printing. Bake and cool cookies.
- Ice cake fluffy; leave smooth front area where name will be printed. Imprint message with press. Pipe message using tip 4. Add tip 8 bead bottom border. Randomly place Sprinkles pieces.
- Cover styrofoam pieces with foil and insert in center of cake. Attach grim reaper to center of cube with dots of icing. Insert cookies in round styrofoam piece. Add a variety of lengths and colors of curling ribbon.

Serves 20.

Getting Up There!

Pop In The Gamewinner!

- 4 Pc. Basketball Cookie Cutter Set, p. 125
- Tips 2, 3, 4, p. 116
- Royal Blue, Kelly Green, Lemon Yellow, Brown, Copper (Lt. Skintone), Red-Red Icing Colors, p. 110
- Basketball Candy Mold, p. 121
- 4 and 8 in. Lollipop Sticks (1 pkg. each needed), p. 121
- Disposable Decorating Bags, p. 114
- Candy Melts® * - White, Red, Pastel Mix, Orange, Light Cocoa, p. 120
- Roll-Out Cookie Dough Recipe, p. 94
- Snow-White Buttercream Icing, p. 92
- Cup, styrofoam, popcorn

- Mold a variety of candy lollipops (see p. 104). Refrigerate to set.
- Before baking cookies, insert lollipop sticks; bake and cool cookies.
- Decorate cookies with buttercream. Outline backboard with tip 3. Pipe tip 2 strings for net. Pipe tip 4 "jump shot" message. Pipe in tip 2 hair and facial features on basketball player. Add tip 4 jersey and shorts; tip 2 shoes, waistline and socks.
- Position styrofoam, cut to fit, in cup; insert lollipops and cookies. Add popcorn.

Each serves 1.

Bowl The Fans Over!

- 11 x 15 in. Sheet Pan, p. 164
- First & Ten Football Pan, p. 169
- Tips 2, 3, 4, 14, 18, 21, p. 116-117
- Brown, Kelly Green, Royal Blue, Copper (Lt. Skintone) Icing Colors, p. 110
- 4 Pc. Football Cookie Cutter Set, p. 125
- Cake Boards, Fanci-Foil Wrap, p. 159
- Decorating Comb, p. 160
- Wooden Dowel Rods, p. 156
- Roll-Out Cookie Dough Recipe, p. 94
- Buttercream Icing, p. 92
- Heavy-duty aluminum foil, mini round hard candies, tape or hot glue gun

- Bake and cool 1 layer sheet cake, football cake, player and touchdown cookies.
- Outline cookies with tip 3; pipe in player and touchdown cookies with tip 3 (smooth with finger dipped in cornstarch). Cover football cookies with tip 14 stars and zigzag stripes; add tip 2 stitching. Print tip 3 names.
- Ice sheet cake smooth. Comb sides of cake. Pipe tip 4 string yard markers every 1 1/2 inches on cake top. Pipe tip 2 numbers. Pipe tip 4 bead top border. Add tip 18 shell bottom border. Prepare for stacked construction (see p. 96).
- Cover football cake with tip 21 stars. Pipe tip 21 string seam on ball and add tip 3 stitches.

- **To construct stadium (p. 103):** Tape two 13 x 19 in. cake boards together and cover with fanci-foil wrap. Cut 4 lengths of heavy-duty aluminum foil, each measuring 24 inches long. Fold pieces lengthwise in quarters to measure 24 in. x 4 1/2 in. Fold each piece up 1 in. from bottom to form a lip. Tape this lip edge to bottom of cake board. Pleat corners to conform to shape of stadium. Overlap pieces for added strength and tape all pieces together.
- **To construct bleachers:** Using Fanci-Foil Wrap, cut 6 pieces 13 in. x 10 in. and 4 corner pieces 13 in. x 7 in. Fold all pieces lengthwise in half and pleat at 1/4 in. intervals. Tape bottom of each pleated piece to edge of 13 x 19 in. boards and pull up and over top edge of stadium. Cut the 13 in. x 7 in. pieces on angles to cover corners, pleat at 1/4 in. intervals and tape to boards. Attach mini round candies to bleachers with buttercream icing.
- **Make "scoreboard":** Cover 3 1/2 in. x 3 1/2 in. cardboard piece with Fanci-Foil Wrap and glue to center of bleachers. Attach "Touchdown" cookie to board with buttercream icing. Cut an additional 1 x 6 in. piece of foil to cover seam on opposite side; tape in place. Position football player cookie on football cake. Position cake in stadium. Position football cookies around stadium.

Serves 53.

TOUCH DOWN

. . . And The Crowd Goes Wild!

SLAM DUNK

BASKET BALL

MATT

CHRIS

Fancy Pansy Garden

Love Tokens

- Mini Heart Pan, p. 173
- Tips 1, 2, 3, 4, 103, 352, p. 116-119
- Violet, Lemon Yellow, Willow Green Icing Colors, p. 110
- 9 Pc. Flower Former Set, p. 113
- Meringue Powder, p. 111
- Cake Boards, Fanci-Foil Wrap, p. 159
- '97 Pattern Book (Tendril Pattern), p. 108
- Royal, Buttercream, Quick-Pour Fondant Icing Recipes, p. 92
- Waxed paper, fine artist's paint brush

Note: Using Royal Icing and tip 103, make 1 spatula striped white/violet pansy and 2 yellow/violet pansies (p. 99) for each cake. Add tip 1 loop centers to all. Make extras to allow for breakage. Let all dry completely on flower formers. Use artist's brush to add center throat after flowers have dried.

- Position Tendril Pattern on cardboard and cover with waxed paper. Using Royal Icing, pipe tip 3 tendril, then overpipe with tip 1. Make at least 6 tendrils for each heart (make extras to allow for breakage). Let dry.
- Prepare and cover cakes with poured fondant. Let set. Position flowers, add tip 352 leaves. Add tip 4 bottom bead border and tip 1 dot accents. Position tendrils.

Each serves 1.

shown on our cover...

Pansy Basket

- 8 in. Round Pan (3 in. Deep), p. 164
- 4 Pc. Sports Ball Pan Set, p. 169
- Tips 2, 2B, 45, 103, 104, p. 116-119
- Violet, Lemon Yellow, Burgundy, Kelly Green, Moss Green, Brown, Ivory Icing Colors, p. 110
- Flower Nail No. 7, 9 Pc. Flower Former Set, p. 113
- Meringue Powder, p. 111
- Cake Board, 10 in. Round White Doilies, p. 159
- Buttercream, Royal Icings, p. 92
- Waxed paper squares, fine artist's paint brush

Combine brown, ivory and a little violet for basket color.
Combine moss green and a little brown for leaf color.

- Use royal icing to make flowers and leaves; make extras to allow for breakage. Make approximately 50 pansies (p. 99) in assorted colors – fifteen tip 104, thirty-five tip 103, both with tip 2 loop centers; including some using brush striping and color striping techniques (p. 93). Make approximately 50 tip 104 ruffled leaves (p. 99); brush striped with kelly green. Place in and on flower formers to dry. When dry, paint pansies using artist's brush and icing color thinned with water.
- Assemble cake, placing half ball cake on top of 1 layer 3 in. deep round. Cover sides with tip 45 basketweave; overpipe vertical lines for added dimension. Add tip 2B smooth side up band around top of cake. Using spatula, build up icing mound on cake top around ball cake.
- Position flowers and leaves.

Serves 15

Say It With Flowers

- 7, 10 in. Round Pans, p. 164
- Tips 1, 2, 2B, 3, 14, 16, 18, 21, 103, 224, 349, 352, p. 116-119
- Violet, Moss Green, Lemon Yellow, Burgundy Icing Colors, p. 110
- '97 Pattern Book (Spanish Alphabet Pattern), p. 108
- Flower Nail No. 9, 9 Pc. Flower Former Set, p. 113
- Decorator Brush Set, p. 120
- Dowel Rods, p. 156
- Cake Board, Fanci-Foil Wrap, p. 159
- Meringue Powder, p. 111
- Crystalique Butterfly Picks, p. 136
- Buttercream, Royal Icings, p. 92
- Using royal icing, make the following in advance: 10 tip 2B smooth side up arched bands on medium flower formers; 70 tip 224 drop flowers with tip 1 dot centers; a variety of 30 tip 103 pansies (p. 99) with tip 1 center string loops. Make extras of all to allow for breakage and let dry.
- Ice 2-layer 7 in. and 10 in. cakes smooth and prepare for stacked construction (see p. 96)
- **On 7 in. cake:** Pipe tip 16 top and tip 18 bottom shell borders.
- **On 10 in. cake:** Mark cake top edge at 2 in. intervals. Pipe tip 3 triple drop strings, 1½ in. deep. Pipe tip 18 top and tip 21 bottom shell borders. Add tip 14 S-curves around bottom shells.
- Use Spanish Alphabet Pattern to trace message. Pipe tip 1 and 2 name.
- Position arched bands on cake; add flowers and tip 352 leaves. Position flowers on shells and add tip 349 leaves. Add flowers and tip 352 leaves to 7 in. cake top. Position butterfly picks.

Serves 34.

A Worthy Tribute

- 10 in. x 3 in. deep Round Pan, p. 161
- Tips 2, 9, 11, p. 116-119
- Ready-To-Use Rolled Fondant (2 pkgs. needed), p. 112
- Cake Board, Fanci-Foil Wrap, p. 159
- Candy Melts®*- Light Cocoa (1 bag needed), p. 120
- Disposable Decorating Bags, p. 114
- 30-Pc. Gum Paste Flowers Kit, p. 112
- Candy Clay Recipe, p. 105
- Buttercream Icing, p. 92
- Ready-to-use chocolate icing, corn syrup, pre-melted unsweetened chocolate packets (Five 1 oz. pkgs. needed)

- Using candy clay and "Modeling A Candy Clay Rose" instructions on p. 105, make three 1 ³/₄ in. roses, thirteen 1 in. roses, 16 leaves and 3 rosebuds. Set aside.
- Prepare 10 in. x 3 in. round cake for rolled fondant (see p. 92). To make chocolate rolled fondant, knead 1 ¹/₂ boxes of fondant with five 1-oz. packages of pre-melted unsweetened chocolate. Store remaining fondant.
- Using ready-to-use icing and disposable bags, pipe tip 9 and 11 triple bead border (p. 99). Pipe tip 9 bead border 1 in. away from top edge.
- Attach roses and leaves with buttercream. Pipe tip 2 message.

Serves 16.

Stirrup That Cowpoke!
- Western Boot Pan, p. 170
- Tips 1, 2, 3, 5, 8, 16, 21, p. 116-119
- Brown, Golden Yellow, Ivory Icing Colors, p. 110
- '97 Pattern Book (Boot Stitching Pattern), p. 108
- Cake Boards, Fanci-Foil Wrap, p. 159
- Li'l Cowpoke, p. 134
- Buttercream Icing, p. 92

Note: To achieve gold color shown, mix golden yellow and brown.

- Ice cake top and sides smooth. Mark pattern on top using toothpick. Outline boot using tip 3, outline pattern using tip 5. Cover with tip 16 stars. Pipe tip 8 strings for heel and sole.
- Pipe message using tips 1 and 2. Add tip 21 bottom rope border. Position topper.

Serves 12.

Chocolate Illusion
- 8 in., 10 in. Square Pans, p. 161
- Numbers Pan Set, p. 170
- Tips 7, 9, p. 116
- Cake Boards, Fanci-Foil Wrap, p. 159
- Candy Melts®*- Lt. Cocoa, Dark Cocoa, White (1 bag each needed), p. 120
- Hidden Pillars, p. 156
- Disposable Decorating Bags, p. 114
- Chocolate Buttercream Icing, p. 92
- Your favorite mocha icing recipe, waxed paper

*brand confectionery coating

- Combine ³/₄ bag lt. cocoa and ¹/₄ bag white Candy Melts and melt following package directions. Mold a candy plaque using 8 in. square pan (p. 105). Melt dark cocoa candy and mold ¹/₄ in. thick plaques in numbers pans. Pipe tip 7 message on waxed paper; refrigerate to set.
- Prepare 3 disposable bags filled with white, lt. cocoa and dark cocoa melted candy; alternately drizzle top of 8 in. plaque. Let set. Position plaque on board with waxed paper and pipe tip 7 candy bead border. Add piped message and number plaques, securing with dots of melted candy. Let set completely.

- Spatula ice 1-layer 10 in. cake. Pipe tip 7 top and tip 9 bottom bead borders.
- Cut hidden pillars: One 3 ¼ in., two 2 ¾ in., one 2 ½ in. Visualizing a clock face on cake top, position 3 ¼ in. pillar at 11:00, 2 ¾ pillars at 7:00 and 2:00, and 2 ½ in. pillar at 4:00. Coat pillar tops with a small amount of melted candy and position plaque.

Serves 14.

He's Our Mane Man!

- **Jungle Lion Pan, p. 167**
- **Tips 2, 3, 8, 16, 21, p. 116-119**
- **Golden Yellow, Black, Red, Brown Icing Colors, p. 110**
- **'97 Pattern Book (Lion Face and Crown Patterns), p. 108**
- **Cake Board, Fanci-Foil Wrap, p. 159**
- **Buttercream Icing, p. 92**
- **Black shoestring licorice**

Note: To achieve face color mix Golden Yellow with Brown.

- Trace Crown Pattern on cake board; cut and cover with foil. Set aside.
- Ice cake smooth. Trace Lion Face Pattern with toothpick. Outline face with tip 3. Pipe in nose, mouth and eyes with tip 8 (smooth with finger dipped in cornstarch). Pipe tip 8 tongue and teeth.
- Cover face and ears with tip 16 stars. Pipe tip 3 string eyebrows. Pipe tip 21 pull out star mane. Pipe tip 21 reverse shell bottom border.
- Pipe tip 2 dots on muzzle. Print tip 2 message on crown and insert into cake. Pipe additional tip 21 pull-out mane over crown. Add licorice whiskers.

Serves 12.

NO "LION" DAD you're the BEST!

LOOK WHO'S 26

Tepee Treat

- Christmas Tree Cookie Treat Pan, p. 180
- Tips 2, 5, 12, 67, p. 116-119
- Ivory, Orange, Lemon Yellow, Christmas Red, Black, Copper (Lt. Skintone) Icing Colors, p. 110
- Cookie Treat Sticks, p. 122
- Buttercream Icing, p. 92

*brand confectionery coating

- Bake and cool cookies following pan recipe and baking instructions.
- Ice cookie smooth. Pipe tip 5 bands on tepee. Pipe tip 5 dot sun (flatten) with tip 2 line rays. Pipe tip 12 ball head (flatten and smooth with finger dipped in cornstarch). Pipe tip 2 string hair, eyes and mouth; dot nose. Add tip 2 zigzag headband and tip 67 pull-out feather.

Each serves 1.

Rough Landing

- Snowman Cookie Treat Pan, p. 180
- Tips 2, 3, 5, 7, 16, 67, p. 116-119
- Sky Blue, Orange, Christmas Red, Black, Brown, Kelly Green, Lemon Yellow Icing Colors, p. 110
- Cookie Treat Sticks, p. 122
- Buttercream Icing, p. 92
- Pretzel sticks

- Bake and cool cookies following pan recipe and instructions. Ice fluffy with yellow icing. Pipe tip 5 dot eyes with tip 2 dot pupils (smooth with finger dipped in cornstarch). Add tip 67 pull-out feathers; tip 16 pull-out "hair". Pipe tip 7 beak.
- Position pretzel for perch; pipe tip 3 string "claws".

Each serves 1.

All Smiles

- Bunny Cookie Treat Pan, p. 174
- Tips 2, 3, 12, p. 116-119
- Black, Christmas Red, Pink, Brown, Copper (Lt. Skintone) Icing Colors, p. 110
- Cookie Treat Sticks, p. 122
- Buttercream Icing, p. 92

- Bake and cool cookies following pan recipe and baking instructions.

- Ice face smooth. Outline and pipe-in mouth with tip 2. Pipe tip 2 string eyes. Pipe tip 3 dot nose, cheeks and tongue. Add tip 2 string hair. Pipe tip 12 bow (smooth with finger dipped in cornstarch).

Each serves 1.

A New Twist

- Jack-O-Lantern Cookie Treat Pan, p. 177
- Tips 1, 1A, p. 116-119
- Brown, Lemon Yellow Icing Colors, p. 110
- Cookie Treat Sticks, p. 122
- Buttercream Icing, p. 92

- Bake and cool cookies following pan recipe and baking instructions.
- Add a small amount of Lemon Yellow to Brown Icing. Pipe tip 1A pretzel shape on cookie. Pipe tip 1 dot salt.

Star Power

- 6 Pc. Nesting Star Cookie Cutters (2nd largest size used), p. 123
- Tips 2, 9, p. 116-119
- Lemon Yellow, Red-Red Icing Colors, p. 110
- Rainbow Nonpareils Sprinkle Decorations, p. 126
- Roll-Out Cookie Dough Recipe, p. 94
- Buttercream Icing, p. 92

- Cut out cookies. Bake and cool. Ice smooth. Pipe tip 9 band around top edge of cookie. Pipe tip 2 name. Sprinkle nonpareils on band.

Each serves 1.

Flying Colors

- Butterfly Perimeter Cookie Cutter, p. 123
- Tips 2, 3, p. 116-119
- Lemon Yellow, Sky Blue, Red-Red Icing Colors, p. 110
- Roll-Out Cookie Dough Recipe, p. 94
- Buttercream Icing, p. 92

- Cut out cookies. Bake and cool.
- Ice cookie smooth, outline using tip 2. Pipe tip 3 body; add dot and string designs with tips 2 and 3.

Each serves 1.

No Melting!

- Ice Cream Cone Perimeter Cookie Cutter, p. 123
- Tip 10, p. 116-119
- Lemon Yellow, Pink, Leaf Green Icing Colors, p. 110
- Rainbow Nonpareils Sprinkle Decorations, p. 126
- Chocolate Roll-Out Cookie Dough Recipe, p. 94
- Buttercream Icing, p. 92

- Cut out cookies and score cone marks with paring knife before baking. Bake and cool. Pipe tip 10 mounds of "ice cream". Sprinkle with nonpareils.

Each serves 1.

Set Sail

- Sailboat Perimeter Cookie Cutter, p. 123
- Tips 2, 4, 5, 9, 14, p. 116-119
- Brown, Sky Blue, Red-Red, Lemon Yellow, Copper (Lt. Skintone) Icing Colors, p. 110
- '97 Pattern Book (Stand Pattern), p. 108
- Roll-Out Cookie Dough Recipe, p. 94
- 8 in. Angled Spatula, p. 111
- Buttercream Icing, p. 92

- Cut sailboat, stand (using pattern) and two 1 in. squares out of cookie dough. Bake and cool.
- Ice sailboat and stand smooth. Cover boat with tip 4 strings. Using tips 2, 5, and 9, figure pipe sailor (see p. 000).
- Attach sailboat to stand with dots of icing. Make an easel in a "L" shape to support the sailboat by attaching with icing one cookie square to back of sailboat and one cookie square to the stand.
- Using tip 14, pipe a double row of waves.

Each serves 1.

It's A Slice!

- Circle Perimeter Cookie Cutter, p. 123
- Tips 3, 7, 8, p. 116-119
- Pink, Leaf Green, Black Icing Colors, p. 110
- Disposable Decorating Bags, p. 114
- Roll-Out Cookie Dough Recipe, p. 94

- Prepare cookie dough, tinting 1/2 dough pink, 1/2 dough green and 1/8 dough black. Leave remainder plain.
- Roll out and cut pink circles with cookie cutter. Slice circle in half and place on cookie sheet. Thin green and white cookie dough with water to pipe through a tip. Pipe tip 7 white line on watermelon; pipe tip 8 green rind. Pipe tip 3 black dot seeds. Bake and cool.

Each serves 1.

Make A Face

- Star, Heart, Round Cookie Treat Pans, p. 122
- Orange, Leaf Green, Sky Blue, Lemon Yellow, Violet, Pink Icing Colors, p. 110
- Cookie Treat Sticks, p. 122
- Candy Melts®*, White, p. 120
- Disposable Decorating Bags, p. 114
- Roll-Out Cookie Dough Recipe, p. 94
- Small paring knife; fabric bows; shredded coconut; assorted candy trim: rolled fruit sheets, candy wafers, candy-coated chocolate dots (regular and mini size), candy jellies

*brand confectionery coating

- Tint cookie dough. Bake cookies following pan recipe and instructions. Cool.
- Tint coconut with icing color (see p. 103); cut rolled fruit with paring knife into desired shapes for mouths. Attach coconut and candy trim using melted Candy Melts. Tie fabric bows on sticks.

Each serves 1.

Cookie Cupboard

The Party Begins

Use tip 3; Lemon Yellow, Red, Royal Blue, Orange and Kelly Green Icing Colors; Balloons Standard Baking Cups; Rainbow Peanut Bits Sprinkle Decorations.

Just Say No!

Use tips 3, 16; No-taste Red and Lemon Yellow Icing Colors; Balloons Standard Baking Cups; Rainbow Nonpareils Sprinkle Decorations.

Totally

Use tips 3, 47(smooth side); Orange, Royal Blue, Lemon Yellow and No-taste Red Icing Colors; Crayons Standard Baking Cups; Rainbow Jimmies Sprinkle Decorations.

Singular Celebration

Use tip 2110 (1M); Lemon Yellow Icing Color; Balloons Standard Baking Cups; Rainbow Nonpareils Sprinkle Decorations.

Petite Treats

Slam Dunk

Use tip 3; Ivory and Brown Icing Colors; Basketball Standard Baking Cups; Basketballs Icing Decorations; 4 in. Lollipop Sticks.

What A Catch

Use tips 3, 12, 104; Royal Blue, No-taste Red, Black and Copper (Lt. Skintone) Icing Colors; Baseball Standard Baking Cups; Baseball Mitts Icing Decorations.

Goal In Sight

Use tips 2, 3, 233; Royal Blue and Kelly Green Icing Colors; Soccer Standard Baking Cups; Soccer Balls Icing Decorations.

Hit The Jackpot

Use tips 1, 2B, 3, 5; Black, No-taste Red and Kelly Green Icing Colors; Gold Foil Petite Loaf Baking Cups; yellow candy-coated chocolate dots, peppermint stick, mini jaw breakers.

Surrounded By Fun

Use tip 3; No-taste Red and Lemon Yellow Icing Colors; Gold Foil Petite Loaf Baking Cups; Clowns and Balloons Icing Decorations; mini jaw breakers.

Strawberry & Cream

Use Tips 1, 2110 (1M); Gold Foil Petite Loaf Baking Cups; Lt. Cocoa Candy Melts®*; Stabilized Whipped Cream Icing (p, 92); fresh strawberry.

Jump To It

Use tips 1, 3,; Lemon Yellow, Orange, Kelly Green, Royal Blue, No-taste Red and Black Icing Colors; Teddy Bears Standard Baking Cups; Teddy Bears Icing Decorations.

And The Winner Is...

Use tips 3, 125; Red-Red Icing Color; White Standard Baking Cups; strawberry rolled fruit sheets.

Desert Dessert

Use tips 2, 131, 362; Juniper Green, Brown Pink, and Lemon Yellow Icing Colors; Western Standard Baking Cups; large marshmallow, granulated brown sugar.

First Down

Use tip 3; Royal Blue and Kelly Green Icing Colors; Football Standard Baking Cups; Footballs Icing Decorations; Rainbow Nonpareils Sprinkle Decorations.

The Cat's Meow

Use tips 2, 3, 12, 352; Lemon Yellow, Pink and Black Icing Colors; Kittens Standard Baking Cups; black string licorice.

Dog Spotted

Use tips 2, 3, 12; Black and No-taste Red Icing Colors; Dalmatians Standard Baking Cups.

Play It Again

Use tips 3, 47 (smooth side); Black, Royal Blue, Red (no-taste) and Leaf Green Icing Colors; Green Foil Petite Loaf Baking Cups.

Makes The Grade

Use tips 3, 21; Black, Brown, No-taste Red and Leaf Green Icing Colors; Red Foil Petite Loaf Baking Cups; Bite-Size Apple Cookie Cutter; Roll-out Cookie Recipe, p. 94.

Hearts & Roses

Use Tips 10, 13, 103, 352; No-taste Red and Kelly Green Icing Colors; Hearts Petite Loaf Baking Cups.

*brand confectionery coating

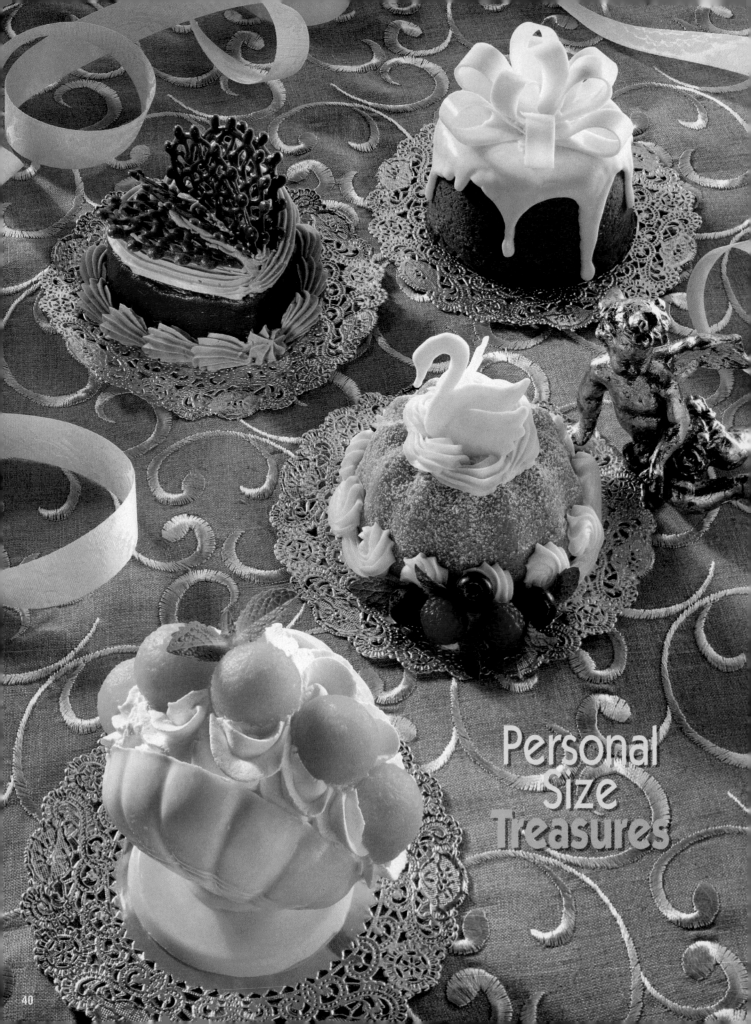

Personal
Size
Treasures

Good Things Come In Small Packages
- Mini Angel Food Pan, p. 166
- White Candy Melts®* (1 pkg. needed), p. 120
- 8 in. Round Gold Doilies, p. 159
- 8 in. Angled Spatula, p. 111 • Favorite chocolate cake recipe
- Freezer paper • Ready-To-Use Canned Icing (optional)

*brand confectionery coating

- Make 12 candy bow loops: Melt candy following package directions. Cut freezer paper into twelve strips, 1/2 in. wide x 3 1/2 in. long. Spread an even layer of candy on the shiny side of each strip, covering to the edges. Clean the edges of each strip with your fingers. Set strips aside until they are partially set, but still pliable (approximately 4-5 minutes, candy should still be wet, but not run off strips). Fold over and pinch ends of each strip together, coated surfaces touching. Place each loop on its side to set completely.
- Pour melted candy or icing over cooled cake. Peel paper off candy loops, assemble bow on cake using additional melted candy: position 8 loops horizontally at base of bow, position 4 center loops at a slight vertical angle. Let set.

Each serves 1.

Fancy Filigree Hearts
- Mini Embossed Heart Pan, p. 173
- Tips 2, 21, p. 116-117
- Lt. Cocoa Candy Melts®*, p. 120
- '97 Pattern Book (Half Filigree Heart Pattern), p. 108
- Disposable Decorating Bags, p. 114
- 8 in. Round Gold Doilies, p. 159
- Chocolate Buttercream Icing, p. 92
- Your favorite mocha icing, waxed paper

*brand confectionery coating

- Melt candy following package directions. Make 5 Half Filigree Hearts: Cover patterns with waxed paper; using tip 2, outline half hearts and pipe cornelli-style filigree. Let set and carefully peel off paper.
- Ice cake smooth in chocolate buttercream. Using tip 21 and mocha buttercream pipe heart outline on top edge of cake, continue piping outlines until cake top is covered; add tip 21 bottom shell border.
- Position filigree hearts on cake top.

Each serves 1.

Little Swan Lake
- Petite Fancy Ring Mold Pan, p. 166
- Tip 21, p. 117
- '97 Pattern Book (Petite Swan Pattern) p. 108
- White Candy Melts®* (1 bag needed), p. 120
- 8 in. Round Gold Doilies, p. 159
- Disposable Decorating Bags, p. 114 •Buttercream Icing, p. 92
- Waxed paper, fresh fruit and mint, confectioners sugar

*brand confectionery coating

- Melt candy following package directions. Make swan: Cover pattern with waxed paper. Using a disposable bag and melted candy, outline and fill-in swan body and two wings. Let set, turn over and overpipe. Let dry completely. Attach wings with melted candy.
- Bake and cool cakes. Pipe tip 21 top shell and bottom c-shell borders. Sprinkle with powdered sugar. Position swan on cake top. Add fruit and mint.

Each serves 1.

Harvest Of Treasures
- Mini Shell Pan, Muffin Caps® Pan, p. 165
- Tip 2110 (1M), p. 117
- Candy Melts®*- White (1 bag needed to make 2 complete dishes), p. 120
- 8 in. Round Gold Doilies, p. 159
- 4 Pc. Candy Colors Set, p. 120
- Disposable Decorating Bags, p. 114
- Stabilized Whipped Cream, p. 92
- Fresh fruit, packaged pound cake

- Make Candy Plaque shells and bases (see p. 104) using pans and melted Candy Melts. (Note: To achieve marblized effect, orange and red candy colors were mixed into melted white candy.)
- To assemble shell, attach 2 candy shell halves to muffin cap base with melted candy. Let set.
- To serve, cut pound cake into bite-sized pieces and place in bottom of shell. Add swirls of whipped cream with tip 2110 (1M). Garnish with fresh fruit. Serve immediately or refrigerate.

Each serves 1.

Teddy's Ready Quickly!
- Mini Bear Pan, p. 171
- Candy Melts®*- Lt. Cocoa, Orange, (1 bag each needed), p. 120
- Disposable Decorating Bags, p. 114
- Favorite crisped rice cereal treat recipe

*brand confectionery coating

- Prepare crisped rice cereal treat recipe according to directions. Spray pan with vegetable spray. Press rice mixture into pan three-fourths full. Let set.
- When rice treats are set, pour melted candy over tops while still in pan. Refrigerate until candy is set (approximately 30 minutes).
- Remove from pan and pipe facial features and paws with melted candy in cut disposable bag.

Each serves 1.

Met Him On A Sundae!
- Mini Loaf Pan, p. 163
- Tip 21, p. 117
- Candy Melts®*- White (1 bag needed), 4 Pc. Candy Colors Set, p. 120
- Loving Bears Lollipop Mold, p. 121
- Chocolate syrup, mini marshmallows
- Rainbow Peanut Bits Sprinkle Decorations, p. 126
- Cake Board, Fanci-Foil Wrap, p. 159
- Buttercream Icing, p. 92
- Favorite mocha icing recipe

*brand confectionery coating

- Melt candy following package directions. Tint and mold teddy bears using "painting" method (p. 104). (Note: Do not use lollipop stick.)
- Ice cakes smooth. Pipe tip 21 reverse shells on top of cake and bottom border. Add mini marshmallows to cake top. Drizzle with chocolate syrup. Position bear and pipe tip 21 drops of icing on bear's head and hand. Add sprinkles.

Each serves 1.

Colorful Kids

- Mini Gingerbread Boy Pan, p. 183
- Tips 2, 3, 9, p. 116-119
- Leaf Green, Sky Blue, Copper (Lt. Skintone), Christmas Red, Brown Icing Colors, p. 110
- Crayon Icing Decorations, p. 126
- Candy Melts®*, White (1 bag yields 3 molded candies), p. 120
- Buttercream Icing, p. 92

*brand confectionery coating

- Melt candy following package directions. Place cakes on rack over drip pan. Cover with melted candy; let set.
- Pipe tip 9 ball heads, flatten with finger dipped in cornstarch. Add tip 3 string body outlines, secure icing decorations with dots of melted candy. Pipe tip 3 dot hands and feet; outline skirt and pipe tip 3 zigzag to fill in. Add tip 2 dot and string eyes, mouth and hair.

Each serves 1.

Home Sweet Home

- Mini Angel Food Pan, p. 166
- Tips 2, 3, 7, 16, 2110 (1M), p. 116-119
- Pink, Lemon Yellow, Christmas Red, Leaf Green Icing Colors, p. 110
- Rainbow Nonpareils Sprinkle Decorations, p. 126
- Party Bear Candle Set, p. 129
- Buttercream Icing, p. 92
- Cherries (candy or maraschino)

- Each "cupcake house" requires one mini angel food cake to complete.
- Pipe tip 7 windows and door, smooth with spatula; outline using tip 3. Cover sides with tip 7 vertical strings, piping from bottom up. Pipe tip 16 star flowers, add tip 2 dot centers and tip 3 pull-out leaves.
- Pipe tip 2110 (1M) in a spiral motion on top of house. Add sprinkle decorations. Position candles and cherry.

Each serves 1.

Total Wackos!

- Mini Heart Pan, p. 173
- Tips 7, 16, p. 116-119
- Black, Red-Red, Lemon Yellow, Leaf Green Icing Colors, p. 110
- Buttercream Icing, p. 92
- Large marshmallows, square gum pieces, candy coated chocolates

- Using tip 7, pipe in mouth area (smooth with finger dipped in cornstarch).
- Flatten marshmallows and position for eyes.
- Cover remainder of face with tip 16 stars. Pipe tip 16 green stars around eyes. Attach candy pupils with dots of icing.
- Add tip 16 pull-out star hair.
- Build up nose area with another layer of tip 16 stars. Pipe tip 7 dot nostrils.
- Position gum teeth.

Each serves 1.

Scentimental Guy

- Aluminum Panda Mold, p. 171
- Tips 1A, 2, 2A, 3, 9, 12, 16, 131, 349, p. 116-119
- Black, Pink, Lemon Yellow, Leaf Green, Christmas Red Icing Colors, p. 110
- Meringue Powder, p. 111
- '97 Pattern Book (Skunk Tail Pattern), p. 108
- Buttercream, Royal Icings, p. 92

- Make skunk's tail at least a day ahead of time. Position waxed paper over tail pattern. With royal icing and tip 1A, fill in tail; with tip 12, fill in spikes. Let dry. When completely dry remove waxed paper, turn tail over and repeat same process on back. Let dry.
- Using royal icing, pipe four tip 131 drop flowers with tip 3 dot centers. Make extras to allow for breakage and let dry.
- After cake is baked, cut ears off. Build up leg area with tip 2A. Pull-out tip 3 claws.
- Outline white area of face and tummy with tip 3. Pipe tip 9 ball ears (smooth with finger dipped in cornstarch). Add tip 16 pull-out fur on ears. Outline tip 3 mouth. Pipe in tip 3 facial features and tongue (smooth with finger dipped in cornstarch). Pipe tip 2 line between nose and mouth.

Mini Mania!

- Position tail, inserting spikes into cake. Cover skunk with tip 16 stars. Add tip 16 pull-out stars on tail and white streaks on head and back.
- Position flowers, add tip 349 leaves and tip 3 string stems.

Each serves 1.

Star For A Day
- Mini Star Pan, p. 170
- Tips 3, 18, p. 116-119
- Teal, Pink, Lemon Yellow Icing Colors, p. 110
- Carousel Horse Candles Set, p. 129
- Buttercream Icing, p. 92
- Ice top of cake smooth. Pipe tip 18 zigzags on sides of cake. Pipe tip 3 outline on cake top. Position candle.

Each serves 1.

Something's Fishy
- Mini Balloon Pan, p. 168
- Tips 4, 8, 16, 32, p. 116-119
- Orange, Black Icing Colors, p. 110
- '97 Pattern Book (Eyes and Mouth Pattern), p. 108
- Buttercream Icing, p. 92
- Ice cake smooth; trace pattern for eyes and mouth. Pipe tip 32 pull-out star fins on sides and back of fish. Pull out tip 16 "hair". Pipe in mouth with tip 4. Pipe tip 8 lips and tail, add tip 32 pull-out star fins to tail. Add tip 4 bead tongue and dot eyes (smooth with finger dipped in cornstarch).

Each serves 1.

Dinomite Party!
- Mini Dinosaur Pan, p. 168
- Tip 2, p. 116-119
- Leaf Green, Orange Icing Colors, p. 110
- Candy Melts®*- Yellow, Orange (1 bag each needed), p. 120
- Dinosaur Mix Sprinkle Decorations, p. 126
- Parchment Triangles, p. 114
- Ice Cream
- To achieve color shades, add desired amount of icing color to batter. Bake and cool cakes.
- In parchment triangle, fitted with tip 2, add melted candy and pipe spots and facial features. Add sprinkles.

Each serves 1.

Fast Food
- Muffin Caps® Pan, p. 165
- Tips 2A, 4, 103, 362, p. 116-119
- Brown, Leaf Green, Golden Yellow, Red-Red Icing Colors, p. 110
- Buttercream Icing, p. 92
- Bake and cool "bun" cakes.
- Pipe tip 2A circular motion string hamburger to cover bottom bun. Pipe tip 362 circular motion string onion. Pipe-in tip 4 ketchup and cheese. Add tip 103 ruffle lettuce. Position inverted top bun.

Each serves 1.

Diaper Divers
- Mini Balloon Pan, p. 168
- Tips 1, 2, 3, 5, 7, 16, 225, p. 116-119
- Brown, Copper (Lt. Skintone), Royal Blue, Pink, Black, Golden Yellow Icing Colors, p. 110
- Buttercream Icing, p. 92

- Pipe tip 225 drop flowers (4 for each cake) with tip 2 dot centers. Let dry.
- Ice cakes smooth. Pipe tip 3 parachute outlines and strings. Cover parachute with tip 16 stars.
- Figure pipe babies (p. 102) with tip 7 bodies, tip 5 arms and feet. Pipe in tip 3 diapers and tip 3 bow. Pipe tip 1 pull-out hair and dot and string facial features.
- Position flowers. Add tip 3 rosette on top of balloon.

Each serves 1.

Rockin' Lullaby!
- 26 Pc. Alphabet Cookie Cutter Set, p. 124
- Royal Blue Icing Color, p. 110
- Roll-Out Cookie Dough Recipe, p. 94

- Tint cookie dough. Cut out cookies, bake, cool. Position around cake.

Each serves 1.

Shake It Up, Baby!
- Cute Baby Pan, p. 168
- Tips 3, 5, 7, 16, 364, p. 116-119
- Copper (Lt. Skintone), Royal Blue, Pink, Brown, Black, Lemon Yellow Icing Colors, p. 110
- '97 Pattern Book (face, guitar, hands patterns), p. 108
- Cake Board, Fanci-Foil Wrap, p. 159
- Buttercream Icing, p. 92

- Cut guitar pattern from cake board and cover with foil. Pipe tip 3 center of guitar, outline and strings. Pipe tip 3 dot tuning pegs. Set aside.
- ce cake smooth. Mark face and hands pattern with toothpick. Outline face, body, booties and facial features with tip 3. Pipe in tongue, sunglasses with tip 7 (smooth with finger dipped in cornstarch). Cover cake with tip 16 stars. Build up nose with tip 7.
- Add tip 16 pull-out hair. Pipe tip 3 string eyebrows. Positon guitar on cake. Outline tip 3 hands; fill in with tip 16 stars.
- Pipe tip 16 star pom poms on booties. Pipe tip 5 musical notes on sides of cake. Add tip 364 star bottom border.

Serves 12.

Sweet Baby Lamb
- 2 Pc. 3-D Cuddly Bear Pan Set, p. 171
- Tips 2, 3, 4, 8, 10, 12, 16, 18, p. 116-119
- Pink, Black Icing Colors, p. 110
- 4 Pc. Baby Blocks Set (3 sets needed), p. 133
- Buttercream Icing, p. 92

- Trim off back area from ears. Extend ear length by piping tip 8 ear centers edged with tip 18 reverse shells. Build up muzzle area with 16 stars. Outline mouth and eyes with tip 3.
- Ice bottoms of feet smooth. Cover face with tip 16 stars. Build up arms with tip 12. Cover arms and body with tip 18 reverse shells.

- Attach block to lamb with icing. Outline hooves with tip 3, pipe in with tip 10. Pipe tip 2 pull-out eyelashes. Pipe in tip 4 nose and bead tongue (smooth with finger dipped in cornstarch). Position remainder of blocks around cake.

Serves 12.

Wishing Stars
- 6 Pc. Nesting Star Cooki Cutter Set (2 smallest cutters used), p. 123
- Tip 2, p. 116-119
- Lemon Yellow Icing Colo p. 110
- Roll-Out Cookie Dough, p. 94
- Poured Cookie Icing, p. 92

- Bake and cool cookies. Pour on icing. Decorate with tip 2 dots and strings.

Each serves 1.

Pooh's Bedtime Stories
- Winnie The Pooh Pan, p. 185
- Tips 4, 16, 20, p. 116-119
- 2 Pc. Pooh Icing Colors Set, Royal Blue, Black, Burgundy, Teal Icing Colors, p. 185
- '97 Pattern Book (Bedtime Pooh Pattern), p. 108
- Cake Board, Fanci-Foil Wrap, p. 159
- Buttercream Icing, p. 92

- Ice sides and lightly ice top of cake smooth. Using toothpick, mark pattern.
- Ice book and bottom of feet smooth. Outline body, nightshirt stripes, book and hat with tip 4 strings. Pipe tip 4 dot eyes and nose. Pipe in tip 4 mouth and tongue (smooth with finger dipped in cornstarch).
- Cover body, shirt, hat and face with tip 16 stars. Add tip 16 pull-out star tassel on hat. Add tip 20 star bottom border.

Serves 12.

A Blessed Day

- 4-Pc. Oval Pan Set (10³/₄ x 7⁷/₈ in., 13 x 9 ⁷/₈ in., 16 x 12³/₈ in. pans used), p. 161
- Tips 1, 2, 3, 4B, 10, 12, 32, 103, 104, 352, 362, p. 116-119
- Flower Nail No. 9, p. 113
- Sky Blue Icing Color, p. 110
- Tube Decorating Gels - Blue, Yellow, Pink, Green, Orange, (1 each needed), Meringue Powder, p. 111
- Cake Board, Fanci-Foil Wrap, p. 159
- Chapel Windows, p. 152
- Wooden Dowel Rods, p. 156
- Italic Message Press Set, p. 113
- Communion Boy Cake Topper, p. 133
- Buttercream, Royal Icings, p. 92

- At least 1 day in advance, sparingly pipe chapel windows with Tube Decorating Gels. With royal icing, pipe tip 3 dots around windows. Let dry.
- With tip 3 and thinned down royal icing, pipe a 2 in. circle on waxed paper to be used as a foundation for topper. Let dry. Attach Communion Boy Topper with dots of royal icing. Let dry.
- Using royal icing, make 14 tip 104 roses with tip 12 bases and 10 tip 103 roses with tip 10 bases. Make 12 tip 103 rose buds. Make extras to allow for breakage and let dry.
- Ice 1-layer cakes smooth and prepare for stacked construction (see p. 96).
- **On top tier:** Pipe tip 32 crown border. Pipe tip 362 line on alternating crowns. Add tip 3 double drop strings with tip 3 dots. Pipe tip 32 shell bottom border.
- **On middle tier:** Pipe tip 32 crown border. Pipe tip 362 shells on alternating crowns. Add tip 3 double drop strings with tip 3 dots. Pipe tip 32 shell bottom border.
- **On bottom tier:** Alternate, piping tip 32 and tip 4B crown borders. On tip 32 crowns, add tip 362 line; on tip 4B crowns, add 362 shells. Add tip 3 double drop strings with tip 3 dots. Pipe tip 32 shell bottom border.
- Imprint message on bottom tier and write with tip 2; add tip 1 dots. Position windows, topper with base and flowers. Add tip 352 leaves.

Serves 72.

Touched By The Spirit

- Cross Pan, p. 175
- Tips 1, 2, 3, 5, 7, 10, 14, 16, 45, 102, 103, 352, p. 116-119
- Flower Nail No. 9, p. 113
- Lemon Yellow, Buttercup Yellow, Juniper Green Icing Colors, p. 110
- Cake Board, Fanci-Foil Wrap, p. 159
- Color Flow Mix, Meringue Powder, p. 111
- '97 Pattern Book (Dove and End Piece Designs), p. 108
- Designer Pattern Press, p. 113
- Color Flow Icings, p. 101
- Royal, Buttercream Icing, p. 92

Note: Mix Lemon Yellow and Buttercup Yellow to achieve shade shown.

- Using Dove, End Piece Design Patterns and color flow icing, outline patterns with tip 2. When dry, flow-in with thinned icing (see p. 101). Let dry. When dry, overpipe tip 2 yellow outline on end pieces. Let dry.
- Using royal icing, make 8 tip 103 roses and 11 tip 102 roses, both with tip 10 bases. Make 50 tip 102 rosebuds. Make extras of each to allow for breakage, let dry.
- Ice smooth top of cross in yellow and sides in white. Pipe tip 45 band cross on top of cake. Pipe tip 3 beads on edge and down center of band and at edge of yellow cross area. Imprint curlique pattern press on sides of cake. Pipe imprinted design with tip 7, overpipe with tip 14. Pipe tip 5 bead border on top edge of cake. Pipe tip 16 shell bottom border.
- Attach roses and rosebuds with buttercream. Add tip 2 sepals on rosebuds; tip 352 leaves and tip 1 vines. Position Color Flow* dove and end piece designs.

Serves 12.

*Note: Since buttercream icing will break down color flow, position on a piece of plastic wrap cut to fit, sugar cubes or mini marshmallows.

A Gift From Above

- 8 in., 12 in. Round Pans, p. 162
- Tips 1, 2, 3, 103, 125, 225, 233, 363, p. 116-119
- Rose, Moss Green, Sky Blue, Brown, Black Icing Colors, p. 110
- Ready-To-Use Rolled Fondant (4 pkgs. needed), Gum Paste Flowers Kit, p. 112
- 3 Pc. Egg Making Set, p. 174
- 14 in. Ruffle Board, p. 159
- Meringue Powder, Piping Gel, p. 111
- Small Doves, p. 151
- Dowel Rods, p. 156
- Decorator Brush Set, p. 120
- 6 in. Decorator Preferred Separator Plate, p.157
- 56 Pc. Make Any Message Letter Press Set, p. 113
- 2 Pc. Sleeping Angels Set, p. 133
- Royal, Buttercream Icing, p. 92
- Granulated sugar

- Using 1 box of fondant, color ½ Rose, ¼ Moss Green and a small amount Brown.
- **Make bassinet:** Following instructions included in kit and using the medium egg mold, make a solid sugar egg half using the bottom mold. Make a hollow sugar egg half using the top mold; before scooping out sugar, cut approximately 1½ in. off the wider end. Let dry

completely. Cover the outside of bottom egg half with a light coating of piping gel, then with rolled fondant. Imprint with tip 225 for a quilted look. Attach a piece of rolled fondant to cover the inside of the top using piping gel; trim even with edges. Roll 2 strips of fondant and attach to outside of the top to create folds. Attach a piece of fondant over folds, trim even with edges and imprint with tip 225. Place a piece of fondant on inside of bottom where baby will lay. Assemble egg pieces using piping gel, press to adhere. Using royal icing, pipe tip 125 ruffle around outside of top; add tip 1 trim. Pipe tip 103 ruffle around outside of top and bottom. Cut wings off baby and position in bassinet; cut a piece of fondant, fold and lay over baby to look like a blanket. Pipe tip 1 dots.
- Make teddy bear using rolled fondant (p. 102).
- Thin royal icing and paint doves; let dry.
- Prepare 1-layer 8 in. and 2-layer 12 in. rounds for stacked construction. Ice lightly in buttercream icing and cover in rolled fondant. Cut 2 in.

wide strips of tinted fondant and attach at bottom border of 12 in. tier using drops of water. Cut 22 fondant flowers using calyx cutter and attach to border using drops of water. Add center dots using royal icing and tip 3.
- Make 1 large and 2 small roses using rolled fondant and instructions in Gum Paste Flowers Book incorporating these changes: Cut petals with the tulip cutter, cut petals apart and add more rows. Cut leaves using large leaf cutter. Set aside.
- **12 in. tier:** Pipe tip 363 shell bottom border. Edge top of band with tip 3 beads. **8 in. tier:** Pipe tip 363 shell bottom border. Edge shells with tip 3 zigzags and add dots.
- Imprint message on 12 in. tier and outline using tip 2; overpipe using tip 1 dots.
- Position plate on top of 8 in. tier. Ice plate in royal icing and position bassinet. Pipe tip 233 pull-out grass. Attach birds using dots of icing and position teddy bear. Position roses and leaves on bottom tier.
Serves 42.

A Storybook Romance
- Two Mix Book Pan, p. 168
- Tips 1, 1D, 2, 126, 131, 225, 349, 6, 116-119
- Rose Petal Pink, Copper (Lt. Skintone), Ivory, Moss Green Icing Colors, p. 110
- '97 Pattern Book (Letter "A" Pattern), p. 108
- Decorating Comb, p. 160
- Bomboniere!® Wedding Couple with Black Tuxedo, p. 147
- Meringue Powder, p. 111
- 6 Pc. Enchanted Coach Set, p. 132
- 56 Pc. Make Any Message Letter Press Set, p. 113
- Cake Board, Fanci-Foil Wrap, p. 159
- Buttercream, Royal Icings, p. 92

NOTE: To achieve flower color, combine Ivory, Pink and Copper.

- Using royal icing, make 24 tip 225 drop flowers and 65 tip 131 drop flowers, both with tip 2 dot centers. Make extras to allow for breakage. Let dry.
- Ice cake smooth. Comb sides to resemble pages. Pipe tip 1D smooth side up band around top edge of cake. Outline and fill in a 1 3/4 in. square block that will go under the letter "A". Smooth with spatula. Trace Letter "A" Pattern on block with toothpick. Pipe letter using tip 2. Pipe base of letter with C-motion. Edge with strings; pipe zigzags between strings. Pipe tip 1 filigree lines around the letter. Imprint message; pipe message and write names with tip 2.
- Pipe tip 2 vines around top edge of cake. Pipe tip 126 ruffle bottom border. Edge with tip 2 beads. Position flowers and add tip 349 leaves.
- Position coach set and wedding couple.
Serves 24.

Vintage Victorian
- 14 in. Round Pan, p. 161
- Viennese Swirl Pan, p. 166
- Tips 2, 3, 4, 5, 349, 352, p. 116-119
- Rose Petal Pink, Ivory, Moss Green Icing Colors, p. 110
- Ready-To-Use Rolled Fondant (3 pkgs. needed), 30 Pc. Gum Paste Flowers Kit, p. 112
- Cake Board, 16 in. Ruffle Board, p. 159
- Decorator Brush Set, p. 120
- Wooden Dowel Rods, p. 156
- Musical Water Globe Ornament, p. 137
- Buttercream Icing, p. 92

- Tint 2 packages of fondant, combining pink and ivory. Leave 1 package white.
- Cut a 3 1/2 in. circle from cake board to support ornament. Cover with white fondant. Set aside.
- Using fondant and cutters in Gum Paste Kit, make the following flowers: **70 small blossoms** using forget-me-not cutter. Cup flower around end of stick to shape. Add tip 2 dot centers with buttercream. **36 medium blossoms** using apple blossom cutter. Add tip 3 dot centers with buttercream. **30 double petal flowers** using pansy cutter and apple blossom cutter. Cup apple blossom around round end of stick and attach to pansy blossom using decorator brush and water. Add tip 3 dot centers with buttercream. Make extras to allow for breakage.
- Make 30 fondant ribbon loops (5 needed for each bow; make extras to allow for breakage): Cut fondant into strips 1/2 in. wide by 3 1/2 in. long. Brush end of strips with water, press together and form loops. Place loops on side and let dry overnight.
- Prepare 1-layer round and swirl cakes for rolled fondant (p. 92) and stacked construction (p. 96).
- Pipe tip 4 bead bottom border on Viennese Swirl and tip 5 bead bottom border on round cake. Attach ribbon loops with icing at 7 in. intervals on round cake. Attach flowers to both tiers with icing; add tip 349 leaves to Viennese Swirl cake and tip 352 leaves to round cake.
- Add tip 2 dots to loops and on sides of cake.
- Position fondant base and ornament.
Serves 35.

Love's Shelter
- 2 Pc. 9 in. Round Pan Set, p. 164
- 4 Pc. Hexagon Pan Set (15 in. pan used), p. 161
- Tips 1D, 2, 3, 16, 18, 66, 102, 225, 349, 352, p. 116-119
- Rose Petal Pink, Ivory, Moss Green Icing Colors, p. 110
- '97 Pattern Book (Threshold Arch and Side Oval Patterns), p. 108
- 1 in. Filigree Bells (1 pk. needed), Small Doves (1 pk. needed), p. 151
- 7 in. Grecian Pillars (4 needed), p. 156
- 8 in. Decorator Preferred Separator Plate (1 needed), p. 157
- 9 Pc. Flower Former Set, Flower Nail No. 7, 8 Pc. Lily Nail Set, Cake Dividing Set, p. 113
- Pearl Stamens (1 pk. needed), p. 112
- Meringue Powder, p. 111
- Plastic Dowel Rods, p. 156
- Cake Boards, Fanci-Foil Wrap, p. 159
- First Dance Ornament, p. 148
- Royal, Buttercream Icings, p. 92
- Nylon thread

- **Make Threshold Arch at least 3 days in advance.** Place waxed paper over one full and two half Threshold Arch Patterns. Using royal icing, pipe tip 1D band (smooth side up) over patterns. Let dry overnight. Turn over dried arch pieces and overpipe with tip 1D.

- Immediately overpipe tip 2 lattice. Let dry overnight. Turn arch pieces again; pipe tip 2 lattice. Let dry completely.
- **To Assemble Threshold Arch:** Using royal icing, secure pillars to plate; attach full arch piece between pillars. Attach half arch pieces. Attach nylon thread through filigree bells and hang over arch. Pipe tip 16 shells on top and bottom edges of arch. Let dry overnight.
- Using royal icing, make 135 tip 225 drop flowers with tip 2 dot centers; 75 tip 102 forget-me-nots with tip 3 centers; 40 tip 66 bluebells on 1 1/4 in. Lily Nail, with tip 3 dot centers and three stamens. Make extras to allow for breakage, let dry.
- Bake and cool two 9 in. round cakes, 1 1/2 in. high, and 2-layer hexagon cake. Ice and prepare cakes for stacked construction (p. 96).
- **On round cake:** Using Cake Dividing Set, divide cake into 6ths; mark center of garland 1 3/4 in. down from top. Pipe tip 2 lattice in garland area. Pipe tip 16 top and tip 18 bottom shell borders. Edge plate with tip 16 c-motion shells.
- **On hexagon cake:** Mark oval pattern on side panels of cake. Pipe tip 1D band (smooth side up) around bottom of cake. Pipe tip 2 lattice work on side panels. Pipe tip 2 beads around ovals. Pipe tip 16 shells on top border and on vertical edges. Pipe tip 18 bottom shell border.
- Position flowers and add tip 349 and 352 leaves to arch and on both cakes. Position ornament; attach doves.
Serves 56.

A Country & Western Union
- 6, 10, 14 in. Square Pans, p. 164
- Tips 4, 8, 18, 21, 48, p. 116-119
- Ivory Icing Color, p. 110
- Floating Tiers Cake Stand Set, p. 154
- Petite Country & Western Ornament, p. 140
- Crystal-Look Bowl (2 needed), p. 152
- Cake Board, Fanci-Foil Wrap, p. 159
- Buttercream Icing, p. 92
- Fresh flowers, greenery
- Lightly ice 2-layer cakes smooth. Pipe tip 8 and 48 basketweave (p. 100)on all cakes. On 6 in. cake, pipe tip 18 shell top and bottom borders. On 10 in. and 14 in. cakes, pipe tip 18 top and tip 21 bottom shell borders. On all cakes, edge bottom shells with tip 4 zigzag.
- At reception, place cakes on stand. Position flowers in crystal-look bowls and ornament.
*Serves 148** *

Flourishing Together
- 4 Pc. Petal Pan Set (15 in. pan used), p. 161
- 6 in., 10 in. Round Pans, p. 164
- Tips 2A, 3, 18, 21, 113, 125, 131, 224, 225, 349, 352, p. 116-119
- 3 in. Flower Nail, p. 113
- Aster Mauve, Juniper Green Icing Colors, p. 110
- Two 8 in. Plates from Crystal Clear Cake Divider Set, p. 154
- 14 in. Decorator Preferred Separator Plate, p. 157
- Piping Gel, Meringue Powder, p. 111
- Candlelight Cake Stand, p. 154
- Wire Lace Separator, p. 158
- Dowel Rods, p. 156
- Cake Boards, Fanci-Foil Wrap, p. 159
- Cake Dividing Set, p. 113
- White Ribbon Roses, p. 146
- Precious Love Ornament, p. 136
- White Artificial Leaves, 4 mm White Pearl Beading* (1 pk. needed), p. 151
- Royal, Buttercream Icing, p. 92
- Taper candles
- Use royal icing to make the following flowers: Eight tip 125 2-tone roses with tip 2A bases; thirty five tip 131 drop flowers with tip 3 dot centers; four hundred tip 225 drop flowers with tip 3 dot centers; one hundred ninety tip 224 drop flowers with tip 3 dot centers. Make extras to allow for breakage and let dry.
- Ice smooth 2-layer cakes; prepare for stacked construction (p. 96).
- **6 in. Tier:** Divide tier into 16ths. Position flowers on cake sides in crescent shape, 2 in. deep, at each division mark. Add tip 349 leaves. Pipe tip 18 shell bottom border.
- **10 in. Tier:** Divide tier into 8ths. Mark garlands, 1 1/2 in. deep, between division marks. Position drop flowers at top border. Position drop flowers for garland and at each garland point. Add tip 352 leaves. Pipe tip 18 shell bottom border.
- **15 in. Tier:** Mark garland, 1 1/2 in. deep, on each petal division. Position drop flowers at top border. Position drop flowers for garland and at each garland point. Position roses, add tip 113 leaves. Pipe tip 21 zigzag puff bottom border. Position drop flowers on bottom border. Add tip 352 leaves.
- At reception, assemble tiers on stand and position ornament. Pipe tip 3 dots with piping gel on all cakes. Make bouquets by twisting together wired ends of ribbon roses and artificial leaves. Position behind wire lace separator. Attach pearl beading to edge of cake board.Position candles.
*Serves 101** *

*Remove pearls before cutting and serving.
**NOTE: The top tier is often saved for the first anniversary. The number of servings given does not include the top tier.

Today
and
Forever

Victorian Lace

- 8, 12, 16 in. Round Pans, p. 161, 164
- Tips 4, 21, 32, p. 116-117
- Ivory*, Rose Petal Pink* Icing Colors, p. 110
- Cake Dividing Set, p. 113
- 5 in. Grecian Pillars (4 pks. needed), p. 156
- Decorator Preferred Separator Plates (two 18 in., two 14 in., two 10 in. needed), p. 157
- Designer Bridesmaids, Blush; Designer Groomsmen, p. 149
- Florist Wire, p. 112
- Scrolls (9 pks. needed), p. 152
- Filigree Stairways (4 needed), p. 153
- Mini Lights (4 sets needed), p. 137
- Meringue Powder, p. 111
- Our Dance Ornament, p. 139
- Buttercream, Royal Icings, p. 92
- Ivory tulle, 1 in. wide green ribbon, silk flowers

*Combine these to produce Victorian peach color shown
Note: Scrolls and stringwork on bottom borders are added at reception. All stringwork on both cake sides and hanging from scrolls is done using royal icing.

- Ice and prepare 2-layer 8, 12 and 16 in. tiers for pillar construction (p. 96).
- **8 in. Tier:** Using Cake Dividing Set, divide top border into 8ths. Centered between each division mark, ³⁄₄ in. down on sides, pipe tip 4 triple drop strings, 2 in. wide; add tip 4 dots. Pipe tip 21 and 4 crown border. Position 3 scrolls at each division mark. Pipe tip 32 shell bottom border to align with scallops on plate.

- **12 in. Tier:** Divide top border into 8ths. Centered between each division mark, 1 in. down on cake sides, pipe two sections of tip 4 triple drop strings, 2 in. wide; add tip 4 dots. Pipe tip 21 and 4 crown border. Position 3 scrolls at each division mark. Pipe tip 32 shell bottom border to align with scallops on plate.

- **16 in. Tier:** Divide top border into 12ths. Centered between each division mark, 1½ in. down on cake sides, pipe tip 4 double drop strings, 2 in. wide. On each side, pipe a 2½ in. wide triple drop string section. Add tip 4 dots. Pipe tip 21 and 4 crown border. Position 3 scrolls at each division mark. Pipe tip 32 shell bottom border to align with scallops on plate. Pipe tip 21 scallop on edge of plate on cake top.

- **At reception:** Assemble tiers on pillars; attach stairways. Gather tulle into puffy bows and secure with florist wire. Position tulle, lights and flowers between tiers. Beginning at top tier, position bottom scrolls and pipe stringwork and dots using tip 4 (see p. 99); work from the inside out: On 8 in. tier, position scrolls at every other shell; on 12 in. Tier, position scrolls at every shell, alternating placement; on 16 in. Tier, position scrolls at every shell. On 16 in. Tier, pipe double drop strings on each scroll. Overpipe dropstrings between alternating scrolls. Add dots. Position stairways, bridesmaids, groomsmen. Position Our Dance ornament on top tier.
Serves 156.

Love Above All

- Oval Pan Set, p. 161
- Tips 2, 4, 364, p. 116-117
- '97 Pattern Book (Scallop Pattern), p. 108
- 9 Pc. Flower Former Set, Decorator Favorites Pattern Press Set, p. 113
- Ready-To-Use Rolled Fondant (7 pks. needed), p. 112
- Cake Boards, Fanci-Foil Wrap, p. 159
- 31 Pc. Gum Paste Flowers Kit, p. 112
- 7 in. and 9 in. Disposable Pillars (1 set each needed), p. 156
- Oval Separator Plates (one 8 1/2 x 6 in. and one 11 1/2 x 8 1/2 in. needed), p. 157
- Meringue Powder, p. 111
- Plastic Dowel Rods (1 pk. needed), p. 156
- Decorator Brush Set, p. 120
- Happiness Ribbon Tier Top, Floral Puff Accent, p. 151
- Dedication Ornament, p. 139
- Buttercream, Royal Icings, p. 92
- plastic ruler, cornstarch, ribbon

- Using rolled fondant and the wild rose cutter in the Gum Paste Flowers Kit, make approximately 65 flowers. Cut 2 flowers to make each flower. Thin and enlarge one flower using round end of modeling stick; cup petal slightly. Using decorator brush, dab a little water in center of one flower, attach second flower on top of first flower; add tip 2 dot center using royal icing. Make extras to allow for breakage; dry flowers in Flower Formers dusted with cornstarch.
- Using pattern and 3/16 in. thick rolled fondant, cut 9 scallops. Score lines using edge of plastic ruler, taking care not to cut through fondant. Let air dry completely, at least 48 hours. In areas of high humidity, allow extra drying time. Make extras to allow for breakage.
- Prepare 2-layer 7 x 5 in., 10 x 7 in. and 13 x 9 in. tiers for rolled fondant (p. 92) and push-in leg construction (p. 96). Prepare 1-layer 16 x 12 in. tier for stacked construction.
- Using small, medium and large c-scrolls from pattern press set, imprint design on tiers to form a vine. Outline using tip 4, overpipe using tip 2. Pipe tip 364 shell bottom borders on all tiers. Attach flowers using dots of icing.
- Position fondant scallops, securing with royal icing. Cut nine 5 x 3 1/2 in. pieces of rolled fondant. Gather the long ends to form a drape, position drapes over scallops, securing with royal icing. Attach flowers with royal icing.
- At reception: Assemble tiers on pillars. Position Tier Top and Floral Puff Accent between tiers and ornament on top. Attach ribbon to edge of cake board.

Serves 105.

Flights Of Fancy

- 7, 10, 14 in. Round Pans, p. 164
- Tips 1, 3, 8, 10, p. 116
- '97 Pattern Book (Script Alphabet Pattern), p. 108
- Ready-To-Use Rolled Fondant (8 pks. needed), p. 112
- Crystalique Ribbon Arch Fresh Flower Holder, Heart/Dove Pick, p. 137
- Crystal-Look Bowl, p. 152
- Flower Holder Ring, p. 153
- 7 in. Crystal-Look Pillars (1 pk. needed), 13 3/4 in. Crystal-Look Pillars (4 needed), p. 156
- 10 in. Crystal-Look Plates, 17 in. Crystal-Look Plates (2 each needed), p. 157
- Kolor-Flo Fountain, p. 153
- Decorator Brush Set, p. 120
- Buttercream Icing, p. 92
- Fresh flowers

- Make 332 fondant loops at least 1-2 days ahead. **To make loops:** roll out fondant to about 1/8 in. thick. Cut loops 1/2 in. wide and 4 to 6 in. long. Form into loops by brushing a small amount of water on one end of fondant strip and pressing it together with other end of strip. Lay on side on waxed paper to dry. Reserve leftover fondant for decoration.
- Prepare 2-layer cakes for rolled fondant (p. 92) and stacked and pillar construction (p. 96).
- Pipe tip 8 bottom bead border on all cakes. Attach loops to cakes with dots of icing. Position 200 loops on 14 in. cake, 20 loops on 10 in. cake, 100 loops on 7 in. cake.
- Roll out leftover fondant to about 1/8 in. thick. With small end of tip 10, cut out fondant pieces and randomly attach to cake with dots of icing. Make indention marks in dots with end of decorator brush.
- Trace monogram pattern on cake with toothpick. Pipe monogram with tip 3; outline with tip 1.
- At reception: Set up fountain, flower ring, pillars. Assemble cake and position flower holder and pick. Accent with remaining loops.

*Serves 116.***

Heart Contrast

- 4 Pc. Heart Pan Set (6 in., 9 in. 15 in. pans used), p. 173
- Tips 4, 17, 18, 21, 32, p. 116-117
- Rose Icing Color, p. 110
- 8 in. Heart Separator Plate, p. 157
- Fresh Flower Holders (1 pk. needed), p. 158
- 9 in. Crystal-Look Spiked Pillars (1 pk. needed), Dowel Rods, p. 156
- Fanciful Ornament, Fancy Pearl Tier Top, p. 136
- Parchment Roll, Cake Boards, Fanci-Foil Wrap, p. 159
- 4mm, 6mm White Pearl Beading* (1 pk. of 6mm, 2 pks. of 4mm needed), p. 151
- Buttercream Icing, p. 92
- Fresh flowers

- Use parchment paper and heart pans as patterns to make half-heart templates. These templates will be used to cover one side of cake while the other is being iced. Ice tops and sides of 2 layer cakes and prepare for stacked and pillar construction (see p. 96).
- **On 6 in. heart:** Divide white half of cake into four equal sections, approximately 2 1/2 in. wide and 2 in. deep. Pipe tip 17 zigzag garland. Position 6mm pearl beading on zigzag garland and 4mm pearl beading below garland. Pipe tip 2 dots at garland points; add 4 mm pearls on top edge of garland. Add tip 17 top and tip 21 bottom shell borders; add 4mm pearls around shells (white half only).
- **On 9 in. heart:** Divide white half of cake into five equal sections, approximately 2 3/4 in. wide and 2 in. deep. Decorate as for 6 in. heart.
- **On 15 in. heart:** Divide white half of cake into 8 equal sections, approximately 3 in. wide and 2 in. deep. Pipe tip 18 zigzag garland. Position pearl beading as above. Add tip 17 top and tip 32 bottom shell borders. Add 4mm pearls around bottom border shells.
- Pipe tip 18 shells around bottom of pillars and tip 4 beads to divide each section.
- At reception, position flowers in holders and add to cake. Position ornament and tier top.

*Serves 100***

*Remove pearls before cutting and serving.
**NOTE: The top tier is often saved for the first anniversary. The number of servings given does not include the top tier.

Each Year A Treasure

- Embossed Heart Pan, 6 in. Heart Pan, p. 173
- 1, 1s, 2, 16, 21, 349, p. 116-119
- Lemon Yellow, Juniper Green Icing Colors, p. 110
- Ready-To-Use Rolled Fondant (2 pkgs. needed), p. 112
- 4 mm. White Pearl Beading* (1 pkg. needed), p. 151
- Cake Board, Fanci-Foil Wrap, p. 159
- 30 Pc. Gum Paste Flowers Kit, p. 112
- 9 Pc. Flower Former Set, p. 113
- Petite Anniversary Years Topper, p. 145
- Buttercream Icing , p. 92

- Bake and cool cakes. Trim off raised center heart from embossed heart cake. Tint 1 ½ packages of fondant and prepare both cakes for rolled fondant (p. 92).
- Roll out remaining fondant and use gum paste cutters to make: 60 baby's breath, 50 apple blossoms, 45 forget-me-nots and 30 pansies (make extras to allow for breakage). Let dry on flower formers. When dry, use buttercream icing to pipe center dots: tip 1s on baby's breath, tip 2 on apple blossoms and pansies, tip 1 on forget-me-nots.
- Position 6 in. heart on embossed heart cake. Pipe tip 21 shell border on 6 in. heart. Pipe tip 16 zigzag puff bottom border on embossed heart. Add pearl beading.
- Position flowers, trim with tip 349 leaves, tip 1 dots and tip 1 string tendrils. Add topper and remaining flowers.

Serves 16.

*Remove pearls before cutting and serving.

Document Their Love

- 11 x 15 in. Sheet Pan, p. 164
- Tips 1, 3, 364, p. 116-119
- Burgundy, Willow Green, Ivory, Black Icing Colors, p. 110
- '97 Pattern Book (Number Pattern), p. 108
- Cake Board, Fanci-Foil Wrap, p. 159
- 30 Pc. Gum Paste Flowers Kit, Gum Paste Mix, Florist Wire, p. 112
- Italic Letter Press Set, 9 Pc. Flower Formers Set, p. 113
- Decorator Brush Set, p. 120
- Plastic Dowel Rods, p. 156
- 25th Silver Anniversary Couple, p. 149
- Ready-To-Use Rolled Fondant (3 pkgs. needed), p. 112
- Buttercream Icing, p. 92
- Cornstarch, non-toxic pastel chalk, tea strainer

- Prepare gum paste mix following instructions on package. Make gum paste flowers and leaves following instructions in book (included in kit). Using medium and large rose cutters, make roses on wires: 3 full-size (7 petal), 4 medium (5 petal), 4 small (buds). Snip wires close to blooms, then attach calyx. Using baby's breath cutter, make 60 lily of the valley blooms. Using small and large leaf cutters, make 12 small and 18 large leaves; dust flower formers with cornstarch and position leaves to dry. When all flowers and leaves are completely dry, dust with pastel chalk. Using a tea strainer, make a powder by grating chalk sticks. Mix the powder with a small amount of cornstarch and brush on flowers and leaves.
- **Make scroll:** Tint half package of fondant; roll out and cut rectangle approximately 11 x 7 in. Imprint message press and trace numbers pattern on scroll. Dust dowel rods with cornstarch and roll opposite corners. Let dry overnight. When dry, slide dowel rods out and dust edges with pastel chalk as above.
- Lightly ice 1-layer cake in buttercream icing. Partially knead icing color into 2 packages of fondant to marbleize; cover cake with fondant.
- Position scroll on cake top, add tip 3 message. Pipe tip 364 bottom shell border. Attach flowers and leaves with tip 3 dots of buttercream; pipe tip 1 stamens in lily of valley blooms. Position ornament.

Serves 20.

An Unforgettable Anniversary

Picture Perfect Memories

- 7, 16 in. Round Pans, 10 in. Round Pan (3 in. deep), p. 164
- 1, 2, 7, 10, 16, 101, 102, 103, 104, 352, 504, p. 116-119
- Flower Nail No. 9, p. 113
- Creamy Peach Icing Color, p. 110
- 12, 18 in. Tall Tier Stand Separator Plates, 7³⁄₄ in. Center Columns (2 needed), Cake Corer Tube, Top Column Cap Nut, Bottom Column Bolt, p. 154
- '97 Pattern Book (Scallop Patterns), p. 108
- Florist Wire, p. 112
- 50th Anniversary Ornament, p. 142
- Meringue Powder, p. 111
- Bomboniere!® Gold Lurex-Edge Tulle Circles (2 pkgs. needed), Bomboniere!® ³⁄₁₆ in. Gold Instant Bow Ribbon (2 spools needed), Bomboniere!® Filigree Heart Boxes (2 pkgs. needed), p. 147
- Cake Dividing Set, p. 113
- 1¹⁄₄ in. Gold Artificial Leaves (1 pkg. needed), Flower Spikes (1 pkg. needed), p. 151
- Buttercream, Royal Icings, p. 92
- White florist tape, 1/4 in. wide white satin ribbon, glue gun, family photos

- Using royal icing, make 42 tip 103 roses with tip 10 bases; 20 tip 102 roses with tip 7 bases; 110 tip 101 apple blossoms with tip 1 dot centers; 50 tip 104 rosebuds. Make extras of all flowers to allow for breakage. Let dry.
- **To make corsages:** (See p. 95 for "To Attach Flowers & Leaves to Wire Stems" instructions.) Attach 12 tip 103 roses, 12 tip 102 roses, 18 apple blossoms, 54 gold leaves and 24 rosebuds to florist wire with royal icing. Make 6 corsages; each consisting of 2 tip 102 roses, 2 tip 103 roses, 3 apple blossoms, 9 leaves, 4 rosebuds and 3 tulle circles. To make corsage, layer tulle circles on top of each other; fold in half. Gather tulle by bringing left and right sides together toward center and tie with wire. Cover all wires with floral tape. Fluff the tulle above gathering point by carefully pulling apart layers and gently pulling outward. Place wired flowers and leaves together with tulle and floral tape together; arrange each corsage.
- Ice smooth and prepare 7 in. and 10 in. round cakes (both 3 inches high) and 2-layer 16 in. round cake for center column construction (p. 96).
- **For 7 and 10 in. cakes:** Divide into 8ths. Mark garlands at each division point, measuring 1¹⁄₄ in. down at lowest point of garland. Pipe tip 1 cornelli lace on cake top and down to garland area. Position apple blossoms along garland. Pipe tip 352 leaves on all cakes. (Pipe bottom borders at reception.)
- **For 16 in. cake:** Divide into 12ths. Mark scallop pattern on cake top, on side of cake mark garlands 1³⁄₄ in. down at lowest point. Ice smooth inside top area peach. Pipe tip 1 cornelli lace between top scallop and side garlands. Pipe tip 16 zigzag garland on sides. Add tip 16 zigzags around top scallop area and add tip 16 rosettes at each scallop point.
- Insert flower spikes into top edge of 16 in. cake. Add apple blossoms at alternating scallop points.
- Add pictures to front of heart boxes with hot glue. Attach instant bows and 4 to 6 in. ribbon lengths to hearts with glue.
- **At reception:** Attach two 7³⁄₄ in. columns together and bolt to 18 in. plate and bottom column bolt; then add 12 in. plate and top column cap nut. Position 10 in. and 7 in. cakes on plate and pipe tip 504 shell bottom borders on all cakes. Attach roses and rosebuds to center of 16 in. cake and trailing up the center column; add gold leaves. Add tip 102 roses and gold leaves on all cakes. Position flower corsages in spikes on 16 in. cake. Position ornament.

Serves 84.

It Bears Celebrating

- 4-Pc. Oval Pan Set (13 in. x 9 in. pan used), p. 161
- Aluminum Panda Mold, p. 171
- Tips 1, 2, 4, 5, 7, 10, 48, 352, p. 116-119
- Brown, Black, Lemon Yellow, Sky Blue, Violet, Pink, Leaf Green Icing Colors, p. 110
- 8 ½ in. x 6 in. Oval Separator Plate, p. 157
- '97 Pattern Book (Small and Large Flower Patterns), p. 108
- Meringue Powder, p. 111
- Cake Board, Fanci-Foil Wrap, p. 159
- Buttercream, Royal Icings, p. 92
- Pretzel Rods

- Make 11 large and 15 small flowers: Place waxed paper over patterns. Using royal icing, pipe tip 10 petals for large flowers and tip 7 petals for small flowers; tip 5 dot centers. Let dry.
- Ice 1-layer oval cake smooth. Position plate on top.
- For bear cakes: Build up muzzle and tail areas with tip 7 dots. Ice smooth inside of ears and inside of paws. Pipe tip 4 whites of eyes; pipe tip 2 dot pupils and lips, tip 1 dot glint in eyes. Add tip 1 string and pull-out eyelashes on female bear, add tip 7 ball bow in hair.
- Cover bears with tip 5 looping motion "fur". Pipe tip 4 dot noses and paw pads.
- Position bears on plate in kissing pose. Press one pretzel log the length of both arms connected together on each side of bears. Cover arms with tip 5 looping motion "fur".
- Pipe tip 5 message and outline in tip 2 black, then tip 1 pink strings.
- Pipe tip 48 ridged side up latttice on sides of cake. Edge plate, top and bottom borders with tip 10 beads. Position flowers and add tip 352 leaves.
Serves 22.

Years of **Togetherness**

Kicking Up Their Heels!

- 4-Pc. Hexagon Pan Set (12 in. pan used), p. 161
- Tips 2, 5, 224, 225, 233, 349, p. 116-119
- Ivory, Kelly Green, Sky Blue, Pink, Violet, Lemon Yellow Icing Colors, p. 110
- Meringue Powder, p. 111
- Line Dancing Couple, 4-Pc. Cactus Set, 4-Pc. Rustic Fence Sets (2 needed), p. 134
- 6-Pc. Script Pattern Press Message Set, p. 113
- Cake Board, Fanci-Foil Wrap, p. 159
- Buttercream, Royal Icings, p. 92

- Using royal icing, make approximately 50 tip 224 and 50 tip 225 drop flowers (assorted pink, violet, yellow, blue) with tip 2 dot centers. Make extras to allow for breakage. Let dry.
- Ice 2-layer cake smooth. Pipe tip 2 vines and tip 349 leaves on cake sides. Add drop flowers with dots of icing. Add tip 233 pull-out grass, position fence.
- Pipe tip 5 bead top border.
- Imprint message and pipe message and freehand names with tip 2. Position couple, add flowers to cacti with dots of icing and position on cake.
Serves 28.

Pumped To Make The Jump!

- Proud Graduate Pan, p. 176
- Tips 3, 10, 16, p. 116-119
- Royal Blue, Black, Brown, Lemon Yellow, Copper (Lt. Skintone), Red-Red Icing Colors, p. 110
- '97 Pattern Book (Graduate Pattern), p. 108
- Cake Board, Fanci-Foil Wrap, p. 159
- Buttercream Icing, p. 92
- Ice top and sides of cake smooth. Using toothpick, mark pattern. Outline pattern and facial features with tip 3 strings. Pipe in mouth and tongue with tip 3; pipe in shoes and inside of gown with tip 10 (smooth with finger dipped in cornstarch).
- Cover remaining areas with tip 16 stars; overpipe nose with tip 16 stars. Pipe tip 3 strings and ball for tassel. Add tip 10 ball border. Add tip 3 string eyes, eyebrows, double outline diploma. Print tip 3 message.

Serves 12.

Honor Roll Appetizers

- Tips 21, 32, p. 117
- Parchment Triangles, p. 114
- Assorted crackers; flour tortillas
- Vegetables: celery sticks, cucumber slices, cherry tomatoes
- Fillings: softened cream cheese, cheese spread
- Garnishes: pimento, dill, green onion, chives
- Prepare vegetables, dry well. Pipe tip 21 and 32 cream cheese and cheese spread zigzags and rosettes on vegetables and crackers. Add garnish. Spread fillings on tortillas, roll, cut into sections and tie on chives for garnish.

Cookie Congrats

- 4 Pc. Graduation Cookie Cutter Set, p. 176
- Tip 4, p. 116
- Disposable Decorating Bags, p. 114
- Red-Red, Royal Blue, Lemon Yellow, Kelly Green Icing Colors, p. 110
- Roll-Out Cookie Dough Recipe, p. 94
- Tint a variety of cookie dough. Cut out cookies.
- Thin dough with water to pass through tip 4. Pipe tip 4 message. Bake and cool cookies.

Each serves 1.

Bear Most Likely To Succeed

- Mini Bear Pan, p. 171
- Tips 3, 16, p. 116-119
- Brown, Black Icing Colors, p. 110
- Graduation Candy Molds, p. 176
- Candy Melts®*- Light Cocoa, Pastel Mix, Yellow, Red, White (1 bag each needed), 3 Pc. Decorator Brush Set, Candy Melting Plate, p. 120
- Disposable Decorating Bags, p. 114
- Cake Board, Fanci-Foil Wrap, p. 159
- Buttercream Icing, p. 92

*brand confectionery coating

- Mold a variety of candies using "painting" method, p. 104.
- Ice sides of cakes smooth. Pipe tip 3 dot eyes, nose. Pipe in mouth, ears and paws with tip 3; smooth with finger dipped in cornstarch. Cover bear with tip 16 stars.
- Position cap and diploma candies. Overpipe tip 16 star paws to hold diploma. Pipe tip 16 star bottom border.

Each serves 1.

Celebrate Success

- 6, 12 in. Round Pans, 8 in. Round Pan 3 in. deep, p. 161
- Tips 3, 6, 10, 12, 102, 103, 104, 352, 501, 502, 504, p. 116-119
- Golden Yellow, Kelly Green Icing Colors, p. 110
- Flower Nail No. 7, Cake Divider Set, p. 113
- Decorator Preferred Separator Plates (two 14 in. round needed), p. 157
- 3 in. Grecian Pillars (1 pk. needed), p. 156
- '97 Pattern Book (Fleur-de-lis Pattern), p. 108
- Meringue Powder, p. 111
- Glowing Grad Cake Topper, p. 176
- Royal, Buttercream Icings, p. 92
- Fresh flowers
- Use royal icing for the following: Make 12 tip 504 fleur-de-lis using pattern. Make roses:10 tip 102 with tip 6 bases, 20 tip 103 with tip 10 bases, 20 tip 104 with tip 12 bases, 12 tip 103 rosebuds. Make extras to allow for breakage and let dry.
- Prepare 1-layer 6 in. and 8 in. tiers and 2-layer 12 in. tier for stacked construction.
- Divide 6 in. and 12 in tiers into 12ths using Cake Dividing Set.
- Decorate tiers: **6 in.:** Pipe tip 3 double drop strings 1 1/4 in. deep between division marks. Add tip 501 top and tip 502 bottom shell borders. **8 in.:** Pipe tip 502 top and tip 504 bottom shell borders. Add tip 103 ruffle edge to bottom border. Pipe tip 3 message. **12 in.:** Position fleur-de-lis at division marks. Pipe tip 3 triple drop strings, attaching to bottom of fleur-de-lis so that strings drop without touching cake. Add tip 501 stars to string ends. Pipe tip 504 shell bottom border. Alternately position tip 103 and tip 104 roses, add tip 352 leaves.
- Assemble pillars, fresh flowers; position ornament, tip 102 roses and rosebuds. Add tip 352 leaves.

Serves 50.

Tough Act To Follow
- 8 in. Round Pan, 12 in. Square Pan, p. 161
- Tips 3, 7, 10, 13, 18, 21, 102, 103, 352, p. 116-119
- Flower Nail No. 9, 8 Pc. Designer Pattern Press Set, p. 148
- Golden Yellow, Kelly Green Icing Colors, p. 110
- Cake Board, Fanci-Foil Wrap, p. 159
- Meringue Powder, p. 111
- Dowel Rods, p. 156
- Scrolls (1 pkg. needed), p. 152
- Buttercream, Royal Icing, p. 92

- Using royal icing, make 7 tip 103 roses with tip 10 bases; 10 tip 102 roses with tip 7 bases; 24 tip 103 rosebuds. Make extras to allow for drying.
- Prepare 2 layer cakes for stacked construction (p. 156) and ice smooth.
- On 8 in. round cake: Pipe tip 3 vines and stems. Add tip 3 leaves. Pipe tip 18 bottom shell border; edge shells with tip 3 zigzags.
- On 12 in. square cake: Imprint corner flourish press on top corners of cake. Overpipe designs with tip 13 and add tip 3 dots. Pipe tip 18 top reverse shell and tip 21 bottom shell borders. Press scrolls into sides of cake. Position roses and rosebuds. Pipe tip 352 leaves and tip 3 sepals and calyxes. Serves 27.

62

Paradise Found

- Horseshoe Pan, p. 168
- Tips 1s, 2, 3, 14, 18, 21, 131, 224, 225, 352, p. 116-119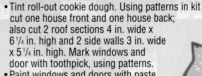
- Rose, Violet, Royal Blue, Lemon Yellow, Kelly Green, Black Icing Colors, p. 110
- '97 Pattern Book (Bridge, State Patterns), p. 108
- 3 Pc. Spruce Tree Set (2 pkgs. needed), 2 Pc. All Terrain Vehicles Set, p. 134
- Cake Board, Fanci-Foil Wrap, p. 159
- Meringue Powder, p. 111
- Royal, Buttercream Icing, p. 000
- Sugar cubes, candy discs

- Using royal icing, make 24 tip 131 rose drop flowers, 35 tip 224 yellow drop flowers, 35 tip 225 violet drop flowers, 35 tip 225 blue drop flowers; all with tip 2 dot centers. Make extras to allow for breakage, let dry.
- Cut Bridge Pattern from cake board and cover with foil. Ice smooth. Set aside.
- Ice cake smooth. Trace State Patterns on cake (patterns may be sized as desired on copy machine). Outline states with tip 3 and fill in with tip 14 stars. Add tip 18 reverse shell top border and tip 21 bottom shell border. Place bridge in center of cake; pipe tip 3 road markings and arrow. Position flowers and add tip 352 leaves.
- Print tip 2 names on states and tip 3 message on cake.
- In front seats of all terrain vehicle, pipe tip 3 ball bodies and insert candy discs for faces. Pipe tip 2 fingers, hair and tip 1s facial features. Attach sugar cube packages to vehicle with royal icing. Position trees.
Serves 12.

A Lucky Punch!

- Santa Checking List Pan, p. 183
- Tips 1, 3, 5, 7, 8, 16, 18, 21, 44, 47, p. 116-119
- Orange, Black, Christmas Red, Royal Blue, Creamy Peach, Brown, Pink, Ivory Icing Colors, p. 110
- '97 Pattern Book (Retiree Pattern), p. 000
- Cake Board, Fanci-Foil Wrap, p. 000
- Buttercream Icing, p. 000

NOTE: Combine Red with Orange for hair color.

- Ice cake smooth. Lightly trace pattern on cake with toothpick. Ice time clock area smooth; outline with tip 5 strings. Outline body and facial features with tip 3 strings.
- Build up nose with tip 16 stars. Pipe in mouth and tongue with tip 7 (smooth with finger dipped in corn-starch). Cover face, body and shoes with tip 16 stars. Pipe tip 18 swirl motion hair. Pipe tip 3 dot earrings.
- Pipe tip 1 numbers, hands and message on clock. Pipe tip 44 white bar slots on clock and smooth side tip 47 vertical bar. Outline explosion burst with tip 3 lines and fill in with tip 8. Add tip 3 squiggle lines on clock. Pipe tip 21 bottom star border.
Serves 12.

Welcome Home

- Gingerbread House Kit, p. 182
- Tips 2, 3, 4, 8, p. 116-119
- Round Perimeter Cookie Cutter, 6 Pc. Nesting Star Cookie Cutter Set, p. 123
- 5 Pc. Bite-Size Geometric Cookie Cutter Set (round cutter needed), p. 122
- Rose, Kelly Green, Red-Red, Royal Blue, Lemon Yellow, Black, Copper (Lt. Skintone), Brown Icing Colors, p. 110
- Candy Melts®*, White (1 bag needed), 4 Pc. Candy Colors Set, Decorator Brush Set, p. 120
- Disposable Decorating Bags, p. 114
- Rainbow Nonpareils Sprinkle Decorations, p. 126
- Cake Boards, Fanci-Foil Wrap, p. 159
- 4 in. and 8 in. Lollipop Sticks, p. 121
- Roll-Out Cookie Dough Recipe, p. 000
- Styrofoam block, shredded coconut, gumdrops, candy sticks

*brand confectionery coating

- Tint roll-out cookie dough. Using patterns in kit cut one house front and one house back; also cut 2 roof sections 4 in. wide x 6 1/4 in. high and 2 side walls 3 in. wide x 5 1/4 in. high. Mark windows and door with toothpick, using patterns.
- Paint windows and doors with paste color and brush. Thin cookie dough with small amounts of water until thin enough to pass through decorating tip and pipe decorations before baking. Pipe tip 3 trim on windows and door; add tip 2 dot flowers and leaves on window ledges.
- Add sprinkles to roof; using a lollipop stick, poke 12 holes on each roof side, twirling stick to enlarge holes. Pipe tip 8 house numbers. Bake and cool.
- Using two smallest star cutters, cut approximately 16 stars. Pipe tip 3 outline in thinned dough and add sprinkles. Bake and cool.
- **To assemble:** Attach stars, numbers and faces onto lollipop sticks using melted Candy Melts. Set aside.
- Cut styrofoam block to fit inside of house; cover with foil. Attach to board with melted candy.
- Pipe message on house front with melted candy in cut disposable bag. Assemble house front, back, side walls and roof around styrofoam block using melted candy as glue.
- Spread melted candy on board, position gum drops, tinted coconut. Arrange cookies on sticks in holes on roof.

It's the little Things...

Kaleidoscope Hearts
- Petite Heart Pan, p. 173
- Pink, Violet, Lemon Yellow, Leaf Green Icing Colors, p. 110
- Disposable Decorating Bags, p. 114
- Cooling Grid, p. 160
- Poured Cookie Icing Recipe, Shortbread Cookie Recipe, p. 104
- Bake cookies following recipe directions. Let cool. Tint icing and place cookies on grid over drip pan. Using a cut bag, pipe icing in random stripes over cookies. Let set.

Sweethearts Candy Box
- Heart Perimeter Cookie Cutter, p. 172
- Tip 3, p. 116-119
- Pink Icing Color, p. 110
- Disposable Decorating Bags, p. 114
- Bon Bon Candy Mold, p. 121
- Candy Melts®*- White, Light Cocoa, Red, Yellow, Green (1 bag each needed), p. 120
- Cherry licorice bites candy, cherry fruit rolls
- Roll-Out Cookie Dough Recipe, p. 94

*brand confectionery coating

- Make assorted bon bons. Pipe swirl designs on bon bons with melted candy in cut disposable bag. Let set.
- Tint cookie dough; cut out and bake cookies. Two will be needed for each box.
- Attach cherry licorice bites to edge of bottom heart with white Candy Melts and tip 3 in a disposable bag. Use same bag to pipe tip 3 beads around bottom of heart.
- Attach bow for lid with melted candy: position one fruit roll strip flat against cookie, cut and fold other strips into loops. Fill heart with bon bons.

Each serves 1.

Under Lock And Key
- Mini Heart Pan, p. 173
- No-Taste Red, Black, Pink Icing Colors, p. 110
- '97 Pattern Book (Key, Keyhole Patterns), p. 108
- Ready-To-Use Rolled Fondant, p. 112
- Red licorice, white curling ribbon
- Tint fondant; cover mini heart cakes. Using patterns, cut out keyhole from black fondant and red fondant on cakes. Cut out pink fondant key. Cut licorice into 4 in. length, bend and attach. Attach ribbon to keys and lock; position keyhole on cake.

Each serves 1.

Love Cub Cookie Clusters

- Heart Cookie Treat Pan, p. 173
- Tips 3, 8, p. 116-119
- Sky Blue, Violet, Lemon Yellow Icing Colors, p. 110
- Heart Lollipop Mold, Loving Bears Candy Mold, p. 121
- Cookie Treat Sticks, p. 122
- 8 in. Lollipop Sticks, p. 121
- Candy Melts®*- Pastel Mix, Red, Light Cocoa, White, (1 bag each needed), p. 120
- Buttercream Icing, p. 92
- Container to hold bouquet, styrofoam, grass

*brand confectionery coating

- Mold assorted lollipop candies. Let set.
- Prepare cookie recipe from Treat Pan label. Bake and cool cookie pops as directed.
- Attach candy bears to center of cookie treats with dots of icing. Pipe tip 3 outline around edge of cookies. Pipe tip 8 double outline around tip 3 outline.
- Cut styrofoam piece to fit inside container. Position cookie pops, lollipops and ribbon.

Each serves 1.

Catching Some Rays

- Standard Muffin Pan, p. 165
- Tip 9, p. 116
- Pink Icing Color, p. 110
- Candy Melts*--Red (1 bag needed), p. 120
- Hearts Standard Baking Cups, p. 172
- Disposable Decorating Bags, p. 114
- Hearts II Candy Mold, p. 172
- Buttercream Icing, p. 92

*brand confectionery coating

- In advance, mold candy hearts and let set.
- Ice cupcakes smooth. Pipe tip 9 dot nose. Position heart candies. Fill disposable bag with melted candy, cut tip and pipe mouth and arms on glasses. Let set.

Each serves 1.

A Heart Overflowing
- Heart Ring Pan, p. 173
- Pink Icing Color, p. 110
- Hearts II Candy Mold, p. 121
- Hearts Mix Sprinkle Decorations, p. 126
- Wilton Clear Vanilla Extract, p. 111
- **Favorite cinnamon roll recipe or hot roll mix (2 pkgs. needed), granulated sugar, cinnamon, icing glaze (recipe below), strawberry jelly, butter**

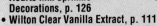

- Mold heart butter: Combine softened butter and jelly, spread in heart candy mold, freeze and unmold.
- Prepare hot roll mix following recipe on package. Roll dough into 14 x 10 in. rectangle, spread 2 tablespoons softened butter on dough, sprinkle with sugar and cinnamon. Roll up starting on 10 in. side. Place in side half of greased heart pan. Repeat with second roll mix to complete heart shape; pinch seam edges. Cover with plastic wrap and damp towel, let rise 30 minutes in warm area. Bake at 375° F for approximately 25 to 20 minutes. Remove from pan.
- Make icing glaze combining 3 cups confectioners' sugar, 3 tablespoons softened butter, 1 teaspoon Wilton Clear Vanilla Extract and 4-5 tablespoons milk; blend until smooth and of pouring consistency. Reserve 1 cup and tint pink. Pour icing glaze over warm bread. Drizzle on tinted icing glaze. Add Heart Mix Sprinkle Decorations.
Serves 24.

Hearts A-Flutter
- 9 in., 12. in. Heart Pans, p. 161
- Tips 2, 3, 11, 15, 32, 103, 104, 352, 363, p. 116-119
- Flower Nail No. 9, p. 113
- Rose Icing Color, p. 110
- Meringue Powder, p. 111
- Ready-To-Use Rolled Fondant (2 packages needed), p. 112
- 12-Pc. Decorator Favorites Pattern Press Set, p. 113
- Cake Board, Fanci-Foil Wrap, p. 159
- Kissing Love Birds Topper, p. 151
- Buttercream, Royal Icings, p. 92

- Using royal icing, make 5 tip 103 roses and 5 tip 104 roses with tip 11 bases. Make extras to allow for breakage and let dry.
- Tint fondant and prepare 1-layer 12 in. and 9 in. cakes for rolled fondant and stacked construction (see p. 96).
- On 9 in. cake, pipe tip 2 triple drop strings, 1 1/4 in. deep at lowest point, at 2 in. intervals. Pipe tip 2 dots at points.
- Imprint vine press on 12 in. heart, reversing for opposite sides. Pipe tip 363 scrolls over imprints. Pipe tip 3 scrolls above tip 363 scrolls; add tip 2 dots. Pipe tip 32 bottom shell border; pipe tip 15 diagonal zigzags over each shell. Edge shells with tip 2 zigzags.
- Position roses, add tip 352 leaves. Position topper.
Serves 24.

Berry & Mousse Cameo
- Embossed Heart Pan, p. 173
- Tips 14, 18, p. 116-119
- Rose Icing Color, p. 110
- Disposable Decorating Bags, p. 114
- Red Crystal Sprinkle Decorations, p. 126
- Cream Cheese Mousse Recipe, p. 104
- Stabilized Whipped Cream Icing, p. 92
- Cake Board, Fanci-Foil Wrap, p. 159
- Fresh strawberries, fresh mint leaves

- Prepare Cream Cheese Mousse according to recipe and add rose icing color. Pour mixture in pan and refrigerate until firm.
- Unmold mousse (dip pan in warm water for easier unmolding). Fill center with fresh strawberries. Pipe tip 14 reverse shells on top indentations. Pipe tip 18 c-shell bottom border. Add red crystal sprinkles, then mint leaves. Keep refrigerated until serving.
Serves 16.

Sweet Love Note
- Heart Springform Pan, p. 173
- Cake Board, Fanci-Foil Wrap, p. 159
- Pink Floral Spray Set, p. 113
- Tube Decorating Gel – Red, Green (1 each needed), p. 111
- **Favorite cheesecake or no-bake cheesecake recipe**

- Bake cheesecake according to recipe directions. Unmold. Using red decorating gel, pipe scallop design around top inner edge of cake. Add dots.
- Position flower spray and add green decorating gel vines. Write red decorating gel message.
Serves 12.

Egg Hunter
- **Mini Loaf Pan, p. 163**
- **Happy Easter Bunny Candy Making Kit, p. 174**
- **Kelly Green Icing Color, p. 110**
- **4 Pc. Candy Colors Set, Candy Melts®*- Lt. Cocoa (1 bag yields 4 bases), p. 120**
- **Disposable Decorating Bags, p. 114**
- **4 Pc. Rustic Fence Set, p. 134**
- **Decorator Brush Set, p. 120**
- **Shredded coconut, small zip plastic bag, jelly beans**

*brand confectionery coating

- **Make bases:** Melt Lt. Cocoa candy following package directions (reserve some candy for assembly). Mold candy plaques in Mini Loaf Pan (see p. 104). Set aside.
- **Mold bunny:** Melt candy following kit directions; tint a small amount of candy yellow for basket and pink for eyes and ears (reserve a small amount of yellow for assembly). Paint details inside mold, let set, fill with remaining candy and chill until firm. Unmold.
- Attach bunny to base using melted candy. Place coconut in plastic bag, add a small amount of green icing color and knead until coconut is tinted to desired shade. Spread additional melted candy on base, add fence, coconut and jelly beans. Attach jelly beans to basket with dots of yellow melted candy.

Do The Bunny Pop
- **Bunny Cookie Treat Pan, p. 174**
- **6 in. Cookie Treat Sticks, p. 122**
- **Candy Melts®*- White, Lt. Cocoa, Pink, p. 120**
- **Disposable Decorating Bags, p. 114**
- **Cooling Grid, p. 160**
- **Favorite cookie recipe**
- **Plastic eggs, pipe cleaners**

*brand confectionery coating

- Press cookie dough into pan cavities, insert sticks and bake following pan directions. Let cool.
- Position cookies on cooling grid over drip pan. Melt candy following package directions and pour over cookies. Let set.
- Fill disposable bags with melted candy and pipe facial features. Let set.
- Attach pipe cleaner and plastic egg to stick with melted candy. Wrap pipe cleaner around plastic egg.

Each serves 1.

There's Spring In His Step!

- Peek-A-Boo Bunny Pan, Mini Egg Pan, p. 175
- Tips 3, 5, 10, 14, 21, 233, p. 116-119
- Black, Pink, Leaf Green, Royal Blue, Violet, Lemon Yellow Icing Colors, p. 110
- '97 Pattern Book (Bunny Pattern), p. 108
- Ready-To-Use Rolled Fondant (1 pkg. needed), p. 112
- Cake Board, Fanci-Foil Wrap, p. 159
- Buttercream Icing, p. 92
- **To make rolled fondant eggs:** Bake and cool egg cakes; prepare for rolled fondant (see p. 92). **For stripes:** Divide package of fondant into five equal sections; reserve one white, tint the remaining four pink, violet, yellow and blue. Take a small amount of each color and roll colors into logs; position side by side. Carefully roll into single sheet and position on egg. Save colored scraps.

Bunny Parade

- **For Dots:** Cover egg with white fondant, hand roll pea-sized pieces of tinted fondant and press on fondant. **For Marble Effect:** Take leftover scraps of fondant and gently knead together (do not overmix). Roll out and cover egg.
- Ice cake smooth. Mark pattern with toothpick. Ice inside of ears smooth with spatula. Outline eyes with tip 3 and pipe-in with tip 5. Build up nose with tip 5 (smooth with finger dipped in cornstarch). Pipe-in mouth with tip 5.
- Position fondant egg in bunny's paws. Build up tail area with tip 10. Pipe outline areas with tip 233 pull-out fur. Cover body, tail and paws with tip 233 pull-out fur. Pipe tip 14 pull-out grass.
- Add tip 21 star bottom border.
Cake serves 12.
Each egg serves 1.

Speedy Bunny Cupcakes

- Standard Muffin Pan, p. 165
- Tips 2, 3, 233, p. 116-119
- Kelly Green, Lemon Yellow, Orange Icing Colors, p. 110
- Easter Standard Baking Cups, p. 127
- Easter Bunny Icing Decorations, p. 126
- Buttercream Icing, p. 000
- Jellybeans
- Bake and cool cupcakes.
- **For smooth cupcakes:** Ice smooth with spatula. Add icing decorations. Pipe tip 3 pull-out carrot and dot paws. Add tip 2 pull-out stems on carrot.
- **For grass cupcakes:** Cover top with tip 233 pull-out grass. Position jelly beans.
Each serves 1.

Joyful Respite
- 18 in. Half Round Pan, p. 161
- 2 Pc. Stand-Up Lamb Pan Set (only front half of pan used), p. 175
- Tips 1, 2, 3, 16, 18, 59, 59S, 102, 103, 104, 224, 352, p. 116-119
- Flower Nail No. 9, 9 Pc. Flower Formers Set, p. 113
- Pink, Lemon Yellow, Royal Blue, Kelly Green, Violet, Brown Icing Colors, p. 110
- Cake Board, Fanci-Foil Wrap, p. 159
- Meringue Powder, p. 111
- Buttercream, Royal Icings, p. 92
- Granulated sugar, waxed paper
- With royal icing, make 12 daffodils using tip 104 for petals, tip 3 for string circles, tip 1 for zigzag centers. Make 18 tip 103 daisies with tip 3 centers; 12 tip 102 forget-me-nots with tip 3 centers; 10 tip 59S violets with tip 2 dot centers; 10 tip 59 violets with tip 2 dot centers; 15 tip 224 drop flowers with tip 2 dot centers. Make extras to allow for breakage and place on flower formers to dry.
- Ice half-round cake smooth.
- On a separate cake board, ice bottom of lamb cake smooth. Pipe tip 3 facial features: outline mouth, pipe dot eyes and nose. Using tip 3, outline legs and add zigzag hooves. Cover face, inside ears and legs with tip 16 stars. Cover top of head, ears and body with tip 18 rosette swirled fur.
- Position lamb cake on half-round cake. Pipe tip 18 shell top and bottom borders. Add flowers; pipe tip 352 leaves and tip 3 stems. Print tip 2 message.

Serves 30.

Spend Easter with Friends!

Little Lambs
- Mini Lamb Pan, p. 175
- Tips 2, 5, 14, 224, 225, 349, p. 116-119
- Pink, Brown, Kelly Green, Sky Blue, Lemon Yellow, Violet Icing Colors, p. 110
- Meringue Powder, p. 111
- Cake Boards, Fanci-Foil Wrap, p. 159
- Buttercream, Royal Icing, p. 92
- Make a variety of drop flowers, 7 for each lamb, using royal icing and tips 224 and 225; add tip 2 dot centers. Make extras to allow for breakage and let dry.

- Sandwich cakes together with icing. Trim face off back cake.
- Ice face area and ears smooth. Pipe tip 2 dot and string facial features. Outline and pipe tip 5 hooves. Overpipe tip 5 leg area. Cover lamb with tip 14 reverse shells. Attach flowers, pipe tip 349 leaves.
Each serves 1.

Wise Crackers
- **Petite Egg Pan, p. 175**
- **Muffin Munchies® Pan, p. 165**
- **Candy Melts®*- Yellow, Light Cocoa, Pastel Mix, White, Orange (1 bag each), p. 120**
- **Parchment Triangles, p. 114**
- **Easter Treats Candy Molds, p. 174**
- **Craft Knife**

*brand confectionery coating

- Mold chick candies using Candy Melts. Let set. Mold Muffin Munchies candy bases. Let set.
- For broken eggs, using melted candy in parchment bags, pipe candy halfway inside egg pan, making jagged edges. For whole eggs, fill pan cavities entirely. Refrigerate until set.
- To assemble hatching chicks: Attach two bottom egg halves and two top egg halves with melted candy. Let set. Pipe a small amount of melted candy on base, attach bottom egg to base and let set. Follow same procedure with chick and top of egg.
- To assemble whole eggs: Using melted candy, attach both halves together, let set. Attach to base with melted candy. Let set. With craft knife, cut cracked effect into egg.
Each serves 1.

Basket Assembly Line
- **3-D Egg Pan Set, p. 175**
- **Tips 1, 3, 5, 12, 18, 47, 233, 352, p. 116-119**
- **Lemon Yellow, Leaf Green, Sky Blue, Pink, Black, Orange Icing Colors, p. 110**
- **Cake Board, Fanci-Foil Wrap, p. 159**
- **Buttercream Icing, p. 92**
- **Jelly beans**

- Bake and cool cake using half of egg pan. Ice smooth in blue. Pipe tip 47 (serrated side up) basketweave on bottom half. Add tip 18 rope handle. Pipe tip 233 pull-out grass around top edge of basket. Using tips 1, 3, 5, 12 and 352, figure pipe chicks directly on cake (see p. 103).
- Position jelly beans.
Serves 6.

Old Glory Cake

- Star Pan, p. 170
- '97 Pattern Book (Star Background Pattern), p. 108
- Tip 8, p. 116-119
- Red-Red, Royal Blue Icing Colors, p. 110
- Ready-To-Use Rolled Fondant (2 pkgs. needed), p. 112
- Cake Board, Fanci-Foil Wrap, p. 159
- Bite-Size Star Cookie Cutter, p. 122
- Buttercream Icing, p.92
- Ice cake smooth.
- Divide 1 package of fondant in half; tint ½ red and ½ blue. Roll out blue fondant to a ⅛ in. thickness. Cut Star Background Pattern from blue fondant and position on cake, aligning top points with cake star points. Trim with knife.
- **To make stripes:** Separately roll out ⅛ in. thick red and white rectangles, each 16 in. long and 5 in. wide. Cut 1 in. stripes and position on cake, trimming off excess fondant to fit. Gently blend seams together with fingers.
- Cut out and position stars. Pipe tip 8 ball border.
Serves 12.

Stars and Stripes Cookie Pops
- Star Cookie Treat Pan, p. 122
- Tips 2, 3, 4, 12, 14, p. 116-119
- Royal Blue, Red-Red, Copper (Lt. Skintone) Icing Colors, p. 110
- Cookie Treat Sticks, p. 122
- Patriotic Mix Sprinkle Decorations, p. 176
- Fanci-Foil Wrap, p. 159
- Buttercream Icing Recipes, p. 92
- Poured Cookie Icing Recipe, p. 104
- ¼ in. wide red and blue ribbon, styrofoam block
- Bake and cool cookies, using recipe on pan package. Place cookies on rack and cover with Poured Cookie Icing. Let set.
- **For Uncle Sam Cookie:** Pipe tip 12 face; smooth with finger dipped in cornstarch. Pipe in tip 4 string arms and tip 3 dot hands. Add tip 4 bow tie (flatten with finger dipped in cornstarch). Pipe tip 4 string hat; tip 2 string mouth and tip 3 swirl motion hair. Add tip 14 zigzag border.
- **For Happy 4th of July Cookie:** Pipe tip 3 lines and print tip 2 message. Add tip 14 zigzag border with tip 3 dots.
- **For Starburst Cookie:** Add sprinkles immediately after pouring icing. Let set. Add tip 14 zigzag border.
- Add red and blue ribbons to cookie sticks. Wrap styrofoam block in foil. Insert decorated cookies in styrofoam block.
Each serves 1.

Confetti Cupcakes
- 6 Cup Standard Muffin Pan, p. 165
- Tip 2110 (1M), p. 117
- Stars and Stripes Standard Baking Cups, Patriotic Mix Sprinkle Decorations, Stars and Stripes Icing Decorations, p. 176
- Buttercream Icing, p. 92
- Bake and cool cupcakes. Pipe tip 2110 swirl on cupcake tops. Add Sprinkle Decorations and Icing Decorations.
Each serves 1.

July 4!

Brownies Jubilee
- Mini Star Pan, p. 170
- Favorite brownie recipe or mix, ice cream, cherry or blueberry pie filling
- Bake and cool brownies. Add ice cream and fruit filling.

Each serves 1.

Miss Liberty
- Proud Graduate Pan, p. 170
- Petite Loaf Pan, p. 163
- Tips 1, 1s, 3, 7, 8B, 16, 21, p. 116-119
- Christmas Red, Royal Blue, Black, Brown, Lemon Yellow, Copper (Lt. Skintone) Icing Colors, p. 110
- '97 Pattern Book (Miss Liberty Pattern), p. 108
- Cake Board, Fanci-Foil Wrap, p. 159
- Patriotic Mix Sprinkle Decorations, p. 126
- Buttercream Icing, p. 92
- Small cake-style ice cream cone

- Position 2 Petite Loaves for arm holding torch and ice together. Carefully trim ridged portion on top area of head to flatten. Ice sides and background area of cake smooth. Trace Miss Liberty Pattern with toothpick. Ice windows in crown smooth. Outline robe, crown and facial features with tip 3. Pipe in tip 3 eyes and mouth. Pipe in tip 3 dot pupils and bead tongue. Add tip 1 glint to eyes.
- Cover crown, face, robe, arms and feet with tip 16 stars. Build up nose and right arm with tip 16 stars. Pipe in book with tip 7 (pat smooth with finger dipped in cornstarch). Pipe tip 16 pull-out star hair. Pipe tip 3 dot faces in windows with tip 1s facial features.
- **For torch:** Cut ice cream cone vertically in half, fill with icing and position on arm. Outline torch with tip 3; fill in with tip 16 stars. Outline fingers with tip 3 and fill in with tip 16 stars. Spatula stripe bag fitted with tip 8B (see p. 93) and pipe swirl motion flame. Pipe tip 21 star bottom border. Add sprinkle decorations.

Serves 12.

Spine Tinglers!

Here Lies Harry
- Petite Loaf Pan, p. 163
- Tip 233, p. 116
- Moss Green Icing Color, p. 110
- Halloween Petite Loaf Baking Cups, p. 177
- Candy Melts®*– Pastel Mix, Dark Cocoa, White, Orange (1 bag each needed)
- Haunted House Candy Mold, Halloween 4-Mix Sprinkle Set (Halloween Mix Used), p. 178
- Disposable Decorating Bags, p. 114
- Buttercream Icing, p. 92
- Mini Pretzel Sticks

*brand confectionery coating

- Mold candy. To achieve grey shade used in tombstone, 3 parts pink were added to 1 part blue. Refrigerate to set.
- To make arms, dip pretzels in melted candy and position on waxed paper. Pipe fingers on end of arms with melted candy in cut disposable bag. Refrigerate to set.
- Ice tops of cakes smooth. Pipe tip 233 pull out grass; add sprinkles. Position candy.

Eac' serves 1.

Silly Spider
- Mini Pumpkin Pan, p. 179
- Tips 5, 234, p. 116
- Black, Lemon Yellow Icing Colors, p. 110
- Buttercream Icing, p. 92
- Black licorice pieces and twists, candy corn

- Cover cakes with tip 234 pull-out hair. Pipe tip 5 ball eyes and nose (smooth with finger dipped in cornstarch). Position licorice twist legs, attach licorice pieces for feet with tip 5 dots of icing. Add candy corn teeth.

Each serves 1.

Cookie Shrieks
- 10 Pc. Spooky Halloween Cookie Cutter Set, p. 177
- Tip 2, p. 116
- Orange, Leaf Green Icing Colors, p. 110
- Candy Melts*, Lt. Cocoa, p. 120
- Disposable Decorating Bags, p. 114
- Roll-Out Cookie Dough Recipe, p. 94

*brand confectionery coating

- Tint cookie dough; cut out, bake and cool cookies.
- Melt candy following package directions. Using a disposable bag and tip 2, outline cookies using melted candy.

Each serves 1.

Friendly Frankie
- Over The Hill Tombstone Pan, p. 170
- Tips 2, 2A, 3, 6, 7, 12, 16, 21, p. 116-119
- Leaf Green, Black Icing Colors, p. 110
- Cake Board, Fanci-Foil Wrap, p. 159
- '97 Pattern Book (Frankenstein Pattern), p. 108
- Buttercream Icing, p. 92
- Chocolate nougat candy rolls

- Ice cake smooth. Trace Frankenstein Pattern with toothpick. Outline mouth with tip 2 strings. Pipe in mouth with tip 3 (smooth with finger dipped in cornstarch). Pipe tip 2 dot teeth.
- Build up icing on face: pipe tip 2A line for extended forehead. Pipe tip 12 ball nose. Cover cake with tip 16 stars. Pipe tip 6 string scars and jaw line. Pipe in tip 7 eyes (smooth with finger dipped in cornstarch).
- Form nougat into 2 "bolts" and insert into neck. Add tip 21 pull out hair, first piping about 5 rows on side of cake, then working from top down.

Serves 12.

Ghostly Glow
- Jack-O-Lantern Pan, p. 179
- Tips 4, 16, 18, p. 116-117
- Red-Red, Orange, Leaf Green, Lemon Yellow Icing Colors, p. 110
- Cake Board, Fanci-Foil Wrap, p. 159
- '97 Pattern Book (Pumpkin Message Pattern), p. 108
- Buttercream Icing, p. 92

- Ice top of cake smooth.
- Mark pattern with toothpick. Outline shaded area of pattern with tip 4 strings.
- Cover cake with tip 16 stars.
- Pipe tip 18 pull out stars for stem, then pipe a tip 18 swirl at top of stem.

Serves 12.

He's Up For Halloween!

- Over The Hill Pan, p. 170
- Tips 1D, 2, 2A, 3, 6, 12, 16, 18, p. 116-119
- Brown, Black, Leaf Green Icing Colors, p. 110
- '97 Pattern Book (Bag Top, Bottom and Side Patterns; Arm Pattern), p. 108
- Cake Board, Fanci-Foil Wrap, p. 159
- Candy Melts®* - Orange (1 bag needed), p. 120
- Halloween Candy Kit, p. 179
- Buttercream Icing, p. 92
- Black shoestring licorice

*brand confectionery coating

- Mold a variety of candy and let set in refrigerator.
- To make candy bag, place wax paper over patterns. Outline patterns with melted candy in cut disposable bag. Let set. Pipe in with candy. Refrigerate to set. When set, attach bag pieces with melted candy. Let set.
- Ice cake smooth. Mark Arm Pattern with toothpick.
- Overpipe top edge of cake with smooth side tip 1D. On top of tip 1D border, pipe s-scroll design, overpiping with tips 3 and 2. Pipe tip 6 beads on both sides of scrolls and at bottom border.
- Outline and fill in sleeve with tip 12; cover with tip 18 stars. Pipe tip 2A arm and tip 12 fingers; smooth both with fingers dipped in cornstarch. Position candy bag, add licorice handle and overpipe fingers with tip 12.
- Pipe tip 2 string stitches on arm.
- Ice grassy area fluffy with spatula and add tip 16 pull-out grass.
- Pipe message with melted candy in cut disposable bag. Position candy in bag. *Serves 12.*

Check Under The Hood!

- Mini Ghost Pan, p. 179
- Tips 2, 3, 5, p. 116
- Leaf Green, Black Icing Colors, p. 110
- Jack-O-Lantern Grid, p. 179
- '97 Pattern Book (Ghost Face), p. 108
- Buttercream Icing, p. 92

- Ice cakes smooth. Trace Ghost Face Pattern with toothpick.
- Pipe in face and inside sleeves with tip 5 (smooth with finger dipped in cornstarch). Pipe tip 2 dot eyes. Build up eyebrows and nose with tip 3 lines. Outline sleeves and face with tip 5 strings; pipe tip 2 string fingers. Pipe tip 5 pull-out for top of hood. Place cakes on grid. *Each serves 1.*

Going Batty

- 2-Pc. Stand-Up Jack-O-Lantern Pan Set, p. 179
- Tips 4, 10, 12, 21, p. 116-117
- Orange, Black, Violet, Leaf Green Icing Colors, p. 110
- '97 Pattern Book (Bat Ears and Wings Patterns), p. 108
- Roll-Out Cookie Dough Recipe, p. 94
- Buttercream Icing, p. 92
- Tint cookie dough. Cut Bat Ears and Wings using patterns. Thin cookie dough with water (see p. 94) to a piping consistency. Using tip 4 and thinned cookie dough, outline bat wings. Bake and cool. Set aside.
- Trim stem from jack-o-lantern cake. Ice mouth area smooth. Cover cake with tip 21 stars; overpipe eyebrow and nose areas. Pipe tip 12 eyes, flatten with fingers dipped in cornstarch. Add tip 10 dot eye centers. Pipe tip 12 pull-out teeth.
- Position cookie ears and wings, securing with dots of icing, if necessary.

Serves 12.

Heads On A Platter

- Petite Jack-O-Lantern Pan, p. 179
- Orange Icing Color, p. 110
- Candy Melts®*- Yellow, Lt. Cocoa, p. 120
- Disposable Decorating Bags, p. 114
- Shortbread Cookie Recipe, p. 104
- Waxed paper

*brand confectionery coating

- Tint shortbread dough. Grease pan and press dough into pan cavities. Bake, remove from pan and cool.
- Melt candy following package directions. Dip bottom of cookies in melted candy, let set on waxed paper. Outline and pipe in facial features. Let set.

Scarecrow Jamboree

- Boy Perimeter Cookie Cutter, p. 123
- Tip 2, p. 116
- Violet, Kelly Green, Brown Icing Colors, p. 110
- 8 in. Jack-O-Lantern Lollipop Mold, p. 121
- Candy Melts®*- Yellow, Orange, Dark Cocoa, p. 120
- Disposable Decorating Bags, p. 114
- Roll-Out Cookie Dough Recipe, p. 94

*brand confectionery coating

- Using melted Candy Melts and following package directions, mold jack-o-lantern candy. Refrigerate to set. Using a cut disposable decorating bag and melted candy, pipe in facial details. Let set.
- Tint cookie dough Violet, Kelly Green, Brown and Orange; cut boys out of Orange dough. Thin Violet, Brown and Kelly Green dough with water (see p. 94); using tip 2, cover pants, shirt and shoes with tight zigzags. Bake and cool cookies.
- Attach jack-o-lantern candy to cookies using dots of melted candy. Using melted candy and tip 2, pipe pull-out dots for straw and dot buttons.

Scary Sticks

- Halloween Pretzel Candy Mold, p. 178
- Candy Melts®*–White, Lt. Cocoa, Orange, Green, Yellow, Decorator Brush Set, p. 120
- Disposable Decorating Bags, p. 114
- Pretzel rods

*brand confectionery coating

- Mold candies following directions on package. After pouring in the final layer, position pretzels and refrigerate until set. Unmold.

Each serves 1.

Bake up a Halloween cookie fest with our 12 Pc. Jack-O-Lantern Cookie Cutter Canister Set (p. 177). Serve the cookies right out of the canister and delight all your trick-or-treaters! Set features ten different spooky cutters in a storage canister and Goblin Goodies Cookie Recipe.

Pumpkin Patch Cookie Bash!
- Jack-O-Lantern Cookie Treat Pan, p. 177
- Tips 2, 5, 6, 10, 14, 349, p. 116-119
- Black, Red-Red, Orange, Leaf Green Icing Colors, p. 120
- 5 Pc. Bite Size Halloween Cookie Cutter Set, p. 177
- 6 in. Cookie Treat Sticks (1 pk. needed), p. 122
- 8 in. Lollipop Sticks (1 pk. needed), p. 121
- 4 Pc. Rustic Fence Set, p. 134
- Fanci-Foil Wrap, p. 159
- Roll-Out Cookie Dough Recipe, p. 94
- Buttercream Icing, p. 92
- Styrofoam block, paper grass, hot glue gun

- Tint cookie dough. Cut out ghost and bat cookies, insert 8 in. lollipop sticks; bake and cool. Prepare Jack-O-Lantern cookies on sticks using Cookie Treat Pan. Bake and cool.
- **Decorate ghosts and bats:** Place ghost cookies on wire rack over drip pan. Thin icing and pour over cookies. Let set. Add tip 2 dot eyes and mouths. **Decorate Jack-O-Lanterns:** Pipe tip 10 eyes, tip 6 mouths with tip 5 teeth and tip 5 noses; shape with finger dipped in cornstarch. Add tip 2 dot freckles and string eye lines. Cover stems with tip 14 pull-out stars and zigzags, add tip 2 string vines and tip 349 leaves.
- Cut styrofoam into 5 x 5 x 2 ½ in. high block. Cover with Fanci-Foil Wrap. Hot glue grass to top and sides of block, glue fence sections to sides. Push sticks into block to arrange cookies.

Each serves 1.

Turkeys In The Straw
- Jack-O-Lantern Cookie Treat Pan, p. 177
- Thanksgiving Candy Mold, p. 178
- 4 Pc. Rustic Fence Set, p. 134
- 6 in. Cookie Treat Sticks (1 pk. needed),   p. 122
- 4, 8 in. Lollipop Sticks (1 pk. each needed), p. 121
- Disposable Decorating Bags, p. 114
- Decorator Brush Set, Candy Melts®*- Orange (2 bags needed), Light Cocoa, Green, Yellow (1 bag each needed), p. 120
- Fanci-Foil Wrap, p. 159
- Styrofoam block (5" x 5" x 2½), excelsior, hot glue gun

*brand confectionery coating

- Using sugar cookie recipe on pan label, bake and cool Jack-O-Lantern cookies.
- Place cooled cookies on rack and cover with melted candy. Let dry and cover again with melted candy. Fill disposable bag with orange melted candy and pipe indentation lines in pumpkin. Fill disposable bag with green melted candy and pipe stems. Let set and overpipe stems to build up.
- Mold a variety of turkey candies using "painting" method (p. 104).
- Cover styrofoam block with Fanci-Foil Wrap. Glue excelsior and fence to block with hot glue gun. Insert cookies and candy into block.

Each serves 1.

Harvest Loaves
- Petite Loaf Pan, p. 163
- Tips 3, 14, p. 116-117
- Orange, Brown, Golden Yellow, Ivory Icing Colors, p. 110
- Petite Loaf Baking Cups - Gold Foil, p. 127
- Buttercream Icing, p. 92

- Bake and cool cakes.
- Ice cakes smooth with spatula. Pipe tip 14 string fenceposts. Pipe tip 14 pull-out haystacks. Pipe tip 3 ball pumpkins with tip 3 pull-out stems.

Each serves 1.

American Classic Pie
- Pumpkin Pie Pan, p. 179
- Tip 2, p. 116
- Leaf Green, Brown Icing Colors, p. 110
- '97 Pattern Book (Stem & Leaves Pattern), p. 108
- Make Any Message Letter Press Set, p. 113
- Parchment Triangles, p. 114
- Decorator Brush Set, p. 120
- Favorite pie crust and pumpkin pie filling recipe, flour

- Make your favorite pumpkin pie recipe, reserving 3 tablespoons pumpkin mixture and extra crust. Ten minutes before pie is done, remove from oven and gently imprint message in filling using individual letters from Letter≈ Press Set. Mix 3 tablespoons reserved pumpkin mixture, 1 teaspoon flour and brown icing color, place tip 2 in parchment bag and outline message. Return pie to oven and bake 10 minutes or until done.
- Roll out reserved pie crust and cut out Stem & Leaves Pattern. Thin a small amount of green icing color with water and paint crust. Mix a small amount of remaining pie crust with 1 teaspoon water and 1 teaspoon granulated sugar, to the consistency of icing; add more water, a little at a time, if necessary. Tint mixture and pipe out lines with tip 2. Bake 15 minutes or until lightly browned. Cool and position on pie.

Serves 12.

HAPPY THANKSGIVING

Jaunty Ginger Kid
Bite-Size Gingerbread Boys Pan; Tips 2 and 8; Christmas Red Icing Color.

Simply Seasonal
Mini Muffin Pan; Tip 4B; Kelly Green Icing Color; Red and Green, White Mini Size Candy and Party Cups; Christmas Tree Mix Sprinkle Decorations.

Visions Of Christmas Pops
Santa's Treats 29 Pc. Candy Making Kit; Christmas Pretzel Candy Mold; Lt. Cocoa, Christmas Mix, White Candy Melts*; 2-Pc. Christmas Party Taper Candles Set; 4 and 8 in. Lollipop sticks; foil streamers, curling ribbon, foil, styrofoam block, cookie tin, ribbon, pretzel rods.

We need a little Christmas!

Little surprises make big holiday smiles! Individual holiday treats are easy to make, using Wilton Pans and Products, Roll-Out Cookie Dough Recipe (p. 94), Buttercream or Royal Icing Recipes (p. 92) and assorted accents.

Elfin Cheer
Mini Snowman Pan; Tips 2, 8, 17, 352; Copper, Kelly Green, Christmas Red, Brown, Black Icing Colors; peppermint sticks, jelly candies.

Spruced Up
Standard Muffin Pan; Tip 19; Green, White Candy Melts*; Plaid Standard Baking Cups; Rainbow Nonpareils Sprinkle Decorations; Edible Glitter; sugar ice cream cone, peppermint stick.

Personality Pines
Petite Christmas Tree Pan; Green, White, Lt. Cocoa Candy Melts*; Roll-Out Cookie Dough Recipe (p. 94).

Santa Surrounded
Standard Muffin Pan; Tips 2, 2A, 4, 12, 16 (see figure piping section for piping Santa); Kelly Green, Christmas Red Icing Colors; Santa Claus & Elves Standard Baking Cups; Santa Claus Icing Decorations; mini jawbreakers.

Never Sees Red
Mini Christmas Tree Pan; Tips 6 and 12; Brown, Black Icing Colors; pretzels, giant gumball.

Snowed Under
Muffin Caps Pan (to mold base); Lt. Cocoa, White Candy Melts*; Truffle Candy Recipe (stack for body; p. 104); jelly candies, mini pretzel stick.

Creative Celebrations
Noel: Petite Loaf Pan; Tips 2 and 352; Golden Yellow, Christmas Red Icing Colors; Holly Mix Sprinkle Decorations; Gold Foil Petite Loaf Baking Cups; peppermint sticks. **Love:** Petite Loaf Pan; Christmas Tree Petite Loaf Baking Cups; Peppermint Crunchies Sprinkle Decorations; Christmas Lollipop Candy Mold; White, Yellow, Lt. Cocoa, Green Candy Melts*; mini candy canes.

Dreaming Of Santa
Mini Gingerbread Boy Pan; Tips 2 and 2A; Christmas Red, Kelly Green, Brown, Royal Blue Icing Colors.

Trim-A-Tree
Petite Christmas Tree Pan; Green, White Candy Melts*; Rainbow Nonpareils Sprinkle Decorations; Petite Wreath and Snowman Icing Decorations.

*brand confectionery coating

Snow Much Fun!

- 11 x 15 in. Sheet Pan, p, 161
- Tips 1, 2, 3, 4, 5, 10, 11, 13, 18, 21, 46, p, 116-119
- Kelly Green, Christmas Red, Black, Royal Blue, Copper (Lt. Skintone), Lemon Yellow, Brown Icing Colors, p. 110
- '97 Pattern Book (Snow Kids Patterns), p. 108
- 56-Pc. Make Any Message Letter Press Set, p. 113
- Cake Boards, Fanci-Foil Wrap, p. 159
- Edible Glitter, p. 112
- Buttercream Icing, p. 92
- Ice cream sugar cones, powdered sugar, tea strainer

- Use stiffened buttercream for the following: Make 3 snow kids using patterns and tips 1, 2, 3, 4, 5, 10, 11, 13, 46 (p. 101). Trim ice cream cones to varying sizes and make 5 trees using tip 18 pullout (p. 101). Make extras to allow for breakage and let dry.
- Ice 1-layer cake sides smooth; ice top fluffy. Using a spatula, smooth area for message, use the back of a spoon to smooth areas for snow kids. Imprint message using Pattern Press Set; outline using tip 2.
- Pipe tip 21 bottom shell border. Position trees and snow kids. Using tip 5, outline snow kids, blend edges using spatula. Sprinkle Edible Glitter on cake top; sprinkle powdered sugar on trees using tea strainer.

Serves 22.

The Other List

- Santa Checking List Pan, p. 183
- Tips 1, 2, 4, 16, 21, p. 116-119
- Lemon Yellow, Royal Blue, Christmas Red, Copper (Lt. Skintone) Kelly Green, Black Icing Colors, p. 110
- Cake Boards, Fanci-Foil Wrap, p. 159
- '97 Pattern Book (Elf Pattern), p. 108
- Buttercream Icing, p. 92
- Mini jaw breakers

- Ice cake sides and list areas smooth. Mark Elf Pattern using toothpick. Build up icing on gloves, arm and nose areas for dimension. Using small angled spatula, shape rolled scroll end. Add outlines as follows: Tip 4 body, clothing details and scroll; tip 2 mouth; tip 1 ears and eyelashes. Fill in mouth and eyes using tip 4; add tip 2 dots for glint in eyes.
- Using tip 16, cover face, gloves and clothing with stars; add zigzags to stripes on hat; cover beard and add hair using pull-out stars. Add tip 1 green and tip 2 red message. Pipe tip 21 bottom rosette border; position mini jawbreaker candies.

Serves 12.

LET IT SNOW
LET IT SNOW
LET IT SNOW...

THINGS TO PACK IN SLEIGH

- *Jumper Cables (for Rudolph)*
- *Antler Defroster*
- *Fuzzy Dice*
- *Sleigh Phone*
- *Chimney Grease*
- *Roof Repair Kit*
- *Radar Detector*
- *Airline Schedules*

Letters To Santa

- Smiling Santa Pan, p. 183
- Tips 3, 16, 20, p. 116-119
- Red-Red, Copper (Lt. Skintone), Black, Icing Colors, p. 110
- Cake Board, Fanci-Foil Wrap, p. 159
- Buttercream Icing, p. 92
- Cover face and hat with tip 16 stars. Build up nose with tip 16 stars. Pipe tip 16 zigzag eyebrows and tip 3 string eyes.
- Pipe tip 20 reverse shell pom-pom and hat trim. Pipe in mouth. Pipe in tip 3 bead tongue (smooth with finger dipped in cornstarch). Ice beard and moustache fluffy with spatula. Position "Spelling Out The Season" cookies (see below).

Serves 12.

Fast 'N Festive Poinsettia Cake

- Double-Tier Round Pan, p. 167
- Tip 3, p. 116
- Ready-To-Use Poinsettia Icing Decorations, Cinnamon Sprinkle Decorations, p. 181
- Cake Board, Fanci-Foil Wrap, p. 159
- Boiled Icing Recipe, p. 92
- Spearmint leaves, peppermint sticks, jelly candies, Christmas hard candies
- Ice cake fluffy. Position peppermint sticks, poinsettias and leaves on cake. Use tip 3 to add dots of icing to backs of candies and spearmint leaves to secure on cake. Attach jelly candy "flames" to peppermint sticks.

Serves 14.

Spelling Out The Season

- 26-Pc. Alphabet Cookie Cutters, p. 124
- Tips 3, 16, p. 116-119
- Kelly Green, Red-Red, Lemon Yellow Icing Colors, p. 110
- Roll-Out Cookie Dough Recipe, p. 94
- Tint cookie dough red, yellow and green. Cut out cookies. Thin part of dough with water to a consistency that can easily be piped through tips 3 and 16. For decorated cookies, using thinned dough, pipe tip 3 dots, tip 16 stars; tip 3 string bows. Bake and cool.

Each serves 1.

Joyous Gingerbread!

Custom Christmas Ornaments!

- Tree, Star Perimeter Cookie Cutters, p. 180
- Tips 1, 2, 3, 4, 6, 8, 13, p. 116-119
- Kelly Green, Black, Brown, Christmas Red, Copper (Lt. Skintone), Royal Blue, Lemon Yellow Icing Colors, p. 110
- Rainbow Nonpareils Sprinkle Decorations, p. 126
- Meringue Powder, p. 111
- Decorator Brush Set, p. 120
- Grandma's Gingerbread Recipe, p. 94
- Royal Icing Recipe, p. 92
- Ribbon or yarn
- Cut and bake cookies. Make holes in tops of cookies with a round tip before baking. Let cool.

- **For star ornament:** Ice smooth. Figure pipe (see p. 102) tip 3 head, tip 6 body, tip 1 facial features, decorating bag and pull out hair. Pipe tip 13 pull out wings and tip 3 feet. Add tip 2 wavy outline around star. Add nonpareils around border; pipe tip 2 message.
- **For tree ornament:** Ice smooth. Figure pipe (see p. 102) tip 8 bear body, head, legs and arms. Pipe tip 1 facial features. Pipe decorating bag with tip 4; add tip 1 fingers. Use tip 2 to outline cookie and add "icing" from bag. Add sprinkles lights.
- Let cookies dry, string with ribbon or yarn to hang on tree.

Candyland Cabin

- Gingerbread House Kit, p. 182
- 6-Cavity Standard Muffin Pan, p. 165
- Jelly Roll Pan, p. 166
- Tips 1, 2110 (1M), 2, 3, 6, 8, 18, p. 116-119
- Christmas Red, Kelly Green, Brown Icing Colors, p. 110
- 13 x 19 in. Cake Boards, (1 pkg. needed); Fanci- Foil Wrap, p. 159
- Holly Mix, Rainbow Nonpareils Sprinkle Decorations, p. 126
- 5-Pc. Bite Size Christmas Cookie Cutter Set, 4 Pc. Gingerbread Family Cookie Cutter Set, p. 180
- Candy Melts®*- White (3 pkgs. needed), Yellow (1 pkg. needed), p. 120
- Silver Foil Standard Baking Cups, p. 127
- Meringue Powder, p. 111
- Parchment Paper Triangles, p. 114
- Grandma's Gingerbread Recipe (prepare 2 recipes – one using regular molasses, one using dark molasses), p. 94
- Royal Icing, p. 92
- Candy canes and sticks, assorted sizes; giant candy canes (2 needed); candy-coated chocolate dots; jelly fruit slices; spice drops (2 sizes); mini jaw breakers; giant gum balls; large marshmallows

*brand confectionery coating

- Enlarge Basic House pattern pieces A, B, and D from Gingerbread House Kit by 30% (1.30) using a copy machine. Make one batch gingerbread using regular molasses, and one batch using dark robust or black bead molasses. Using Gingerbread Family Cookie Cutter Set, cut desired number of people from lighter dough. Knead remaining light dough together with darker dough, adding Brown Icing Color to deepen dough color. Cut 2 "A" House Front & Back, 2 "D" Side Wall, 2 "C" Straight Roof and 1 door canopy 2 in. x 4 in. Following kit directions, bake all and cool.
- Line a jelly roll pan with parchment paper. Place a single layer of white Candy Melts in pan. Set

BACK VIEW

SIDE VIEW

pan in warm 200°F oven for 2-3 minutes, until candy appears wet and shiny. Remove from oven and sprinkle with Rainbow Nonpareils Sprinkle Decorations. Place pan in refrigerator or freezer for approximately 5 minutes until set.
- Make a cupcake candy shell. Coat the inside of a foil cupcake liner with melted Candy Melts, place in Muffin Pan and chill in refrigerator to set. Peel off liner, fill candy with large

A Very Cool Gift!

- Holiday Tree Grid, p. 183
- Tips 2, 6, p. 116
- Christmas Red, Kelly Green, Golden Yellow Icing Colors, p. 110
- 10 Pc. Christmas Cookie Collection Set, p. 180
- Disposable Decorating Bags, p. 114
- Grandma's Gingerbread Recipe, Roll-Out Cookie Dough Recipe, p. 94
- Gold ribbon
- Cut cookies from gingerbread dough. Color and thin down cookie dough with water until it will pass through tip 2. Outline and pipe in designs on cookies with tip 2. Bake. While still warm, use opening of tip 6 to make hole in tops of cookies. Let cool and tie to grid with ribbon.

Each serves 1.

marshmallows and cover with tip 2110 royal icing spiral. Position gumball on top and let dry completely.
- Pour remaining melted yellow Candy Melts onto parch-ment paper lined pan; when partially set, cut out 2 stars using cookie cutter; cut six 2 x 2 in. house windows and one 2 x 1½ in. door window using sharp knife. Remove excess candy and let set completely.
- Reinforce gingerbread before assembling house. Cut cake boards to same size as main house pieces; attach to inner sides of gingerbread with royal icing and let set. Follow kit directions and

assemble house on foil-covered triple thick corrugated board or plywood base using brown royal icing and tip 8; let set.
- Using tip 18 and royal icing, position Candy Melts on roof starting at bottom and working up. Overlap rows slightly, trim candy to size when necessary. Attach candy to front and back eaves. Pipe zigzags at roof peak and position giant gum balls; attach stars to front and back eave peaks.
- Attach windows using dots of icing and outline with tip 6. Using tip 2, add window crossbars, attach holly mix. Attach jelly fruit slice shutters. Position giant candy canes at door and secure

with dots of icing, attach door canopy. Attach candy canes and candy sticks to house corners. Pipe tip 18 stars around doorway and windows; attach candy trim. Spatula icing fluffy around house and smooth at walkway. Position spice drops around bottom border. Let dry completely and position cupcake on canopy.
- Decorate gingerbread family. Outline and fill-in clothing using tip 3. Using tip 2, add zigzag trim and dot buttons. Add dot and string facial features: Use tip 2 for parents, tip 1 for kids. Position around house.

Cookie Wonderland

- 4 Pc. Christmas Cutter Set, 4 Pc. Christmas Treats Set, p. 180
- Blue, Red, Black, Orange, Green, Yellow, White (Clear), Pink, Chocolate (Brown) Tube Decorating Gel, p. 111
- Edible Glitter, p. 112
- Roll-Out Cookie Dough Recipe, p. 94

- Bake cookies and cool. Decorate with assorted decorating gel colors. Sprinkle desired areas with edible glitter. *Each serves 1.*

The House That Love Built

- Ready-To-Use Gingerbread House Kit (includes pre-baked and formed gingerbread pieces, meringue powder for royal icing, cinnamon dots, spice drops, gumballs, decorating bag, tip 16 and instruction book), p. 182
- 3-Pc. Spruce Tree Set (2 sets needed), p. 134
- Cake Board, Fanci-Foil Wrap, p. 159
- Peppermint candies, assorted hard candies, shredded coconut, favorite photos

- Assemble house on wrapped, double-thick cake board, according to kit instruction book. Attach photos with dots of royal icing.
- Pipe tip 16 zigzag "frames" around pictures and at house corners; attach candies. Using spatula, ice roof and make mounds of icing around base of house; sprinkle with coconut. Position trees and favorite candles or figurines.

Holiday Snowman Centerpiece

- Christmas Tree and Snowman Cookie Treat Pans, p. 180
- Tips 1, 3, 13, 349, p. 116-119
- Lemon Yellow, Black, Red-Red, Brown, Kelly Green Icing Colors, p. 110
- Bite-Size Boy Cookie Cutter, Cookie Treat Sticks, p. 122
- Meringue Powder, p. 111
- Rainbow Peanut Bits Sprinkle Decorations, p. 126
- Mini Wreaths Icing Decorations, p. 181
- Cake Dividing Set, p. 113
- Cake Board, Fanci-Foil Wrap, p. 159
- Roll-Out Cookie Dough Recipe, p. 94
- Royal Icing, p. 92
- Styrofoam circle (8 in. round x 2 in. high), 12 small candy canes (2 1/2 in.)

- Prepare roll-out cookie dough recipe and tint 1/4 of the dough brown for boys. Press remaining dough into cookie treat pans over sticks.
- Bake and cool cookies. For mini boys (make 14): Using royal icing, pipe tip 1 dot eyes and buttons, tip 1 string for mouth. Add mini wreaths to boys with dots of icing. For trees: Pipe tip 13 pull-out star branches; tip 1 garland and sprinkle decoration ornaments. For snowman: Ice smooth, pipe tip 3 dot facial features, buttons and zigzag scarf and hat brim. Pipe in tip 3 arms, position candy cane in hand and pipe tip 3 mittens. Add tip 349 holly leaves and tip 3 dot berries on hat.
- Ice styrofoam circle with royal icing and divide into 12ths. Add candy canes and boys to circle while icing is still soft. Insert trees and snowman into top of circle.

Swing On A Star

- Star Cookie Treat Pan, Cookie Treat Sticks, p. 122
- Tip 4, p. 116
- 8 in. Santa/Tree Lollipop Mold, p. 181
- Candy Melts®*- Christmas Mix, White, Light Cocoa, Yellow (1 pkg. each needed), 3 Pc. Decorator Brush Set, Candy Melting Plate, p. 120
- Disposable Decorating Bags, p. 114
- Fruit stripe gum, red shoestring licorice, mini round candies

- Mold Santa candy using "painting" method on p. 105.
- Bake and cool star cookies on sticks, using pan recipe and instructions. Place cookies on rack over drip pan, cover with melted white candy; let set. Using disposable bag fitted with tip 4 and melted yellow candy, pipe top edge and cover sides of cookies. Position mini round candies.
- Cut two 3 inch lengths of licorice for each swing. Make 3 holes in gum, using a round decorating tip, that will accommodate licorice and lollipop stick. Attach Santa to stick with melted candy. Position licorice and gum. Pipe name with tip 4 and melted candy.

Each serves 1.

Victorian Pastels

Renaissance Carolers

- 10 1/2 in. Ring Mold, p. 166
- Tips 1, 10, 70, 101, 103, 352, p. 116-119
- Willow Green, Rose Icing Colors, p. 110
- Flower Nail No. 7, p. 113
- Cake Board, Fanci-Foil Wrap, p. 159
- Angel Duet (2 pkgs. needed), p. 150
- 6mm White Pearl Beading* (1 pkg. needed), p. 151
- Buttercream Icing, p. 92
- White tulle 6 in. x 3 ft. (to be used for bow)*

- Using stiffened buttercream icing, make 6 tip 103 roses with tip 10 bases and 12 tip 101 apple blossoms with tip 1 dot centers. Let set.
- Ice cake smooth. Position 3 rows of pearl beads around bottom border. Randomly pipe tip 70 and tip 35 leaves. Position flowers and angels. Add tulle bow.

Serves 14.

*Remove before cutting and serving.

Bountiful Holiday Blossoms

- Treeliteful Pan, p. 183
- Tips 2, 4, 17, 46, 789, p. 116-119
- Rose, Willow Green Icing Colors, p. 110
- 30 Pc. Gum Paste Flowers Kit, Gum Paste Mix, p. 112
- Cake Board, Fanci-Foil Wrap, p. 159
- 16 in. Featherweight Decorating Bag, p. 114
- 3 Pc. Decorator Brush Set, p. 120
- 9 Pc. Flower Former Set, p. 113
- Buttercream Icing, p. 92
- Non-toxic pastel chalks

- Prepare gum paste mix. Using gum paste kit, make 60 baby's breath, 50 forget-me-nots, 50 apple blossoms and 32 holly leaves. Let dry on small flower formers. Grate pastel chalks through a tea strainer to make a powder. Using a brush, dust outer edge of forget-me-nots; attach flower to centers of apple blossoms using a moistened decorator's brush. Add tip 2 dot centers to all flowers.
- Ice sides of cake using bag fitted with tip 789. Ice top and trunk of tree smooth. Pipe tip 46 ribbed side lattice on trunk of tree. Cover top of tree with tip 17 stars. Pipe tip 4 bead top and bottom borders.
- Position flowers and holly leaves on cake. Use remaining gum paste to hand roll berries and randomly place on cake.

Serves 12.

Christmas By Candlelight

- 2 Pc. Stand-Up Tree Pan Set, p. 183
- 12 in. Round Pan, p. 164
- Tips 3, 7, 10, 68, 102, 103, 352, p. 116-119
- Willow Green, Rose Icing Colors, p. 110
- Cake Board, p. 159
- Ready-To-Use Rolled Fondant (3 boxes needed), p. 112
- Meringue Powder, p. 111
- Flower Nail No. 9, Cake Dividing Set, p. 113
- 4 mm Pearl Beading* (1 pkg. needed), p. 151
- Candlelight Cake Stand, p. 154
- Decorator Brush Set, p. 120
- 14 in. Decorator Preferred Plate, p. 157
- Plastic Dowel Rods, p. 156
- Buttercream, Royal Icings, p. 92
- Taper candles, fresh flowers, waxed paper

*remove beading before cutting and serving.

- With royal icing, make 30 tip 102 roses with tip 7 bases and 25 tip 103 roses with tip 10 bases. Make extras to allow for breakage and let dry.
- Using 1 package of fondant, tint ¼ green and ¾ rose. On waxed paper covered board, roll out fondant to about ⅛ in. thick. For small bows on sides of cake, cut 50 strips of fondant (make extras to allow for breakage) measuring ³⁄₈ in. x 3 in.; for large bow on top of cake, cut 15 strips of fondant measuring ⅝ in. x 5 ½ in.

*Remove before cutting and serving.

Loop in half, seal loops with water and let dry. Cut 6 fondant "streamers" measuring from 4 to 6 in. long; stand streamers on edge and shape into flowing ribbons. Let dry. Save remainder of rose fondant to later drape on cake.

- Prepare 2-layer cake for fondant (see p. 92) and stacked construction (see p. 96). Divide 12 in. round cake into 8ths. Make 8 lengths of fondant, approximately 5 x 3 in. for draping. Roll and cut out pieces; immediately pinch at both ends and form drape look. Attach fondant drapes between each section with brush dipped in water.
- Attach loops for bows with icing. Roll green fondant into ½ in. wide x 38 in. diameter rope (may be done in 3 separate pieces). String pearl beading around rope before positioning on bottom border of cake.
- Cover tree with tip 68 leaves. Add roses, tip 352 leaves and tip 3 berry clusters. Position cake on candlelight stand, then add tree on cake board. Attach top ribbon and streamers to cake with icing.

Serves 49.

INSTRUCTIONAL

Easy Baking & Decorating Guide
Everyone Can Enjoy Cake Decorating!

Beginners and hobbyists alike will find cake decorating fun, easy and very rewarding. A personally decorated special occasion cake will delight the recipient and prove rewarding for the decorator. The following guide will provide you with the basics of cake decorating as well as more advanced techniques. With just a little practice, you can make specific decorations described in this section that will enable you to create cakes in the "idea" section of this Yearbook. And, if you've already gained some experience with cake decorating, the pages ahead are great for review and new inspirations.

Cake Decorating Terms to Know

These words are frequently used in cake decorating. Use this as a reference when decorating your cakes.

Attach
To secure royal or buttercream icing flowers or plastic decorations, pipe dots of icing to "attach" the decoration to an iced cake. Royal icing dries hard and is more permanent than buttercream. Use your icing to attach as you would use "glue."

Border
A continuous decoration used around the top, side or base of a cake.

Elongated
When we use the term elongated shells, leaves, etc.,it means to taper an icing decoration by relaxing bag pressure and moving before stopping the technique.

Figure Piping
Decorating technique used to form figures out of icing.

Filling
Frosting, preserves or pudding that's spread between cake layers and holds them together.

Leveling
Removing the "crown" of a cake to provide a flat surface for frosting or decorating.

Outline or Strings
When the outlining method is used, the icing that flows out of the tip to follow contours of a shaped cake or to cover pattern design marks are called "strings" or outlines.

Piping
Squeezing icing out of a bag to form decoration. Also see figure piping.

Score
Using your spatula edge to make a mark in icing or marzipan by gently pressing it against the surface.

Baking Hints

- If you like to plan ahead, do so. Your baked cake will stay fresh up to three months wrapped in heavy-duty foil in the freezer. Always thaw cake completely before icing. Your cake will still be fresh and easy to ice because it will be firm.

- Wilton Bake-Even Cake Strips will help prevent crowns from forming on basic shaped cakes as they bake.

- Packaged, two-layer cake mixes usually yield 4 to 6 cups of batter, but formulas change, so always measure. Here's a handy guide: one 2-layer cake mix will make any of the following: two 8-in. round layers, or one 10-in. round layer, or one 7x11x2-in. sheet, or one character cake, or one Wonder Mold cake, or one mini-tier cake.

- If you're in doubt as to how many cups of batter you need to fill a pan, measure the cups of water it will hold first and use this number as a guide. Then, if you want a cake with high sides, fill the pan 2/3 full of batter. For slightly thinner cake layers, fill 1/2 full. Never fill cake pans more than 2/3 full. Even if the batter doesn't overflow, the cake will have a heavy texture.

- For 3-in. deep or 3-D pans, we recommend pound or pudding-added cake batters. Fill pan half full only.

- For 3-D cakes: When using the baking core, it's essential to be exact about baking time, as it's very difficult to test 3-D cakes for doneness. Be sure to preheat the oven. If your 3-D cake is to be given away or sold, after baking you can remove the baking core and insert crumpled aluminum foil into the opening for support.

- Hints for cakes-to-go! Use our Cake Pan Cover to protect sheet cakes in our 9x13-in. pan (p. 164). The Cake Saver is a great way to take cakes places (p. 164). The 9 x 13 inch and 11 x 15 inch Sheet Cake Pans with Covers (p. 166) are perfect for transporting cakes and baked goods, too!

Baking Your Cake

The First Step to Success! For a beautiful cake, follow these easy instructions. A properly baked cake is the best foundation for your icing and your decorations. NOTE: If you're using one of the Wilton shaped pans, follow the specific instructions included with the pan. For 3-dimensional stand-up cakes, use batters that bake a firm-textured cake such as a pound cake.

GREASE	FLOUR	SHAKE	PLACE RACK	REMOVE

- Preheat oven to temperature specified in recipe or on packaged mix.
- Thoroughly grease the inside of each pan with solid vegetable shortening **or use a vegetable cooking spray**. Use a pastry brush to spread the shortening evenly. Be sure sides, corners and all indentations are completely covered.
- If solid vegetable shortening is used, sprinkle flour inside of pan and shake back and forth so the flour covers all the greased surfaces. Tap out excess flour and if any shiny spots remain, touch up with more shortening and flour. This tip is essential in preventing your cake from sticking. If you prefer, the bottom of a simple geometric shaped pan (round, square, hexagon, etc.) may be lined with waxed or parchment baking paper after greasing. This eliminates flouring pan. Your cake will unmold easily but with more crumbs on side.

- Bake the cake according to temperature and time specifications in recipe or on package instructions. Remove cake from oven and let cool 10 minutes in pan on a cake rack. Larger cakes over 12-in. diameter may need to cool 15 minutes.
- So cake sits level and to prevent cracking, while in pan, cut away the raised center portion with serrated knife. To unmold cake, place cake rack against cake and turn both rack and pan over. Remove pan carefully. If cake will not release, return it to a warm oven (250ºF) for a few minutes, then repeat procedure. Cool cake completely, at least 1 hour. Brush off loose crumbs and frost.

All About Icing

Proper consistency is the key to making decorating icing that will shape the petals of a flower, show the details of a border or cover the surface of a cake. It's important that you use the recommended icing and consistency for any technique. As a general rule, flowers require a stiff icing consistency, borders a medium-stiff consistency and writing or leaves a slightly thinned consistency.

Icing that can peak to an inch or more is stiff, less than that is medium consistency. Icing that flows easily from a tip without running is a thin consistency. Every Wilton icing recipe is tested for taste and other important qualities. This chart will tell you each recipe's qualities, so you can determine which is the right one for your cake.

Icing	Recommended Uses	Tinting	Flavor & Consistency	Storing Icing	Special Information
Buttercream (Wilton Mix or Homemade)	• Borders, writing • Roses, drop flowers & sweet peas • Figure piping • Icing cakes smooth	• Deep colors • Most colors deepen upon setting	• Sweet, buttery flavor • Thin-to-stiff consistency	• Refrigerate icing in an airtight container for 2 weeks	• Iced cake can be stored at room temperature for 2-3 days • Flowers remain soft enough to be cut with a knife
Snow-White Buttercream	• Borders, writing • Roses, drop flowers & sweet peas • Figure piping • Icing cakes smooth	• Deep colors • Most colors deepen upon setting • Gives true colors	• Sweet, almond flavor • Thin-to-stiff consistency	• Refrigerate icing in an airtight container for 2 weeks	• Iced cake may be stored for 2-3 days • Air-dried flowers have translucent look • Flowers remain soft enough to be cut with a knife • Good for wedding cakes • Tints true colors due to pure white color
Cream Cheese	• Basic borders, writing, stars, shells, drop flowers • Icing cakes smooth	• Pastels	• Cream cheese • Thin-to-medium consistency	• Refrigerate icing in an airtight container for 2 weeks	• Iced cake must be refrigerated • Cream cheese flavor is especially good with spice cakes, carrot cakes • All-purpose
Stabilized Whipped Cream	• Borders, writing • Icing cakes smooth	• Pastels only • Paste colors are best to use	• Creamy, delicate sweetness • Light, thin-to-medium consistency	• Use immediately	• Iced cake must be refrigerated • Texture remains soft on decorated cake • Especially good on cakes decorated with fruits
Quick-Pour Fondant Icing	• For icing	• Pastels	• Very sweet flavor • Pourable consistency	• Use immediately, excess fondant drippings can be reheated & poured again	• Dries to a shiny, smooth surface to coat cakes, petit fours and cookies • Seals in freshness
Rolled Fondant Icing	• For covering heavy pound or fruit cake • Cutting small decorations and ruffles	• Pastels	• Rich, sweet flavor • Dough-like consistency	• Excess can be refrigerated 3 weeks • Bring to room temperature before kneading	• Gives a perfectly smooth, satin-like surface • Seals in freshness and moisture • Always decorate with royal icing • Cake can be stored at room temp. 3-4 days
Royal (made from pasteurized egg whites)	• Flower-making, figure piping, making flowers on wires • Decorating cookies & gingerbread houses	• Deep colors • Some colors may fade upon sitting in bright light	• Very sweet and hard • Thin-to-stiff consistency	• Store in airtight grease-free container at room temperature for 2 weeks	• Dries candy-hard for lasting decorations • Flowers and other decorations will last for months. Air dry. • Bowl & utensils must be grease free • Cover icing with damp cloth to prevent crusting
Fluffy Boiled Icing 100% Fat-free!	• Borders • Figure piping • Writing stringwork • Icing cakes smooth and fluffy.	• Pastel & deep shades	• Marshmallow-like flavor • Very fluffy consistency	• Use immediately	• Serve within 24 hours • Sets quickly! Ice smooth or fluffy, immediately • Ideal for figure piping

Cake Icing Hints

• Thinning buttercream icing with light corn syrup makes consistency best for easy spreading.

• When icing small areas or sides of a shaped cake, be sure to ice a little past the area or edge or top to create a neat surface that can be outlined or covered with stars.

• To smooth the icing surface on 3-dimensional cakes such as the ball, egg, bear, lamb or bunny cakes, let buttercream icing crust slightly. Then place plastic wrap over the icing and smooth over the surface gently with your hands. Carefully remove wrap. For a textured surface, follow the same procedure using a cloth or paper towel.

• To make clean-up easier and quicker when decorating with buttercream icing, use a degreaser liquid soap to dissolve icing from tools. It is especially important to have grease-free utensils when using royal or color flow icings.

Torting

By simply cutting a cake into layers, you can enhance its taste and create impact! Classic and novelty shapes are easy to torte, especially with our Cake Leveler! It cuts perfectly-even layers on cakes up to 10 inches in diameter and adjusts to desired height. Slice the cake horizontally into two or four layers. Make layers the same thickness. Follow package directions for using our Cake Leveler or use a serrated knife. Hold knife level at desired height and with a gentle sawing motion, rotate the cake against blade of knife.

• For easy handling, slide the sliced layer onto a cake board (for each layer follow this procedure).

• Fill bottom layer. Slide next layer off board onto filled layer.

Decorating Hints

• Tips from the same basic group that are close in size may be substituted for one another. The effect will be a slightly smaller or larger decoration.

• Use tip 20, 21 or the super fast Triple-Star Tip, when you're covering a large area with stars. You can also use zigzags or side-by-side stripes to fill in large areas.

• When using parchment bags, you can place a tip with a smaller opening over the tip you're using and tape it in place. This saves time changing bags and tips when you're using the same color icing.

• Stock up on the bags and tips in the sizes you use the most. Your decorating will go faster if several are filled and ready to use. Cover tips securely with convenient Tip Covers.

• Overpiping: Outlining a piped decoration with the same technique will add dimension and make it stand out. Overpiping with a different technique in a contrasting color creates an eye-catching effect.

Icing Recipes

Buttercream Icing

½ cup solid vegetable shortening
½ cup butter or margarine*
1 teaspoon Clear Vanilla Extract (p. 111)
4 cups sifted confectioners sugar
 (approx. 1 lb.)
2 tablespoons milk**

Cream butter and shortening with electric mixer. Add vanilla. Gradually add sugar, one cup at a time, beating well on medium speed. Scrape sides and bottom of bowl often. When all sugar has been mixed in, icing will appear dry. Add milk and beat at medium speed until light and fluffy. Keep icing covered with a damp cloth until ready to use. For best results, keep icing bowl in refrigerator when not in use. Refrigerated in an airtight container, this icing can be stored 2 weeks. Rewhip before using.
YIELD: 3 cups

*Substitute all-vegetable shortening and ½ teaspoon Wilton Butter Flavor (p. 111) for pure white icing and stiffer consistency.

**Add 3-4 tablespoons light corn syrup per recipe to thin for icing cake.

Chocolate Buttercream

Add ¾ cup cocoa or three 1 oz. unsweetened chocolate squares, melted, and an additional 1 to 2 tablespoons milk to recipe. Mix until well blended. For a unique change of pace, add Wilton Candy Flavors (p.120), in place of vanilla extract.

Snow-White Buttercream

⅔ cup water
4 tablespoons Meringue Powder Mix (P. 111)
12 cups sifted confectioners' sugar (approx. 3 lbs.)
1¼ cups solid shortening
¾ teaspoon salt
½ teaspoon Almond Extract (p. 111)
½ teaspoon Clear Vanilla Extract (p. 111)
¼ teaspoon Butter Flavor (p. 111)

Combine water and meringue powder; whip at high speed until peaks form. Add 4 cups sugar, one cup at a time, beating after each addition at low speed. Alternately add shortening and remainder of sugar. Add salt and flavorings; beat at low speed until smooth. YIELD: 7 cups
Note: Recipe may be doubled or cut in half. If cut in half, yield is 2⅔ cups.

Frozen Non-Dairy Whipped Topping

Non-dairy whipped topping must be thawed in the refrigerator before coloring or using for decorating. Can be used for decorating techniques similar to stabilized whipped cream. Do not allow to stay at room temperature, as it becomes too soft for decorating. After decorating, store cake in refrigerator.

Packaged Topping Mix

Whipped topping mix can be used for decorating similar to stabilized whipped cream. However, use immediately after preparing. Do not allow to stay at room temperature, as topping becomes too soft for well-defined decorations.

Confectioners' Sugar Glaze

Drizzle on dessert cakes, muffins and cookies.
1¼ cups confectioners sugar
3 tablespoons milk
Stir milk into sugar.
 YIELD: ½ cup

Royal Icing

3 level tablespoons Meringue Powder (P. 111)
4 cups sifted confectioners' sugar (approx. 1 lb.)
6 tablespoons water*
Beat all ingredients at low speed for 7 to 10 minutes (10 to 12 minutes at high speed for portable mixer) until icing forms peaks.
YIELD: 3 cups

*When using large counter top mixer or for stiffer icing, use 1 tablespoon less water.

Stabilized Whipped Cream Icing

1 teaspoon unflavored gelatin
4 teaspoons cold water
1 cup heavy whipping cream
¼ cup confectioners' sugar
½ teaspoon Clear Vanilla Extract (p.111)

Combine gelatin and cold water in small saucepan. Let stand until thick. Place over low heat, stirring constantly, just until gelatin dissolves. Remove from heat and cool, do not let set. Whip cream, sugar, and vanilla until slightly thickened. While beating slowly, gradually add gelatin to whipped cream mixture. Whip at high speed until stiff.
YIELD: 2 cups.

Cakes iced with whipped cream must be stored in the refrigerator.

Fluffy Boiled Icing Recipe

Meringue:
3 tablespoons Meringue Powder (p. 111)
½ cup cold water

Syrup:
2 cups granulated sugar
¼ cup corn syrup
½ cup water

Beat meringue powder and cold water until stiff, about 4 minutes. In large microwave-safe measuring cup stir sugar, corn syrup and water. In microwave oven, bring syrup mixture to a boil (approximately 5 minutes). Remove when boiling stops. Slowly add syrup to meringue mixture while beating on low. Beat on HIGH for 4 minutes until stiff and glossy.
YIELD: 8 cups

For top of range: Mix sugar, corn syrup and water in 2 quart saucepan. Bring to a boil; cool slightly and follow directions above.

Cream Cheese Icing

½ cup (1 stick) butter, softened
8 oz. package cream cheese, softened
1 lb. (4 cups) confectioners' sugar
1 tablespoon milk

Note: Do not use light cream cheese or butter substitute. If margarine is used, icing will be softer. In a medium mixer bowl cream butter and cream cheese until smooth. Add sugar and milk. Beat on high speed until smooth (only 30 seconds to 1 minute). Thin to ice cake smooth; use full strength for piping borders. YIELD: 2 ¾ cups

Wilton Creamy White Icing Mix

You'll love its creamy taste and convenience. Ideal for icing smooth and decorating (p.111). Just add butter and milk, the shortening's already in the mix. For chocolate icing: Mix icing according to package directions. Stir in 2-oz. melted, unsweetened baking chocolate. If too stiff, add a few drops of milk.
For Deluxe Buttercream: Use 6 tablespoons butter and ¼ cup whipping cream.

Heated Wilton Ready-To-Spread Icing

Open icing container, remove foil. Microwave on 50% power for 1 minute; stir. Continue to
microwave at 30 second intervals until ready to pour. If a microwave is unavailable, icing can be heated on a warming tray or in a pan on a stove.

Quick-Pour Fondant Icing

6 cups confectioners' sugar, sifted
½ cup water (4 ounces)
2 tablespoons white corn syrup
1 teaspoon Wilton Almond Extract (p. 111)
Wilton Icing Colors (p. 110), optional

Combine water and corn syrup. Add to sugar in a saucepan and stir over low heat until well-mixed and heated to 92°F, thin enough to be poured, but thick enough so it won't run off the cake. Stir in extract and Icing Color, if desired. To cover cake, ice smoothly with buttercream and let icing crust, or cover with apricot glaze (recipe below). Place cake on cooling rack with a cookie sheet beneath it. Pour fondant over iced cake, flowing from center and moving out in a circular motion. Touch up sides with a spatula. Excess fondant can be stored, tightly covered, in refrigerator for weeks. Reheat to use again.
YIELD: 4 cups, enough to cover a 10 in. round cake. Recipe may be doubled or tripled.

Chocolate Poured Fondant: Follow recipe above, but increase amount of water by 1 ounce. After fondant is heated, stir in 3 ounces of melted, unsweetened chocolate, then add flavoring.

Apricot Glaze: Heat 1 cup of apricot preserves to boiling, strain, then brush on cake while still hot. It will dry to a hard finish in 15 minutes or less. Ideal for crumb-coating cakes before icing.

Rolled Fondant

This icing is rolled out and used as a covering for a pound or fruit cake, which is traditionally first covered with a layer of marzipan to seal in flavor and moistness of the cake. A light layer of buttercream may also be used. Cakes covered with rolled fondant can be decorated with royal or buttercream icing. Wilton also has convenient, ready-to-use Rolled Fondant (p. 112)– for easy-to-handle fondant with no mixing.

Rolled Fondant Recipe
1 tablespoon unflavored gelatin
¼ cup cold water
½ cup Glucose (p. 112)
1 tablespoon Glycerin (p. 111)
2 tablespoons solid vegetable shortening
2 lbs. confectioners' sugar
2-3 drops liquid food color and flavoring, as desired.

Combine gelatin and cold water; let stand until thick. Place gelatin mixture in top of double boiler and heat until dissolved. Add glucose and glycerin, mix well. Stir in shortening and just before completely melted, remove from heat, add flavoring and color. Mixture should cool until lukewarm. Next, place 1 lb. confectioners' sugar in a bowl and make a well. Pour the lukewarm gelatin mixture into the well and stir with a wooden spoon, mixing in sugar and adding more, a little at a time, until stickiness disappears. Knead in remaining sugar. Knead until the fondant is smooth, pliable and does not stick to your hands. If fondant is too soft, add more sugar; if too stiff, add water (a drop at a time). Use fondant immediately or store in airtight container in refrigerator. When ready to use, bring to room temperature and knead again until soft. This recipe yields enough to cover a 10 x 4-in. high cake.

To Roll Fondant

Spray work surface and rolling pin with vegetable oil pan spray and dust with a mixture of confectioners' sugar and cornstarch. Here are two ways to prepare cake for fondant. Coat with piping gel or apricot glaze, then cover with rolled marzipan. Coat again with piping gel or glaze. Add fondant. Or ice cake with buttercream icing, let set, then cover with rolled fondant or use new Wilton ready-to-use Rolled Fondant. Roll out fondant into a circle the diameter of the cake plus double the height of the cake you are covering. As you roll, lift and move the fondant to prevent it from sticking to the surface. Gently lift fondant over rolling pin and place over cake. Smooth and shape fondant on cake, using palm of hand. If large air bubbles are trapped under fondant, prick with a pin and continue to smooth. Trim excess from base. A fondant-covered cake may be kept for several days.

Coloring Your Icing

Color brings cake decorations to life; therefore it's essential that you learn how to tint icings to achieve different decorating effects. Wilton Icing Color is concentrated color in a creamy, rich base. It gives icing vivid or deep, rich color without changing icing consistency. See page 110 for a complete selection of quality Wilton Icing Colors. Icing Color Kits are also available.

Tinting

• Start with white icing and add the color a little at a time until you achieve the shade you desire. Use a toothpick to add icing color; (use more depending on amount of icing). Hint: Tint a small amount of icing first, then mix in with remainder of white icing. Colors intensify or darken in buttercream icings 1 to 2 hours after mixing, so keep this in mind when you're tinting icing. You can always add extra color to deepen the icing color, but it's difficult to lighten the color once it's tinted. Use White-White Icing Color to make your buttercream icing the purest snow-white!

• To mix deep or dark color icing (such as red for roses), you may need a larger amount of Wilton Icing Color. The color should still be added gradually, but use a clean small spatula each time to add the color. Red No-Taste Color has no after-taste! It's ideal for decorating large areas. Red-Red or Christmas Red Color is still better to use in royal icing and for accent color, as each offers more color intensity. If you plan to use flavorings, make icing stiff consistency, then use enough flavoring to improve taste.

• Always mix enough of any one color icing. If you're going to decorate a cake with pink flowers and borders, color enough icing for both. It's difficult to duplicate an exact shade of any color. As you gain decorating experience, you will learn just how much of any one color icing you will need.

Important Hints For Coloring

• Royal icing requires more base color than buttercream to achieve the same intensity.

• Use milk, not water, in buttercream icing recipe when using Violet Icing Color, otherwise the icing may turn blue.

• Substitute chocolate icing for dark brown colors. Use 6 tablespoons unsweetened cocoa powder, or 2 one-ounce squares, of melted unsweetened baking chocolate, 1 tablespoon milk, and add to 1 1/2 cups white icing.

• Add color to piping gel, color flow, gum paste, cookie dough, marzipan, cream cheese, sugar molds and even cake batter for striking decorating effects!

• To restore the consistency of Wilton Icing Colors that have dried out, add a few drops of Wilton Glycerin. Mix until proper consistency is reached.

• Use a clean toothpick or spatula to add Wilton Icing Colors each time, until you reach desired shade.

Icing the Cake

Think of your cake as the canvas that your beautiful icing decorations will be presented upon. So it's essential that it be smooth and free of crumbs. By following our 5-easy-steps icing method, we feel you'll get the results you want.

1. Leveling
There are two ways to remove the slight crown your baked cake will have. Cool cake for 10 minutes in the pan. Carefully slice off the raise center with a serrated knife. Or after cake is cooled completely as per directions on p. 90, invert so that its brown top crust is uppermost and trim away the crust for a flat surface (see pic. 1). Our Bake-Even Strips will help prevent crowns from forming on basic shaped cakes (see p. 164 for details).

2. Filling Layers
Place one cake layer on a cake board or circle atop a cake stand or plate, top side up. Hint: To prevent cake from shifting, place a few stripes of icing on base surface before positioning cake. Fit bag with coupler and fill with icing. Make a dam by squeezing out a band of icing about 3/4-in. high around the edge. With your spatula, spread icing, jam, pudding or other filling in center. Position top layer with bottom side up.

3. Icing The Top
Thin your buttercream icing with light corn syrup (approximately 2 teaspoons for each cup). The consistency is correct when your spatula glides over the icing. With large spatula, place mound of icing in center of top and spread across cake, pushing excess down onto sides. Always keep spatula on the iced surface. Pulling toward the cake surface will mix in crumbs. Hint: To keep your serving base free of icing, place 3-in. wide strips of waxed paper under each side of cake.

4. Icing The Sides
Cover the sides with excess icing from the top, adding more icing if necessary. Work from top down, forcing any loose crumbs to the cake base. Again, be sure spatula touches only icing. You'll find that an angled spatula is ideal for icing sides. When you're icing a curved side, hold the spatula upright against the side of the cake and, pressing lightly, turn cake stand slowly around with your free hand without lifting the spatula from the side surface. Return excess icing to bowl and repeat procedure until sides are smooth. For angled sides such as on a cross cake, do each straight side individually; hold spatula firmly to smooth.

5. Smooth Top
Place spatula flat on one edge of cake top and sweep it across to center of cake. Lift off, remove excess icing and repeat, starting from a new point on edge of cake top. Repeat procedure until entire top surface is smooth. To smooth center, apply an even pressure to spatula as you turn cake stand around in a full circle. Lift off spatula and any excess icing.

Sheet & Other Flat Surfaced Cakes
Use the same icing procedure as shown here for sheet cakes, heart, oval, square and other shaped cakes with flat surfaces.

To Ice Areas on Shaped Cakes
The sides of shaped cakes are usually the only areas iced smooth. Just place icing on side with your spatula and spread. After sides are covered, run spatula lightly over icing in the same direction. Sometimes small background areas or facial features on top are iced smooth. Use a small spatula or decorating tip (3 or 4) and squeeze icing onto area, then smooth with finger dipped in cornstarch.

The Cake Icer Tip Will Save You Time (No.789)
If you haven't discovered this versatile tip (pg. 119) you should! You'll love how quickly and easily you can cover flat-surfaced cakes with wide bands of icing. Just hold tip flat against cake surface, serrated side up, and squeeze out a ribbed band. Holding the smooth side up gives you a smooth band. To cover side, turn cake stand clockwise as you squeeze out a band of icing, wrapping it around the cake. When your cake is completely iced, use a fork to blend ribbed seams; a spatula to join smooth bands together.

Coloring for Special Effects

BRUSH STRIPING
Striping is a method used to give multiple or deep color effects to icing. To do this, one or more colors are applied to the inside of the parchment paper bag with a brush. Then the bag is filled with white or pastel-colored icing and, as the icing is squeezed past the color, out come the striped decorations!

SPATULA STRIPING
Use a spatula to stripe the inside of a decorating bag with pastel-colored icing. Then fill the bag with white icing, or another shade of the same color as the striping, and squeeze out decorations with pastel contrasts. Use the above color techniques when figure piping for exciting results. It's fun to experiment with color! Try to achieve natural-looking flower colors by using the spatula striping method. (Roses look especially beautiful with this effect.)

3 Essentials of Bag and Tip Decorating

1. Icing Consistency

Remember, if the consistency of your decorating icing isn't exactly right, your decorations won't be either. Follow the general guidelines on p. 91.

90° Angle

45° Angle

2. Bag Position

To hold the decorating bag correctly, grip the bag near the top with the twisted or folded end locked between your thumb and fingers. Guide the bag with your free hand.

Generally, there are two basic positions for the decorating bag — the 90° angle with the bag straight up, perpendicular to the surface. And the 45° angle with the bag half-way between vertical and horizontal.

Pointing the back end of your decorating bag in the right direction is also important. Sometimes instructions will tell you to hold the back end of bag pointing to the right or towards you.

Left-handed decorators do things differently. Hold the decorating bag in your left hand and guide the decorating tip with the fingers of your right hand. If the instructions say to hold the decorating bag over to the right, you should hold your decorating bag over to the left. A right-handed person will always decorate from left to right. A left-handed person should always decorate from right to left. The only exception to this rule is when you are writing or printing. When decorating a cake on a turntable, rotate the stand counter-clockwise. For flower making on a flower nail, turn nail clockwise in right hand as you pipe petals using left hand.

HEAVY   **MEDIUM**   **LIGHT**

3. Pressure Control

The size and uniformity of your icing design are directly affected by the amount of pressure you apply to the decorating bag and the steadiness of the pressure--how you squeeze and relax your grip on the decorating bag. Strive to apply pressure so consistently that you can move the bag in a free and easy glide while just the right amount of icing flows from the tip. Practice to achieve this control.

Cookie Recipes

Grandma's Gingerbread Recipe

5 to 5 ½ cups all-purpose flour
1 tsp. baking soda
1 tsp. salt
2 tsps. ginger
2 tsps. cinnamon
1 tsp. nutmeg
1 tsp. cloves
1 cup shortening
1 cup sugar
1 ¼ cups unsulphured molasses
2 eggs, beaten

Preheat oven to 375°F. Thoroughly mix flour, soda, salt and spices. Melt shortening in large saucepan. Cool slightly. Add sugar, molasses and eggs; mix well. Add four cups dry ingredients and mix well.

Turn mixture onto lightly floured surface. Knead in remaining dry ingredients by hand. Add a little more flour, if necessary, to make a firm dough. Roll out on a lightly floured surface to ¼ in. thickness for cut-out cookies. Bake on ungreased cookie sheet. Small and medium-sized cookies for 6-10 minutes, large cookies for 10-15 minutes. One recipe of this gingerbread dough will yield 40 average-size cookies.

Note: If you're not going to use your gingerbread dough right away, wrap it in plastic and refrigerate. Refrigerated dough will keep for a week, but be sure to remove it 3 hours prior to rolling so it softens and is workable.

Decorating Step-by-Step

Basic Shapes

- Outline design
- Pipe in small areas. Fill in areas with stars, zigzags, etc.
- Add message
- Add top and bottom borders
- Ruffles and "overpiped" decorations
- Attach trims such as flowers, cookies, color flow and candy. Note: if a decoration doesn't seem secure enough, just add a few dots of icing
- Pipe leaves on flowers.
- Position Wilton cake tops or wedding ornaments.

Novelty Shapes

When decorating a cake that's basically covered with stars, here are the easy steps involved.

1. Ice sides and other areas per instructions smooth.

2. Outline details.

3. Pipe in facial features, small details, window, doors, etc.

4. Cover areas with stars, stripes, zigzags or hair.

5. Add message.

6. Edge top and base with borders Attach flowers or trims.

Decorating Guidelines

These easy-to-follow guidelines outline the basic steps in decorating. Our steps are very general because each cake you decorate has special needs. We hope these guidelines will inspire you to design original cakes on your own.

We suggest that flowers, candy, cookies or any special accent be made ahead of time, perhaps while your cake cools. To allow for breakage, make extras of any fragile addition. Heavy trims that protrude out of cake should be attached to a craft stick or coffee stirrer with royal icing. When using cookie trims, easel backs can be cut out of dough and attached with royal icing.
• Before icing or decorating, place each cake to be decorated on a cake circle or board cut to fit. Other than wedding cakes, if a small cake is to be set atop a larger cake, we usually recommend that you decorate both cakes first, then put them together. To transfer, let icing set (a slight crust will form and be more workable), then slip a wide spatula under cake and lift. Position cake and slowly pull spatula out (to prevent sticking, lightly dust spatula with cornstarch). If cake is large, support with free hand and redecorate areas that may get damaged.
• Marking design: Use a toothpick, pattern press or cookie cutter. Patterns for more intricate designs are included in the '97 Pattern Book (contains easy pattern transfer instructions). Often geometric shaped cakes are divided into 6ths, 8ths, 12ths, etc. You'll find dividing a round cake is quick 'n easy when you use our Cake Dividing Set (instructions included).

Decorating with Thinned Cookie Dough

Before baking, cookies can be decorated with thinned cookie dough. This easy method gives the appearance of colorful icing and is perfect for lasting centerpieces and novelty decorations. To thin dough, mix a small amount of tinted cookie dough with 1 tsp. water at a time until thin enough to pass through tip 2. Pipe desired decorations onto unbaked cookies. Bake according to recipe.

Roll-Out Cookies

1 cup butter
1 cup sugar
1 large egg
1 tsp. vanilla
2 tsps. baking powder
3 cups flour

Preheat oven to 400°F. In a large bowl, cream butter and sugar with an electric mixer. Beat in egg and vanilla. Mix baking powder and flour, add one cup at a time, mixing after each addition. The dough will be very stiff; blend last flour in by hand (if dough becomes too stiff, add water, a teaspoon at a time). Do not chill dough.

Note: Dough can be tinted with Icing Color. Add small amounts until desired color is reached. **For chocolate cookies:** Stir in 3 ounces melted, unsweetened chocolate. Divide dough into 2 balls. On a floured surface, roll each ball into a circle approximately 12 inches in diameter and ⅛ in. thick. Dip cutters in flour before each use. Bake cookies on an ungreased cookie sheet on top rack of oven for 6-7 minutes, or until cookies are lightly browned. Makes 20-24 average size cookies.

Large Batch Roll-Out Cookies

1 ¼ cups butter
2 cups sugar
2 eggs
5 cups flour
2 tsps. baking powder
1 tsp. salt
½ cup milk
1 tsp. almond or vanilla flavoring

Preheat oven to 375°F. Cream butter and sugar together, then add eggs and beat until fluffy. Sift dry ingredients together and add alternately to creamed mixture with milk. If mixture is too sticky, add a little more flour so that it is easy to handle. Roll dough ⅛ in. thick and cut. Dip cutters in flour before each use. Bake for 8 minutes, or until edges are lightly browned. Makes 36-42 average size cookies.

Making a Rose

The flower nail (p. 110) is used to make the most popular flower of all, the rose. Use flower nails No. 7 and 9 for small and average size blooms. Large flowers would use a 2 or 3-in. flower nail.

The key to making any flower on the nail is to coordinate the turning of the nail with the formulation of a petal. The stem of the nail is held between your left thumb and forefinger, so you can turn the flat nailhead surface at the same time you're piping a flower with your right hand.

Make roses on the nail with royal or stiffened buttercream icing (see p. 92), and the tips specified for each flower. Air dry flowers made in royal icing, and freeze buttercream flowers (buttercream roses can also be placed directly on iced cake) until firm at least 2 hours. (Snow White Buttercream Icing flowers can be air dried).

For each flower you make, attach a 2-in. square of waxed paper to the nailhead with a dot of icing. Make a flower; remove waxed paper and flower together.

Note: Left-handed decorators should use the nail opposite of above instructions.

Make The Rose Base
- Use tip 10 or 12. Hold the bag perpendicular at a 90⁰ angle to nail with tip slightly above center of nailhead. Squeeze with a heavy pressure, keeping bottom of tip in icing until you've made a full, round base.
- Ease pressure as you raise tip up and away from nailhead, narrowing base to a dome head. The base is very important for successful rose-making. Be sure that it is secure to nail and can support all the petals.

The Center Bud
- Use tip 104. Hold bag at a 45⁰ angle to nail with wide end of tip just below top of dome, and narrow end pointed in slightly. Back of bag should be pointed over your shoulder.
- Now you must do three things simultaneously...squeeze, pull tip up and out away from top of dome stretching icing into a ribbon band, as you turn the nail counterclockwise. Relax pressure as you bring band of icing down around dome, overlapping the point at which you started.

1st Row of 3 Petals
- Hold bag at 45⁰ angle with end of bag pointed over your shoulder. Touch wide end of tip 104 to midpoint of bud base. Turn nail counterclockwise and move tip up and back down to midpoint of bud base forming first petal of rose.
- Start slightly behind end of 1st petal and squeeze out 2nd petal same as first.
- Start slightly behind end of 2nd petal and add a 3rd petal, ending this petal overlapping starting point of 1st petal. Now you have a full rosebud made on a nail to use just as you would a rosebud made on a flat surface (at right).

2nd Row of 5 Petals
- Touch wide end of tip 104 slightly below center of a petal in 1st row, angle narrow end of tip out slightly more than you did for 1st row of petals. Squeeze and turn nail counterclockwise, moving tip up, then down to form 1st petal in second row.
- Start slightly behind this last petal and make a 2nd petal. Repeat this procedure for a total of 5 petals, ending last petal overlapping the 1st petal's starting point.

3rd Row of 7 Petals
- Touch wide end of tip 104 below center of petal in 2nd row, again angling narrow end of tip out a little more. Squeeze and turn nail counterclockwise and move tip up and down forming 1st petal. Repeat for a total of 7 petals.
- Slip waxed paper and completed rose off nail. Attach another square of waxed paper and start again. **HINT:** An easy way to place a buttercream icing rose directly on your cake is to slide open scissors under the base of rose and gently lift flower off waxed paper square and flower nail. Position flower on cake by slowly closing scissors and pushing base of flower with stem end of flower nail.

Flat Surface Flowers
Rosebuds, Half Roses & Sweet Peas
These pretty blossoms look great in royal or stiffened buttercream icing. Royal icing flowers must be made in advance and air dried; stiffened buttercream flowers may be frozen until firm at least 2 hours for later use or can be made directly on your cake.

A. Rosebud
- Make base petal. Hold bag at a 45⁰ angle so that the end of bag points over your right shoulder, finger tips gripping bag facing you. Touch wide end of tip 104 to surface, point narrow end to the right. Squeeze, move forward ¼ in.; hesitate so icing fans out, then move back as you stop pressure.
- Make overlapping center petal. Hold bag in same position as above with wide end of tip touching inside right edge of base petal, narrow end of tip pointing slightly up above base petal. Squeeze as icing catches inside edge of base petal and rolls into interlocking center bud. Stop pressure; touch large end back to surface and pull tip away.
- Make sepals and calyx directly on cake with tip 3 and thinned icing. Hold bag at a 45⁰ angle to base of bud with end of bag pointing towards you. Touch tip to bud. Squeeze and pull tip up and away from flower, relaxing pressure as you draw calyx to a point. Add three tip 3 sepals.

B. Half Rose
- Make a rosebud without sepals and calyx. To make right petal: Hold bag at a 45⁰ angle so the end of bag points to the left. Touch wide end of tip to bottom right side of bud base. Squeeze, move up, around to the left and down to center of bud base. Stop pressure, pull tip away.
- To make left petal: Hold bag at a 45⁰ angle so the end of bag points to the right, finger tips gripping the bag should face you. Touch wide end of tip 104 to bottom left side of bud. Squeeze, move it up, around to the right and down, relaxing pressure.
- Make sepals and calyxes with tip 3 and thinned icing. Follow same procedure as for step 3 of rosebud, starting at bottom center of half rose.

C. Sweet Pea
- Make center petal. Hold bag at a 45⁰ angle to surface so that back end of bag points towards you. Touch wide end of the tip to surface with narrow end of tip straight up. Squeeze, raise tip slightly and let icing roll into center petal. Stop pressure, lower tip, pull away.
- Make side petals. Touch wide end of tip to bottom left edge of center rolled petal, point narrow end up and out to the left. Squeeze, lift tip slightly, stop pressure, lower tip, pull away. Repeat procedure for right petal, starting at bottom edge of center petal.
- Add calyx to flower base with tip 3 and thinned icing. Hold bag at 45⁰ angle to surface so that end of bag points towards you. Insert tip into flower base and hold in place as you squeeze to build up pressure as you draw tip down, narrowing calyx to a point.

D. To Attach Flowers & Leaves To Wire Stems.
- **For Flowers:** On waxed paper square, using royal icing, pipe a dot base with tip 4. Make ⅛ in. hook on one end of 4 in. florist wire and insert hook into base. With slightly moistened decorator's brush, smooth and taper icing on the wire. Push other end of wire into a piece of styrofoam to dry base. Remove waxed paper and attach flower with dots of icing.
For Leaves: Pipe tip 3 royal icing dot on a waxed paper square and immediately push in hooked end of wire. Use tip 352 and royal icing to pipe a leaf directly on top of wire. Again, push into styrofoam to dry. Then remove waxed paper square. **Note:** Use only royal icing for attaching flowers to stems.

Two-Tone Roses

Create a dramatic effect by making the center petals of your rose contrast with the outer petals. You'll need to pipe the base, center bud and 1st row of petals with one color. Then in your contrasting shade, add remaining petals.

All About Tier Cakes

There are many methods of constructing tiered cakes. Here are some of the most popular:

To Prepare Cake For Assembly

Place base tier on a sturdy base plate or 3 or more thicknesses of corrugated cardboard. For heavy cakes, use masonite or plywood. Base can be covered with Fanci-Foil Wrap and trimmed with Tuk-N-Ruffle or use Wilton Ruffle Boards®. Each tier of your cake must be on a cake circle or board cut to fit. Smear a few strokes of icing on boards to secure cake. Fill and ice layers before assembly.

To Dowel Rod Cakes for Pillar & Stacked Construction

Center a cake circle or plate one size smaller than the next tier on base tier and press it gently into icing to imprint an outline. Remove circle. Measure one dowel rod at the cake's lowest point within this circle. Using this dowel rod for measure, cut dowel rods (to fit this tier) the same size using pruning shears. If the next tier is 10-in. or less, push seven 1/4 in. dowel rods into cake down to base within circle guide. Generally the larger and more numerous the upper tiers, the more dowels needed. Very large cakes need 1/2 in. dowels in base tier.

Stacked Construction

This method is often combined with pillar construction. Dowel rod bottom tier. Center a corrugated cake circle, same size as the tier to be added, on top of the base tier. Position the following tier. Repeat procedure for each additional tier. To keep stacked tiers stable, sharpen one end of a dowel rod and push through all tiers and cardboard circles to base of bottom tier. To decorate, start at top and work down.

Pillar Construction

Dowel rod tiers. Optional: Snap pegs into separator plates to prevent slipping (never substitute pegs for dowel rods). Position separator plates on supporting tiers, making sure that pillar projections on each tier will line up with pillars below. Mark center backs of cakes. Decorate cakes. At reception, align pillar projections and assemble cakes on pillars.

Fast & Easy Push-In Leg Construction

Dowel rods are not needed because legs attached to separator plates push right through the tiers down to the plate below.

Ice cakes on cake circles. To mark where legs will go, simply center separator plate for tier above (projections down) and gently press onto the tier. Lift plate off. Repeat this procedure for each tier (except top). Position upper tiers on separator plates. Decorate cakes.

To assemble: Insert legs into cake at marks. Push straight down until legs touch cake board. Add plate with cake to legs. Be sure plates are securely fastened to legs. Continue adding tiers in this way until cake is assembled.

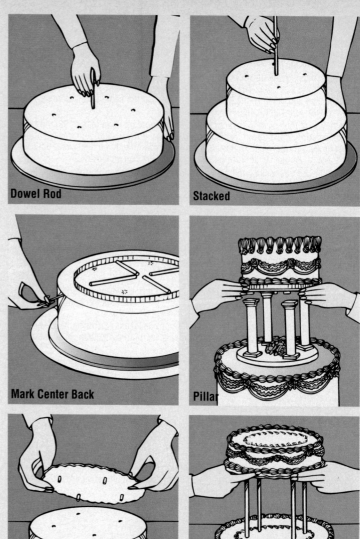

Dowel Rod

Stacked

Mark Center Back

Pillar

Mark Where Legs Go

Push-In Leg

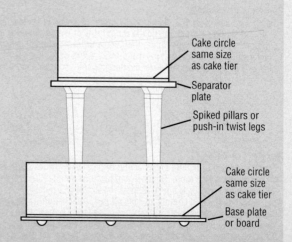

Pillar and Stacked Construction

Cake circle same size as cake tier

Separator plate

Pillars

Plastic pegs

Separator plate

Dowel rods cut to fit

Cake circle same size as cake tier

Sharpened dowel rod

Cake circle same size as cake tier

Base plate or board

Push-In Leg Construction

Cake circle same size as cake tier

Separator plate

Spiked pillars or push-in twist legs

Cake circle same size as cake tier

Base plate or board

Center Column Construction with the Tall Tier Stand

- Each cake involved in this type of construction should be placed on a cake circle or board (cut to fit) with a pre-cut center hole. To do this, trace pan shape on waxed paper. **Note:** To make positioning easier, place top tier on a board slightly larger than cake. Fold pattern into quarters to determine the exact center of each tier. Snip away the point to make a center hole (use cake corer as a guide to size). Trace hole pattern onto boards and cut out.

- Place all tiers on prepared cake boards, attaching with a few strokes of icing. Ice tiers smooth. Core out cake centers by pushing the cake corer down to the cake base. Pull out and press cake out of corer.

- Screw a column to prepared base plate, attaching with the bottom column bolt from underneath the plate. Slip bottom tier over the column to rest on plate.

- The bottom of the plates will not sit level, so to decorate, set plates on the Flower Holder Ring, a pan or bowl.

- Since the column cap nut attaches under the top tier, this cake must be positioned after assembling the Tall Tier Stand. Add base borders after assembling the top tier. Or you may place the top tier on a foil-covered cake circle so decorating can be done ahead.

- To assemble at reception, position plate onto base column section and screw column tight. Continue adding tiers with columns. At top plate, secure columns with cap nut bolt. Position top tier and decorate.

Wedding Cake Data

One cake mix yields 4 to 6 cups of batter. Pans are usually filled ½ to ⅔ full; 3 in. deep pans should be filled only ½ full. Batter amounts on this chart are for pans two-thirds full of batter. Icing amounts are very general and will vary with consistency, thickness applied and tips used. These amounts allow for top and base borders and a side ruffled border. For large cakes, always check for doneness after they have baked for one hour.

Number of servings are intended as a guide only.

Pan Shape	Size	# Servings 2 Layer	Cups Batter/ 1 Layer 2"	Baking Temps.	Baking Time Minutes	Approx. Cups Icing to Frost and Decorate 2 Layer Cake
Oval	7¾ x 5¾"	13	2½	350°	25-30	3
	10¾ x 7⅞"	30	5½	350°	25-30	4
	13 x 9¾"	44	8	350°	25-30	5½
	16 x 12¾"	70	11	325°	25-30	7½
Round	6"	14	2	350°	25-30	3
	8"	25	3	350°	30-35	4
	9"	32	5⅓	350°	30-35	4½
	10"	39	11	350°	35-40	5
	12"	56	7½	350°	35-40	6
	14"	77	10	325°	50-55	7¼
	16"	100	15	325°	55-60	8¾
Round 3" Deep (# Servings for 1 layer)	8"	15	5	325°	60-65	7¼
	10"	24	8	325°	75-80	4¾
	12"	33	11	325°	75-80	5¾
	14"	45	15	325°	75-80	7
Half Round	18"					
2" layer		127†	9*	325°	60-65	10½
3" layer		92††	12*	325°	60-65	10½
Petal	6"	8	1½	350°	25-30	3½
	9"	20	3½	350°	35-40	6
	12"	38	7	350°	35-40	7¾
	15"	62	12	325°	50-55	11
Hexagon	6"	12	1¾	350°	30-35	2¾
	9"	22	3½	350°	35-40	4¾
	12"	50	6	350°	40-45	5¾
	15"	72	11	325°	40-45	8¾
Heart	6"	11	1½	350°	25	2½
	9"	24	3½	350°	30	4½
	12"	48	8	350°	30	5¾
	15"	76	11½	325°	40	8¾
Square	6"	18	2	350°	25-30	3½
	8"	32	4	350°	35-40	4½
	10"	50	6	350°	35-40	6
	12"	72	10	350°	40-45	7½
	14"	98	13½	350°	45-50	9½
	16"	128	15½	350°	45-50	11
	18"	162	18	350°	50-55	13

*Batter for each half round pan.   †Four half rounds.   ††Two half rounds.

Hints for Assembling & Transporting Tiered Cakes

- Before placing separator plate or cake circle atop another tier, sprinkle a little confectioners' sugar or coconut flakes to prevent plate or circle from sticking. Letting icing crust a bit before positioning plate on cake will also prevent sticking.

- You will have less crumbs when icing if cakes are baked a day in advance.

- When filling or torting large layers, use less than you usually would. Your dam of icing should also be far enough from edge so filling doesn't form a bubble.

- The cake icer tip (789) is an invaluable timesaver in icing wedding tiers.

- When transporting tiers, place cakes on damp towels or carpet foam and drive carefully.

- To keep balance, cut cakes on the Tall Tier Stand from top tier down.

- To divide tiers, use the Cake Dividing Set (p. 113). The Wheel Chart makes it easy to mark 2 in. intervals on 6 to 18 in. diameter cakes. The triangle marker gives precise spacing for stringwork and garlands. The raised lines on separator plates can also be followed for each dividing.

- When using Spiked Pillars and stacked construction, double cake boards or use separator plates between layers to prevent the weight of tiers from causing the pillars to pierce through cake.

Wedding Cake Cutting Guide

The first step in cutting is to remove the top tier, and then begin the cutting with the 2nd tier followed by 3rd, 4th and so on. The top tier is usually saved for the first anniversary so it is not figured into the serving amount.

Cutting guides for shapes not shown can be found in other Wilton publications. The diagrams below show how to cut popular shaped wedding tiers into pieces approximately 1 in. x 2 in. by two layers high (about 4 in.). Even if you prefer a larger serving size, the order of cutting is still the same.

To cut oval tiers, move in 2 in. from the outer edge and cut across. Then slice 1 in. pieces of cake. Now move in another 2 in. and slice again until the entire tier is cut.

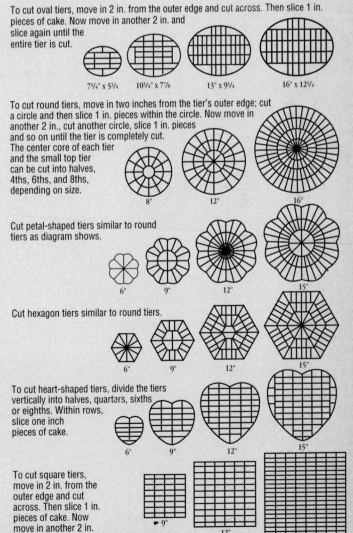

To cut round tiers, move in two inches from the tier's outer edge; cut a circle and then slice 1 in. pieces within the circle. Now move in another 2 in., cut another circle, slice 1 in. pieces and so on until the tier is completely cut. The center core of each tier and the small top tier can be cut into halves, 4ths, 6ths, and 8ths, depending on size.

Cut petal-shaped tiers similar to round tiers as diagram shows.

Cut hexagon tiers similar to round tiers.

To cut heart-shaped tiers, divide the tiers vertically into halves, quarters, sixths or eighths. Within rows, slice one inch pieces of cake.

To cut square tiers, move in 2 in. from the outer edge and cut across. Then slice 1 in. pieces of cake. Now move in another 2 in. and slice again until the entire tier is cut.

The Techniques

The size and shape of the opening on a decorative tip identifies the basic group to which the tip belongs and determines the type of decorations the tip will produce.

Plain or Round Tips

Use to outline details, filling and piping in areas, printing and writing messages, figure piping, stringwork, beads, dots, balls, stems, vines, flower centers, lattice, cornelli lace. These tips are smooth and round — small plain tips include numbers 1, 2, 3, 4; medium 5, 6, 7, 8, 9, 10, 11, 12; large 1A, 2A. For fine stringwork, use 1S, 1L, 2L, 0L, 00L, 000. For Philippine method flower making, oval tips 55 and 57. Writing tip 301 pipes fine, flat lines.

Printing and Writing

Use a small round tip and thin icing consistency. **Hint:** With a toothpick or Message Pattern Presses draw guidelines to follow. With practice, you'll achieve control and soon be piping out messages free-handed. (Some special writing techniques are shown on p. 105)

To Print: Hold bag at 45° angle with tip resting lightly on surface with back of the bag to the right for horizontal lines, toward you for vertical. With a steady, even pressure, squeeze out a straight line, lifting tip off surface to let icing string drop. Be sure to stop squeezing before you lift the tip to end the line so a tail doesn't form.

To Write: You must move your whole arm to write effectively with icing. Hold bag at a 45° angle with back of bag to the right. The tip should lightly touch the cake as you write.

Outlining

Use thin icing consistency and bag at a 45° angle and touch tip (usually 3 or 4) to surface. Now raise the tip slightly and continue to squeeze. The icing will flow out of the tip while you direct it along the surface. To end an outline, stop squeezing, touch tip to surface and pull away.

To Pipe In: After area is outlined, squeeze out tip 3 or 4 zigzag motion strings to fill area. Immediately smooth over strings with finger tip or spatula dipped in cornstarch.

To Fill In: Follow same procedure as Pipe In, but thin icing before piping.

Dots

Use medium icing consistency. Hold bag at a 90° angle with tip slightly above surface. Squeeze and keep point of the tip in icing until dot is the size you want. Stop pressure, pull away; use tip to clean point away or smooth with finger dipped in cornstarch. To make large dots or balls, lift tip as you squeeze to allow greater icing build-up.

Beads

Use medium consistency. Hold bag at 45° angle with tip slightly above surface and end of bag pointing to the right. Squeeze and lift tip slightly so icing fans out into base. Relax pressure as you draw tip down and bring bead to point. Ideal for borders or pipe in side-by-side rows to cover large areas.

For Hearts: Pipe two beads side by side and smooth together with finger dipped in cornstarch.

Triple Bead Border

Pipe tip 11 band around base of cake. Using tip 9, pipe bead border above and below band; add a third border of beads on top of band.

Cornelli Lace

With thin icing, use a 90° angle with tip slightly above surface. Pipe a continuous string of icing, curve it up, down and around until area is covered. Stop pressure; pull tip away. Make sure strings never touch or cross.

Drop Strings

Use stiff consistency icing that has been thinned with corn syrup. Icing is the right consistency if you can drop a loop of icing from your finger. With toothpick, mark horizontal intervals in desired widths. Hold bag at 45° angle to surface so that end of bag points slightly to the right. Touch tip to first mark and squeeze, holding bag in place momentarily so that icing sticks to surface. Then pull tip straight out away from surface, allowing icing to drop into an arc. Stop pressure as you touch tip to second mark to end string. Repeat procedure, attaching string to third mark and so on, forming row of drop strings. It's very important to let the string, not your hand, drop to form an arc. Try to keep your drop strings uniform in length and width.

For Double Drop Strings: Start at first mark again, squeeze bag. Let icing drop into a slightly shorter arc than arc in first row. Join end of string to end of corresponding string in first row and repeat procedure.

Always pipe longest drop strings first and add shorter ones. This technique is ideal for cake sides. Practice is important in making drop strings uniform.

Dropped Lattice Garlands: With stiff consistency icing, connect garland marks with drop string guidelines. Cover strings with three rows of tip 16 zigzags (overpipe rows). Ease pressure at ends so icing doesn't build up too high. Drop a string guideline directly on top of zigzags. From cake to edge of string, pipe tip 3 diagonal lines across area. From the opposite side, work strings in the other direction. Cover edges of lattice with tip 3 strings. Follow same technique to cover any area with lattice; use tip directed.

Star Tips

The star-shaped openings create the most popular decorations...stars, zigzags, shells, rosettes and more. The most often used star tips are numbers 13 through 22. Star tips range in size from small to extra large. For deep ribbed decorations, try tips 23-31, 133 and 195. Large star tips include numbers 32, 96, 4B, 6B and 8B. Fine cut star tips are numbers 362, 363, 364, 172, and 199. For these techniques use medium icing consistency.

Stars

Hold bag at 90° angle with tip slightly above surface. Squeeze bag to form a star, then stop pressure and pull tip away. Increase or decrease pressure to change star size. An entire cake or just one area can be covered with stars made very close together so that no cake shows between stars. Use the triple-star or use large star tips to save time.

For Pull-Out Stars: Hold bag at 45° angle to surface. As you squeeze out icing, pull tip up and away from cake. When strand is long enough, stop pressure and pull tip away. Work from bottom to top of area to be covered with pull-out stars.

For Star Puffs: Use a large tip and hold tip in place to allow icing to build up.

For Star Flowers: Squeeze and keep tip in icing until star petals are formed. Stop pressure and pull tip away. Add tip 2 or 3 dot centers.

Ropes

Hold bag at 45° angle to surface with end of bag pointing over right shoulder. Touch tip to surface; squeezing bag, move tip down, up and around to the right forming a slight "s" curve. Stop pressure, pull tip away. Tuck tip under bottom arch of first "s" and repeat procedure. Continue joining "s" curves to form rope.

Zigzags

Hold bag at 45° angle to surface, so that end of bag points out to the right and fingers on the bag are facing you. Allow the tip to touch the surface lightly. Steadily squeeze and move hand in a tight side-to-side motion. To end, stop pressure and pull tip away.

Elongated Zigzags: Follow procedure but keep an even pressure as you move hand in the desired length. Very large areas can be covered in this manner.

Relaxed Zigzags: Simply relax pressure as you move bag along.

Zigzag Garlands

Hold bag as for basic zigzag procedure. Allow tip to touch the surface lightly and use light-to-heavy-to-light pressure to form curves of garland. To end, stop pressure, pull tip away. Practice for rhythmic pressure control so garlands are uniform.

The Techniques (cont.)

Zigzag Puffs
Hold bag at 45⁰ angle to surface, fingertips on bag facing you. Touch tip to surface and use a light-to-heavy-to-light pressure and zigzag motion to form puff. Repeat procedure again and again as you move tip in a straight line to form row of puffs. To end row, stop pressure, pull tip away.

C & E - Motion (only "E" motion shown)
Hold bag at 45⁰ angle to surface, finger tips on bag facing you. As you squeeze out icing, move tip down, up to the right and around as if writing the letter "c" or "e". Use a steady, even pressure as you repeat procedure. To end, stop pressure, pull tip away.

Swirl Waves
Using tip 18, pipe c-motion and reverse c-motion waves. Randomly overpipe some using tip 4.

Shells
Hold bag at 45⁰ angle with tip slightly above surface and end of bag pointing to the right. Squeeze with heavy pressure and slightly lift tip as icing builds and fans out into a full base. Relax pressure as you pull bag down to the right as you make the tail. Stop pressure completely, pull tip away. When you make the shells, always work to the right; starting each new shell slightly behind tail of previous shell.

For Elongated Shells: Extend tail while relaxing pressure, until desired length is achieved.

For Upright Shells: Hold bag at 90⁰ angle to cake sides. Follow same procedure as elongated shells.

Note: Once you've mastered the motion of shell making, you can create unique borders with other tip groups such as leaf and ruffle.

Reverse Shells
Hold bag at 45⁰ angle with tip slightly above surface. Squeeze to let icing fan out as if you were making a typical shell, then swing tip around to the left in a semi-circular motion as you relax pressure to form tail of a shell. Stop pressure, pull tip away. Repeat procedure, only this time, swing tip around to the right as you form tail of shell. Continue procedure, alternating directions for a series of reverse shells.

Fleur-De-Lis
Make a shell. Keep bag at 45⁰ angle and starting at the left of shell, squeeze bag to fan icing into shell base. Then as you relax pressure to form tail, move tip up slightly around to the right, relaxing pressure, forming tail similar to reverse shells. Join to tail of the first shell. Repeat procedure to right side of first shell. Variation: Substitute beads for shells.

Scrolls
Hold bag at 45⁰ angle to surface so that end of bag points to the right. Use tip 3 to draw an inverted "C" center and use circular motion to cover inverted "C." You may overpipe (go over lines) with tip 13 or any small star tip. Use a heavy pressure to feather the scroll, relaxing pressure as you taper end. Add side petals like reverse shells.

Reverse Scrolls
With tip 3 squeeze out an inverted "C" scroll. Then, starting at the top of this "C," squeeze and move tip down, up and around for a backward "C." Cover outlines with tip 13. Add reverse shell side petals.
Hint: Use our Scroll Pattern Presses to imprint an easy-to-follow guide on cake top or sides.

Embellished Fleur-de-lis Imprint (p. 25)
Imprint upside down Fleur-de-lis pattern press from Decorator Favorites Pattern Press Set. Use Small C-Scroll pattern press to overprint additional curls onto fleur-de-lis as follows: Match lines and overprint c-scroll on bottom of in fleur-de-lis; match lines at top of fleur-de-lis and overprint c-scroll on left and right side of center line; move c-scroll down approximately 1 in., match lines and overprint c-scroll on left and right side of center line. Outline imprints using tip 16, beginning with small c-scrolls and lastly piping the large scrolled lines in the center.

Rosettes
Hold bag at 90⁰ angle with tip slightly above surface. Squeeze and move hand to the left, up and around in a circular motion to starting point. Stop pressure and pull tip away. For a fancy effect, trim center with a star.

Spirals
Follow rosettes technique. Starting at outer edge, move tip in a clockwise direction in a continuous circular motion, decreasing size of circles until center is reached. Stop pressure and pull tip away.

Drop Flower Tips
These are the easiest flowers for a beginning decorator to do. The number of openings on the end of the tip determines the number of petals the flower will have. Each drop flower tip can produce two different flower varieties-plain or swirled. Swirled drop flowers cannot be made directly on cake. Some form center holes. Small tips include numbers 107, 108, 129, 224, 225; medium tips are 109, 131, 135, 140, 190, 191, 193, 194, 195; for large flowers, tips 1B, 1C, 1E, 1G, 2C, 2D, 2E and 2F.

Drop Flowers
Icing consistency should be slightly stiffer. Hold bag at a 90⁰ angle with tip touching surface and pipe as you would a star.

For swirled flowers: Turn wrist around to the left as you squeeze out icing, bring wrist back to the right. Stop pressure, pull tip away. Add tip 2 or 3 dot centers.

Leaf Tips
The v-shaped openings of these tips give leaves pointed ends. With any leaf tip you can make plain, ruffled or stand-up leaves. Make leaves with center veins from small 65s, 65-70, to large, 112-115. Other popular numbers are 73, 75, 326, 349, 352.

Basic Leaf
Use thin icing consistency and hold bag at a 45⁰ angle to surface, back of bag facing you. Squeeze and hold tip in place to let icing fan out into base, then relax and stop pressure as you pull tip towards you and draw leaf to a point.

Stand Up Leaf
Hold bag at a 90⁰ angle. Touch tip lightly to surface and squeeze, holding tip in place as icing fans out to form base. Relax and stop pressure as you pull tip straight up and away, creating stand-up leaf effect.

Ruffled Leaf
Use tip 104 and Flower Nail No. 7. Hold bag at 45⁰ angle to nail center, with wide end lightly touching surface and narrow end lifted slightly. Begin squeezing and move tip out towards edge of nail, moving hand in a back and forth motion to create ruffles. Gradually move hand upwards as you turn nail. After curve is formed, move hand back down to starting position. Let dry on Flower Formers.

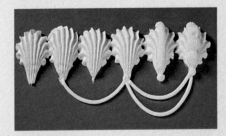

Crown Border
Use tip 32 and pipe a row of side-by-side shells over the top edge of cake. Start each shell just at the edge of the tier, apply pressure to let the shell build up and curve over the edge of the tier, then relax pressure and move down. Pipe tip 4 dots on shell ends.

Crown Border with Stringwork
Pipe Crown Border as described above, eliminating tip 4 dots on shell ends. Use tip 3 to pipe double drop strings on shell ends. Pipe tip 16 stars at shell points.

Victorian Lace Drop Stringwork (p. 52)

8 in. Tier: Pipe triple drop strings between alternating scrolls, add dots. Pipe double drop strings at middle point of alternating scrolls. Pipe double drop strings at outside points of scrolls, add dots. **12 in. Tier:** Dropstrings are attached onto only the lower group of scrolls. Pipe triple drop strings between scrolls at lowest point. Add double drop strings between alternating scrolls at middle point; add triple drop strings on same alternating scrolls at highest point. Add dots.

Petal Tips

These tips have an opening that is wide at one end, narrow at the other. This teardrop-like shaped opening yields a variety of petals that form flowers like the rose, carnation, daisy, pansy and more (see pages 95; 100-101). Petal tips can also make ribbons, drapes and swags; bows and streamers. Plain rose tips include numbers 101s, 101, 102, 103, 104, 124, 125, 126, 127 and giant roses, tip 127D. Swirled rose tips that make instant-curled petals are 97 and 116. Others include 59s, 59, 60, 61, 121, 123, 62, 64 and 150.

Ruffle

Use medium icing consistency. Hold bag at 45° angle to surface, finger tips on bag facing you. Touch wide end of tip to surface, angle narrow end out about 1/4 in. away from surface. As you squeeze, move hand up and down slightly to ruffle the icing. **For Stand-Up Ruffle** just turn tip so wide end is pointing up and away from the surface.

Swag/Drape

Use same procedure as for ruffle. As you squeeze, swing tip down and up to the right forming ribbon drape.

Bows

Creating bows with a petal tip is different from a round or star tip because of the shape of tip but otherwise the technique is the same. With tip 103 or 104 and medium icing consistency, hold bag at a 45° angle to surface. The wide end of the tip should touch the surface and the narrow end should point straight up. While squeezing, move the tip up and around to the starting point and continue around, making a second loop on the left. The two loops should form a figure 8. Still holding bag in the same position, return to the center and squeeze out two streamers. Bows can also be piped with round tips, star tips and basketweave tips.

Ribbon Stripe Bow

To make a bow with a basketweave tip, hold bag at a 45° angle with the ribbed side of tip up. Start in center and move bag up and to the right. As you bring bag down to form loop, turn tip so that the ribbed side is now down. Repeat procedure for left loop. Pipe streamers with smooth or ribbed side up.

Flutes

A pretty effect to add between rows of shells. Hold tip 104 (petal tip) at 45° angle so that wide end of tip is between two shells. Squeeze and move tip up slightly as icing fills in between shell. Stop pressure, lower tip, pull away.

Stripe/Basketweave Tips

These are decorating tips with a smooth side for making smooth, wide icing stripes and/or one serrated side for making ribbed, wide icing stripes. When short ribbed horizontal stripes are interwoven in vertical rows the effect is that of a basketweave. Tips are 46 and 47. For smooth stripes, 44 and 45. For ribbed stripes, 48. Large ribbon tips include 1D, 2B and 789 (Cake Icer).

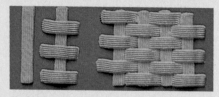

Basketweave

Use star or basketweave tips and medium consistency icing. For an interesting effect, use a round tip to make vertical lines.

- Hold bag at 45° angle to cake with serrated side of tip facing up (or use round tip). Touch tip lightly to surface and squeeze out a vertical line of icing.
- Next, hold bag at 45° angle to surface, finger tips gripping bag facing you. Touch tip, serrated side facing up, to top left side of vertical line and squeeze out a horizontal bar. Add two more horizontal bars, each about a tip width apart, to cover vertical line.
- With bag and tip at 45° angle, make another vertical line of icing to right of first one, overlapping ends of horizontal bars. Use same procedure as step two to cover this line with horizontal bars, piping them in spaces of bars in first row.
- Repeat entire procedure, alternating vertical lines and horizontal bars, to create a basketweave effect. Other tips may be used for basketweave, but serrated tips 46-48 give icing a ribbed basket effect.

Stripes

This versatile technique can be made with star and ribbon tips. They can be piped straight, curved or side-by-side to fill in an area. Hold decorating bag at 45° angle to surface. As you squeeze out icing with steady, even pressure, move tip in vertical direction laying out a ribbed stripe of icing. Stop pressure and pull tip up and away. When covering an area, stripes can be slightly overlapped for added dimension.

Flower Nail Flowers

For best results, use royal icing to pipe these impressive blooms. To curve petals, dry on convex or concave flower formers. Instructions will indicate the number of flowers needed, so make extras to allow for breakage.

Pansy

Use tip 103 or 104 and Flower Nail No. 7. Hold bag at 45° angle to nail center. Pipe two back petals, squeezing and moving tip out to edge of nail. Turn nail while squeezing, relax pressure as returning to nail center. Repeat to form second back petal. Use the same sequence to add two shorter petals atop the first two.

Squeeze out a base petal that equals the width of the back petals, using a back and forth hand motion for a ruffled effect.

Use a fine artist's brush to paint thinned icing color veins, edging and highlights to flower after it has dried. Add tip 2 string loop center. See p. 93 for brush striping techniques to pipe multi-colored pansies.

Daisy

- Use royal icing and tip 103 or 104. Dot center of flower nail with icing as guide for flower center. Hold bag at a 45° angle with tip almost parallel to nail surface, wide end of tip pointing to nail center, narrow end pointing out. Now, starting at any point near outer edge of nail, squeeze and move tip towards center icing dot. Stop pressure, pull tip away. Repeat procedure for a total of twelve or more petals.
- Add tip 4 flower center and press to flatten. For pollen-like effect, dampen your finger, press in edible glitter, then flatten center.
- For Brown-Eyed Susans: Make yellow petals, brown centers, and use granulated brown sugar for pollen at centers.

Apple Blossom

- Use tip 101 and hold bag at a 45° angle to flower nail with wide end of tip touching nail center, narrow end pointed out 1/8 in. away from nail surface.
- Squeeze bag and turn nail as you move tip 1/8 in. out from nail center and back, relaxing pressure as you return to starting point.
- Repeat procedure to make four more petals. Add five tip 1 dots for center.

Forget-Me Not

Very similar to the apple blossom. Use tip 101S and move tip out just 3/8 in. from center, curve around and return, letting the turn of the nail form petals. Dot center with tip 1. Use large flower nail No. 7 and pipe several at once!

Violet

Use tip 59s and same procedure as for apple blossom to make three 3/4 in. long petals and two 1/4 in. base petals. Add two tip 1 center dots.

Daffodil And Jonquil

Use tip 104 for daffodil or tip 103 for jonquil. Hold bag at a 45° angle to flower nail, with large end of tip touching nail, narrow end pointed out and almost parallel to nail surface. Squeeze and as you turn nail, move tip out about 1/2 in. and back to center of nail to form petal. Repeat procedure for five more petals. Dip fingers in cornstarch and pinch ends of petals to form points. For center coil pipe row-upon-row of tip 2 string circles and top with tip 1 zigzag for center.

Narcissus

Use tip 102 and same procedure as for daffodil to make six 3/4 in. long petals. Add tip 1 coil center and tip 1 zigzag.

Wild Rose

Use tip 103 and hold bag at a 45° angle. Touch nail with wide end of tip with narrow end just slightly above nail surface. Begin at center of nail and press out first petal, turning nail as you move tip out toward edge of nail, and return to center of nail as you stop squeezing. Repeat 4 more times. Pull out tiny stamens with tip 1.

Holly Leaf

With tip 68, follow basic leaf method and use medium consistency royal icing to pipe desired size leaf. While icing is wet, pull out tiny points around edge with a dampened Decorator's Brush. Let dry on flower formers for a curved look. Do not make directly on cake.

Color Flow Icing Recipe

(Full-Strength for Outlining)
1/4 cup water + 1 teaspoon
1 lb. sifted confectioners' sugar (4 cups)
2 Tablespoons Wilton Color Flow Icing Mix

In an electric mixer, using grease-free utensils, blend all ingredients on low speed for 5 minutes. If using hand mixer, use high speed. Color Flow icing "crusts" quickly, so keep it covered with a damp cloth while using. Stir in desired icing color. In order to fill an outlined area, this recipe must be thinned with 1/2 teaspoon of water per 1/4 cup of icing (just a few drops at a time as you near proper consistency). Color Flow is ready for filling in outlines when a small amount dropped into the mixture takes a full count of ten to disapppear. Use grease-free spoon or spatula to stir slowly.

Note: Color Flow designs take a long time to dry, so plan to do your Color Flow piece at least 2-3 days in advance.

Lily Nail Flowers

The Wilton Lily Nail Set lets you make natural-looking flowers with bell-like shapes and cupped, turned-up petals. Different lily nail sizes relate to the size of flowers you can make. The larger the nail, the larger the flowers. Always use royal icing for flowers made on the lily nail since softer icing will not hold their deeply-cupped shapes. Lightly spray aluminum foil square with vegetable oil spray. To make any flower on the lily nail, place an aluminum foil square in bottom half of nail. Press in top half to form a foil cup. Remove the top half. This makes it easier to remove from foil after icing has dried and reduces breakage. Pipe a flower on the foil cup and lift out flower and foil to dry.

Morning Glory

Line a 1 5/8 in. lily nail with foil; use royal icing. Using tip 104 and white icing, keep wide end of tip down and form a shallow cup within nail. With violet icing and tip 103, pipe a ruffled cup slightly above first, increasing pressure in five places to form points. Smooth colors together with damp decorator brush. With tip 1 and thinned white icing, pipe five lines from base of flower to edge; pipe tip 2 center dot.

Easter Lily

Line a 1 5/8 in. lily nail with foil; use royal icing. Use tip 67 and lily nail. Touch center well of nail with tip and squeeze, pulling petal up and over edge of foil cup. Decrease pressure as you reach tip of petal and hesitate before you stop pressure and pull tip away, drawing petal to a point. Pipe 2 more petals, then pipe 3 more petals in between the open spaces. Add tip 14 star center and push in artificial stamens.

Color Flow
Color Flow Technique

- Tape pattern and waxed paper overlay to your work surface. (The back of a cookie pan makes a great work surface.) For curved decorations, use flower formers. Use full-strength Color Flow icing and tip 2 or 3 to outline the pattern with desired colors. If you're going to use the same color icing to fill in the outlines, let the icing outlines dry a few minutes until they "crust." If you're going to fill in with icing that differs in color from the outlines, then let outlines dry thoroughly (1-2 hours) before filling in.

- Thin icing for filling in pattern outlines as specified in recipe. Don't use a tip for filling in outlines; instead, cut a very small opening in end of parchment bag. Begin filling in along the edges of the outline first, squeezing gently and letting the icing flow up to the outline almost by itself. Work quickly; filling in design from the outside edges in and from top to bottom. If you have several outlined sections, fill in one at a time. If you're filling in a large area, have two half-full parchment bags ready, otherwise icing could "crust" before you finish filling in the patttern.

Hint: For curved decorations, use flower formers. Since buttercream icing will break down color flow, either position color flow decoration on cake shortly before serving or place a piece of plastic wrap cut to fit on area first and set atop sugar cubes.

To easily remove dried Color Flow, pull waxed paper backing over the edge of a table with one hand, while holding decoration with other hand. Waxed paper will pull off naturally. Or, with dried Color Flow resting on cookie sheet, place cardboard sheet over Color Flow, lift and turn over so that top of decoration rests on cardboard. Lift off waxed paper.

Figure Piping

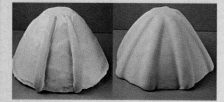

Fairy Dress (p. 8)

Roll eight 7 in. long x ¾ in. diameter logs of fondant; position vertically and space evenly around side of cake to create skirt pleats. Taper at top and smooth evenly. Cover with rolled fondant.

Magical Carousel Hearts (p. 11)

Tape Heart Pattern to the convex side of largest flower former. Tape waxed paper over pattern. Using royal icing and tip 16, pipe zigzag heart. Let dry at least 1-2 days. Position drop flowers on heart with dots of icing. Add tip 352 leaves. Let dry completely.

Fire Truck Clowns (p. 18)

With tip 4B and medium pressure, pipe body. Add tip 32 legs. Pipe tip 4B back arm, then overpipe top arm. Pipe-in tip 8 hands and feet. Pipe tip 5 hose between hands, then start hose again under arm and down. Pipe tip 8 mound on head for hat. Add tip 102 edge around hat. Pipe-in tip 2 white front area of hat and tip 2 number. Position in body.

Merry Clown Go-Round (p. 21)

For handles: Roll out red fondant into a log ½ in. in circumference. Cut eight 1½ in. lengths from log and let set.

For Clown Go-Round: Cut pattern from two 12 in. cake circles (reverse grain for added strength). Test to insure that Clown Go-Round will turn freely in column, trimming center hole if necessary. Cover with foil and position on column. Place column with Clown Go-Round in styrofoam block for support.

For Clowns: Using royal icing and tip 6B, hold bag at 90° angle and pipe swirl motion body trunk for all four clowns. Let dry. Attach fondant "handles" with tip 6 dots of royal icing. Let dry. Pipe tip 21 arms and tip 9 hands directly on handle. (Smooth hands with finger dipped in cornstarch.) Position jelly bean feet. When cake is decorated, transfer merry-go-round and column to cake center and screw in place with bottom column bolt. (Make sure feet do not touch cake.) Attach center gumball knob with royal icing.

Spotlight Guy (p. 28)

Use buttercream and pipe directly on cake. Use tip 14 to pipe black shadow; tip 12 to pipe head. Pipe in tip 12 shirt and arms. Pipe tip 9 leg using medium pressure. (Smooth with finger dipped in cornstarch.) Add tip 4 dot eyes; tip 2 pupils and mouth. Add tip 3 ears. Pipe tip 233 pull-out hair. Add tip 9 shoes; tip 3 hands and fingers.

Sailor (p. 36)

Pipe tip 9 ball head, smooth with finger dipped in cornstarch. Using tip 5, pipe shirt, tuck tip into sides and pipe sleeves; using tip 2, pipe ball hands, tuck in tip and add pull-out fingers. Add tip 2 dot and string facial features and hair.

Half Filigree Heart (p. 41)

Cover Half Filigree Heart pattern with waxed paper and tape down. Using tip 2 and melted Candy Melts brand confectionery coating, outline and pipe cornelli-style filigree. Let set and carefully peel off waxed paper. Make extras to allow for breakage.

Parachute Babies (p.44)

Pipe tip 7 bead for body. Tuck tip 5 into sides and pipe pull-out arms and legs. Using tip 3, pipe diaper (smooth with finger dipped in cornstarch) and string bow. Using tip 1, add pull-out hair and fingers, dot and string facial features.

Teddy Bear (p. 47)

Tint Ready-To-Use Rolled Fondant and assemble using drops of water. Roll large ball of fondant for body, medium ball for head and four small balls for paws. Flatten a round piece of fondant for muzzle, flatten and shape two pieces for ears. Using royal icing add tip 1 string and dot facial features. Imprint stitch marks using end of toothpick.

Chicks in Basket (p. 71)

Use medium consistency buttercream icing and pipe directly on cake. Hold bag at a 90° angle and with tip 12 pipe ball for head and tip 5 for cheeks. Add tip 352 pull-out beak and hair. Add tip 352 pull-out feather on wings. Pipe tip 1 dot eyes and inside mouth.

Snow Kids (p. 82)

Using tip 10, pipe a line of icing for body, tuck tip into sides and pull-out arms and legs. Add tip 11 ball of icing for head, flatten with finger dipped in cornstarch. Using tip 1, add dot eyes and dot and string hair. Pipe tip 2 outline and pipe-in mouths and tongue, tip 5 earmuffs and hats, add tip 13 star snowflake on tongue. Pipe tip 3 dot buttons, tip 4 string belt, tip 5 boots and mittens, tip 46 smooth side scarves.

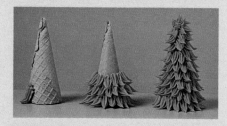

Trees (p. 82)

Trim ice cream cones to varying lengths. Beginning at the bottom, pipe tip 18 pull-out stars around base, turning cone as you decorate. Repeat, overlapping each successive row until cone is covered. Pipe an upright pull-out star at tree top. Let dry.

Custom Ornaments (p. 84)

Angel: Pipe tip 3 ball head; using tip 6, pipe elongated body, tuck tip into side and add arms. Pipe tip 13 pull-out star wings. Add tip 3 feet. Using tip 1, add dot facial features. pull-out string hair and pipe decorating bag (smooth and shape with finger dipped in cornstarch).

Bear: Using tip 8, pipe elongated shape for body; add ball head, dot ears and muzzle; tuck tip into sides and add pull-out legs. Add tip 1 dot eyes, nose and string mouth. Add tip 4 decorating bag (shape and smooth with finger dipped in cornstarch). Add tip 1 pull-out dot fingers.

Stadium Cake (p. 33)

To construct stadium: Tape two 13 x 19 in. cake boards together and cover with foil wrap. Cut 4 lengths of heavy-duty aluminum foil, each measuring 24 inches long. Fold pieces lengthwise in quarters to measure 24 in. x 4 ½ in. Fold each piece up 1 in. from bottom to form a lip. Tape this lip edge to bottom of cake board. Pleat corners to conform to shape of stadium. Overlap pieces for added strength and tape all pieces together.

To construct bleachers: Using Fanci-Foil Wrap, cut 6 pieces 13 in. x 10 in. and 4 pieces 13 in. x 7 in. Fold all pieces lengthwise in half and pleat at ¼ in. intervals. Tape bottom of each pleated piece to edge of 13 x 19 in. boards and pull up and over top edge of stadium. Cut the 13 in. x 7 in. pieces on angles to cover corners, pleat at ¼ in. intervals and tape to boards.

Double Petal Flowers (p. 49)

Using rolled fondant and gum paste cutters, cut 30 pansy and 30 apple blossoms. Cup apple blossom around round end of stick and attach to pansy blossom using decorator brush and water. Add tip 3 dot centers with buttercream icing. Make extras to allow for breakage and let dry.

Fondant Loops (p. 54)

Roll fondant to about ⅛ in. thick. Cut loops ½ in. wide and 4 to 6 in. long. Form into loops by brushing a small amount of water on one end of fondant strip and pressing it together with the other end of strip. Lay loops on side on waxed paper to dry 1 to 2 days.

Mini Cakes

The quickest way to cover a mini cake is with a poured icing, such as Quick-Pour Fondant (p. 92), Ganache Glaze (p. 104) or melted Candy Melts. Place cake on rack over drip pan and pour on icing to cover, let set. Remove cakes from rack using a spatula and position on individual foil-covered boards or larger serving tray. Rolled fondant may also be used to cover mini cakes with quick results.

When icing mini cakes with buttercream icing, it's easiest to decorate directly on a cake board, so not to disturb the icing around the bottom border. Secure cake to an individual foil-covered board with a dab of icing. Pipe icing on small areas with a tip and smooth with finger dipped in cornstarch or use a small spatula to smooth areas. Sides of mini cakes can be iced quickly by covering with tip 2B, then smoothing seams.

Recipes

Chocolate Cookie Recipe

¾ cup butter or margarine
¾ cup sugar
2 large eggs
1 teaspoon vanilla
2 ¾ cups flour
2 teaspoons baking powder
⅓ cup unsweetened cocoa powder

Preheat oven to 375°F. Cream butter and sugar. Beat in eggs and vanilla. Add flour, baking powder and cocoa, one cup at a time, mixing well after each addition. If dough is too soft, add enough flour to make a stiff dough. Do not chill. Cut patterns, transfer dough pieces to ungreased cookie sheet with spatula. Bake 8-10 minutes, cool.

Poured Cookie Icing Recipe

This icing dries to a shiny, hard finish and tastes good, too. Great to use for icing or to outline and fill in with tip 2 or 3.

1 cup sifted confectioners' sugar
2 teaspoons milk
2 teaspoons light corn syrup

Place sugar and milk in bowl. Stir until mixed thoroughly. Add corn syrup and mix well. For filling in areas, use thinned icing (add small amounts of light corn syrup until desired consistency is reached.)

Recipes (cont.)

Cream Cheese Mousse

2 ½ cups whipping cream
3 packets unflavored gelatin (2 tablespoons)
⅔ cup cold water
20 oz. cream cheese, softened
1 ¼ cups granulated sugar
2 ½ teaspoons vanilla
1 ¼ cups milk
2 ½ teaspoons lemon juice

With pastry brush, lightly oil pan with vegetable oil. The following mixture will set quickly after gelatin is added; be sure to assemble in the following order. Whip cream until soft peaks form. Set aside. Soften gelatin in cold water, heat in top of double boiler until dissolved; cool. Beat cream cheese and sugar until light and fluffy. Add vanilla, milk and lemon juice, mix. Add gelatin, stir. Immediately fold in whipped cream.

Pour into prepared pan. Refrigerate until firm, at least 6 hours or overnight. Makes 16 servings.

Shortbread

1 cup butter
¾ cup sugar
1 teaspoon vanilla
2 ½ cups flour

Preheat oven to 300°F. Spray pan with vegetable pan spray. In a medium mixing bowl, cream butter, sugar and vanilla. Add flour and mix until dough is smooth. Chill dough one hour. Bake 15-20 minutes, or until very lightly browned. Cool 10 minutes in pans and remove shortbread to cool. Baked shortbread can be stored in an airtight container at room temperature for several weeks or frozen for two months.

Makes 4 dozen small cookies.

Candy Making

Candy Melts are so easy to use!

For melting, molding and dipping directions, refer to the back of the Candy Melts package.

To Flavor: The creamy, rich taste of Candy Melts can be enhanced by adding approximately ¼ teaspoon Wilton oil-based Candy Flavor (p. 120) to 14 oz. (one pkg.) of melted Candy Melts. Never use alcohol based flavorings; they will cause coatings to harden.

To Color: Add Wilton Candy Colors (p. 120) to melted Candy Melts a little at a time. Mix thoroughly before adding more color. Colors tend to deepen as they're mixed. Pastel colored candies are most appetizing, so keep this in mind when tinting.

To Mold Multi-Color Candy

Painting Method – Use a decorator's brush dipped in melted Candy Melts. Paint features or details desired. Let set. Fill mold. Refrigerate until set, unmold.

Layering Method – Pour melted coating into dry molds to desired height. Refrigerate until partially set. Pour contrasting color melted coating to desired height. Refrigerate until partially set. Repeat until desired numbers of layers are formed. Let candy harden in refrigerator. Unmold.

To Mold Candy Plaques

Molding a section or the entire pan out of Candy Melts is easy and impressive. Simply pour your melted coating into center of any shaped or basic pan. Tap pan gently on counter to break up bubbles and spread coating evenly over bottom and up the sides. Coating should be about ⅛ to ¼ in. thick. Place pan in refrigerator for approximately 5-10 minutes (check occasionally, if coating becomes too hard it will crack). Unmold onto hand or soft towel (tap pan gently, if necessary).

Multi-Color Candy Plaque – Use a cut decorating bag and pipe one color at a time. Refrigerate until set, repeat for each additional color. Pour in melted coating to fill remaining area.

Cookie Cutter Plaques – Place cookie cutter on waxed paper, pour in melted candy. Refrigerate to set, unmold.

To Make Candy Shells

Fill pan or mold to the top edge with melted candy. Let chill in refrigerator for 10-15 minutes or until a ¼ in. shell has formed. Pour out excess candy, smooth top edges with spatula and chill for 15-20 minutes longer. Carefully unmold shells (if you have difficulty removing shells, place in freezer for 2-3 minutes, then unmold. Excess candy can be reheated and used again.

Modeling Candy Clay

14 oz. package of Candy Melts
⅓ cup light corn syrup

Melt Candy Melts following package directions. Add corn syrup and stir to blend. Turn out mixture onto waxed paper and let set at room temperature to dry. Wrap well and store at room temperature until needed. Candy Clay handles best if hardened overnight.

To Tint: Candy Clay may be tinted using Wilton Candy or Icing Colors. Knead in color until well blended.

To Use: Candy Clay will be **very hard** at the start; knead a small portion at a time until workable. If Candy Clay gets too soft, set aside at room temperature or refrigerate briefly. When rolling out Candy Clay, sprinkle work surface with cornstarch to prevent sticking; roll to approximately ⅛ in. thickness.

To Store: Prepared Candy Clay will last for several weeks at room temperature in a well sealed container.

Modeling a Candy Clay Rose

Start with the base and mold a cone that's approximately 1½ in. high from a ¾ in. diameter ball of modeling candy. Next, flatten a ⅜ in. ball of modeling candy into a circular petal that's about ¼ in. thick on one side and about the diameter of a dime. Make several petals this size. Wrap first petal around the point of the cone to form a bud. Now press three more petals around the base of the bud. Gently pinch edges of petals. Make five more petals using slightly larger balls of modeling clay. Flatten, then thin edge with finger and cup petals. Press petals under first row of petals. Continue adding petals, placing them in between and slightly lower than previous row. For a fuller flower, continue adding petals in this manner.

Candy Recipes

Ganache Glaze Recipe

14 oz. package of Candy Melts®
½ cup whipping cream

Chop Candy Melts (you can use a food processor). Heat whipping cream in saucepan just to boiling point. DO NOT BOIL. Remove from heat, add chopped Candy Melts, stir until smooth and glossy. If mixture is too thick, add 1 to 2 Tablespoons whipping cream. Position cake on wire rack over drip pan. Pour glaze into center and work out toward edges.

Note: Cake may be iced first in buttercream. Let icing set, then pour on ganache. If cake has a perfect surface, no other icing is needed.

Truffles Recipe

One (14 oz.) package Wilton Candy Melts in desired flavor and color
½ cup Whipping Cream

Chop Candy Melts coarsely; set aside. Place cream in a small saucepan over medium heat and bring to a boil, stirring constantly. Once cream reaches a boil, remove from heat; add chopped Candy Melts and cover pan. Let stand approximately 5 minutes, or until coating has melted; 1 tablespoon Liqueur can be added at this point for flavor, if desired. Stir until smooth and creamy. Refrigerate until firm. Roll into balls. Truffles may be rolled in a variety of coatings (Wilton Sprinkle Decorations, chopped nuts, powdered sugar), used as centers for dipping or served plain. Store truffles in refrigerator up to 3 weeks.
Yield: Approximately 28-30 ¾ in. diameter centers.

Variations:
Lemon-Coconut: Follow truffle recipe using Wilton White Candy Melts and stir in 1 teaspoon lemon flavoring. Roll centers to coat in 2 cups tinted shredded coconut.
Mint: Follow truffle recipe; stir in ½ teaspoon Wilton Peppermint Candy Flavor. Drizzle melted Green Candy Melts (flavored with Peppermint) over truffles.
Cocoa: Follow truffle recipe. Roll centers to coat in ¾ cup cocoa.

Sugar Molding

Sugar Mold Recipe

2 cups granulated sugar
4 teaspoons water

Place sugar in a large mixing bowl. Mix sugar so there are no lumps in it. Make a well in sugar and add water (if you want to tint sugar, blend icing color into water at this point). Rub mixture in hands and knead for about 1 minute or until well-blended and mixture packs like wet sand. Be sure there are no lumps in mixture.

NOTE: Keep sugar mixture covered with a damp cloth when not in use.

- Mix sugar according to recipe. Dust mold half with cornstarch to prevent sticking. Pack sugar mixture into mold, pressing firmly with heel of hand. Scrape a metal spatula at a 45° angle over mold to remove excess sugar. Unmold at once by placing cardboard circle over mold and turning upside down. To loosen, tap top of mold with spatula and carefully lift mold off. Allow to dry for 3 to 4 hours.

- When dry, turn mold over and carefully hold in palm of hand. Do not squeeze or move molded sugar while it's in your hand or it will crack. Use a spoon to mark ¼ in. thick shell on the inside rim. Gently scoop out remaining soft sugar. Smooth inside and edge with your fingers. Place molded sugar, open side up, on cardboard circle to finish drying for about 24 hours, or place on cookie sheet in 200°F oven for 20 minutes. Allow to cool to room temperature before touching.

Just for fun...

Add pizazz to your cake messages using Wilton Presses and the techniques below. It's fun, easy, and another exciting Wilton way to add personality to your cakes!

Wilton Letter Press Sets are available in Italic, Block and Script designs – see page 113 for sets available. Easy to use – just ice cake smooth and imprint message, outline using smaller round tips 1, 2, or 3.

1. Overpiping

Add dimension and highlight your message! For a different look, overpipe portions of letters, or just the first letter in each word. You'll like the effect when you overpipe tinted gels with icings.

2. Dots

Have fun using dots to accent letters and words. Pipe dots directly on letters. Surround individual letters or complete words with dot borders. Pipe different color dots all in a row to create letters that complement other cake colors.

3. Outlining

Surround letters in electrifying multiple colors! Pipe completely around letters, or just along one edge. Try outlining the first letter of each word in the message.

4. "Loose" Lettering

Create excitement with lettering that shouts action! Imprint letters individually following the shape of the cake, the party theme or your mood. Vary spacing between the letters to create your own distinctive look.

5. Fancy Capitals

Begin your message with a bang! Embellish the first letter by using a different script, color or technique. Mix italic and script presses with block lettering to create impact. You can also add fun to fancy capitals by piping dots and stripes, outlining or overpiping.

Party Theme Product Index

Product Index

Pan Index

Italics indicate page numbers for designs which feature these pans.

The Wilton School
of Cake Decorating and Confectionery Art
Woodridge, IL

LEARN HOW TO DECORATE FROM THE EXPERTS!

Since 1929, when Dewey McKinley Wilton first opened the Wilton School, hundreds of thousands of students have learned classic decorating The Wilton Way. Students begin with The Master Course, a thorough program in the fundamentals; later courses expand their expertise and creativity in specific methods.

MASTER COURSE — 2 weeks, 67 hours. The foundation for cake decorating skills. Designed for the cake decorating shop owner, baker, caterer, chef or enthusiast.
TUITION: $575   Plus Registration Fee $75*

INTRODUCTION TO GUM PASTE –
12 hours - 4 afternoons during the Master Course. Learn the art of making lovely gum paste flowers, bouquets and more.
TUITION: $100   Plus Registration Fee $25*

ADVANCED GUM PASTE / ROLLED FONDANT –
1 week, 35 hours. For the more serious decorator. This class covers gum paste flowers, roses, carnations, rose buds, orchids and others. Also rolled fondant cakes including crimping and embossing, appliqué work plus frills, bows and ribbons and a color flow centerpiece.
TUITION $400   Plus Registration Fee $50*

LAMBETH CONTINENTAL COURSE – 1 week, 40 hours. Intricate overpiping of borders on royal icing and rolled fondant-covered cakes. Previous decorating experience required.
TUITION $320   Plus Registration Fee $50*

PULLED SUGAR COURSE – 9 hours, 3 afternoons during Master Course. Use pulled sugar to cover a cake, make flowers, candy dishes, ribbons, bows and more.
TUITION $250   Plus Registration Fee $25*

CHOCOLATE ARTISTRY WITH ELAINE GONZALEZ –
5 days, 30 hours. Well-known chocolatier and author of Chocolate Artistry presents professional techniques for creating and decorating fabulous candies—from molded treats to delicious truffles.
TUITION $400   Plus Registration Fee $50*

CAKES FOR CATERING –
5 days, 40 hours. Ice and decorate cakes to serve large or small groups. Covers wedding and other tiered cakes, sheets, large rounds, squares and petit fours. Design theme party cakes and get special tips for quick and easy, but spectacular designs. Decorating experience required.
TUITION $320   Plus Registration Fee $50*

The Wilton School has a Certificate of Approval to operate issued by the Illinois State Superintendent of Schools. Course enrollment is limited. Apply early!

For more information, or to enroll, write to:
School Secretary, Wilton School
of Cake Decorating and Confectionery Art
2240 West 75th Street, Woodridge, IL 60517
Or call: **708-963-7100** for free brochure and schedule.
After August 3, 1996 call **630-963-7100.**

You may charge courses on
VISA, MasterCard or Discover Card.

* When registering for multiple classes, the MAXIMUM Registration Fee is only $100.

Wilton Home Study Course in Cake Decorating

Even if you've never tried cake decorating before, The Wilton Home Study Course will show you how to decorate beautiful cakes for every occasion. Easy-to-follow 5-lesson course includes the specialty tools you need plus the step-by-step instructions, illustrations and photographs that make it easy!

Enroll in the Wilton Home Study Course in Cake Decorating now. The cost is only $17.99 plus $4.75 postage and handling per lesson. See details on card facing page 96.

LESSON 1

Discover the easy way to pipe buttercream icing stars, zigzag borders and more! Learn how to prepare and color icing for your decorating bag, the correct angle to use, and how to control the pressure for expert results. Make a "Happy Birthday" cake.

Lesson 1 includes: Notebook Easel and Lesson Pages, Decorating Tips 4, 16 and 18, Quick-Change Plastic Coupler, Two Jars of Paste Icing Color, Shaped "Happy Birthday" Cake Pan, 12" Featherweight Decorating Bag , Pattern Sheets and Practice Board,Cardboard Cake Circle, Cake Decorating Easy As 1-2-3 Book.

LESSON 2

Make royal icing drop flowers, star flowers and leaves. Mold a sugar basket. Create a blooming basket cake. Learn how to achieve special effects with color and floral sprays plus how to print or write personalized messages!

Lesson 2 includes: Lesson Pages, Flower Basket Sugar Mold, Large Stainless Steel Angled Spatula, Decorating Tips 3, 20, 67 and 131, Two Jars of Paste Icing Color, Meringue Powder (4 oz. canister), Pack of 50 Parchment Paper Triangles, Cardboard Cake Circle, 6 Pattern Sheets.

LESSON 3

Learn the proper techniques for making shells, rosebuds, sweet peas, ruffles, bows and more! Learn to make bouquets on a heart-shaped cake for anniversaries, birthdays, Valentine's Day, weddings, showers.

Lesson 3 includes: Lesson Pages, Two 9" Heart-Shaped Aluminum Pans, Decorating Tips 22, 103 and 104, 12" Featherweight Decorating Bag , Quick-Change Plastic Coupler, Jar of Paste Icing Color, Cardboard Cake Circle, 4 Pattern Sheets.

LESSON 4

Pipe daisies and chrysanthemums using a flower nail. Weave basketweave stripes. Create symmetrical cake designs, pipe rope borders and more. Use your new cake turntable to decorate a round cake.

Lesson 4 includes: Lesson Pages, Trim 'N Turn Cake Stand, Decorating Tips 48 and 81, Flower Nails 7 and 9, Jar of Paste Icing Color, Wilton Cake Marker, 6 Pattern Sheets.

LESSON 5

Shape a magnificent icing rose! Pipe stringwork and create a mini-tiered cake using the pans and separator set we'll send. After this lesson you'll qualify for your Wilton Certificate of Completion!

Lesson 5 includes: Lesson Pages, Round Mini-Tier Kit (includes 3 cake pans, separator plates and columns), Decorating Tips 2, 12, 87 and 102, Cardboard Cake Circle, 4 Pattern Sheets.

Publications

GIFTS FROM THE KITCHEN
For those who love to share and receive the gift of food. Over 65 recipes and ideas for appetizers, breads, entrees and desserts; plus pretty and practical hints on packaging, wrapping and sending food gifts. Soft cover, 96 color pages. 8 1/4 x 10 3/4 in.
902-D-1223 $7.99 each

ENTERTAINING
A year-round serving resource, featuring exciting menu ideas season by season. Create appetizers, breads, entrees and desserts with the Wilton touch – fun, festive and perfect for the occasion. Birthdays for young and old, Mother's and Father's Day, graduations, picnics, showers, holidays, sports parties and more. Complete recipes and instructions. Soft cover, 96 color pages. 8 1/4 x 10 3/4 in.
902-D-7020 $7.99 each

PARTY FAVORS II
Learn step-by-step how to make over 50 easy, beautiful favors – styles for weddings, anniversaries, showers, baby showers, rehearsal dinners and more! Complete instructions on basic techniques, flowers and bows. Soft cover; 36 color pages. See Bomboniere® product selection p. 147.
8 1/4 x 10 3/4 in.
916-D-831 $4.99 each

NEW 1997 YEARBOOK OF CAKE DECORATING
The most complete idea and resource book for the professional baker and hobbyist alike. Over 135 new decorating ideas for cakes, cookies, candy and food creations, plus a spectacular array of wedding cakes. Step-by-step instructions, technique guide, helpful hints and product section included. Soft cover, 192 color pages. 8 1/4 x 10 3/4 in.
1701-D-9700 $6.99 each

NEW 1997 PATTERN BOOK
Duplicate many of the beautiful cake designs and ideas from the 1996 Yearbook. A great source for innovative designs and indispensible decorating outlines you'll use over and over again. Easy-to-follow instructions included. Soft cover; 60 pages; 8 1/4 x 10 3/4 in.
408-D-970 $5.99 each

SANTA'S HOLIDAY TREATS!
Here are recipe cards straight from Santa's file to you – ready for you to share with your family in holiday seasons to come. Discover Santa's secrets for candy and cookie gifts, decorated appetizers, party foods and colorful cakes. Plus a special gingerbread section with construction tips, patterns and wonderful designs. Soft cover, 96 color pgs. 8 1/4 x 10 3/4 in.
902-D-1224 $7.99 each

CHRISTMAS!
The ideal place to begin new holiday traditions, filled with dozens of recipes and ideas. Create festive main dishes, appetizers, cakes, cookies, crafts, gingerbread designs and more, using our easy-to-follow instructions and timely hints. A great source for your holiday party or to add imagination to the family Christmas dinner. Soft cover, 96 color pages. 8 1/4 x 10 3/4 in.
902-D-250 $7.99 each

NEW MINI TREATS RECIPE BOOK
The book that shows you how easy and fun it is to serve personalsized treats! Dozens of exciting recipes for delicious individual treats using the wide variety of Wilton single-serving baking pans and molds. Serve elegant appetizers, aromatic breads, luscious entrees and fun desserts perfect for any occasion. Soft cover; 50 color pages; 5 1/2 x 8 1/2 in.
2104-D-1100 $3.99 each

CAKE DECORATING-EASY AS 1-2-3
Shows and explains the basics of cake decorating in simple terms.
902-D-1792 $1.99 each
902-D-1790 Italian $1.99 each
CANDY EASY AS 1-2-3
Inspiring designs teach basic and advanced candy making. Easy step-by-step instructions.
902-D-2101 $2.99 each
Both books are soft cover; 36 color pages; 5 1/2 x 8 1/2 in.

USES OF DECORATING TIPS
Valuable quick reference/idea book for any decorator, and a marvelous inspiration for the beginner! Features five of the most popular decorating tip families and explains what each does. Shows the versatility and range of many tips by depicting design variations. Full color, soft cover; 48 pages; 8 1/4 x 10 3/4 in.
902-D-1375 $7.99 each

NEW WILTON WEDDINGS
Our most comprehensive book ever for planning and organizing your wedding. Garden Weddings, At-Home and Hotel Receptions, from budgeting to interior design, invitations to rehersal dinners, this book covers it all. A special **pull-out Planning Guide** includes a budget checklist and 12-month organizer, plus tips on getting the most for your wedding dollars. 25 cake designs, with complete instructions, patterns, recipes and more. Soft cover, 136 color pages; 8 1/4 x 10 3/4 in.
908-D-115 $7.99 each

WILTON BRIDAL CAKES
A showcase for many favorite wedding cake styles . . . Victorian, country garden and contemporary. Includes 27 bridal masterpieces, ideal for large or intimate celebrations. Complete instructions, patterns, recipes and wedding cake data and cutting guide make it easy to achieve the cake of your dreams. Soft cover, 96 color pages. 8 1/4 x 10 3/4 in.
908-D-110 $7.99 each

A TREASURY OF WILTON WEDDING CAKES
The most exquisite collection of wedding cakes and ornaments anywhere. This book reflects more than half a century of experience Wilton has in designing wedding cakes. From Victorian to contemporary cakes and designer series porcelain ornaments. Soft cover; 96 color pages; 8 1/4 x 10 3/4 in.in.
908-D-105 $7.99 each

WEDDING CAKES-A WILTON ALBUM
Mark those cherished occasions with a culinary masterpiece. Create wedding, shower and anniversary cakes-from classic to contemporary. Complete, easy-to-follow instructions, patterns, recipes and wedding cake data and cutting guide are also included. Soft cover; 82 color pages; 8 1/4 x 10 3/4 in.
908-D-100 $7.99 each

DRAMATIC TIER CAKES
With this complete Wilton guide, learn the fundamentals of constructing and decorating lavish tier cakes, from the basics of building a cake to the safest way to transport wedding tiers. Includes uses of stairways and fountains, plus tested recipes, decorating descriptions and a complete selection of products needed to make the cakes shown. A must-have for any decorator. Soft cover; 80 color pages; 8 1/2 x 11 in.
902-D-1725 $7.99 each

Publications

OUR THREE PART ENCYCLOPEDIA:
THE WILTON WAY OF CAKE DECORATING

The comprehensive cake decorating reference book for professionals and amateurs alike! Explore this must-have trilogy of techniques, tools, ideas, instructions and hints. All found in three invaluable volumes you'll be constantly consulting.

VOLUME ONE-
BEGIN WITH THE BASICS!
More than 600 full-color photos portray the Wilton method of decorating. Specialty techniques, such as Color Flow, Figure Piping, Sugar Molding and Marzipan Modeling are easy to master. Includes recipes. Hard cover; 328 color pages; 8½ x 11 in.
904-D-100 $29.99 each

VOLUME TWO-
ADVANCED TECHNIQUES
Our 328-page encyclopedia is brimming with Wilton-American and foreign techniques: English (Nirvana and overpiped), Australian, Continental, Mexican, Philippine and South African. Includes gum paste flowers and figures and the art of pulled sugar taught and demonstrated by Norman Wilton. Soft cover; 328 color pages; 8½ x 11 in.
904-D-119 $29.99 each

VOLUME THREE-
USING DECORATING TIPS
More than 400 color photos highlight over 40 beautiful borders, plus dozens of flowers and other decorative motifs. Exciting figure piped and gum paste creations are demonstrated and explained. Hard cover; 328 color pages; 8½ x 11 in.
904-D-348 $29.99 each

Video Home Study

IT'S CONVENIENT...see actual decorating techniques demonstrated right in your own home. Learn step-by-step, how to create these wonderful icing techniques yourself ...then practice them on your practice board right in front of your TV.

IT'S A TREAT...learn from our experts. Now you can gather all the secrets of experienced cake decorators. See and hear all the hints and tips that make decorating easy.

ENROLL IN THE WILTON VIDEO HOME STUDY COURSE NOW.

The cost is only **$29.99** plus $4.75 shipping and handling per lesson...and the videos and all the pans and tools are yours to keep. Don't delay. Return the card on page 96 with your first payment to Wilton and we'll send you Lesson I. If you are not completely satisfied, you can return the materials within 30 days for a full refund or credit.

Lesson 1
Learn the fundamentals of baking and frosting shaped cakes, about icing, how to use decorating tools and more! Learn how to decorate **2 fun, shaped cakes.**
Includes
Lesson I 30 minute VHS video, Lesson Plan/Guide, Huggable Bear shaped pan, 10 in. Soft Touch decorating bag, 3 disposable decorating bags, 4 metal decorating tips, 2 quick-change couplers, practice board with practice sheets, 2 jars of icing color, heavy duty cake board, Trim 'N Turn cake stand, 1997 Wilton Yearbook of Cake Decorating.

Lesson 2
Learn how to torte, how to ice a cake smooth, how to make shells, drop flowers, leaves, figure pipe. Learn how to decorate **2 cakes and a clown cupcake,** using figure piping and drop flowers.
Includes
Lesson II 30 minute VHS video, Lesson Plan/Guide, 9" Round Pan Set, 3 metal decorating tips, large angled spatula, 2 jars of icing color, 3 disposable decorating bags, 30 parchment sheets, 2 cake circles, Clown Heads cake tops.

Lesson 3
Learn how to make the rose and other icing flowers, how to make bows, and how to position flower sprays on cakes. Learn how to decorate **2 heart-shaped cakes** with basketweave and flowers.
Includes
Lesson III 30 minute VHS video, Lesson Plan/Guide, 9" Happiness Heart Pan Set, 3 metal decorating tips, #7 flower nail, 2 jars icing color, a container of meringue powder, 2 cake circles, a decorating comb and a Certificate of Completion.

How To Videos

LET'S DECORATE!
Master essential cake decorating skills with this comprehensive 27-minute video. Provides easy-to-follow one-on-one instruction on borders, flowers, messages and more. Review as often as you need – it's the best way to learn!
VHS 901-D-7580 $19.99 ea.

HOW TO MAKE WEDDING CAKES
Receive invaluable lessons on how to design and assemble dramatic tier cakes for weddings, showers, anniversaries and other special occasions. Hints for transporting and serving also included in this 60 minute video.
VHS. 901-D-128 $19.99 ea.

HOW TO MAKE ICING FLOWERS
Learn how to make roses, Easter lilies, violets, pansies, daisies, poinsettias and more! Five cake designs incorporate all the flowers included in this 60 minute video.
VHS. 901-D-119 $19.99 ea.

CAKE DECORATING - EASY AS 1,2,3!
Zella Junkin, Director of the Wilton School, takes you through the basics. See how to level and frost a cake perfectly, make simple borders, flowers, leaves and more. 60 minutes.
VHS. 901-D-115 $19.99 ea.

CANDY MAKING – EASY AS 1, 2, 3!
Learn how to make truffles, candy novelties, dipped fruit, molded and filled candy. Melting candy in the microwave included. 80 minutes.
VHS. 901-D-125 $19.99 ea.

Color!

Color is vital to your decorating. With color you can add realism to character cakes, personalize special event and holiday cakes and add vibrancy to all your cakes. Wilton Icing Colors are concentrated in a rich, creamy base, are fast-mixing and easy to use, and will not change your icing consistency. Our extensive range of icing colors makes it convenient for you to achieve the colors you need and want.

BUTTERCUP YELLOW 610-D-216	ASTER MAUVE 610-D-222	DELPHINIUM BLUE 610-D-228	JUNIPER GREEN 610-D-234	IVORY 610-D-208	BLACK 610-D-981
LEMON YELLOW 610-D-108	LEAF GREEN 610-D-809	KELLY GREEN 610-D-752	TEAL 610-D-207	SKY BLUE 610-D-700	VIOLET 610-D-604
DAFFODIL YELLOW† 610-D-175	MOSS GREEN 610-D-851	WILLOW GREEN 610-D-855	CORNFLOWER BLUE 610-D-710	ROYAL BLUE 610-D-655	BURGUNDY 610-D-698
GOLDEN YELLOW 610-D-159	TERRA COTTA 610-D-206	COPPER (LT. SKINTONE) 610-D-450	CHRISTMAS RED 610-D-302	ROSE PETAL PINK 610-D-410	ROSE 610-D-401
BROWN 610-D-507	ORANGE 610-D-205	RED (no-taste) 610-D-998	RED-RED 610-D-906	CREAMY PEACH 610-D-210	PINK 610-D-256

ICING COLORS	CONCENTRATED PASTE*	1 oz.	AIR BRUSH*	8 oz.
Buttercup Yellow*	610-D-216	1.59	N/A	
Aster Mauve*	610-D-222	1.59	N/A	
Delphinium Blue*	610-D-228	1.59	N/A	
Juniper Green*	610-D-234	1.59	N/A	
Ivory*	610-D-208	1.59	N/A	
Black	610-D-981	1.69	609-D-15	4.40
Lemon Yellow	610-D-108	1.59	609-D-12	3.80
Leaf Green	610-D-809	1.59	609-D-8	3.80
Kelly Green	610-D-752	1.59	609-D-7	3.80
Teal*	610-D-207	1.59	609-D-2	4.20
Sky Blue	610-D-700	1.59	609-D-17	3.80
Violet	610-D-604	1.59	609-D-13	4.40
Daffodil Yellow†	610-D-175	1.99	N/A	
Moss Green	610-D-851	1.59	N/A	
Willow Green*	610-D-855	1.59	N/A	
Cornflower Blue*	610-D-710	1.59	609-D-3	4.20
Royal Blue	610-D-655	1.59	609-D-4	4.40
Burgundy	610-D-698	1.99	N/A	
Golden Yellow	610-D-159	1.59	N/A	
Terra Cotta*	610-D-206	1.59	609-D-1	4.40
Copper (Lt. Skintone)	610-D-450	1.59	609-D-6	4.20
Christmas Red	610-D-302	1.59	609-D-10	4.40
Rose Petal Pink*	610-D-410	1.59	N/A	
Rose	610-D-401	1.59	N/A	
Brown	610-D-507	1.69	609-D-14	3.80
Orange	610-D-205	1.59	609-D-11	3.80
Red (no-taste)	610-D-998	1.99	N/A	
Red-Red	610-D-906	1.99	609-D-9	4.40
Creamy Peach*	610-D-210	1.59	609-D-5	4.40
Pink	610-D-256	1.59	609-D-16	4.20

BLEND SPECIAL COLORS

Experiment with small amounts of icing first to achieve the perfect color for all your decorating needs! It's easy to create popular school colors like maroon, hunter green, and warm gold using the mixtures shown at right.

ROYAL BLUE	+	small amount of BLACK	=	NAVY BLUE
GOLDEN YELLOW	+	touch of BROWN	=	WARM GOLD
PINK	+	RED-RED	=	RASPBERRY
BURGUNDY	+	RED-RED	=	MAROON
KELLY GREEN	+	small amount of BLACK	=	HUNTER GREEN
5 parts SKY BLUE	+	1 part LEAF GREEN	=	AQUA
9 parts LEMON YELLOW	+	1 part LEAF GREEN	=	CHARTREUSE

ADD COLOR TO YOUR COOKIES!

It's easy to bake color right into cookies — knead small amounts of Icing Color into prepared Roll-Out Cookie Dough (see p. 94) until desired shade is reached. Pipe decorations on unbaked cookies using thinned tinted cookie dough. Thin a small amount of tinted dough with 1 tsp. water at a time until it will pass through a small round decorating tip. Bake following recipe instructions.

COLOR EASTER EGGS TOO!

It's easy to color eggs with Wilton Icing Colors. Put 1 tsp. vinegar into ¾ cup very hot water. Mix in icing color until the water is a very deep hue. Let water set a few minutes, stir until completely dissolved. Experiment with different colors, using a test egg to try out different combinations!

1. 8-ICING COLORS KIT **
½ oz. jars of icing colors. Christmas Red, Lemon Yellow, Leaf Green, Sky Blue, Brown, Orange, Pink, and Violet.
601-D-5577 $8.99 kit

2. 12-ICING COLORS KIT **
½ oz. jars of popular new updated icing colors. Kelly Green, Violet, Pink, Brown, Lemon Yellow, Black, No-Taste Red, Royal Blue, Golden Yellow, Burgundy, Teal and Copper (Lt. Skintone).
601-D-5580 $12.99 kit

3. PASTEL 4-ICING COLORS KIT **
½ oz. jars of icing colors. Petal Pink, Creamy Peach, Willow Green, Cornflower Blue.
601-D-25588 $4.29 kit

4. GARDEN TONE 4-ICING COLORS KIT **
½ oz. jars of icing colors. Buttercup Yellow, Aster Mauve, Delphinium Blue, Juniper Green.
601-D-4240 $4.29 kit

5. PRIMARY 4-ICING COLORS KIT **
½ oz. jars of icing colors. Lemon Yellow, Christmas Red, Sky Blue, Brown.
601-D-5127 $4.29 kit

6. WHITE-WHITE ICING COLOR*
Stir in to whiten icing made with butter or margarine. Perfect for wedding cakes. 2 oz. plastic bottle.
603-D-1236 $2.99 each

NEED HOLIDAY OR CHARACTER COLORS? TURN TO OUR SPECIALTY SHOPS IN BACK!

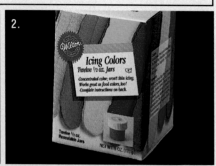

*Special Blend Color **Kosher †Daffodil Yellow is an all-natural color. It does not contain Yellow #5. The color remains very pale.

1. TUBE DECORATING ICINGS** $1.79 each

Our delicious icing is ideal for decorating. The tube can be used with the 5 Pc. Tip Set (below) or Coupler Ring (below) and any standard size Wilton metal tip. The colors match Wilton Icing Colors shown on p. 110. 4.25 oz. tube.

Black	704-D-206	Blue	704-D-248
Chocolate	704-D-254	Green	704-D-224
Orange	704-D-212	Pink	704-D-230
Red	704-D-218	Violet	704-D-242
White	704-D-200	Yellow	704-D-236

2. TUBE DECORATING GELS** $1.29 each

Transparent gels are great for writing messages and decorating cakes and cookies. The colors match Wilton Icing Colors shown on p. 110. .68 oz. tube.

Black	704-D-306	Blue	704-D-348
Brown	704-D-354	Green	704-D-324
Clear	704-D-300	Orange	704-D-312
Pink	704-D-330	Red	704-D-318
Violet	704-D-342	Yellow	704-D-336

3. 5-PC. TIP SET

Designed for use with Wilton Tube Decorating Icings – attach with a twist! Includes Star Tip, Round Tip, Leaf Tip, Petal Tip and Flower Nail.
418-D-47300 $1.79 set

4. 4-PC. COUPLER RING SET

Use to attach Wilton standard size metal decorating tips onto tube icing.
418-D-47306 $1.49 set

5. 16 OZ. READY-TO-USE DECORATOR ICING

Perfect for decorating and frosting. Just stir and use!
710-D-117 $1.99 each

6. CREAMY WHITE ICING MIX

Convenient mix that provides rich, homemade taste. Just add butter and milk. Makes 2 cups.
710-D-112 $2.49 each

7. MERINGUE POWDER MIX**

For Royal icing, meringue, boiled icing. Also stabilizes buttercream icing. New resealable top opens completely for easy measuring. You can fit a tablespoon inside.
4 oz. can 702-D-6007 $4.99 each
8 oz. can 702-D-6015 $7.99 each

8. PIPING GEL**

For glazing, writing, etc. Clear; tint with paste color. 10 oz.
704-D-105 $3.49 each

9. COLOR FLOW MIX**

Add water and confectioners sugar to make color flow designs. 4 oz. can yields about ten 1½ cup batches.
701-D-47 $7.49 each

10. GLYCERIN**

A few drops stirred into dried-out icing color restores consistency. 2 oz.
708-D-14 $1.99 each

11. NO-COLOR BUTTER FLAVOR**

Gives a rich, buttery taste to icing, cakes, cookies.
2 oz. 604-D-2040 $1.79 each
8 oz. 604-D-2067 $4.79 each

12. CLEAR VANILLA EXTRACT**

Perfect for decorating because it won't change the color of your icing. Great for baking, too!
2 oz. 604-D-2237 $1.79 each
8 oz. 604-D-2269 $4.79 each

13. NO-COLOR ALMOND EXTRACT**

Delicious almond flavor for icing, cookies, cakes. 2 oz.
604-D-2126 $1.79 each

STAINLESS STEEL & ROSEWOOD SPATULAS

Strong, flexible blades in designs for every decorating need.

14. 8 IN. TAPERED (4 in. blade)
409-D-517 $2.99 each

15. 8 IN. STRAIGHT (4¼ in. blade)
409-D-6043 $2.99 each

16. 11 IN. STRAIGHT (6 in. blade)
409-D-7694 $4.79 each

17. 8 IN. ANGLED (4½ in. blade)
409-D-738 $2.99 each

18. 12 IN. ANGLED (6¼ in. blade)
409-D-134 $4.99 each

** Kosher

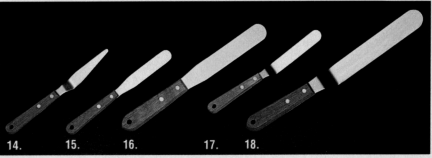

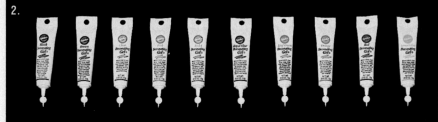

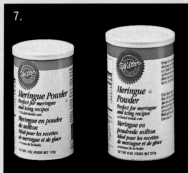

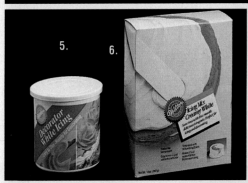

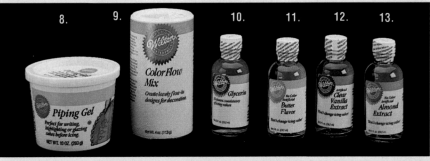

Flowers & Flower Accessories

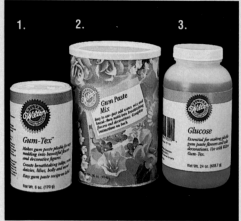

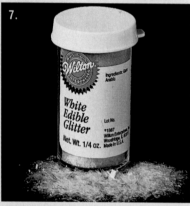

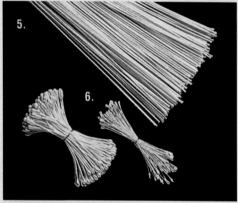

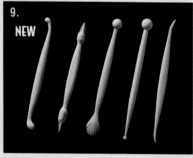

1. GUM-TEX™ KARAYA
Makes gum paste pliable, elastic, easy to shape. New 6 oz. can has a flip-top with a plastic resealable lid.
707-D-117 $7.49 each

2. GUM PASTE MIX
Just add water and knead. Workable, pliable dough-like mixture molds into beautiful flowers and figures. 1 lb. can.
707-D-124 $4.99 each

3. GLUCOSE
Essential ingredient for making gum paste. 24 oz. plastic jar.
707-D-109 $4.49 each

4. 31 PC. GUM PASTE FLOWERS KIT
Make lifelike gum paste flowers. Full color how-to book contains lots of ideas and step-by-step instructions. Kit includes 24 plastic cutters, 1 leaf mold, 3 wooden modeling tools and 2 squares of foam for modeling.
1907-D-117 $15.99 kit
BOOK ONLY   907-D-117 $7.99 each

5. FLORIST WIRE
Medium weight 18 in. long white wires.
409-D-622 $8.99 pk. of 175

6. STAMENS
Make flowers more realistic.
Yellow   1005-D-7875 $1.49 pk. of 144
Pearl White   1005-D-102 $1.49 pk. of 144

7. EDIBLE GLITTER
Sprinkles sparkle on scores of things. 1/4 oz. plastic jar.
White   703-D-1204 $2.49 each

8. READY-TO-USE ROLLED FONDANT*
No mixing necessary — ready to roll and shape! Covers cakes with a perfectly smooth iced surface. Easy to shape into beautiful braid or ribbon borders, flowers and decorations. 24 oz. pkg. covers an 8 in. 2-layer cake plus decorations.
710-D-2076 $5.99 each

9. NEW 5 PC. CONFECTIONERY TOOLS FOR GUM PASTE & FONDANT FLOWERS
Invaluable tools for shaping, imprinting and stenciling – letting you create incredibly lifelike confectionery flowers. Excellent for shaping marzipan fruits and marking patterns in fondant cakes. Set includes Dogbone, Umbrella, Shell, Ball and Veining Tools.
1907-D-1000 $9.99 set

10. PROFESSIONAL CAKE STAND
Heavy-duty aluminum stand is 4 5/8 in. high with 12 in. rotating plate. Super strong; essential for decorating tiered wedding cakes.
307-D-2501 $59.99 each

11. LAZY DAISY SERVER
Stationary stand. Sturdy white plastic with scalloped edges. 5 in. high with 12 in. plate.
307-D-700 $8.99 each

12. TRIM 'N TURN CAKE STAND
Flute-edged white molded plastic. 12 in. plate turns smoothly on hidden ball bearings. Just turn as you decorate.
2103-D-2518 $7.99 each

13. REVOLVING CAKE STAND
Now with easy, rotating ball bearings! Plate turns smoothly in either direction for easy decorating and serving; 3 in. high with 11 in. diameter plate in molded white plastic.
415-D-900 $10.49 each

*Certified Kosher

NOTE: Prices and products offered in this Yearbook may not apply in Canada.

Helpful Tools & Flowers

1. NEW 8 PC. DESIGNER PATTERN PRESS SET
Imprints elegant designs for easy printing. Includes: symmetrical swirl, corner flourish, small and large fleurs de lis, flower, heart bow, scroll and curliques.
2104-D-3112 $5.99 set

2. NEW 12 PC. DECORATOR FAVORITES PATTERN PRESS SET
Set includes: double heart, fleur de lis, open heart, heart, closed scroll, large, medium and small c-scrolls medallion, crest, double scroll and vine.
2104-D-3160 $5.99 set

3. NEW 58 PC. ITALIC MAKE ANY MESSAGE PRESS SET
Imprint any message you want with these pretty and sophisticated letters. Press words up to 10½ in. wide; letters ¾ in. high.
2104-D-2277 $7.99 set

4. 56 PC. MAKE ANY MESSAGE LETTER PRESS SET
You can customize that perfect message. Press words up to 10½ in. wide; letters ¾ in. high.
2104-D-0010 $7.99 set

5. 6 PC. SCRIPT PATTERN PRESS SET
Combine the words Happy, Birthday, Best, Wishes, Anniversary, Congratulations. Word height app. ⅞ in.
2104-D-2061 $3.69 set

6. 6 PC. BLOCK LETTER PATTERN PRESS SET
Includes Happy, Best, Birthday, Anniversary, Congratulations, Wishes. Word height app. ⅞ in.
2104-D-2077 $3.69 set

7. 8 PC. ALL-OCCASION SCRIPT PATTERN PRESS SET
Press and pipe: Merry Christmas, Happy New Year, Easter, Thanksgiving, God Bless You, I Love You, Good Luck. Word height 1 in.
2104-D-2090 $3.99 set

8. 2 PC. CAKE DIVIDING SET
Handy chart marks 2-in. intervals on 6 to 18 in. diameter cakes. Includes instructions.
409-D-800 $8.99 set

9. READY-TO-USE ICING 1⅛ IN. ROSES *
Instant beauty! Made of edible hard icing, with decorating ideas on the package.
Pink 710-C-313 $3.99 pk. of 12

10. FLORAL SPRAY SET * $3.99 set
6 medium roses, 5 rosebuds, 8 leaves.
Pink 710-D-718   White 710-D-720
Red   710-D-717   Yellow 710-D-719

11. ROSEBUDS *   25 buds per pk. $3.99 pk.
Pink 710-D-715

12. LEAVES *
Make all flowers more realistic. Green.
710-D-711 $3.99 pk. of 24

13. 9 PC. FLOWER FORMER SET
Dry icing leaves and flowers in a convex or concave shape. 11 in. long in three widths: 1½, 2, 2½ in. (3 of each size.)
417-D-9500 $5.99 set

14. 8 PC. TREE FORMER SET
Make icing pine trees; dry royal icing or gum paste decorations. 4½ in. high formers; 6 in. holding sticks.
417-D-1150 $1.99 set

15. 3 IN. FLOWER NAIL   Ideal with large petal tips.
402-D-3003 $1.29 each

16. LILY NAIL 1⅝ in. diameter.
402-D-3012   89¢ each

17. 2 IN. FLOWER NAIL Use with curved and swirled petal tips, 118-121, to make large blooms.
402-D-3002 $1.19 each

18. 1½ IN. FLOWER NAIL NO. 7 For basic flower-making.
402-D-3007   99¢ each

19. 1¼ IN. FLOWER NAIL NO. 9 For smaller flowers.
402-D-3009   79¢ each

20. 8 PC. LILY NAIL SET
Essential for making cup flowers. Set includes ½, 1¼, 1⅝ and 2½ in. diam. cups. Sturdy white plastic.
403-D-9444 $1.99 set

*Certified Kosher

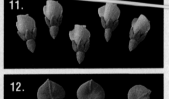

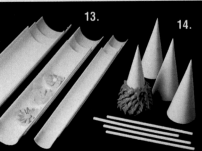

Bags, Couplers & Air Brush

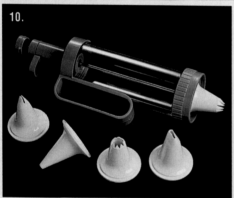
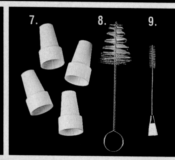

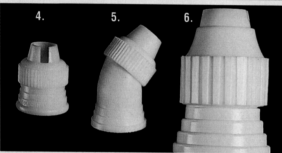
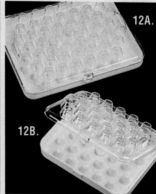
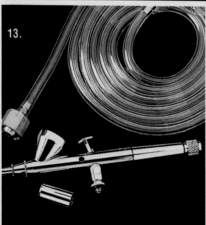
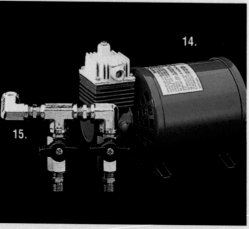

1. FEATHERWEIGHT DECORATING BAGS
Lightweight, strong, flexible polyester bags are easy to handle, soft, workable and never get stiff. Specially coated so grease won't go through. May be boiled. Dishwasher safe. Instructions included.

Size	Stock No.	Each
8 in.	404-D-5087	$2.49
10 in.	404-D-5109	$3.89
12 in.	404-D-5125	$4.89
14 in.	404-D-5140	$6.29
16 in.	404-D-5168	$7.59
18 in.	404-D-5184	$8.29

2. DISPOSABLE DECORATING BAGS
Use and toss — no fuss, no muss. Perfect for melting Candy Melts®* in the microwave, too. Strong, flexible, and easy-to-handle plastic. 12 in. size fits standard tips and couplers.
*brand confectionery coating

2104-D-358 $3.99 pk. of 12
24-Count Value Pack
2104-D-1358 $6.29 pk. of 24

3. PARCHMENT TRIANGLES
Make your own disposable decorating bags with our quality, grease-resistant vegetable parchment paper.
12 in. 2104-D-1206 $4.49 pk. of 100
15 in. 2104-D-1508 $5.49 pk. of 100

PLASTIC COUPLERS
Use to change tips without changing bags when using the same color icing.

4. STANDARD COUPLER
Fits all decorating bags, standard tips.
411-D-1987   59¢ each

5. ANGLED COUPLER
Reaches around sharp angles. Fits all bags and standard decorating tips.
411-D-7365   79¢ each

6. LARGE COUPLER
Fits 14 in. to 18 in. Featherweight bags. Use with large decorating tips.
411-D-1006 $1.19 each

7. TIP COVERS
Slip over tip and save to take filled bags of icing along for touch-ups. Plastic.
414-D-915 99¢ pk. of 4

8. MAXI TIP BRUSH
Gets out every bit of icing fast and easy. 1½ in. wide x 5½ in. long.
414-D-1010 $1.79 each

9. TIP BRUSH
Plastic bristles clean tips thoroughly. ¼ in. wide x 4 in. long.
418-D-1123 $1.19 each

10. DESSERT DECORATOR
Easy-to-control lever lets you decorate cakes, pastries, cookies with one hand. Includes 5 easy-to-change decorating nozzles.
415-D-825 $10.99 each

11. TIP SAVER
Reshape bent tips, large or regular size. Molded plastic.
414-D-909 $2.79 each

12. TIP SAVER BOXES
Keep decorating tips clean and organized.
A. 52-Tip Capacity 405-D-7777 $6.99 each
B. 26-Tip Capacity 405-D-8773 $4.99 each

13. 2 PC. AIR BRUSH AND HOSE SET
Nickel-plated solid brass. Generous capacity angled color-holder cup. Includes 6-ft. PVC hose and airbrush holder.
415-D-4000 $124.99 set

14. AIR BRUSH COMPRESSOR
Professional quality, piston-type compressor. 1/12 horsepower provides maximum pressure of 40 lbs. per square in. Easy to control; on/off switch.
415-D-4001 $224.99 each

15. TWO-BRUSH MANIFOLD ADAPTER
Use 2 air brushes with just one compressor.
415-D-4100 $69.99 each

1. 18 PC. STARTER CAKE DECORATING SET
• Four metal decorating tips: 3, 16, 21, 67.
• Six 12-in. disposable decorating bags
• Two tip couplers
• Five (.067 fl. oz.) liquid color packets
• 10 page Instruction booklet
2104-D-2530 $6.99 set

2. 25 PC. BASIC CAKE DECORATING SET
• Five metal decorating tips: 3, 16, 21, 67, 104.
• Twelve 12-in. disposable decorating bags
• Two tip couplers
• Four ½ oz. icing colors
• 1½ in. Flower Nail No. 7
• 12 page Instruction booklet
2104-D-2536 $9.99 set

3. 36 PC. DELUXE CAKE DECORATING SET
• Ten metal decorating tips: 3, 5, 7, 12, 16, 21, 32, 67, 104, 225.
• Eighteen 12 in. disposable decorating bags
• Two tip couplers
• Four ½ oz. icing colors
• 1½ in. Flower Nail No. 7
• Storage Tray
• 36 page *Cake Decorating, Easy As 1,2,3* book.
2104-D-2540 $18.99 set

4. 52 PC. SUPREME CAKE DECORATING SET
• 18 metal decorating tips: 2, 3, 5, 7, 12, 16, 18, 21, 32, 47, 65, 67, 101, 104, 108, 129, 225, 352.
• Twenty-four 12 in. disposable decorating bags
• Two tip couplers
• Five ½ oz. icing colors
• 1¼ in. Flower Nail No. 9
• 8-in. angled spatula
• Storage Tray
• 36 page *Cake Decorating, Easy As 1,2,3* book.
2104-D-2546 $27.99 set

5. TOOL CADDY
You can take it with you and keep it all beautifully organized. (Tools not included.) Holds 38 tips, 10 icing color jars, couplers, spatulas, books and more. Lightweight, stain-resistant molded polyethylene.
16⅝ x 11½ x 3 in.
2104-D-2237 $19.99 each

6. 28 PC. DELUXE TIP SET
• 26 metal decorating tips • Tip coupler
• Two flower nails • Plastic tipsaver box
2104-D-6666 $20.99 set

7. 55 PC. MASTER TIP SET
• 52 metal decorating tips • Tip coupler
• One flower nail • Plastic tipsaver box
2104-D-7778 $36.99 set

8. 7 PC. PRACTICE BOARD WITH PATTERNS SET
Practice is a must for decorating that gets an A+. Slip practice pattern onto board under wipe-clean vinyl overlay and trace in icing. Includes stand and patterns for flowers, leaves, borders and lettering. 31 designs included. 9 x12 in.
406-D-9464 $6.99 set

NOTE: Prices and products offered in this Yearbook may not apply in Canada.

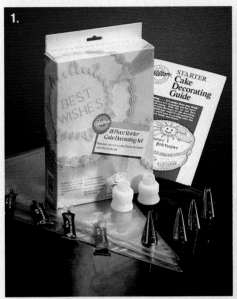

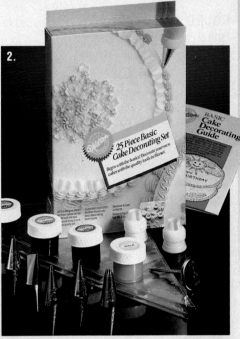

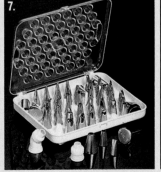

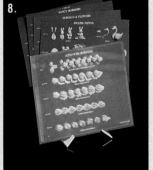

Decorating Tips Guide

Tip Openings and Techniques are shown at 65% size.

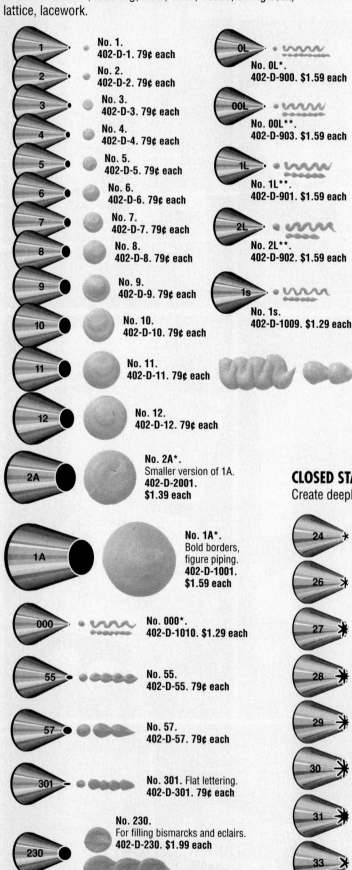

ROUND Outline, lettering, dots, balls, beads, stringwork, lattice, lacework.

No. 1.
402-D-1. 79¢ each

No. 2.
402-D-2. 79¢ each

No. 3.
402-D-3. 79¢ each

No. 4.
402-D-4. 79¢ each

No. 5.
402-D-5. 79¢ each

No. 6.
402-D-6. 79¢ each

No. 7.
402-D-7. 79¢ each

No. 8.
402-D-8. 79¢ each

No. 9.
402-D-9. 79¢ each

No. 10.
402-D-10. 79¢ each

No. 11.
402-D-11. 79¢ each

No. 12.
402-D-12. 79¢ each

No. 2A*.
Smaller version of 1A.
402-D-2001.
$1.39 each

No. 1A*.
Bold borders,
figure piping.
402-D-1001.
$1.59 each

No. 000*.
402-D-1010. $1.29 each

No. 55.
402-D-55. 79¢ each

No. 57.
402-D-57. 79¢ each

No. 301. Flat lettering.
402-D-301. 79¢ each

No. 230.
For filling bismarcks and eclairs.
402-D-230. $1.99 each

No. 0L*.
402-D-900. $1.59 each

No. 00L**.
402-D-903. $1.59 each

No. 1L**.
402-D-901. $1.59 each

No. 2L**.
402-D-902. $1.59 each

No. 1s.
402-D-1009. $1.29 each

MULTI-OPENING Rows and clusters of strings, beads, stars, scallops.

No. 42.
402-D-42. 79¢ each

No. 89.
402-D-89. 79¢ each

No. 134.
402-D-134. $1.59 each

No. 233.
402-D-233. $1.39 each

No. 234.
402-D-234. $1.59 each

No. 235*.
402-D-235. $1.39 each

TRIPLE STAR*.
402-D-2010.
$2.49 each

CLOSED STAR
Create deeply grooved shells, stars and fleur-de-lis.

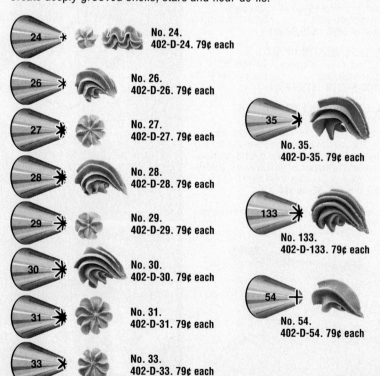

No. 24.
402-D-24. 79¢ each

No. 26.
402-D-26. 79¢ each

No. 27.
402-D-27. 79¢ each

No. 28.
402-D-28. 79¢ each

No. 29.
402-D-29. 79¢ each

No. 30.
402-D-30. 79¢ each

No. 31.
402-D-31. 79¢ each

No. 33.
402-D-33. 79¢ each

No. 35.
402-D-35. 79¢ each

No. 133.
402-D-133. 79¢ each

No. 54.
402-D-54. 79¢ each

*Fits large coupler. **Use with parchment bags only.

Tip Openings and Techniques are shown at 65% size.

OPEN STAR Star techniques and drop flowers; the finely cut teeth of 199 thru 364 create decorations with many ridges; use 6B and 8B with pastry dough too.

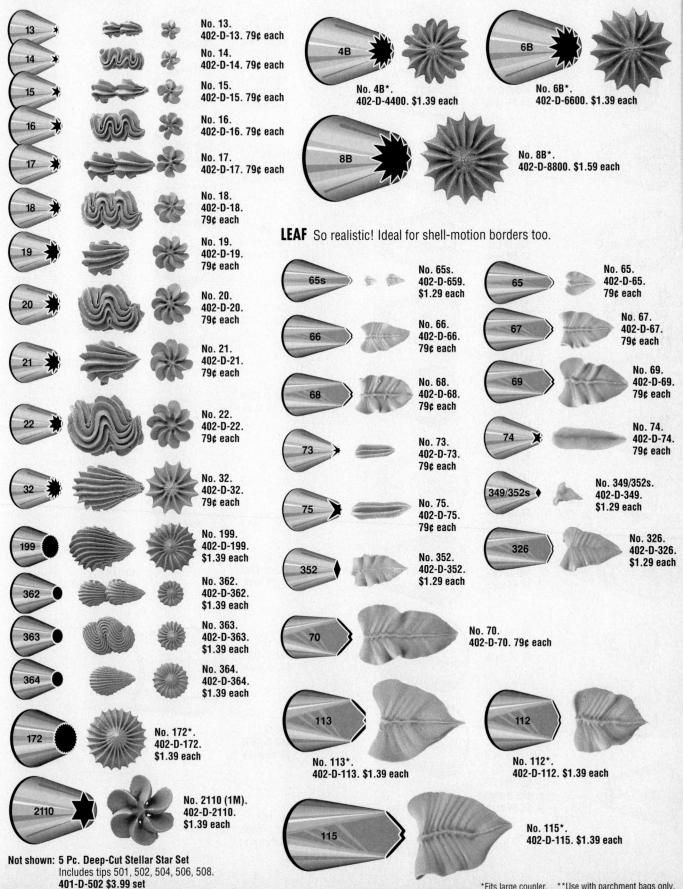

No. 13.
402-D-13. 79¢ each

No. 14.
402-D-14. 79¢ each

No. 15.
402-D-15. 79¢ each

No. 16.
402-D-16. 79¢ each

No. 17.
402-D-17. 79¢ each

No. 18.
402-D-18.
79¢ each

No. 19.
402-D-19.
79¢ each

No. 20.
402-D-20.
79¢ each

No. 21.
402-D-21.
79¢ each

No. 22.
402-D-22.
79¢ each

No. 32.
402-D-32.
79¢ each

No. 199.
402-D-199.
$1.39 each

No. 362.
402-D-362.
$1.39 each

No. 363.
402-D-363.
$1.39 each

No. 364.
402-D-364.
$1.39 each

No. 172*.
402-D-172.
$1.39 each

No. 2110 (1M).
402-D-2110.
$1.39 each

No. 4B*.
402-D-4400. $1.39 each

No. 6B*.
402-D-6600. $1.39 each

No. 8B*.
402-D-8800. $1.59 each

LEAF So realistic! Ideal for shell-motion borders too.

No. 65s.
402-D-659.
$1.29 each

No. 65.
402-D-65.
79¢ each

No. 66.
402-D-66.
79¢ each

No. 67.
402-D-67.
79¢ each

No. 68.
402-D-68.
79¢ each

No. 69.
402-D-69.
79¢ each

No. 73.
402-D-73.
79¢ each

No. 74.
402-D-74.
79¢ each

No. 349/352s.
402-D-349.
$1.29 each

No. 75.
402-D-75.
79¢ each

No. 326.
402-D-326.
$1.29 each

No. 352.
402-D-352.
$1.29 each

No. 70.
402-D-70. 79¢ each

No. 113*.
402-D-113. $1.39 each

No. 112*.
402-D-112. $1.39 each

No. 115*.
402-D-115. $1.39 each

Not shown: 5 Pc. Deep-Cut Stellar Star Set
Includes tips 501, 502, 504, 506, 508.
401-D-502 $3.99 set

*Fits large coupler.   **Use with parchment bags only.

ICING

Decorating Tips Guide

Tip Openings and Techniques are shown at 65% size.

DROP FLOWER Small (106-225); medium (131-194); large (2C-1G) great for cookie dough too.

RUFFLE Plain, fluted, shell-border, special effects.

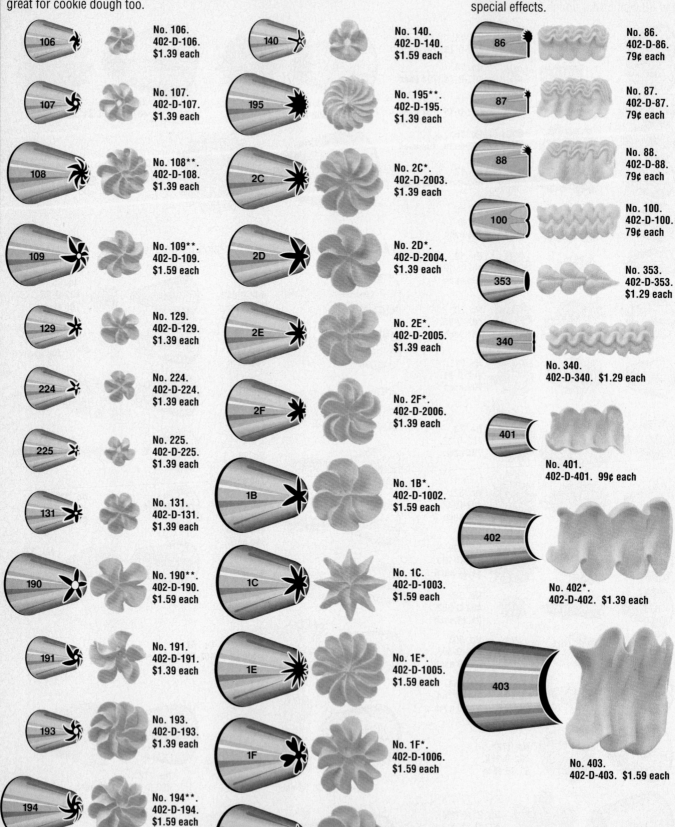

No. 106. 402-D-106. $1.39 each

No. 107. 402-D-107. $1.39 each

No. 108**. 402-D-108. $1.39 each

No. 109**. 402-D-109. $1.59 each

No. 129. 402-D-129. $1.39 each

No. 224. 402-D-224. $1.39 each

No. 225. 402-D-225. $1.39 each

No. 131. 402-D-131. $1.39 each

No. 190**. 402-D-190. $1.59 each

No. 191. 402-D-191. $1.39 each

No. 193. 402-D-193. $1.39 each

No. 194**. 402-D-194. $1.59 each

No. 140. 402-D-140. $1.59 each

No. 195**. 402-D-195. $1.39 each

No. 2C*. 402-D-2003. $1.39 each

No. 2D*. 402-D-2004. $1.39 each

No. 2E*. 402-D-2005. $1.39 each

No. 2F*. 402-D-2006. $1.39 each

No. 1B*. 402-D-1002. $1.59 each

No. 1C. 402-D-1003. $1.59 each

No. 1E*. 402-D-1005. $1.59 each

No. 1F*. 402-D-1006. $1.59 each

No. 1G*. 402-D-1007. $1.59 each

No. 86. 402-D-86. 79¢ each

No. 87. 402-D-87. 79¢ each

No. 88. 402-D-88. 79¢ each

No. 100. 402-D-100. 79¢ each

No. 353. 402-D-353. $1.29 each

No. 340. 402-D-340. $1.29 each

No. 401. 402-D-401. 99¢ each

No. 402*. 402-D-402. $1.39 each

No. 403. 402-D-403. $1.59 each

118 *Fits large coupler. **Use with parchment bags only.

Tip Openings and Techniques are shown at 65% size.

PETAL
Realistic flower petals, dramatic ruffles, drapes, swags and bows.

No. 59s/59°. 402-D-594. 79¢ each

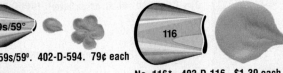

No. 59. 402-D-59. 79¢ each

No. 60. 402-D-60. 79¢ each

No. 61. 402-D-61. 79¢ each

No. 62. 402-D-62. 79¢ each

No. 64. 402-D-64. 79¢ each

No. 97. 402-D-97. 79¢ each

No. 101s. 402-D-1019. $1.29 ea.

No. 101. 402-D-101. 79¢ each

No. 102. 402-D-102. 79¢ each

No. 103. 402-D-103. 79¢ each

No. 104. 402-D-104. 79¢ each

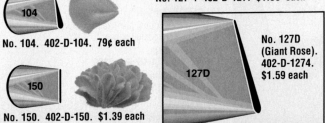
No. 150. 402-D-150. $1.39 each

No. 116*. 402-D-116. $1.39 each

No. 118*. 402-D-118. $1.39 each

No. 121*. 402-D-121. $1.39 each

No. 122*. 402-D-122. $1.39 each

No. 123*. 402-D-123. $1.39 each

No. 124*. 402-D-124. $1.39 each

No. 125*. 402-D-125. $1.39 each

No. 126*. 402-D-126. $1.39 each

No. 127*. 402-D-127. $1.39 each

No. 127D (Giant Rose). 402-D-1274. $1.59 each

BASKETWEAVE
44, 45 make smooth stripes; rest of basketweave tips make both smooth and ribbed stripes.

No. 44. 402-D-44. 79¢ each

No. 45. 402-D-45. 79¢ each

No. 46. 402-D-46. 79¢ each

No. 48. 402-D-48. 79¢ each

No. 47. 402-D-47. 79¢ each

No. 1D. 402-D-1004. $1.59 each

No. 2B*. 402-D-2002. $1.39 each

No. 789 Cake Icer. 409-D-789. $2.59 each

SPECIALTY
Shells, ropes, hearts, Christmas trees, ring candle holders!

No. 98. 402-D-98. 79¢ each

No. 347. 402-D-347. $1.39 each

No. 136. 402-D-136. $1.59 each

No. 77. 402-D-77. 79¢ each

No. 78. 402-D-78. 79¢ each

No. 83. 402-D-83. 79¢ each

No. 96. 402-D-96. 79¢ each

No. 105. 402-D-105. 79¢ each

No. 79. 402-D-79. 79¢ each

No. 80. 402-D-80. 79¢ each

No. 81. 402-D-81. 79¢ each

No. 250. 402-D-250. $1.59 each

No. 252. 402-D-252. $1.59 each

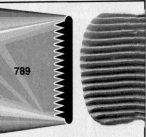
No. 95. 402-D-95. 79¢ each

*Fits large coupler. **Use with parchment bags only.

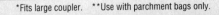

Ingredients & Tools

Mint Flavored!

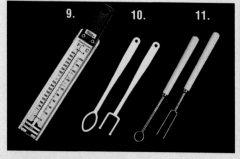

1. CANDY MELTS ® *

Versatile, creamy, easy-to-melt wafers are ideal for all your candy making—molding, dipping and coating. Delicious taste that can be varied with our Candy Flavors. 14 oz. bag. Certified Kosher. **$2.50 each**

White 1911-D-498
Light Cocoa (All natural, cocoa flavor) 1911-D-544
Dark Cocoa (All natural, cocoa flavor) 1911-D-358
Pink 1911-D-447
Yellow 1911-D-463
Green 1911-D-404
Christmas Mix (Red, Green) 1911-D-1624
(Available 9/4-12/15)
Pastel Mix (Pink, Lavender, Blue) 1911-D-1637
(Available 12/1-5/31)
Orange (Available 7/16-10/31) 1911-D-1631
Red (Available 9/4-1/31) 1911-D-499
Chocolate Mint 1911-D-1920
Pastel Mint (Pink, Green, White) 1911-D-1923
(Available 12/1-5/31)

Vanilla flavored, unless otherwise noted. *brand confectionery coating

2. 4 PC. CANDY COLORS SET

Rich, concentrated oil-based color that blends beautifully into Wilton Candy Melts®. Contains red, blue, yellow and orange; 1/4 oz. jars. Convenient, economical.
1913-D-1299 $3.99 set

3. CANDY WAFER AND FONDANT MIX

Perfect for petit four icings and making mint patties. 16 oz. Resealable lid.
1911-D-1427 $3.99 each

4. 4 PC. CANDY FLAVOR SET

It's easy to add your favorite flavor. Cinnamon, Cherry, Creme De Menthe and Peppermint. 1/4 oz. bottles.
1913-D-1029 $4.99 set

5. CREME CANDY FILLING MIX

Create creamy centers that can be dipped or molded for candy favorites. 9 oz.
1911-D-1901 $2.59 each

6. CANDY MELTING PLATE

Microwave-melt up to 11 Candy Melts® colors at one time for less mess! Non-slip grip edge. Includes decorating brush.
1904-D-801 $2.99 each

7. 3 PC. DECORATOR BRUSH SET

Perfect for smoothing icing, striping bags and painting candy molds. Ideal for use with candy melting plate above. Improved design with more durable bristles and easy-to-hold handle.
2104-D-9355 $1.49 set

8. EASY-POUR FUNNEL

Push button controls the flow. 5 x 4 in. wide; nylon.
1904-D-552 $3.99 each

9. CANDY THERMOMETER

Necessary accessory for hard candy, nougat, more.
1904-D-1200 $14.99 each

10. 2 PC. CANDY DIPPING SET

White plastic spoon and fork, each 7 3/4 in. long.
1904-D-800 $2.99 set

11. 2 PC. METAL DIPPING SET

Sturdy metal with wooden handles; 9 in. long.
1904-D-925 $9.49 set

12. CANDY CUPS

Crisply pleated cups, just like professionals use. White glassine-coated paper.

White-1 in. diam.
1912-D-1243 $1.19 pk. of 100
White-1 1/4 in. diam.
1912-D-1245 $1.29 pk. of 75

NOTE: Prices and products offered in this Yearbook may not apply in Canada.

Candy Molds

C A N D Y

1. LOLLIPOP STICKS
Sturdy paper sticks are easy to add to candy molds.
4 in.
1912-D-1006 $1.99 pk. of 50
8 in.
1912-D-9320 $1.99 pk. of 25

2. CLEAR TREAT BAGS
Perfect for candy and cookie treats. Plastic bags are 3 x 4 in.
1912-D-2347 $2.69 pk. of 50

NEW PRETZEL CANDY MOLDS
A pretzel pop is the ultimate lollipop – kids love eating 'em stick and all! Easy to mold; just position pretzel rod, spoon in melted Candy Melts and refrigerate. 6 molds, 1 design. $1.99 each
3. Clown 2115-D-1505
4. Bear 2115-D-1504

NEW SPORTS CANDY MOLDS
Action designs capture favorite games. 9 molds, 4 designs.
5. Football
2115-D-1700 $1.99 each
6. Basketball
2115-D-1701 $1.99 each
7. Baseball
2115-D-1702 $1.99 each
8. Soccer
2115-D-1703 $1.99 each

9-11. 8 IN. LOLLIPOP MOLDS
Designed for longer pops. Sticks line up to fit neatly in the freezer. Also great for 4 in. sticks.
7 molds, 2 designs.
9. Bear
2114-D-2837 $1.99 each
10. Dinosaur
2114-D-2834 $1.99 each
11. Heart
2114-D-2835 $1.99 each

12-16. SINGLE DESIGN CANDY MOLDS

12. TROLLS
8 molds.
2114-D-9210 $1.99 each

13. BON BONS
12 molds.
2114-D-91072 $1.99 each

14. MINT DISCS
12 molds, 1/4 in. deep.
2114-D-91226 $1.99 each

15. BABY BOTTLES
10 molds.
2114-D-9319 $1.99 each

16. ACCORDIAN RUFFLES
10 molds.
2114-D-91013 $1.99 each

17-29. MULTI-DESIGN CANDY MOLDS
17. LOVING BEARS
8 molds, 8 designs.
2114-D-9322 $1.99 each

18. TEDDY BEARS
8 molds, 8 designs.
2114-D-92826 $1.99 each

19. DINOSAURS
9 molds, 4 designs.
2114-D-98888 $1.99 each

20. OVER THE HILL
7 molds, 2 designs.
2114-D-1237 $1.99 each

21. WESTERN
8 molds, 7 designs.
2114-D-9310 $1.99 each

22. GRADUATION
11 molds, 5 designs.
2114-D-92818 $1.99 each

23. BABY ARRIVAL
8 molds, 7 designs.
2114-D-92822 $1.99 each

24. BABY SHOWER
10 molds, 4 designs.
2114-D-92816 $1.99 each

25. BRIDAL TREATS
8 molds, 5 designs.
2114-D-92820 $1.99 each

26. WEDDING SHOWER
3 designs. 12 molds, including 2 lollipops.
2114-D-91104 $1.99 each

27. LEAVES
10 molds, 2 designs.
2114-D-90629 $1.99 each

28. ROSES 'N BUDS
10 molds per sheet; 2 designs, 2 lollipops.
2114-D-91101 $1.99 each

29. ROSES
10 molds, 3 designs.
2114-D-91511 $1.99 each

30. CANDY BOOK - EASY AS 1-2-3!
Learn basic and advanced candy making; create spectacular gifts and favors. 36 full color pages of fun ideas and step-by-step instructions.
2104-D-2101 $2.99 each

31. ALUMINUM PANDA MOLD
Ideal for baking or molding. Sides clip together, base opens for easy filling. 5 x 5 in. Instructions, base and clips included.
518-D-489 $5.99 each

121

Cookie Pops & Bite-Size

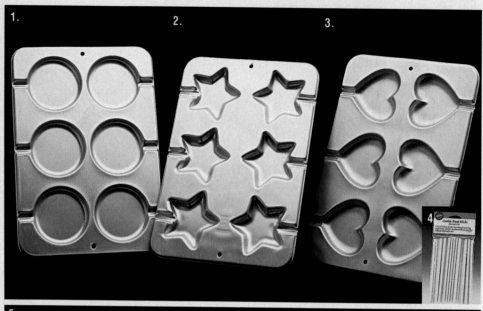

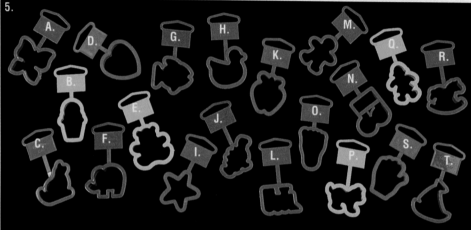

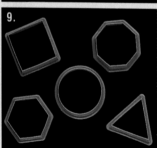

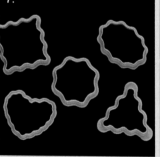

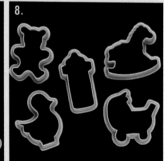

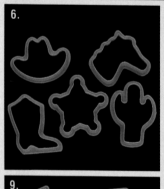

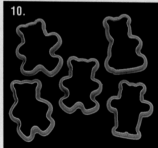

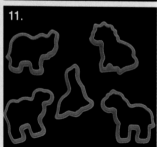

COOKIE TREAT PANS

No rolling or cutting — just press dough in pan for fun cookies or cereal treats on a stick. Great for cookie bouquets! Individual treats are 3 1/2 in. diameter x 1/2 in. deep. Make them easily with our cookie treat sticks and wrap them in a matching Treat Bag (p. 125).

1.	Round	2105-D-8105	$7.99 each
2.	Star	2105-D-8102	$7.99 each
3.	Heart	2105-D-8104	$7.99 each

4. COOKIE TREAT STICKS

Sturdy 6 in. sticks support any type of cookie; designed for use with Wilton Cookie Treat Pans.
1912-D-9319 $1.99 pk. of 20

5. BITE SIZE COOKIE CUTTERS

A great new way to serve kids treats they love! Use these fun shapes to cut cookies, cheese and gelatin treats. Or try on top of gift packages, using painted modeling clay. Each child-safe cutter measures approximately 1 1/2 x 1 1/2 in.

All cutters are 49¢ each.

A.	Butterfly	2303-D-219
B.	Ice Cream Cone	2303-D-205
C.	Cat	2303-D-214
D.	Heart	2303-D-203
E.	Bear	2303-D-204
F.	Elephant	2303-D-211
G.	Fish	2303-D-208
H.	Duck	2303-D-213
I.	Star	2303-D-218
J.	Dinosaur	2303-D-200
K.	Apple	2303-D-209
L.	Locomotive	2303-D-217
M.	Boy	2303-D-215
N.	Musical Note	2303-D-207
O.	Foot	2303-D-202
P.	Puppy	2303-D-206
Q.	Girl	2303-D-212
R.	Rocking Horse	2303-D-216
S.	Hand	2303-D-201
T.	Sailboat	2303-D-210

5 PC. BITE SIZE COOKIE CUTTER SETS

Each child-safe cutter measures approximately 1 1/2 x 1 1/2 in.

6. WESTERN
2303-D-9314 $2.49 set

7. CRINKLE
2303-D-9311 $2.49 set

8. BABY THINGS
2303-D-9313 $2.49 set

9. GEOMETRIC
2303-D-9310 $2.49 set

10. TEDDY BEAR
2303-D-9315 $2.49 set

11. CIRCUS ANIMALS
2303-D-9312 $2.49 set

Prices and products offered in this Yearbook may not apply in Canada.

STANDARD SIZE PERIMETER CUTTERS
A shape for every occasion! 3 in. wide x 4 in. long.
All are 69¢ each

1. PARTY SHAPES
House	2303-D-106
Cowboy Hat	2303-D-160
Ice Cream Cone	2303-D-111
Musical Note	2303-D-140
Umbrella	2303-D-131
4 Leaf Clover	2303-D-134
Cowboy Boot	2303-D-159
Texas	2303-D-158
Saw	2303-D-162
Man In Moon	2303-D-151
Apple	2303-D-104
Dog Bone	2303-D-123
Flower	2303-D-117

2. ANIMALS
Kangaroo	2303-D-157
Duck	2303-D-148
Teddy Bear	2303-D-133
Cow	2303-D-126
Fish	2303-D-128
Dinosaur	2303-D-112
Pig	2303-D-103
Butterfly	2303-D-116
Unicorn	2303-D-108
Elephant	2303-D-145
Kitten	2303-D-118
Puppy	2303-D-137
Stegosaurus	2303-D-154
Rocking Horse	2303-D-127

Not shown, but also available:
Whale	2303-D-155

3. GEOMETRIC
Shell	2303-D-146
Star	2303-D-135
Heart	2303-D-100

Not shown, but also available:
Circle	2303-D-161

4. KIDS/PEOPLE
Foot	2303-D-113
Molar	2303-D-153
Hand	2303-D-147
Girl	2303-D-120
Boy	2303-D-124
Clown	2303-D-109
Baby Bottle	2303-D-150

5. TRANSPORT
Locomotive Engine	2303-D-139
Sailboat	2303-D-129
Airplane	2303-D-101
Bicycle	2303-D-152

Not shown, but also available:
Roller Skate	2303-D-114

6. 4 PC. NESTING DINOSAURS SET
1 3/4 to 5 in. tall;
2 3/4 to 8 wide.
2303-D-190 $2.99 set

7. 6 PC. NESTING HEART SET
1 1/2 to 4 1/8 in.
2304-D-115 $2.99 set

8. 6 PC. NESTING STAR SET
1 5/8 to 4 5/8 in.
2304-D-111 $2.99 set

9. 4 PC. NESTING TEDDY BEARS SET
1 3/4 to 6 3/8 in. tall; 1 3/8 to 4 7/8 wide.
2304-D-1520 $2.99 set

USE YOUR IMAGINATION!
Think of Wilton cutters as "idea makers"— there are so many ways to use them!
• Sandwiches/french toast
• Balloon weights
• Bread dough ornaments
• Window sun catchers
Easy to handle, with deep sides and child-safe edges.

1.

2.

3.

4.

5.

6.

7.

8.

9.

Cutters & Tools

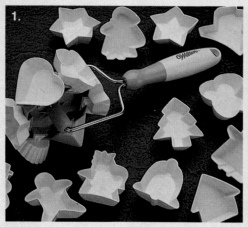

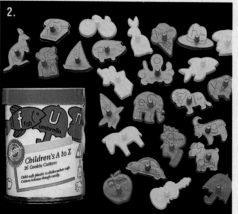

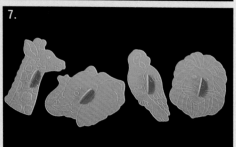

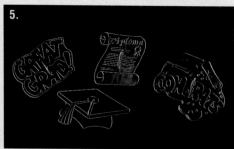

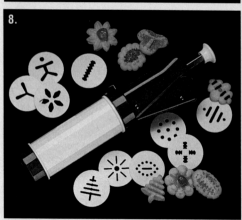

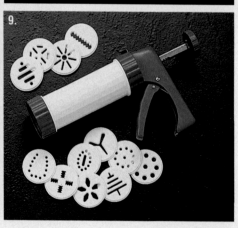

1. 19 PC. ROLL ALONG COOKIE CUTTER SET
18 interchangeable holiday designs. Cuts 6 different designs with one roll. Cutters remove for individual use and fast cleanup. **Each cutter is 1½ x 2 in.**
2104-D-2404 $6.99 set

2. 26 PC. CHILDREN'S A TO Z CANISTER SET*
An entertaining way to learn the ABC's! 26 different cutters, one shape for each letter of the alphabet, in a sturdy storage canister. Each cutter is 2½ x 3 in.
2304-D-91 $5.99 set

3. 26 PC. ALPHABET SET
Have F-U-N from A to Z! Cut out cookies, gelatin treats, cheese and sandwiches that are letter-perfect. Use them for clay play, in the sandbox and for craft and school projects. Each letter is 2 x 1⅛ in.
2304-D-1521 $8.99 set

4. 4 PC. OVER THE HILL SET*
Four friendly reminders of maturity prove that plenty of good times are left. Each cutter is 3 to 4 in.
2304-D-1237 $2.99 set

5. 4 PC. GRADUATION SET*
Class acts — cookies to honor the grad in four terrific shapes. Each cutter is 3 to 4 in.
2304-D-1800 $2.99 set

6. 4 PC. WESTERN SET*
Favorite frontier images blaze new trails for theme parties and after school snacks. Each cutter is 3 to 4 in.
2304-D-1238 $2.99 set

7. 4 PC. JUNGLE ANIMALS SET*
They'll go wild for our menagerie of friendly creature cutters. Each cutter is 3 to 4 in.
2304-D-2095 $2.99 set

8. 11 PC. BITE-SIZE COOKIE PRESS SET
Ten unique shapes in a small size — great for kids and entertaining. Easy one-hand pressing action makes dozens in no time.
2104-D-9311 $9.99 set

9. 13 PC. SPRITZ COOKIE PRESS SET
Easy-squeeze trigger action. Includes 12 plastic disks in classic holiday shapes.
2104-D-4000 $10.99 set

10. COOKIE SPATULA
Precisely angled to remove cookies from pan without breakage. Stainless steel spatula with rosewood handle.
2305-D-134 $3.99 each

* Cookie recipe included.

10.

Cookie Cutters

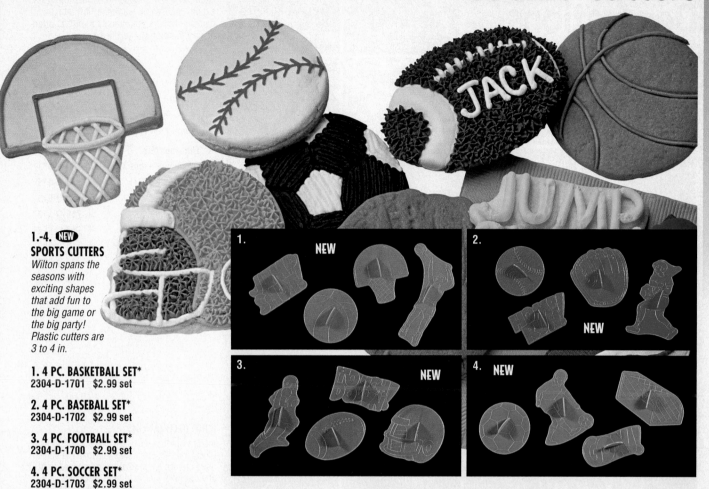

1.-4. NEW
SPORTS CUTTERS
Wilton spans the seasons with exciting shapes that add fun to the big game or the big party! Plastic cutters are 3 to 4 in.

1. 4 PC. BASKETBALL SET*
2304-D-1701 $2.99 set

2. 4 PC. BASEBALL SET*
2304-D-1702 $2.99 set

3. 4 PC. FOOTBALL SET*
2304-D-1700 $2.99 set

4. 4 PC. SOCCER SET*
2304-D-1703 $2.99 set

* Cookie recipe included.

Treat & Lollipop Bags

TREAT BAGS!
Wrap up lollipops, cookie pops, candy and much more the fun way! Perfect for cookie bouquets and party favors – there's a design to match every occasion. Size: 6 in. x 4 in. Each pack contains 40 bags and 40 ties.

1. FOOTBALL
1912-D-1127 $1.89 pk.

2. BASKETBALL
1912-D-1122 $1.89 pk.

3. BASEBALL
1912-D-1126 $1.89 pk.

4. SOCCER
1912-D-1124 $1.89 pk.

5. HEARTS
1912-D-2344 $1.89 pk.

6. OVER THE HILL
1912-D-1237 $1.89 pk.

7. WESTERN
1912-D-1238 $1.89 pk.

8. PARTY
1912-D-1128 $1.89 pk.

9. HAPPY BIRTHDAY
1912-D-2343 $1.89 pk.

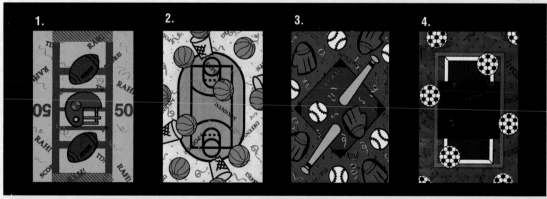

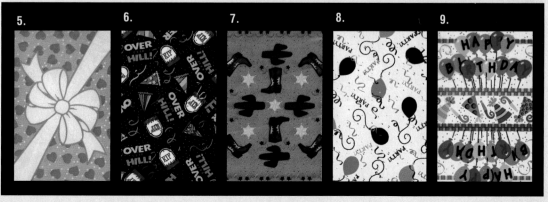

125

Sprinkle Decorations

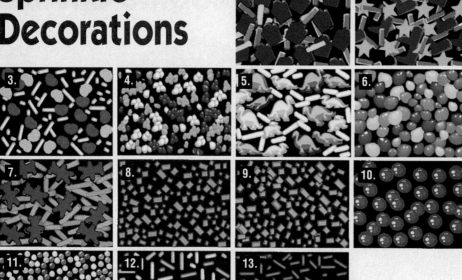

Decorate your cakes, cookies and cupcakes with Wilton Sprinkles! Decorating is easy because our V-shaped spout lets you pour exactly where you want. Our large-size package means you won't run out as often during decorating. Certified Kosher. 4 - 5¼ oz.
$1.99 pk.

1.	Over The Hill Mix	710-D-1237
2.	Western Mix	710-D-1238
3.	Hearts Mix	710-D-806
4.	Peppermint Crunchies	710-D-829
5.	Dinosaur Mix	710-D-828
6.	Rainbow Peanut Bits	710-D-831
7.	Teddy Bear Mix	710-D-832
8.	Red Crystal	710-D-813
9.	Green Crystal	710-D-812
10.	Cinnamon	710-D-814
11.	Rainbow Nonpareils	710-D-800
12.	Rainbow Jimmies	710-D-802
13.	Chocolate Jimmies	710-D-801

Icing Decorations

ICING DECORATIONS
Instant fun for your party cakes and cupcakes. Lively mint-flavored shapes (No. 21 is sugar flavored) are a real treat for kids. Sized to fit any cupcake, jumbo to mini. Packages of 9, except where noted. Certified Kosher. **$1.99 pk.**

14.	**NEW** Script Alphabet		710-D-546
15.	Over the Hill		710-D-535
16.	Western		710-D-537
17.	**NEW** Mini Hearts		710-D-524
18.	Petite Hearts	pk. of 12	710-D-840
19.	Doily Hearts		710-D-510
20.	Jungle Animals		710-D-533
21.	Graduation		710-D-473
22.	Clowns and Balloons		710-D-481
23.	Carousel Horses		710-D-479
24.	Baseball Mitts		710-D-475
25.	Basketballs		710-D-476
26.	Footballs		710-D-478
27.	Soccer Balls		710-D-477
28.	Dalmatians		710-D-487
29.	Kittens		710-D-485
30.	Crayons	pk. of 8	710-D-493
31.	Dinosaurs		710-D-497
32.	Teddy Bears		710-D-499
33.	Baby Things		710-D-495
34.	Alphabet/Numerals	pk. of 68	710-D-494

Wilton cups are more fun! Exclusive designs, holiday themes and favorite patterns that add to the enjoyment of whatever you're serving. Made of grease-resistant, microwave-safe paper. They're great for baking or using to hold candy and nuts.

Baking Cup measurements are:
Jumbo -
2¼ in. diam. bottom x 2 in. high
Standard -
1⅞ in. diam. bottom x 1¼ in. high
Mini -
1¼ in. diam. bottom x ⅞ in. high

$1.49 pk. except where noted.

GRADUATION
Standard 415-D-248 pk. of 50

CRAYONS
Standard 415-D-237 pk. of 50

JUNGLE ANIMALS
Standard 415-D-290 pk. of 50

BALLOONS
Standard 415-D-201 pk. of 50

CAROUSEL HORSES
Standard 415-D-231 pk. of 50

CLOWNS
Standard 415-D-204 pk. of 50

DINOSAURS
Standard 415-D-212 pk. of 50

TEDDY BEARS
Standard 415-D-202 pk. of 50

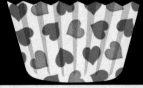

HEARTS
Standard 415-D-210 pk. of 50
Mini 415-D-310 pk. of 75

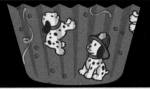

DALMATIANS
Standard 415-D-236 pk. of 50

KITTENS
Standard 415-D-239 pk. of 50

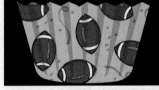

FOOTBALL
Standard 415-D-232 pk. of 50

SOCCER
Standard 415-D-235 pk. of 50

BASKETBALL
Standard 415-D-234 pk. of 50

BASEBALL
Standard 415-D-233 pk. of 50

OVER THE HILL
Standard 415-D-270 pk. of 50

WESTERN
Standard 415-D-271 pk. of 50

WHITE
Jumbo 415-D-2503 pk. of 50
Standard 415-D-2505 pk. of 50
Mini 415-D-2507 pk. of 75

RED (GLASSINE)
Standard 415-D-233 pk. of 50

GLASSINE CUPS
Candy and Party Cups fit large and small Wilton candy mold shapes.
White Mini (1¼ in.)
1912-D-1245 **$1.29** pk. of 75
White Bon Bon (1 in.)
1912-D-1243 **$1.19** pk. of 100

NUT & PARTY CUPS **$1.49 pk.**
White Standard (3¼ oz.)
415-D-400 pk. of 24
Mini (1¼ oz.) 415-D-500 pk. of 36

SILVER FOIL **$1.49 pk.**
Standard (1⅞ in.) **415-D-207**
(24 pure aluminum/24 paper)
Bon Bon (1 in.) **415-D-307**
(36 pure aluminum/36 paper)

GOLD FOIL **$1.49 pk.**
Wax-laminated paper on foil.
Standard (1⅞ in.) **415-D-206** pk. of 24
Bon Bon (1 in.) **415-D-306** pk. of 75

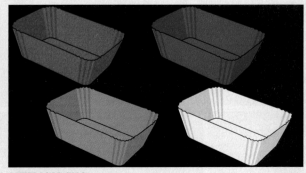

PETITE LOAF CUPS **$1.49 pk.**
Fits Petite Loaf Pan shown on p. 163. 3¼ x 2 x 2½ in.

Red Foil	415-D-106	pk. of 24
Green Foil	415-D-107	pk. of 24
Gold Foil	415-D-452	pk. of 24
White	415-D-450	pk. of 50

Candle & Cake Top Sets

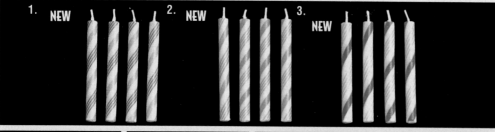

1. NEW
2. NEW
3. NEW

4. NEW
5. NEW
6. NEW
7. NEW

8.
9.

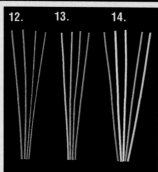

10.
11.
12. 13. 14.
15.

16.
17. 18.
19.

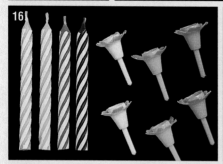

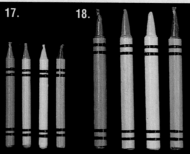

20.
21. 22. 23. 24. 25.

NEW CANDYSTICK CANDLES
Hand-twisted for a look just like old-fashioned candy sticks! 2½ in. high.
$1.99 pk. of 10
1. Pink/Green   2811-D-802
2. Purple/Pink   2811-D-801
3. Red/Blue   2811-D-800

NEW TWOTONE CANDLES
Exciting new color treatments ideal for so many celebrations. 2½ in. high.
69¢ pk. of 18
4. Yellow/Red   2811-D-810
5. Pink/Blue   2811-D-811
6. Yellow/Green   2811-D-812

7. NEW OVER THE HILL RELIGHTING CANDLES 2½ in. high.
2811-D-1220   99¢ pk. of 10

8. CELEBRATION CANDLES
2½ in. high.   69¢ pk. of 24
Asst. 2811-D-215   Pink   2811-D-213
White 2811-D-207   Red   2811-D-209
Black 2811-D-224   Yellow 2811-D-208
Blue   2811-D-210   Green 2811-D-211
Neon   2811-D-225

9. CELEBRATION JUMBO CANDLES
3½ in. high.   69¢ pk. of 10
Asst. 2811-D-222   Neon   2811-D-221

10. RELIGHTING CANDLES 2½ in. high.
2811-D-220   99¢ pk. of 10

11. GLITTER CANDLES
Candleholders included. 2½ in. high.
99¢ pk. of 10
Pink   2811-D-244 Black 2811-D-247
Green 2811-D-245 White 2811-D-248
Blue   2811-D-246 Orange 2811-D-249

12. RED & BLUE SPARKLERS
6½ in. high. 2811-D-704 99¢ pk. of 18

13. SPARKLERS 6½ in. high.
2811-D-1230   99¢ pk. of 18

14. SLENDERS 6½ in. high.
2811-D-1188   79¢ pk. of 24

15. GOLD AND SILVER
Gold   2811-D-9122 $1.49 pk./10
Gold jumbo   2811-D-9124 $1.49 pk./8
Silver   2811-D-9123 $1.49 pk./10
Silver jumbo 2811-D-9125 $1.49 pk./8

16. SPIRAL CANDLES WITH HOLDERS
Candles go in with ease, holders protect cake tops! 2¾ in. high.
2811-D-150 $1.49 pk. of 12 holders,
                      24 spiral candles

17. CRAYON CANDLES
2½ in. high candles in happy hues.
2811-D-227 $1.49 pk. of 10

18. JUMBO CRAYON CANDLES
Color a birthday bright. 3½ in. high.
2811-D-226 $1.49 pk. of 8

19. OVER THE HILL CANDLES
Say it isn't so. All 2¾ in. high.
30 2811-D-9111 $1.99 each
40 2811-D-9112 $1.99 each
50 2811-D-9314 $1.99 each
NEW 60 2811-D-9115 $1.99 each

THEME MUSICAL CANDLES
Fun designs in harmony with your party!
Play "Happy Birthday To You".
Convenient on/off switch.
4¾ in. high. All $4.99 each
20. Over The Hill 2811-D-1237
21. Train 2811-D-1904
22. Clown 2811-D-1761
23. Dinosaur 2811-D-1216
24. Bear 2811-D-1110
25. White 2811-D-1231 $3.49 each

WARNING: Candles not intended to be used by children. Keep out of reach of children.

#1 NUMERAL 3 in. high.
1. **PINK** 2811-D-240 69¢ each
2. **BLUE** 2811-D-241 69¢ each

3. **TEDDY BEAR HAPPY BIRTHDAY**
2 1/4 x 2 3/4 in. high.
2811-D-110 $2.49 each

4. **HAPPY BIRTHDAY**
3 7/8 x 2 1/8 in. high.
2811-D-490 $1.99 each

5. **NUMERAL**
Numbers 0 thru 9 and ?. Confetti
design. All 3 in. high. 69¢ each

1 2811-D-9101	7 2811-D-9107
2 2811-D-9102	8 2811-D-9108
3 2811-D-9103	9 2811-D-9109
4 2811-D-9104	0 2811-D-9100
5 2811-D-9105	? 2811-D-9110
6 2811-D-9106	

Four-piece sets are fast ways to add
personality to your cake! Hand-painted,
clean burning design.

6. **NEW ARRIVAL SET**
Joyous bundles. Height: 1 1/4 to 2 in.
2811-D-9132 $2.99 set

7. **CAROUSEL HORSE SET**
Party performers! Height: 2 5/8 in.
2811-D-243 $3.99 set

8. **DALMATIAN SET**
Height: 1 3/4 to 2 in.
2811-D-9310 $2.99 set

9. **KITTEN SET**
Height: 1 3/4 to 2 in.
2811-D-9312 $2.99 set

10. **TROLL SET**
Height: 2 in.
2811-D-9311 $2.99 set

11. **LITTLE DINOSAUR SET**
Birthday playmates.
Height: 1 1/4 to 1 3/4 in.
2811-D-216 $2.99 set

12. **CIRCUS CLOWN SET**
Height: 1 1/4 to 2 in.
2811-D-761 $2.99 set

13. **PARTY BEAR SET**
Cute celebration cubs!
Height: 1 3/4 in.
2811-D-214 $2.99 set

14. **PLAY BALL SET**
Boys of summer.
Height: 2 in.
2811-D-9134 $2.99 set

*Candle holder sets turn any cake into a
party cake quickly. Sets include theme
coordinating candle holders and candles.*

15. **12 PC. BALLERINA SET**
6 ballerinas, 6 candles.
2113-D-1472 $2.49 set

16. **12 PC. TRAIN SET**
All aboard! 6 train cars 1 1/4 to 1 5/8 in.
high; 6 candles 2 1/2 in. high.
2113-D-9004 $2.69 set

WARNING: Candles not intended to be used by
children. Keep out of the reach of children.

NOTE: Prices and products offered in this Yearbook
may not apply in Canada.

Candle Holder Sets

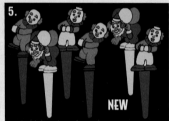

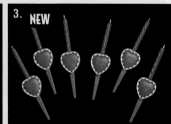

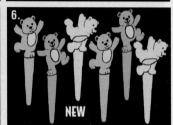

6 Piece Sets

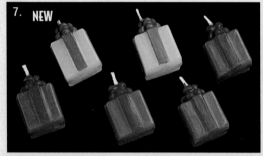

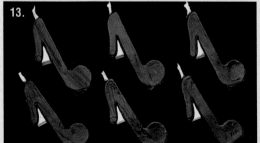

CANDLE HOLDER SETS

New Candle Holder Sets have all the fun of a shaped candle with reusable convenience. Bright plastic holders protect your cake. Candles are 2 1/2 in. high; holders are 2 3/8 in. high.

1. NEW 18 PC. OVER THE HILL
9 candles, 9 holders.
2811-D-151 $2.99 set

2. NEW 26 PC. HAPPY BIRTHDAY
13 candles, 13 holders.
2811-D-153 $2.99 set

3. NEW 12 PC. HEARTS
6 candles, 6 holders.
2811-D-156 $1.99 set

4. NEW 12 PC. DINOSAURS
6 candles, 6 holders.
2811-D-154 $1.99 set

5. NEW 12 PC. CLOWNS
6 candles, 6 holders.
2811-D-157 $1.99 set

6. NEW 12 PC. BEARS
6 candles, 6 holders.
2811-D-155 $1.99 set

No time to decorate? Wilton candles gives you so many ways to add instant fun and personality to any cake, even cupcakes. Designs you won't find anywhere else.

7. NEW GIFT BOXES
1 1/4 in. high.
2811-D-9332 $2.99 set

8. NEW CUPCAKES
1 in. high.
2811-D-9330 $2.99 set

9. GRADUATION
1/2 to 2 in. high.
2811-D-1800 $2.99 set

10. CHAMPAGNE BOTTLES
1 1/4 in. high.
2811-D-163 $2.99 set

11. BEARS
1 1/4 in. high.
2811-D-9329 $2.99 set

12. IN-LINE SKATES
1 in. high.
2811-D-9318 $2.99 set

13. MUSICAL NOTES
2 1/8 in. high.
2811-D-753 $2.99 set

14. COLA BOTTLES
2 1/4 in. high.
2811-D-751 $2.99 set

15. CHOCOLATE BARS
3/8 in. high, 2 in. wide.
2811-D-9321 $2.99 set

15.

No one does novelty candles like Wilton! We make it easy to add the light touch that makes even a plain cake unique. Our great selection of handpainted, clean-burning styles has something for everyone.

1. **NEW** **COMPUTERS**
1 1/2 in. high.
2811-D-9334 $2.99 set

2. **NEW** **TOMBSTONES**
1 3/4 in. high.
2811-D-9331 $2.99 set

3. SOCCER BALLS
2 in. high.
2811-D-9322 $2.99 set

4. GOLF BALLS
2 in. high.
2811-D-9324 $2.99 set

5. BASKETBALLS
1 3/4 in. high.
2811-D-9323 $2.99 set

6. FOOTBALLS
2 1/4 in. high.
2811-D-757 $2.99 set

7. BASEBALL BATS
2 3/4 in. high.
2811-D-750 $2.99 set

8. FISH
2 1/2 in. high.
2811-D-752 $2.99 set

9. BOWLING SET
6 pins, 1 ball. Pin 2 in. high.
2811-D-760 $2.99 set

10. WESTERN BOOTS
1 3/4 in. high.
2811-D-9320 $2.99 set

11. HEARTS
1 1/4 in. high.
2811-D-9328 $2.99 set

12. BEER CANS
1 3/4 in. high.
2811-D-9326 $2.99 set

13. DYNAMITE
2 in. high.
2811-D-9325 $2.99 set

WARNING: Candles not intended to be used by children. Keep out of the reach of children.

1.

2.

3.

4.

5.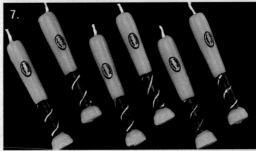

6.

7.

8.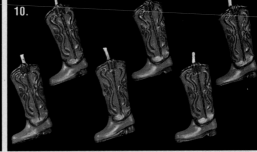

9.

10.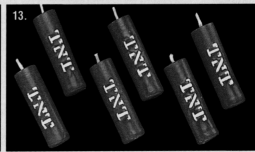

11.

12.

13.

Cake Decorations & Party Favors

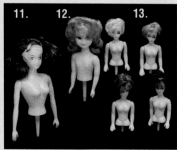

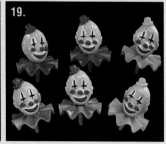

1. 8 PC. CAROUSEL SEPARATOR SET-UPDATED
Bright new colors make any birthday cake come to life. Create an exciting tiered birthday cake in minutes! Snaps together fast – sturdy pony pillars and separator plates provide strong support. Set includes four 9 in. high pony pillars, two 10 in. diameter separator plates.
2103-D-1139 **$11.99 set**

2. 4 PC. CLOWN SEPARATOR SET
Two big-footed clowns balance a 6 in. round cake on top plate. Perfect to set atop a large base cake (be sure to dowel rod). They can stand on their hands or feet. Set includes two 7 in. scalloped-edge plates and two snap-on clown supports. 4 in. high.
301-D-909 **$6.99 set**

3. 25 PC. CAROUSEL CAKE TOP SET
A circus in seconds for 10 in. or larger cakes. Includes one big top and six each of the following: horses, clowns, rails and flags. 9 in. high.
1305-D-9302 **$4.99 set**

4. 4 PC. CIRCUS ANIMALS SET
Brightly handpainted. 2 1/2 to 3 in. high
2113-D-9422 **$3.99 set**

5. 4 PC. DINOSAUR PARTY SET
Earthshaking celebration. 1 3/4 to 2 1/2 in. high.
2113-D-9420 **$3.99 set**

6. 4 PC. JUNGLE ANIMALS SET
Instant party cake - just add these jungle friends. 4 plastic decorations, 1 3/4 to 3 in. high.
2113-D-2095 **$3.99 set**

7. 4 PC. TUMBLING BEARS SET
Adorable acrobats. 2 to 2 1/2 in. high.
2113-D-9421 **$3.99 set**

8. 6 PC. TELEPHONE TEENS SET
Get in on the conversation track with these teens - 3 girls, 3 boys, 1 3/8 to 2 in. high.
1301-D-706 **$3.69 set**

9. DOLLY DRESS UP High style; 4 1/2 in. high.
2113-D-1485 **$2.69 each**

10. 6 PC. ENCHANTED COACH SET
Ride first class. 3 1/2 in. high.
2113-D-1490 **$3.99 set**

11. TEEN DOLL PICK 6 1/2 in. high without pick.
2815-D-101 **$2.99 each**

12. FRECKLE-FACED DOLL PICK
4 in. high without pick.
2113-D-2317 **$2.99 each**

13. 4 PC. MINI DOLL PICK SET
4 1/4 in. high with pick.
1511-D-1019 **$5.99 set**

14. 3 PC. CLOWNS SET 2 1/4 to 2 3/4 in. high
2113-D-9003 **$2.99 set**

15. 3 PC. CIRCUS BALLOONS SET
12 in a bunch. 3 bunches per set. 6 1/2 in. high.
2113-D-2366 **$2.49 set**

16. HONEY BEAR 3 3/4 in. high.
2113-D-2031 **$2.69 each**

17. 4 PC. COMICAL CLOWNS SET
Varied expressions. 2 in. to 3 in.
2113-D-2635 **$3.29 set**

18. JUGGLER CLOWN
Jolly fellow in action. 4 in. high.
2113-D-2252 **$2.29 each**

19. 6 PC. SMALL DERBY CLOWNS SET
Perfect for cupcakes. 2 in. high with pick.
2113-D-2759 **$1.99 set**

*CAUTION: Contains small parts.
Not recommended for use by children 3 years and under.

Cake Decorations & Party Favors

1. 2 PC. BABY SHOES SET
Classic on cakes or to hold candies at the shower. 1 3/4 in. high.
2113-D-424 $2.29 set

2. 4 PC. BABY BLOCKS SET
Spell out the good news. 1 1/4 in. high.
2113-D-418 $1.79 set

3. 2 PC. BABY CRADLES SET
They'll be rocking in style. 2 1/2 in. high.
Pink 2113-D-406 $1.99 set
Blue 2113-D-400 $1.99 set

4. 2 PC. BABY CARRIAGES SET
Great gift and cake accents. 3 1/2 in. high.
2113-D-442 $1.39 set

5. LARGE SAFETY PINS 4 1/2 in. wide.
Blue 1213-D-430 $1.09 pk. of 2
Pink 1213-D-436 $1.09 pk. of 2

6. SMALL SAFETY PINS 1 1/2 in. wide.
Blue 1103-D-19 $1.09 pk. of 12
Pink 1103-D-18 $1.09 pk. of 12

7. 2 PC. ROCKING HORSES SET
Classic baby symbol. 2 1/4 in. high.
2113-D-412 $1.99 set

8. PETITE PACIFIERS 1 in. high.
Pink 1103-D-74 $1.59 pk. of 6
Blue 1103-D-68 $1.59 pk. of 6

9. LARGE PINK & BLUE PACIFIERS 1 3/4 in. high.
1103-D-80 $1.99 pk. of 2

10. MINI BABY BOTTLES 1 1/4 in. high.
Three each, green, yellow, pink and blue.
1103-D-25 99¢ pk. of 12

11. LARGE BABY BOTTLES
One pink, one blue. 3 1/4 in. high.
1103-D-50 $2.15 pk. of 2

12. NEWBORN BABY FIGURINE 1 in. high.
1103-D-62 $1.99 pk. of 6

13. BLUE & PINK BABY BRACELETS 1 1/4 in. high.
1103-D-56 $2.15 pk. of 6

14. BABY LAMBS 1 1/8 in. high.
1103-D-17 $2.15 pk. of 2

15. FUZZY BEARS 1 in. high.
Blue 1103-D-15 $2.15 pk. of 4
Pink 1103-D-14 $2.15 pk. of 4

16. 2 PC. 3 A.M. FEEDING SET 5 in. high.
2113-D-3333 $3.99 set

17. GUARDIAN ANGEL
Watching over the cake. 3 1/2 in. high.
2113-D-7896 $2.99 each

18. 2 PC. SHINING CROSS AND BIBLE SET
For so many religious occasions. 2 1/2 in. high.
2113-D-7890 $1.99 set

19. COMMUNION GIRL* 3 1/2 in. high.
2113-D-7878 $3.49 each

20. COMMUNION BOY* 3 1/2 in. high.
2113-D-7886 $3.49 each

21. 2 PC. SLEEPING ANGELS SET
1 1/2 in. high x 3 in. long.
2113-D-2325 $1.99 set

22. SHINING CROSS
Detachable pick. 3 3/4 in. high.
1105-D-7320 $1.09 each

23. 11 PC. NUMERAL PICKS SET
2 in. high. With picks, about 3 1/2 in. high.
1106-D-7406 $1.39 set

designed by Ellen Williams
© 1995 EHW Enterprises, Inc. Licensee Wilton Enterprises

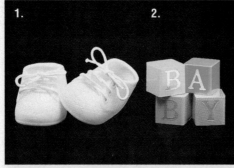
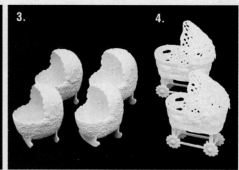
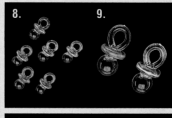

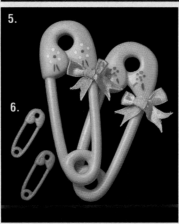

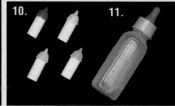

Cake Decorations & Party Favors

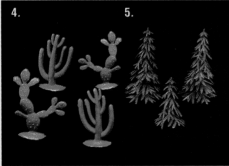

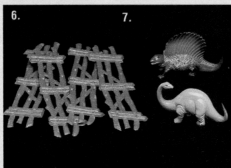

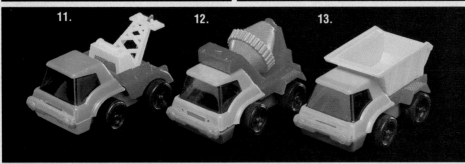

1. GRIM REAPER
Humorous bearer of bad news. 3 1/2 in. high.
2113-D-370 $3.49 each

2. LINE DANCING COUPLE
Keep in step with this dancing craze.
3 1/2 in. high.
2113-D-360 $3.99 each

3. LI'L COWPOKE
Wee buckaroo; 5 1/4 in. high.
2113-D-2406 $2.69 each

4. 4 PC. CACTUS SET
Add the look of the great Southwest.
2 1/4 to 2 1/2 in. high.
2113-D-2086 99¢ set

5. 3 PC. SPRUCE TREE SET
Perfect for holiday or camping motifs, and
much more. 2 to 3 in. high.
2113-D-2092 99¢ set

6. 4 PC. RUSTIC FENCE SET
Create your own outdoor scenes. 5 1/4 in. long.
2113-D-2099 99¢ set

7. 2 PC. REALISTIC DINOSAUR SET
Back to the prehistoric era. 1 1/2 in. high.
2113-D-2072 $1.99 set

8. 2 PC. ALL TERRAIN VEHICLES SET
With moving wheels, they really ride! 3 in. long.
2113-D-2100 $2.99 set

9. 3 PC. JETS SET*
Bring your party to new heights. 3 1/4 x 4 in.
2113-D-2112 99¢ set

10. 2 PC. RACE CARS SET
Real moving parts – fast-paced addition to
celebrations – cars are perfect for after party
play. 2 in. long.
2113-D-2106 $2.99 set

11. TOW TRUCK
With real moving parts. 3 in. long.
2113-D-2130 $1.99 each

12. CEMENT MIXER
Great alone or with other trucks. 3 in. long.
2113-D-2124 $1.99 each

13. DUMP TRUCK
Movable truck doubles as a toy. 3 in. long.
2113-D-2118 $1.99 each

14. 2 PC. GRADUATION CAPS SET
Quick way to decorate for the big day.
2 in. high.
Black 2113-D-1801 $1.99 set
White 2113-D-1800 $1.99 set

15. HAPPY GRADUATE
5 in. high.
2113-D-1818 $2.09 each

16. GLAD GRADUATE
4 1/2 in. high.
2113-D-1817 $2.09 each

17. GLOWING GRAD
4 1/2 in. high.
2113-D-1833 $1.69 each

18. SUCCESSFUL GRAD
4 1/4 in. high.
2113-D-4549 $1.69 each

*CAUTION: Contains small parts.
Not recommended for use by children 3 years and under.

Cake Decorations & Party Favors

1. 9 PC. SOCCER CAKE TOP SET
9 pieces, 1¾ to 2 in. high.
2113-D-9002 $2.69 set

2. GOOD SPORTS COACH
He's game for birthday and sports parties.
4½ in. high.
2113-D-4140 $2.69 each

3. 2 PC. BASKETBALL PLAYER WITH HOOP SET
He's the center of attention on any cake!
Player 2 in. high; hoop 4½ in. high.
2113-D-9360 $2.69 set

4. 6 PC. BASEBALL SET
Batter, catcher, pitcher and 3 basemen.
Handpainted. 2⅛ - 2¾ in. high.
2113-D-2155 $2.99 set

5. 3 PC. "NICE PLAY" BASEBALL SET
1½ to 3⅛ in. high.
2113-D-2473 $2.99 set

6. 2 PC. ARMCHAIR QUARTERBACK SET
Man 3½ in. high; TV 2¼ in. high
2113-D-1302 $2.69 set

7. 10 PC. FOOTBALL SET
Eight 1½ - 2 in. high players and two 4½ in.
high goal posts.
2113-D-2236 $2.99 set

8. FISHY SITUATION
5¼ in. high.
2113-D-2074 $2.69 each

9. END OF DOCK FISHERMAN
5 in. high.
2113-D-4832 $2.69 each

10. FRUSTRATED FISHERMAN
4½ in. high.
2113-D-2384 $3.49 each

11. 3 PC. FISH SET
Fun for small fry or big sports! 2½ in. long.
2113-D-2080 99¢ set

12. 13 PC. GOLF SET*
Includes 4½ in. high golfer plus 3 each: 2½ in.
wide greens, 4 in. high flags, 5 in. clubs and
golf balls.
1306-D-7274 $2.09 set

13. COMICAL GOLFER
2 in. high, 4¼ in. wide, 5⅛ in. long.
2113-D-2554 $2.09 each

14. SHARP SHOOTER
5⅞ in. high.
2113-D-2422 $2.99 each

15. LAZY BONES
3 in. high x 5½ in. long.
2113-D-2414 $2.69 each

*CAUTION: Contains small parts.
Not recommended for use by children 3 years and under.

NOTE: Prices and products offered in this Yearbook may not
apply in Canada.

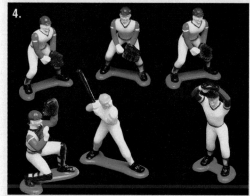

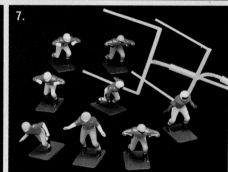

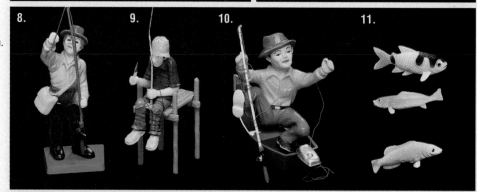

Cake Ornaments & Tier Tops

 1. **NEW**

 2. **NEW**

 3. **NEW**

 4. **NEW**

 5. **NEW**

 6. **NEW**

 7. **NEW**

 8. **NEW**

 9. **NEW**

 10. **NEW**

Perfectly matched in every detail – the two of you, and your cake! Wilton presents a collection of specially designed wedding cake ornaments with matching tier tops.

1. **NEW** **PRECIOUS LOVE ORNAMENT**
Wire filigree heart design embellished with pearls, glitter roses and tulle.
Height: 6 $\frac{1}{2}$ in.
Base: 4 in. diameter
103-D-446 $16.00 each

2. **NEW** **CIRCLE OF LOVE TIER TOP**
Tulle and pearl detail enhance this charming matching design.
Height: 3 in.
Base: 5 in. diameter
211-D-446 $7.50 each

3. **NEW** **HAPPINESS ORNAMENT**
Flowing wire frame and petite song birds celebrated with opulent plumage.
Height: 8 in.
Base: 4 in. diameter
103-D-452 $18.00 each

4. **NEW** **HAPPINESS RIBBON TIER TOP**
Ribbon and tulle accent the lush matching design.
Height: 3 in.
Base: 5 in. diameter
211-D-452 $7.00 each

5. **NEW** **LOVE BIRDS ORNAMENT**
Romantic wire birds accentuated with tulle and iridescent blooms.
Height: 7 in.
Base: 4 in. diameter
103-D-458 $16.00 each

6. **NEW** **LOVE BIRDS TIER TOP**
Ribbon edged tulle and a pair of lovebirds highlight the matching design.
Height: 2 $\frac{1}{2}$ in.
Base: 4 in. diameter
211-D-458 $7.50 each

7. **NEW** **FANCIFUL ORNAMENT**
Pearl beaded heart, pearl spray and abundant floral arrangements complement the lush ribbon edged tulle.
Height: 7 $\frac{1}{2}$ in.
Base: 4 in. diameter
103-D-464 $21.00 each

8. **NEW** **FANCY PEARL TIER TOP**
Pearl wisps, ribbon and tulle adorn the matching design.
Height: 3 in.
Base: 3 $\frac{1}{2}$ in. diameter
211-D-464 $7.00 each

9. **NEW** **ANGELINOS BLESSING ORNAMENT**
Ribbon edged tulle halos the angels on front and back.
Height: 6 $\frac{1}{2}$ in.
Base: 3 $\frac{1}{2}$ in. diameter
103-D-470 $16.00 each

10. **NEW** **ANGELINOS TIER TOP**
Double angels framed in ribbon edged tulle enrich the matching design.
Height: 4 in.
Base: 3 $\frac{1}{4}$ in. diameter
211-D-470 $7.50 each

NOTE: Prices and products offered in this Yearbook may not apply in Canada.

1.-4. NEW CRYSTALIQUE™ ACCESSORIES

Frosted crystal-look accents will add richness and beauty to so many cake styles. Two lovely holder styles let you add popular fresh flower treatments to your cake.

1. NEW CRYSTALIQUE™ FRESH FLOWER & CANDLE/COUPLE HOLDER

Your floral bouquet and candle or couple gain incredible beauty set against the cool texture of this crystal-look base.
Height: 5 ¼ in. Base: 2 in. diameter.
120-D-3303 $15.00 each

2. NEW CRYSTALIQUE™ RIBBON ARCH FRESH FLOWER HOLDER

Ribbon loops grace this beautifully frosted design and allow for fresh or silk flowers to cascade creating a beautiful cake top. The base is designed to set into the cake layer.
Height: 7 ½ in.
Base: 5 ½ in. diameter
113-D-3303 $15.00 each

3. NEW CRYSTALIQUE™ HEART DOVE PICK

Fluttering lovebirds carry dainty ribbon tendrils on our Crystalique heart.
Height: 6 ¼ in. Base: 3 ½ in. diameter
1001-D-3303 $5.00 each

4. NEW CRYSTALIQUE™ BUTTERFLY PICK

Openwork butterflies to soar above your cake. Wonderful accents for wedding, shower or anniversary cakes and toppers.
6 ¼ in. high x 3 ½ in. wide
1001-D-873 $5.00 pk. of 2

5. NEW MINI LIGHTS SET

Softly illuminate floral arrangements and ornaments. 10 bulbs on 20 in. long clear wire. Uses two AA batteries (not included).
1006-D-5 $6.99 set

6. NEW VICTORIAN MUSICAL WATER GLOBE ♪

Precious musical water globe adorned with a trellis of roses, ribbons and doves with floating glitter inside the globe. Plays "Here Comes The Bride".
Height: 6 in.
Base: 4 ½ in. diameter.
215-D-950 $45.00 each

Cake Ornaments

1. FOREVERMORE
Enchanting Art Plas couple adrift on a double-pleated ruffle which echoes the bride's rose motif. Graceful lucite-look backdrop carries a flowing floral arch with "pearl" loops.
Height: 10 $\frac{1}{2}$ in.
Base: 4 $\frac{3}{4}$ in. diameter.
Black Tux
110-D-860 $45.00 each
White Tux/Black Trousers
110-D-859 $45.00 each

2. RIBBON DELIGHT
Swells of shimmering satin-edged ribbon unfurl at the base and in a heart shape behind our blissful Art Plas couple. "Pearl"-trimmed satin bows complete the sparkling look.
Height: 10 in.
Base: 4 $\frac{1}{2}$ in. diameter.
Black Tux
110-D-932 $38.00 each

3. NEW BEGINNING
Intertwined "pearl" arch frames our glamorous Art Plas couple amidst sprays of tulle. Delicate flowers and "pearl" petals add a light and airy touch above a base encircled by a double ruffle and "pearl" band. An excellent value.
Height: 10 in.
Base: 4 $\frac{1}{2}$ x 6 in. oval.
Black Tux
110-D-858 $46.00 each

4. ROSE GARDEN
A glorious floral arch of roses, ribbons and "pearl" sprays frame a loving porcelain bisque couple.
Height: 11 in.
Base: 4 $\frac{1}{2}$ x 6 in. oval.
Black Tux
118-D-475 $75.00 each

5. BEAUTIFUL
Joyous porcelain bisque couple in a mist of tulle, "pearl" leaves, flowers and lace. On a base of leaves trimmed in "pearls".
Height: 7 $\frac{1}{2}$ in.
Base: 4 $\frac{1}{2}$ x 6 in. oval.
Black Tux
118-D-445 $70.00 each

6. TIMELESS
A radiant porcelain bisque couple under a lattice arch of "pearls". Adorned with lovely floral and "pearl" bursts on a lace and "pearl"-trimmed base.
Height: 10 in.
Base: 4 $\frac{1}{2}$ x 6 in. oval.
Black Tux
118-D-455 $75.00 each

Designer Series by

Ellen Williams

7. OUR DANCE
Graceful couple dances under an arched heart frame trimmed with lace. Floral blooms top the lace-edged base. Height: 9 1/4 in. Base: 4 1/2 x 6 in. oval.
Black Tux
118-D-650 $45.00 each

8. ROMANTIC MOMENTS
Lily of the valley spray cascading from an opulent pillar frames the dancing couple. Pearl loops, leaves and lace add the finishing touches. Height: 10 1/2 in. Base: 4 1/2 x 6 in. oval.
White Couple/Black Tux
118-D-651 $50.00 each

9. ALLURE
An enchanting gazebo wrapped with ivory tulle and prettied by a profusion of satin bows. White and ivory flowers enhance this lovely wedding setting. Exquisitely detailed Art Plas couples. Height: 11 in. Base: 5 in. diameter.
White Couple/Black Tux
101-D-1783 $45.00 each
Ethnic Couple/Black Tux
101-D-1785 $45.00 each

10. I DO
Double crystal-look hearts and bells highlighted with blossoms, satin ribbons, "pearls", ivory and white floral accents. Features painstakingly detailed Art Plas couples.
Height: 9 in. Base: 4 1/2 in. diameter.
Ethnic Couple/Black Tux
101-D-1781 $40.00 each
White Couple/Black Tux
101-D-1779 $40.00 each

11. GARDEN DELIGHT
Breathtaking spiral holds a topiary of blooms and long streamers of ribbons and "pearls" accenting lovely detailed Art Plas couples. Crystal-look backdrop adds drama to the scene.
Height: 10 in. Base: 4 3/4 in. diameter.
White Couple/Black Tux
101-D-1775 $42.00 each
Ethnic Couple/Black Tux
101-D-1777 $42.00 each

12. DEDICATION
A trio of chapel windows provides the inspiring backdrop for our magnificent Art Plas Our Day couple. Clusters of roses and bursts of tulle sweep above a band of openwork lace at the base.
Height: 7 in. Base: 4 1/2 x 6 in. oval.
Black Tux
101-D-150 $35.00 each

7.

8.

9.

10.

11.

12.

Cake Ornaments

Designer Series by
Ellen Williams

1. **NEW** PETITE COUNTRY & WESTERN
Whimsical representation of a country kind of love. Art Plas figurine accented with lace, fabric roses and lasso!
Height: 7 in.
Base: 5 in. diameter.
White Couple/ White Tux
104-D-112 $32.50 each

2-3. EXPRESSION OF LOVE
Our linked hearts float behind majestic Art Plas couples adrift in a trail of soft flowers and feather-edge ribbon. A "pearl"-trimmed lace band and ruffled lace at the base complete the romantic scene.
Height: 7 3/4 in.
Base: 4 1/2 in. diameter.
2. Ethnic Couple/Black Tux
101-D-933 $35.00 each
3. White Couple/Black Tux
101-D-931 $35.00 each

4. SWEETNESS
Entwined crystal-look hearts arise from a bounty of tulle surrounding our poised Art Plas couple. Tastefully trimmed with "pearl" accented satin bows, it's a fresh look at an outstanding value.
Height: 7 3/4 in.
Base: 4 1/2 in. diameter.
White Couple/Black Tux
101-D-153 $27.00 each

5. EVERLASTING
A dramatic "pearl"-trimmed gazebo is the setting for this dainty porcelain couple. Tulle sprays tied with ribbons and flowing lily of the valley.
Height: 11 1/2 in.
Base: 5 in. diameter.
Black Tux
118-D-505 $60.00 each

6. PETITE DELICATE JOY
Solitary petite porcelain bisque couple on a lacy ruffled base dotted with floral blooms and streamers.
Height: 6 in.
Base: 3 1/4 in. diameter.
Black Tux
108-D-645 $40.00 each

Designer Series by
Ellen Williams

7. PETITE ROMANCE
Petite couple stands atop a base beautifed with gathered bows and streamers of feather edge and smooth edge ribbon.
Height: 5 1/4 in. Base: 3 1/4 in. diameter.
White Couple/Black Tux
104-D-942 $18.00 each
White Couple/White Tux/White Trousers
104-D-941 $18.00 each

8. PETITE RIBBON DELIGHT
Shimmering satin-edged ribbon heart frames our petite Art Plas couple. Enhanced with ribbon and "pearl" trim.
Height: 7 1/4 in. Base: 3 1/4 in. diameter.
White Couple/Black Tux
104-D-934 $22.00 each
Ethnic Couple/Black Tux
104-D-936 $22.00 each

9. PETITE HEART OF FANCY
Lovely lacy heart crested with a lavish bow and "pearl" ring is a fine backdrop for our petite Art Plas couple.
Height: 7 in. Base: 3 1/4 in. diameter.
Black Tux   104-D-932 $24.00 each

10. PETITE LACE TRELLIS
Cameo-patterned lace arch encircles our petite couples. Lavishly adorned with ribbon bow and "pearl" trim.
Height: 7 1/2 in. Base: 3 1/4 in. diameter.
Ethnic Couple/Black Tux
104-D-940 $22.00 each
White Couple/Black Tux
104-D-938 $22.00 each

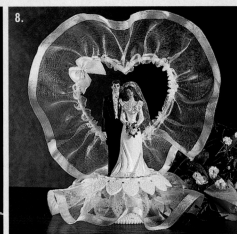

11. NATURAL BEAUTY
Lovebirds beneath filigree heart trimmed with lily of the valley and a smooth satin bow.
Height: 6 in. Base: 3 1/4 in. diameter.
White
106-D-1163 $11.00 each

12. PETITE BELLS OF JOY
Cluster of white filigree bells with fabric roses, lace-covered arches and tulle.
Height: 7 in. Base: 3 1/4 in. diameter.
White
106-D-2658 $14.00 each

13. LA BELLE PETITE
Tolling bell surrounded by tulle and flowers glimmers with iridescence.
Height: 5 1/2 in. Base: 3 1/4 in. diameter.
White
106-D-248 $10.00 each

14. PETITE SPRING SONG
A dainty song bird duet arched in flowers, "pearls" and tulle.
Height: 7 in. Base: 3 1/4 in. diameter.
White
106-D-159 $11.00 each

15. PETITE DOUBLE RING
Graceful doves land on simple wedding bands on heart base. Adorned with tulle puff.
Height: 5 1/2 in. Base: 3 1/4 in. diameter.
White
106-D-4316 $8.00 each

Cake Ornaments

Designer Series by
Ellen Williams

1. SIMPLE JOYS
A trio of blooming roses, exquisite lace and "pearl" wisps decorate this simply beautiful ornament. Glorified by interlocked crystal-look hearts.
Height: 8 in. Base: 4 1/2 in. diameter.
103-D-150 $22.00 each

2. OPULENCE
"Pearl"-adorned wedding bands shimmer on a base of "pearl" leaves and accordion-pleated lace.
Height: 6 1/2 in. Base: 4 1/2 in. diameter.
103-D-420 $40.00 each

3. TRUE LOVE
"Pearl"-embellished swooning doves rest on a pair of "pearl" studded wedding bands. Tufts of tulle and soft roses complete the vision.
Height: 8 1/2 in. Base: 4 5/8 in. diameter.
103-D-410 $40.00 each

4. CROWNING GLORY
Two fluttering doves alight on a lace and "pearl" trimmed heart and satiny bell. Lace also underscores the base.
Height: 9 1/2 in. Base: 4 5/8 in. diameter.
103-D-405 $40.00 each

5. INSPIRATION
The gilded cross is highlighted on a petal base flowing with tulle bursts. A soft bouquet of posies drapes cross and base.
Height: 6 1/2 in. Base: 3 1/4 in. diameter.
106-D-355 $18.00 each

6. MASTERPIECE
Ornately-trimmed bells toll out the happiest of wedding messages. Tied with ribbon and set in a lace-trimmed heart.
Height: 9 1/2 in. Base: 4 1/2 in. diameter.
Ivory **103-D-425 $40.00 each**
White **103-D-430 $40.00 each**

7. EXUBERANCE
Two graceful swans float on a lace-trimmed base. Both glide under a shower of flowing tulle and "pearl" decked buds.
Height: 7 in. Base: 4 7/8 in. diameter
103-D-440 $25.00 each

8. 25TH & 50TH ANNIVERSARY ORNAMENTS
Lovely mementos from the Designer Series by Ellen Williams.
Height: 6 in. Base: 3 1/4 in. diameter.
50th Gold 105 -D-4310 $35.00 each
Not shown , but also available:
25th Silver 105-D-4300 $35.00 each

NOTE: Prices and products offered in this Yearbook may not apply in Canada

Cake Ornaments

1. LUSTROUS LOVE
Bursts of tulle peek from behind lace leaves; dotted with forget-me-nots and rimmed with gleaming "pearls". Satiny roses bloom while "pearls" are suspended on transparent strings around the happy glazed porcelain couple.
Height: 8 in. Base: 4 $\frac{5}{8}$ in. diameter
White 117-D-621 $35.00 each

2. DEVOTION
Crystal-look arch is framed with gathered tulle and lace. Glazed porcelain couple stands on pedestal base in burst of tulle, blooms and "pearl" strands.
Height: 9 $\frac{1}{2}$ in. Base: 4 $\frac{3}{4}$ in. diameter.
White 117-D-425 $25.00 each

3. PROMISE
Simple beauty. Dramatic crystal-look heart frames dainty porcelain couple. Crystal-look base is covered with tulle, ribbons and fabric flowers.
Height: 9 $\frac{5}{8}$ in. Base: 4 $\frac{1}{2}$ in. diameter.
White 117-D-315 $25.00 each

4. REFLECTIONS
Sleek, streamlined and sophisticated. Dramatic crystal-look backdrop reflects porcelain couple, tulle burst, "pearl" sprays and florals.
Height: 8 in. Base: 4 $\frac{3}{4}$ in. diameter.
White 117-D-268 $25.00 each

5. ECSTASY
Sprays of flowers and leaves surround a romantic porcelain pair. Delicate tulle forms a lovely base.
Height: 9 $\frac{1}{2}$ in. Base: 4 $\frac{3}{4}$ in. diameter.
White 117-D-831 $42.50 each

6. GARDEN ROMANCE
Charming porcelain couple stands in a gazebo decked with flowery vines. Clusters of tulle and ribbons complete this romantic hideaway.
Height: 10 $\frac{1}{2}$ in. Base: 5 in. diameter.
White Iridescent 117-D-711 $44.00 each

7. SPLENDID
Sweeping crystal-look curve surrounds adoring glazed porcelain pair. Cylindrical vase holds a matching spray of flowers that accents base. Add real flowers if you wish.
Height: 10 $\frac{1}{2}$ in. Base: 4 $\frac{3}{4}$ in. diameter.
White 117-D-506 $28.00 each

Cake Ornaments

1. LACE CHARM
Luxuriant ruffled lace heart and base display the shimmering wedding bells. "Pearl" sprays and flowers add the final touches.
Height: 11 in.
Base: 4 3/4 in. diameter.
103-D-151 $32.00 each

2. SWEET CEREMONY
Seed pearl heart frames glitter bell accented with tulle. Bell surrounds our classic couple.
Height: 10 in.
Base: 4 5/8 in. diameter.
Black Coat
101-D-22011 $16.00 each

3. SPRING SONG
Perching lovebirds sing their romantic songs in a garden of posies and tulle.
Height: 9 1/2 in.
Base: 4 5/8 in. diameter.
111-D-2802 $20.00 each

4. CIRCLES OF LOVE
Symbolic double rings and doves in a hideaway of flowers and "pearl" sprays.
Height: 10 in.
Base: 4 5/8 in. diameter.
White
103-D-9004 $25.00 each

5. VICTORIAN CHARM
Graceful ribbon loops and fantasy florals layer over romantic satin five-bell cluster.
Height: 7 1/2 in.
Base: 4 1/2 in. diameter.
Ivory
103-D-1586 $23.00 each

6. HEARTS TAKE WING
Romantic beak-to-beak birds perched on a setting of heart-shaped branches and tulle.
Height: 10 1/2 in.
Base: 4 1/2 in. diameter.
103-D-6218 $14.00 each

NOTE: Prices and products offered in this Yearbook may not apply in Canada

Cake Ornaments

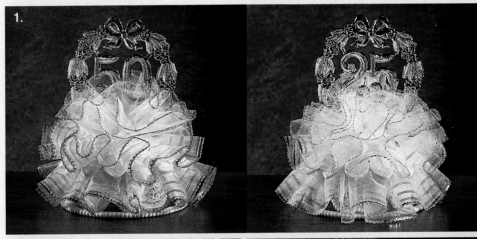

1. LOVE ENDURES
Celebrate the years gone by with an opulent burst of glitter-edged tulle and glimmering ribbon. Topped with the appropriate shimmering number.
Height: 7 1/2 in. Base: 4 5/8 in. diameter.
50th 102-D-151 $22.00 each
25th 102-D-150 $22.00 each

2. 25 OR 50 YEARS OF HAPPINESS
In gold or silver, the number tells the happy story. Accented with blooms and shimmering leaves.
Height: 10 in. Base: 4 5/8 in. diameter.
50th 102-D-223 $18.00 each
Not shown , but also available:
25th 102-D-207 $18.00 each

3. GOLDEN/SILVER JUBILEE
Celebrate the years with gold or silver flowers. Couple stands before numeral wreath of orchids, ferns and puffs of tulle.
Height: 8 1/2 in. Base: 4 5/8 in. diameter.
Silver 102-D-1225 $20.00 each
Not shown , but also available:
Gold 102-D-1250 $20.00 each

4. PETITE DOUBLE RING DEVOTION
Celebrating couple surrounded by rings and the shimmer of "pearls" and ferns.
Height: 5 in. Base: 3 1/4 in. diameter.
50th Gold 105-D-4605 $13.00 each
Not shown , but also available:
25th Silver 105-D-4613 $13.00 each

5. PETITE ANNIVERSARY YEARS
Beautiful blooms, leaves and sprays of tulle add appeal to this versatile favorite. Embossed wreath holds snap-on numbers to mark the milestones—5, 10, 15, 20, 40.
Height: 5 3/4 in. Base: 3 1/4 in. diameter.
105-D-4257 $9.00 each

6. PETITE ANNIVERSARY
Shining numeral wreath is highlighted by two fluttering doves.
Height: 5 1/2 in. Base: 3 1/4 in. diameter.
25th 105-D-4265 $7.00 each
Not shown , but also available:
50th 105-D-4273 $7.00 each

Designer Series by
Ellen Williams

7. JOYFUL DEBUT ORNAMENT WITH LA QUINCEAÑERA
Lavish lace, ribbon and "pearls" encircle the lovely young lady in celebration of her 15th birthday. Art Plas.
Height: 9 in. Base: 4 5/8 in. diameter.
203-D-306 $22.00 each

8. LA QUINCEAÑERA FIGURINE
Sweetly posed Art Plas figurine is a beautiful remembrance of her 15th birthday jubilee. Lovely bridesmaid as well.
Height: 4 1/2 in.
203-D-305 $3.50 each

Gifts & Accessories

On your special day, the details make all the difference. Loving Traditions™ perfects the little touches that make memories . . . a complete selection of lace-lavished keepsakes.

1. CAKE KNIFE & SERVER
Gleaming stainless with acrylic handles. Tied with sprays of flowers, ribbons and "pearls".
Cake Knife
120-D-704 $14.50 each
Cake Server
120-D-705 $14.50 each
2 Pc. Knife & Server Set
120-D-703 $26.00 set

2-3. 2 PC. FLUTED GLASSES SETS
Rosebud motif; trimmed with lace and ribbon. Spiral stem. 2 glasses per set. Height: 8 3/8 in.
2. Bride & Groom Set
120-D-708 $22.00 set
3. Anniversary Set
120-D-707 $22.00 set

4-5. 2 PC. TOASTING GLASSES SETS
Lillies of the valley design with satin ribbons. 2 glasses per set. Height: 4 1/2 in.
4. Bride & Groom Set
120-D-203 $16.00 set
5. Anniversary Set
120-D-205 $16.00 set

6. UNITY CANDLE
Intricately carved pastel candle features ring-bearing doves. 9 in. high x 2 3/4 in. diameter.
120-D-710 $17.50 each

7. NEW BOUQUET OF LACE UNITY CANDLE
Appliqués of lacy roses sparked with iridescence decorate this symbol of love. 9 in. high x 2 3/4 in. diameter.
120-D-711 $17.50 each

8. NEW VICTORIAN LACE UNITY CANDLE
Lace motif surrounds this eternal flame. 9 in. high x 2 3/4 in. diam.
120-D-712 $17.50 each

9. NEW 2 PC. VICTORIAN LACE TAPER CANDLE SET
10. in ivory candles punctuated with pearlized roses. Ideal for use with Candlelight cake stand, p. 158.
120-D-722 $2.50 set

10. PLUME PEN
A signature touch of romance.
120-D-804 $15.00 each

11. GUEST BOOK
An elegant keepsake engraved with gold-leaf lettering.
120-D-800 $14.00 each

12. BRIDE'S GARTERS
Lacy satin band trimmed with ribbons and "pearls", featuring a generous use of lace. Wide elastic band for comfort.
Blue   120-D-402 $5.50 each
Pink   120-D-400 $5.50 each
White 120-D-401 $5.50 each
Ivory   120-D-403 $5.50 each
Black 120-D-404 $5.50 each

13. RING BEARER'S PILLOWS
Satin handmade pillows trimmed with delicate lace, ribbon, and "pearls". Square pillows approximately 10 1/2 in.
Ribbon Square - White
120-D-104 $16.00 each
Ribbon Heart - White
120-D-100 $16.00 each
Lacy Square - Ivory
120-D-107 $20.00 each
Lacy Square - White
120-D-106 $20.00 each

Bomboniere!®
— Party Favors —

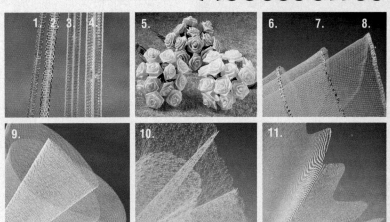

1-4. INSTANT BOW RIBBON
Woven-in pull strings help you create foolproof, perfectly-shaped iridescent bows. Each yard makes one bow.

1. 3/16 in. Gold   1003-D-3204 $6.99 10 yard spool
2. 5/16 in. White   1003-D-3240 $6.99 8 yard spool
3. 5/16 in. Pink   1003-D-3252 $6.99 8 yard spool
4. 5/16 in. Blue   1003-D-3246 $6.99 8 yard spool

5. RIBBON ROSES
Lifelike, beautiful blooms on wired stems are easy to insert in all styles of favors. Pretty on packages too!

Pink   1006-D-85   White 1006-D-84
Blue   1006-D-86   89¢ pk. of 12

TULLE CIRCLES
Sheer mesh fabric for elegant puffs and pleated bows. 9 in. diameter.

6-8. LUREX-EDGE TULLE CIRCLES
6. Silver   1005-D-22   7. Gold   1005-D-21
8. Iridescent   1005-D-20 $7.49 pk. of 12

9. WHITE TULLE CIRCLES
1005-D-1 $3.49 pk. of 25

10. LACE SCALLOPED-EDGE TULLE CIRCLES
White 1005-D-24 $5.39 pk. of 25

11. ORGANZA SCALLOPED-EDGE TULLE CIRCLES
White 1005-D-23 $5.39 pk. of 12

12. TUXEDO BOXES   4 in.   1006-D-48 $2.59 pk. of 2

13. TOP HAT AND CANE
1 in. hat; 4 in. long cane.   1006-D-11 $1.19 pk. of 2

14. FILIGREE HEART BOXES   2 1/4 in.   1006-D-21 $1.19 pk. of 4

15. ROUND BASKETS   3 in.   1006-D-113 $1.39 pk. of 4

16. FLOWER CARTS   4 1/2 in.   1006-D-24 $1.49 pk. of 2

17. PARTY PARASOLS   2 3/4 in.   1006-D-27 $1.79 pk. of 4

18. WEDDING COUPLE WITH GREY TUXEDO
1 7/8 in.   1006-D-14 $1.99 each

19. WEDDING COUPLE WITH BLACK TUXEDO
2 1/2 in.   1006-D-25 $1.99 each

20. LACE BONNET   4 1/4 in. wide.   1006-D-51 $2.39 each

21. SATIN HEART PILLOW   3 1/4 in.   1006-D-26 $1.89 pk. of 2

22. PEARL SWANS   3 in.   1006-D-108 $2.15 pk. of 4

23. CHAMPAGNE GLASSES   2 in.
Silver 1006-D-103 $1.49 pk. of 4
Clear 1006-D-105   85¢ pk. of 4

24. SILK-LOOK PURSE BOX   3 in. wide. 1006-D-47 $1.99 pk. of 2

25. SCALLOP SHELLS   2 in. high.   1006-D-28 $1.79 pk. of 4

26. DOVES ON STEM   1 1/4 in. wide. 1006-D-18   99¢ pk. of 6

27. HEART TAGS   3 1/2 x 1 in.   1006-D-44 $1.99 pk. of 2

28. ANNIVERSARY BANDS   3/4 in. diameter.
Gold 1006-D-19 55¢ pk. of 12   Silver 1006-D-20   55¢ pk. of 12
Gold 1006-D-100 $1.59 pk. of 48   Silver 1006-D-101 $1.59 pk. of 48

29. "PEARL" HEARTS   4 1/2 in.   1006-D-35 $1.49 pk. of 6

30. "PEARL" SPRAYS
4 sprays of 3; 5 1/4 in.   1006-D-31 $2.29 pk. of 12

31. STAMENS   3 in.   1006-D-30 $1.59 pk. of 12

Bomboniere!® products are both imported and made in the United States.

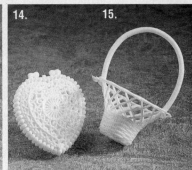

Wedding Figurines

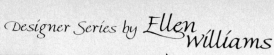
Designer Series by Ellen Williams

1. A DAY TO REMEMBER ♪
Revolving musical ornament plays "Waltz of the Flowers". Supremely detailed with floral embellishments. Height: 8 in. Base: 4 ½ in.
White Couple/Black Tux 215-D-410 $50.00 each

2. SWEET SYMPHONY* ♪
Musical plays "The Wedding March". Hand-painted, detailed Art Plas. Height: 7 ¾ in. Base: 3 ½ in. diam.
Black Tux 215-D-776 $50.00 each

3. NEW PETITE COUNTRY & WESTERN
Lighthearted tribute when country folk wed! Detailed and crafted in Art Plas. Height: 4 in.
214-D-1120 $10.00 each

4. LOVE'S DUET
Captivating detail enhances this elegant Art Plas figure. Height: 6 in.
Black Tux 202-D-402 $12.00 each
White Tux 202-D-403 $12.00 each

5. NEW ETHNIC LOVE'S DUET
Romantic ethnic Art Plas couple complements cake designs with grace and beauty. Height: 6 in.
Black Tux 202-D-412 $12.00 each

6. TOGETHER FOREVER*
Romantic porcelain couple in a traditional bridal pose. Height: 6 ½ in.
Black Tux/White Dress 214-D-415 $35.00 each

7. PETITE TOGETHER FOREVER*
Porcelain figure is perfect for cakes and table decoration. Height: 4 ½ in.
Black Tux 214-D-439 $30.00 each

8. FIRST DANCE
Beautifully defined and detailed enchanted Art Plas couple capture the moment of their first dance. Height: 6 in.
Black Tux 202-D-411 $15.00 each
White Tux 202-D-410 $15.00 each

9. OUR DAY
Adoring Art Plas bride and groom in a striking natural pose. Height: 4 ½ in.
Black Tux 202-D-409 $7.00 each

10. HAPPIEST DAY
Sweetly poised ethnic couple with life-like Art Plas bouquets and headpiece. Height: 4 ½ in.
Black Tux 202-D-306 $7.00 each
White Tux/White Trousers 202-D-305 $7.00 each

11. PETITE HAPPIEST DAY
Graceful ethnic Art Plas couple ideal for cakes and place settings. Height: 3 ½ in.
Black Tux 202-D-404 $6.00 each

12. LASTING LOVE
Lovely bride has a flowing tulle veil. Made of life-like Art Plas material. Height: 4 ½ in.
White Tux/White Trousers 202-D-303 $7.00 each
Black Tux 202-D-302 $7.00 each

13. PETITE LASTING LOVE
Our petite rendition with all the beautiful Art Plas detail intact. Height: 3 ½ in.
Black Tux 202-D-401 $6.00 each
White Tux/White Trousers 202-D-400 $6.00 each

15. DESIGNER BRIDESMAIDS
So many beautiful jewel and soft tones match
many color themes. Art Plas. Height: 4 ½ in.

NEW Ivory   203-D-9122
NEW Blush   203-D-9123
Black   203-D-9110
Raspberry (fuchsia)   203-D-9108
Dark Pink   203-D-9119
White   203-D-9111
Sapphire (dark blue)   203-D-9109
Emerald (dark green)   203-D-9104
Amethyst (purple)   203-D-9107
$4.50 pk. of 2

16. ETHNIC DESIGNER BRIDESMAIDS
Shades that will coordinate well with many
wedding color motifs. Art Plas. Height: 4 ½ in.

NEW Ivory   203-D-9120
NEW Blush   203-D-9121
White   203-D-9114
$4.50 pk. of 2

17. DESIGNER GROOMSMEN
Handsome groomsmen in attractive matte
finish. Art Plas. Height: 4 ½ in.
Black Tux   203-D-9101 $4.00 pk. of 2
White Coat 203-D-9100 $4.00 pk. of 2

18. ETHNIC DESIGNER GROOMSMEN
Groomsmen have the option of exactly
matching their tuxedo to that of the groom.
Art Plas. Height: 4 ½ in.
Black Tux   203-D-9116 $4.00 pk. of 2
White Coat 203-D-9117 $4.00 pk. of 2

19. RING BEARER
Charming young man carries a gold trimmed
pillow and shimmering rings. Highly detailed
cake decoration and keepsake. Height: 3 ¼ in.
203-D-7887 $4.00 each

20. FLOWER GIRL
Exquisitely detailed down to her shimmering
dress and floral basket. Perfect cake decoration
and memento of the occasion. Height: 3 ¼ in.
203-D-7879 $4.00 each

21. ANY ANNIVERSARY & 25TH DESIGNER COUPLE
Precious keepsakes from the Designer
Series by Ellen Williams. Height: 4 ½ in.
Any Anniversary Ivory
203-D-1850 $7.50 each
25th Silver 203-D-1825 $7.50 each

© 1991, 1992, 1995 EHW Enterprises, Inc.,
Licensee Wilton Enterprises

22. ANNIVERSARY COUPLE
Gold or silver gown. Plastic. Height: 3 ½ in.
50th Gold   203-D-1821 $4.00 each
25th Silver 203-D-2828 $4.00 each

23. STYLIZED COUPLE
Glazed porcelain couple. Height: 4 ⅝ in.
202-D-218 $16.00 each

24. LIBERATED BRIDE
A light-hearted approach! Plastic. Height: 4 ½ in.
2113-D-4188 $4.00 each

25. RELUCTANT GROOM
Don't let this one get away! Plastic. Height: 4 ½ in.
1316-D-9520 $5.00 each

26. CLASSIC COUPLE
Designed in plastic. Height: 4 ½ in.
Black Tux 202-D-8110 $4.70 each

149

Cake Accents & Accessories

1. 14 PC. ARCHED TIER SET
Quite dramatic when used with Kolor-Flo Fountain. Includes: Six 13 in. arched columns, two super strong 18 in. round Decorator Preferred Separator Plates and six angelic cherubs to attach to columns with royal icing or glue. See our Gazebo Cake Kit (page 152) that works beautifully with Arched Pillars.
301-D-1982 $49.00 set

Be prepared with replacement pieces for the Arched Tier Set:

18 in. Decorator Preferred Plate
302-D-18 $11.49 each

13 in. Arched Pillars
303-D-9719 $3.99 each

SAVE $4.95 on pack of six Arched Pillars.
301-D-9809 $19.99 pk. of 6

2. 6 PC. HARVEST CHERUB SEPARATOR SET
Includes four 7 in. Harvest Cherub pillars, two 9 in. separator plates (lower plate has 12 in. overall diameter).
301-D-3517 $11.99 set

3. DANCING CUPID PILLARS
This charming character is wonderful on wedding shower or Valentine cakes. 5 1/2 in. high.
303-D-1210 $7.99 pk. of 4

4. CHERUB SNAP-ONS
Accent 5 and 7 in. Grecian pillars. (Pillars not included.) 3 1/2 in. high.
305-D-4104 $1.29 pk. of 4

5. FROLICKING CHERUB
Animated character. 5 in. high.
1001-D-244 $2.79 each

6. ANGEL DUET
Fluttering fancies. A pair per package. 2 1/2 x 2 in.
1001-D-457 $1.90 pk. of 2

7. MUSICAL TRIO
Setting just the right mood. Each 3 in. high.
1001-D-368 $2.29 pk. of 3

8. KNEELING CHERUB FOUNTAIN
Beautiful when accented with tinted piping gel and flowers. 4 in. high.
1001-D-9380 $1.99 each

9. ANGELINOS
Heavenly addition to wedding, birthday and holiday cakes. 2 x 3 in.
1001-D-504 $3.29 pk. of 6

10. CHERUB CARD HOLDER
What neat place markers, too. (Cards not included.) 1 5/8 x 3 3/8 in.
1001-D-9374 $3.49 pk. of 4

11. HEAVENLY HARPISTS
Striking the perfect chord. 3 1/2 in. high.
1001-D-7029 $4.49 pk. of 4

NOTE: Prices and products offered in this Yearbook may not apply in Canada.

Cake Accents & Accessories

1. WHITE PEARL BEADING
With just one continuous row of lustrous pearls you can transform a beautiful cake into a glorious work of art. Stunning and easy to work with, these pearls are a must for all serious decorators. Molded on one continuous 5 yard strand, they can be easily cut to size.
To use: Work with long, continuous strands. Position before icing crusts. Trim after pearls are in position to insure exact measure. Do not trim smaller than 6 in. lengths. Remove pearls before cutting and serving cake.

Size	Stock No.	Price
6 mm	211-D-1990	$3.19 each
4 mm	211-D-1989	$2.69 each

2. FLORAL PUFF ACCENT
$5\frac{1}{2}$ in. tulle puff with soft flowers and "pearl" sprays.
White 211-D-1011 $4.00 each

3. PEARL LEAF PUFF
$5\frac{1}{2}$ in. tulle puff with "pearls".
White 211-D-1125 $4.69 each

4. KISSING LOVE BIRDS
Beak-to-beak romantics. $5\frac{1}{2}$ in. high
1002-D-206 $4.99 each

5. PETITE SONG BIRDS
A note of grace and poise. $2\frac{1}{4}$ in.
1316-D-1210 $2.99 pk. of 4

6. LOVE DOVES
Devoted duo provides the perfect finish. $4 \times 2\frac{3}{4}$ in.
1002-D-1806 $2.99 pk. of 2

7. SMALL DOVES
Elegant atop cakes or favors. $2 \times 1\frac{1}{2}$ in.
1002-D-1710 $1.99 pk. of 12

8. GLITTERED DOVES
$2 \times 1\frac{1}{2}$ in. Coated with non-edible glitter.
1006-D-166 $1.69 pk. of 12

9. FLOWER SPIKES
Fill with water, push into cake, add flowers. 3 in. high.
1008-D-408 $2.49 pk. of 12

10. ARTIFICIAL LEAVES
Green or white cloth; gold or silver foil. $1\frac{7}{8}$ in. and $1\frac{1}{4}$ in. sizes. (Add **1005-D-** prefix before number.)

Color	#Per pk.	$1\frac{7}{8}$" Stock #	Per pk.	$1\frac{1}{4}$" Stock #	Per pk.
Gold	144	6518	$3.49	6712	$2.99
Silver	144	6526	$3.49	6720	$2.99
Green	72	7555	$3.29	7570	$2.99
White	72	7565	$3.29	N/A	N/A

11. PEARL LEAVES $2\frac{1}{4}$ in. long.
211-D-1201 $2.99 pk. of 2

12. FILIGREE BELLS* Beautiful floral detail.

Height	Stock No.	Price	# Per Pk.
1 in.	1001-D-9447	$1.79	12
$1\frac{7}{8}$ in.	1001-D-9422	$1.79	6
$2\frac{1}{4}$ in.	1001-D-9439	$2.29	6

13. GLITTERED BELLS* A shimmering addition.

Height	Stock No.	Price	# Per Pk.
1 in.	1007-D-9061	$2.99	12
$1\frac{7}{8}$ in.	1007-D-9088	$2.49	6

14. OPENWORK BELLS* $1\frac{3}{4}$ in. high.
1006-D-10 $1.79 pk. of 6

15. WHITE FROSTED BELLS* $\frac{5}{8}$ in. high.
1006-D-36 $1.99 pk. of 6

* Ribbon not included.

CAUTION: Contains small parts. Not recommended for use by children 3 years and under

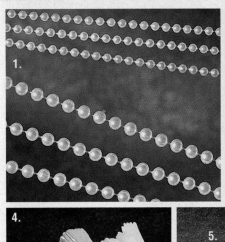

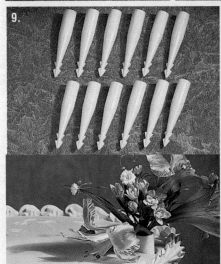

Cake Accents & Accessories

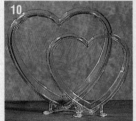

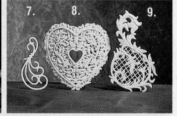

1. 20 PC. GAZEBO CAKE KIT
The delicate cuts and trellis-work openings of the twenty arch and trellis pieces in this kit are accomplished with a laser. The paper is coated and remarkably sturdy. Complete assembly instructions included. For use only with: two 10 in. Wilton Separator Plates and four 6 1/2 in. Wilton Arched Pillars (top layer); and two 18 in. Wilton Separator Plates and six 13 in. Wilton Arched Pillars (bottom layer). Pillars and plates sold separately (p.156-7).
2104-D-350 **$9.99 kit**

2. 10 PC. CATHEDRAL CAKE KIT
Includes: 5 easy-to-assemble white church pieces, 4 white plastic cake supports, a church window that can be illuminated from within.
2104-D-2940 **$15.99 kit**

3. CHAPEL WINDOWS
Refelective back window setting adds a glimmering effect. Use with Oval Base (shown below) or alone. Size: 6 1/2 x 5 x 1 in. deep.
205-D-3060 **$3.99 each**

4. GAZEBO SET 5 x 9 in. Easy to assemble.
205-D-8298 **$4.69 set**

5. SEED PEARL HEART 7 x 6 1/2 in.
205-D-1006 **$3.69 pk. of 3**

6. FILIGREE HEART FRAMES
7 x 6 1/2 in.   205-D-1501 **$2.69 pk. of 3**
4 x 4 in.   205-D-1527 **$1.69 pk. of 3**

7. SCROLLS 2 3/4 x 1 1/4 in.
1004-D-2801 **$2.29 pk. of 24**

8. LACY HEARTS 3 3/4 x 3 1/2 in.
1004-D-2306 **$2.49 pk. of 12**

9. FILIGREE SWIRLS 4 x 2 1/4 in.
1004-D-2100 **$2.49 pk. of 12**

10. CRYSTAL-LOOK HEARTS
5 1/2 in.   205-D-1674 **$1.99 each**
4 1/4 in.   205-D-1672 **$1.79 each**

11. DOUBLE WEDDING BANDS 3 1/2 in. diam.
201-D-1008 **$1.99 each**

12. CRYSTAL-LOOK BOWL
4 1/2 in. diameter, 1 1/2 in. deep.
205-D-1404 **$2.69 each**

13. IRIDESCENT GRAPES 2 x 2 in.
1099-D-200 **$3.79 pk. of 4**

14. IRIDESCENT DOVES 2 in. wide.
1002-D-509 **$3.49 pk. of 6**

15. CIRCLES OF LACE
Lacy alcove with tulle and a shimmery bell. Height: 10 in. Base: 4 5/8 in. diameter.
210-D-1986 **$10.00 each**

16. FLORAL ARCH
Botanical arch covered with gleaming flowers. Height: 10 in. Base: 4 5/8 in. diam.
210-D-1987 **$9.00 each**

17. ROMANTIC HEART BASE 2 pieces, 2 base sizes, both 1 1/2 in. high.
Base: 4 5/8 in. diameter.
201-D-7332 **$2.99 each**
Base: 3 1/4 in. diameter.
201-D-7847 **$2.69 each**

18. FLORAL BASE
White. Height: 1 1/2 in. Base: 4 7/8 in. diam.
201-D-1815 **$1.99 each**

19. CRYSTAL-LOOK BASE
Height: 1 3/4 in. Base: 4 1/2 in. diameter.
201-D-1450 **$2.99 each**

20. IVORY FLORAL SCROLL BASE
Height: 2 1/2 in. Base: 4 1/2 in. diameter.
White 201-D-1303 **$2.99 each**
Ivory 201-D-305 **$2.99 each**

21. OVAL BASE Bead border. 4 1/2 x 6 in.
201-D-420 **$2.99 each**

Cake Fountains & Stairways

1. THE KOLOR-FLO FOUNTAIN

Water pours from three levels. Remove top levels for smaller fountain arrangement. Intricate light system with two bulbs for extra brilliance. Use with 14 in. or larger plates, 13 in. or taller pillars for tallest cascade. Coordinates with our Crystal-Look Tier Set, p. 155. Plastic fountain bowl is 9 3/4 in. diameter. 110-124 V, AC motor with 65 in. cord. Pumps water electrically. Directions and replacement part information included.

306-D-2599 $109.99 each

Replacement Parts		
Pump	306-D-1002	$41.99 each
Piston	306-D-1029	$ 2.99 each
Pump/Bulb		
Bracket	306-D-1037	$ 3.99 each
Light Socket	306-D-1045	$ 4.99 each
Light Bulb	306-D-1053	$ 3.99 each
Cascade/Pump		
Connector	306-D-1088	$ 2.59 each
Floater Switch	306-D-1096	$13.99 each
Upper Cascade	306-D-1118	$ 6.99 each
Middle Cascade	306-D-1126	$ 7.99 each
Lower Cascade	306-D-1134	$ 9.99 each
Bowl	306-D-1142	$15.49 each
Bottom Base	306-D-1169	$12.49 each

FANCI FOUNTAIN (not shown)

This dramatic fountain electrically pumps water. Control ring adjusts fountain flow. Instructions included.

306-D-2000 $59.99 each

Fanci Fountain Replacement Parts		
Bulb	306-D-1790	$ 1.79 each
Cascade Set	306-D-1791	$ 9.99 each

2. 4 PC. FOUNTAIN CASCADE SET

Dome shapes redirect water over their surface in nonstop streams. Set includes 4 pieces: 2 1/2 in., 4 1/2 in., 8 in. and 11 1/2 in. diam. (Kolor-Flo Fountain sold separately).

306-D-1172 $14.99 set

3. FLOWER HOLDER RING

Put at base of Kolor-Flo Fountain. Size: 12 1/2 in. diam. x 2 in. high. Plastic.

305-D-435 $4.99 each

4. NEW FRESH FLOWER HOLDERS

Inserts easily under cake tiers to hold cascading blooms. greenery, pearl sprays, tulle puffs and more. Use with floral oasis to keep flowers looking fresh.

205-D-8500 $2.99 pk. of 2

5. 3 PC. CRYSTAL BRIDGE AND GRACEFUL STAIRWAY SET

Includes two stairways (16 3/4 in. long) and one platform (4 3/4 x 5 in.). Plastic.

205-D-2311 $14.99 set

ONE STAIRWAY ONLY

205-D-2315 $ 7.99 each

6. 3 PC. FILIGREE PLATFORM AND STAIRWAY SET

Bridge the gap between lavish tiers. Includes two stairways (16 1/4 in. long) and one platform (4 3/4 x 5 in.). Plastic.

205-D-2109 $11.99 set

ONE STAIRWAY ONLY

205-D-1218 $4.99 each

7. 24 PC. STAIRSTEPS SET

Twenty-four 1 in. high stairs snap together with 3 in. candleholders.

1107-D-8180 $5.49 set

8. SUPER STRONG CAKE STAND

Holds up to 185 pounds of cake! High impact polystyrene and underweb of ribbing make stand super strong. Height: 2 3/4 in. Diameter: 18 in., to accommodate larger cakes.

307-D-1200 $14.99 each

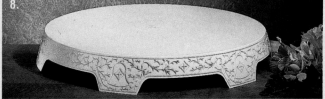

Wedding Cake Stands

1. GARDEN CAKE STAND
An elegant way to present your cake. Its dramatic scrolls and rich wrought-iron look are inspired by the revival in metalwork —a style that's particularly lovely surrounded by greenery. Fast and easy to use—simply place cakes on plates and set on the stand. Painted metal stand is 23 in. high x 22 in. wide and uses any standard 10 in., 14 in. and 18 in. separator plates. Satellite garden cake stands sold individually below.
307-D-860 $149.99 each
SATELLITE GARDEN CAKE STAND
Painted metal stand coordinates with garden cake stand above. Holds a 12 in. separator plate. Sold individually.
307-D-861 $40.00 each
Separator Plates sold separately on page 157.

2. NEW CANDLELIGHT CAKE STAND
Updated look emphasizes swirls of beautiful scrollwork and hearts. Now reinforced with a crossbar for more support. Sturdy enameled metal design holds up to 40 lbs. Ideal for 3 stacked tiers supported by a 14 in. separator plate. Stand is 21 1/2 in. diam. (13 1/4 in. center cake area) x 5 in. high and uses standard 7/8 in. candles. Our taper candle set, shown on p. 146, is a perfect complement to this stand. (Plates and candles not included.)
307-D-871 $35.00 each

3. 4 PC. FLOATING TIERS CAKE STAND SET
Display three tiers on this graceful metal cake stand. Fast and easy to use! Set includes 17 in. high stand and 8 in., 12 in. and 16 in. smooth separator plates and instructions.
307-D-825 $64.99 set
Additional plates available.
(Same plates as Crystal-Clear Cake Divider Set).

Plate	Number	Price
8 in.	302-D-9749	$3.99 each
12 in.	302-D-9765	$6.99 each
16 in.	302-D-9780	$10.99 each

4. 30 PC. CRYSTAL-CLEAR CAKE DIVIDER SET
Plastic separator plates 1/2 in. diameter x 7 1/2 in. high. Clear plastic twist legs penetrate cake and rest on plate (dowel rods not needed). Includes 6 in., 8 in., 10 in., 12 in., 14 in. and 16 in. plates plus 24 legs.

SAVE 25% ON SET   301-D-9450 $47.99 set
Additional plates available.

Plate	Number	Price
6 in.	302-D-9730	$2.99 each
8 in.	302-D-9749	$3.99 each
10 in.	302-D-9757	$4.99 each
12 in.	302-D-9765	$6.99 each
14 in.	302-D-9773	$8.99 each
16 in.	302-D-9780	$10.99 each

7 1/2 IN. TWIST LEGS 303-D-9794 $3.99 pk. of 4
9 IN. TWIST LEGS Add more height. **303-D-977 $3.99 pk. of 4**

5. 13 PC. TALL TIER STAND SET
Five twist-apart columns 6 1/2 in. high with 1 bottom and 1 top bolt; 18 in. footed base plate; 8 in., 10 in., 12 in., 14 in. and 16 in. separator plates (interchangeable, except footed base plate). Plastic.

SAVE 25% ON SET   304-D-7915 $45.99 set
Additional plates and columns available.

Plate	Number	Price
8 in.	302-D-7894	$3.99 each
10 in.	302-D-7908	$4.99 each
12 in.	302-D-7924	$5.99 each
14 in.	302-D-7940	$8.99 each
16 in.	302-D-7967	$11.99 each
18 in.	302-D-7983	$14.99 each

Column	Number	Price
6 1/2 in.	303-D-7910	$1.59 each
7 3/4 in.	304-D-5009	$2.59 each
13 1/2 in.	303-D-703	$4.49 each

TOP COLUMN CAP NUT   304-D-7923 79¢ each
GLUE-ON PLATE LEGS   304-D-7930 59¢ each
BOTTOM COLUMN BOLT   304-D-7941 99¢ each

6. TALL TIER 4-ARM BASE STAND
Replace Tall Tier Base Plate (see No. 5) with this heavy-duty plastic support; add separator plates up to 12 in. For proper balance, add up to 3 graduated tiers to center column. Includes base bolt.
304-D-8245 $11.99 each
BASE BOLT ONLY 304-D-8253 59¢ each

7. CAKE CORER TUBE
Prepare tiers quickly and neatly for the Tall Tier Stand column. Serrated edge removes cake centers with one push. Ice cake before using. 7 in. long solid center fits into 6 1/2 in. long hollow corer to eject cake bits. Cleans easily.
304-D-8172 $1.99 each

1. 54-PC. GRECIAN PILLAR AND PLATE SET

A deluxe money-saving collection for the serious cake decorator. Decorator Preferred scalloped-edge separator plates and 5 in. pillars. Includes: two each 6 in., 8 in., 10 in., 12 in. and 14 in. plates; 20 Grecian pillars and 24 pegs.

SAVE 22% ON SET
301-D-8380 **$45.99 set**

2. 8 PC. SIX-COLUMN TIER SET

Includes six 13 ³/₄ in. Roman columns and two super strong 18-in. round Decorator Preferred Separator Plates. A lovely set to use with the Kolor-Flo Fountain (sold on p. 153). Plastic.
301-D-1981 **$34.99 set**

3. 14 PC. ARCHED TIER SET

Quite dramatic when used with Kolor-Flo Fountain. (sold on p. 153) Includes: Six 13 in. arched columns, two super strong 18 in. round Decorator Preferred Separator Plates and six angelic cherubs to attach to columns with royal icing or glue. Recommended for use with Gazebo Wedding Cake Kit (sold on p. 152).
301-D-1982 **$49.00 set**

4. 6 PC. CRYSTAL-LOOK TIER SET

The ideal style and height to work with the Kolor-Flo Fountain and a beautiful way to present any tiered cake. Plastic set includes two 17 in. plates; four 13 ³/₄ in. pillars.
301-D-1387 **$41.99 set**

5. 6 PC. HARVEST CHERUB SEPARATOR SET

An idyllic setting for a most romantic cake. Pillars simply snap on to plates for strong support. Set includes four 7 in. Harvest Cherub pillars and two 9 in. separator plates (lower plate has 12 in. overall diameter).
301-D-3517 **$11.99 set**

6. 10 PC. CLASSIC SEPARATOR SETS

Stately Grecian pillars and scalloped-edge plates create beautiful settings for all tiered cakes. Sets include 2 Decorator Preferred Plates, 4 pillars and 4 pegs.

6 IN. PLATE SET; 3 IN. PILLARS
2103-D-639 **$6.49 set**

8 IN. PLATE SET; 5 IN. PILLARS
2103-D-256 **$7.49 set**

10 IN. PLATE SET; 5 IN. PILLARS
2103-D-108 **$9.49 set**

12 IN. PLATE SET; 5 IN. PILLARS
2103-D-124 **$11.49 set**

CRYSTAL SEPARATOR SET (not shown)

Unique crystal-look set adds height and sparkling illusion to cakes. Each set includes 2 plates and 4 contoured crystal pillars.

7 IN. PLATE SET; 3 IN. PILLARS
301-D-1507 **$10.49 set**

9 IN. PLATE SET; 5 IN. PILLARS
301-D-1509 **$13.49 set**

11 IN. PLATE SET; 5 IN. PILLARS
301-D-1511 **$16.49 set**

13 IN. PLATE SET; 7 IN. PILLARS
301-D-1513 **$19.99 set**

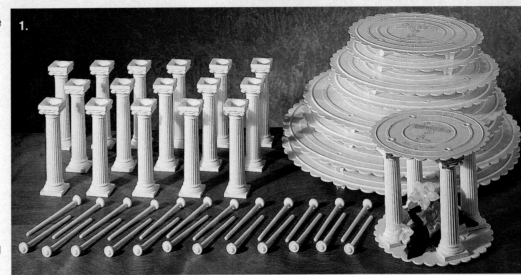

Pillars & Dowels

1. GRECIAN PILLARS
Elegantly scrolled and ribbed.
3 in. 303-D-3606 $2.09 pk. of 4
5 in. 303-D-3703 $3.19 pk. of 4
7 in. 303-D-3705 $4.19 pk. of 4

2. GRECIAN SPIKED PILLARS
Eliminates need for separator plates on cake tier tops. Push into cake to rest on separator plate or cake circle beneath. Wide diameter bottom for increased stability.
5 in. 303-D-3708 $2.09 pk. of 4
7 in. 303-D-3710 $3.19 pk. of 4
9 in. 303-D-3712 $4.19 pk. of 4

3. CRYSTAL-LOOK SPIKED PILLARS
Push into cake to rest on separator plate or cake circle beneath. Double cake circles for extra support.
7 in. 303-D-2322 $4.19 pk. of 4
9 in. 303-D-2324 $5.19 pk. of 4

4. DISPOSABLE PILLARS WITH RINGS
7 IN. PILLARS WITH RINGS
303-D-4000 $2.79 pk. of 8 (4 each)
9 IN. PILLARS WITH RINGS
303-D-4001 $2.87 pk. of 8 (4 each)

5. "HIDDEN" PILLARS
Designed to separate cake tiers slightly and create a floating illusion—adapted from the English method of cake decorating. Pushed into cake tiers as dowel rods, hidden pillars fit onto all white separator plates except Tall Tier. Trimmable, hollow plastic.
6 in. 303-D-8 $1.99 pk. of 4

6. LATTICE COLUMNS
Flattering garden-inspired designs.
3 in.   303-D-2131 $2.49 pk. of 4
5 in.   303-D-2151 $3.49 pk. of 4
13 in. 303-D-2113 $3.49 each

7. ARCHED PILLARS
Grecian-inspired with arched support.
4 $1/2$ in. 303-D-452 $2.99 pk. of 4
6 $1/2$ in. 303-D-657 $4.99 pk. of 4
13 in.   301-D-9809 $19.99 pk. of 6

8. ROMAN COLUMNS
Handsome pillars may be used with Kolor-Flo Fountain.
10 $1/4$ in. 303-D-8135 $2.59 each
13 $3/4$ in. 303-D-2129 $2.99 each

9. CRYSTAL-LOOK PILLARS
Combine with crystal-look plates and Crystal Bridge and Stairway Set.
3 in.   303-D-2171 $3.19 pk. of 4
5 in.   303-D-2196 $4.19 pk. of 4
7 in.   303-D-2197 $4.69 pk. of 4
*13 $3/4$ in. 303-D-2242 $3.99 each
*(Use only with 17 in. crystal plate sold on p. 157.)

10. SWAN PILLARS
Grecian pillars with romantic swan bases add grace to your masterpiece. Height: 4 in.
303-D-7725 $2.99 pk. of 4

11. SNAP-ON CHERUB
Accent 5, 7 in. Grecian pillars. 3 $1/2$ in. high.
305-D-4104 $1.29 pk. of 4

12. DANCING CUPID PILLARS
Wedding shower, Valentine cakes. 5 $1/2$ in. high.
303-D-1210 $7.99 pk. of 4

13. PLASTIC DOWEL RODS
Heavy-duty hollow plastic provides strong, sanitary support for all tiered cakes. Can be cut with serrated knife to desired length. Length: 12 $3/4$ in. Diameter: $3/4$ in.
399-D-801 $2.29 pk. of 4

14. WOODEN DOWEL RODS
Cut and sharpen with strong shears and knife. Length: 12 in. Diameter: $1/2$ in.
399-D-1009 $2.99 pk. of 12

15. PLASTIC PEGS
Insure that cake layers and separator plates atop cakes stay in place. These pegs do not add support, so dowel rod cake properly before using. Length: 4 in.
399-D-762 $1.44 pk. of 12

1. **GUARANTEED NON-BREAKABLE!**

Decorator Preferred®

- *Guaranteed Non-Breakable*
- *Circles of Strength Construction*
- *Lovely Scalloped Edges*
- *Easy Size Identification*
- *Smooth Back*

1. DECORATOR PREFERRED® SEPARATOR PLATES

Our best, strongest separator plates with the strength and beauty serious cake decorators require.

6 in.	302-D-6	$ 2.09 each
7 in.	302-D-7	$ 2.29 each
8 in.	302-D-8	$ 2.59 each
9 in.	302-D-9	$ 3.19 each
10 in.	302-D-10	$ 3.59 each
11 in.	302-D-11	$ 4.19 each
12 in.	302-D-12	$ 4.69 each
13 in.	302-D-13	$ 5.49 each
14 in.	302-D-14	$ 5.79 each
15 in.	302-D-15	$ 6.99 each
16 in.	302-D-16	$ 7.79 each
18 in.	302-D-18	$11.49 each

BAKER'S BEST®

2. DISPOSABLE SINGLE PLATES

Baker's Best® Disposable Separator Plates are the perfect option for busy decorators. Use these sturdy plates with pillars and adjustable pillar rings sold on page 156. All are made of recyclable plastic.

6 in. Plate	302-D-4000	$1.49 each
7 in. Plate	302-D-4001	$1.69 each
8 in. Plate	302-D-4002	$1.99 each
9 in. Plate	302-D-4003	$2.49 each
10 in. Plate	302-D-4004	$2.89 each
12 in. Plate	302-D-4006	$3.79 each
14 in. Plate	302-D-4008	$4.89 each

3. CRYSTAL-LOOK PLATES

Use with crystal-look pillars sold on p. 156.

7 in.	302-D-2013	$ 3.49 each
9 in.	302-D-2035	$ 4.49 each
11 in.	302-D-2051	$ 5.99 each
13 in.	302-D-2078	$ 7.49 each
*17 in.	302-D-1810	$14.49 each

*(Use only with 13 3/4 in. crystal pillars)

4. HEART SEPARATOR PLATES

8 in.	302-D-2112	$2.99 each
11 in.	302-D-2114	$3.99 each
14 1/2 in.	302-D-2116	$7.99 each
16 1/2 in.	302-D-2118	$8.99 each

5. OVAL SEPARATOR PLATES

8 1/2 x 6 in.	302-D-2130	$3.99 each
11 1/2 x 8 1/2 in.	302-D-2131	$4.99 each
14 1/2 x 8 1/2 in.	302-D-2132	$5.99 each

6. SQUARE SEPARATOR PLATES

7 in.	302-D-1004	$2.99 each
9 in.	302-D-1020	$3.99 each
11 in.	302-D-1047	$4.99 each
13 in.	302-D-1063	$5.99 each

7. HEXAGON SEPARATOR PLATES

7 in.	302-D-1705	$2.99 each
10 in.	302-D-1748	$3.99 each
13 in.	302-D-1764	$5.99 each
16 in.	302-D-1799	$7.99 each

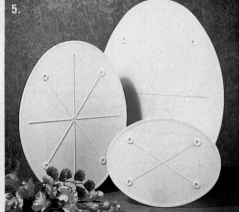

Fresh Flowers & Accessories

THE MAGIC OF CANDLELIGHT

Unforgettable – your wedding cake basking in the glow of our updated candlelight cake stand. Redesigned for a more romantic look, with an abundance of graceful scrollwork that works beautifully with arrangements of flowers and greenery. Our new wire lace collection of accents perfectly complements this beautifully scrolled stand...delicate openwork designs to enhance any wedding cake.

1. NEW CANDLELIGHT CAKE STAND
Updated look emphasizes swirls of beautiful scrollwork. Now reinforced with a crossbar for more support. Sturdy enameled metal design holds up to 40 lbs. Ideal for 3 stacked tiers supported by a 14 in. separator plate. Stand is 21 1/2 in. diam. (13 1/4 in. center cake area) x 5 in. high and uses standard 7/8 in. candles. Ideal for use with our Victorian Lace Taper Candles shown on p. 146. (Plates and candles not included).
307-D-871 **$35.00 each**

2. NEW FRESH FLOWER HOLDERS
Insert between tiers to hold cascading blooms, greenery, pearl sprays, tulle puffs and more. Use with flower oasis (not included). 2 1/4 in. high with 1 1/4 in. well.
205-D-8500 **$2.99 pk. of 2**

3. NEW WIRE LACE SEPARATOR
Flowing filigree design gracefully separates wedding tiers. 2 in. high; 6 1/2 in. diameter.
303-D-870 **$6.00 each**

4. NEW WIRE LACE UNITY CANDLE HOLDER
Openwork lace design holds candles up to 3 1/2 in. wide. 1 1/2 in. high.
120-D-870 **$3.50 each**

5. NEW MINI LIGHTS
Softly illuminate floral arrangements, pillars and wedding ornaments. 10 bulbs on 20 in. long clear wire. Uses two AA batteries (not included)
1006-D-5 **$6.99 each**

6. NEW WIRE LACE HEART PICK
Interwoven lilies and heart design enhances floral arrangements. 3 1/2 in. high with 3 1/2 in. pick stem.
1001-D-870 **$2.99 each**

7. NEW WIRE LACE LOVEBIRDS PICK
Intricate flowing lines complement cake design. 3 1/2 in. high with 3 1/2 in. pick stem.
1001-D-872 **$2.99 each**

8. NEW WIRE LACE BELL PICK
Free-hanging bell adds a distinctive touch. 4 in. high with 1 3/4 in. stem.
1001-D-871 **$2.99 each**

NOTE: Prices and products offered in this Yearbook may not apply in Canada.

1. RUFFLE BOARDS®
Ready to use, it's a cake board and ruffle in one. The Ruffle Board® line features bleached white cake boards with all-white ruffling already attached.

8 in. (for 6 in. round cake)	415-D-950	$2.29 each
10 in. (for 8 in. round cake)	415-D-960	$2.79 each
12 in. (for 10 in. round cake)	415-D-970	$3.29 each
14 in. (for 12 in. round cake)	415-D-980	$3.79 each
16 in. (for 14 in. round cake)	415-D-990	$4.69 each
18 in. (for 16 in. round cake)	415-D-1000	$6.29 each

2. SHOW 'N SERVE CAKE BOARDS
Scalloped edge. Food-safe, grease-resistant coating.

8 in.	2104-D-1125	$3.99 pk. of 10
10 in.	2104-D-1168	$4.49 pk. of 10
12 in.	2104-D-1176	$4.99 pk. of 8
14 in.	2104-D-1184	$5.49 pk. of 6
14 x 20 in. Rectangle	2104-D-1230	$5.99 pk. of 6

3. CAKE CIRCLES & BOARDS Corrugated cardboard.

6 in. diameter	2104-D-64	$2.99 pk. of 10
8 in. diameter	2104-D-80	$3.99 pk. of 12
10 in. diameter	2104-D-102	$4.99 pk. of 12
12 in. diameter	2104-D-129	$4.99 pk. of 8
14 in. diameter	2104-D-145	$4.99 pk. of 6
16 in. diameter	2104-D-160	$5.99 pk. of 6
10 x 14 in.	2104-D-554	$4.49 pk. of 6
13 x 19 in.	2104-D-552	$4.99 pk. of 6

4. TUK-N-RUFFLE
Attach to serving tray or board with royal icing or tape.
60 ft. Bolt

Pink	802-D-702	$14.99 per bolt
Blue	802-D-206	$14.99 per bolt
White	802-D-1008	$14.99 per bolt
6 ft. Package-White	802-D-1991	$2.99 each

DOILIES
Greaseproof quality makes a flawless presentation. Round and rectangular shapes have lace borders sized to fit around your decorated cakes.

5. GOLD DOILIES

4 in. Round	2104-D-90104	$2.49 pk. of 24
8 in. Round	2104-D-90012	$2.49 pk. of 12
10 in. Round	2104-D-90013	$2.49 pk. of 6
12 in. Round	2104-D-90014	$2.49 pk. of 4
10 x 14 in. Rec.	2104-D-90015	$2.49 pk. of 4

6. SILVER DOILIES

4 in. Round	2104-D-90114	$2.49 pk. of 24
8 in. Round	2104-D-90006	$2.49 pk. of 12
10 in. Round	2104-D-90007	$2.49 pk. of 6
12 in. Round	2104-D-90008	$2.49 pk. of 4
10 x 14 in. Rec.	2104-D-90009	$2.49 pk. of 4

7. WHITE DOILIES

4 in. Round	2104-D-89997	$1.99 pk. of 40
5 in. Round	2104-D-89998	$1.99 pk. of 36
6 in. Round	2104-D-89999	$1.99 pk. of 28
8 in. Round	2104-D-90004	$1.99 pk. of 16
10 in. Round	2104-D-90000	$1.99 pk. of 12
12 in. Round	2104-D-90001	$1.99 pk. of 8
14 in. Round	2104-D-90002	$1.99 pk. of 8
10 x 14 in. Rec.	2104-D-90003	$1.99 pk. of 8

8. FANCI-FOIL WRAP
Serving side has a non-toxic grease-resistant surface. FDA approved for use with food.
Continuous roll: 20 in. x 15 ft. **$7.99 each**

Rose	804-D-124	White	804-D-191
Gold	804-D-183	Silver	804-D-167

PARCHMENT
Non-stick parchment lines pans, prevents sticking and withstands temperatures to 400°F.

9. RECTANGLES
Fits 9 x 13 in. pans (actual size 8 7/8 x 12 3/4 in.)
415-D-998 $2.49 pk. of 15
Fits 11 x 15 in. pans (actual size 10 7/8 x 14 3/4 in.)
415-D-999 $2.49 pk. of 15

10. PARCHMENT ROLL
Professional grade, silicone-treated parchment. Oven safe to 450°F, great in microwaves, too. Double roll contains 41 sq. feet. (15 in. x 33 ft.)
415-D-680 $4.99 roll

11. SELECT-A-SIZE PARCHMENT CIRCLES
One sheet that helps you cut the exact size you need to line your pan — pre-marked circles can fit round pans from 6 to 12 in. Non-stick paper for easy release; oven-safe to 400°F.
415-D-994 $3.99 pk. of 20

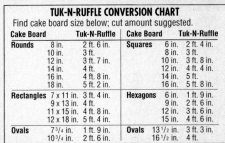

All white board . . . no brown edges!

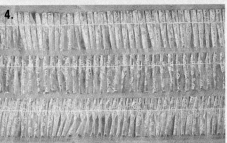

TUK-N-RUFFLE CONVERSION CHART
Find cake board size below; cut amount suggested.

Cake Board		Tuk-N-Ruffle	Cake Board		Tuk-N-Ruffle
Rounds	8 in.	2 ft. 6 in.	Squares	6 in.	2 ft. 4 in.
	10 in.	3 ft.		8 in.	3 ft.
	12 in.	3 ft. 7 in.		10 in.	3 ft. 8 in.
	14 in.	4 ft.		12 in.	4 ft. 4 in.
	16 in.	4 ft. 8 in.		14 in.	5 ft.
	18 in.	5 ft. 2 in.		16 in.	5 ft. 8 in.
Rectangles	7 x 11 in.	3 ft. 4 in.	Hexagons	6 in.	1 ft. 9 in.
	9 x 13 in.	4 ft.		9 in.	2 ft. 6 in.
	11 x 15 in.	4 ft. 8 in.		12 in.	4 ft. 6 in.
	12 x 18 in.	5 ft. 8 in.		15 in.	5 ft. 6 in.
Ovals	7 3/4 in.	1 ft. 9 in.	Ovals	13 1/2 in.	3 ft. 3 in.
	10 3/4 in.	2 ft. 6 in.		16 1/2 in.	4 ft.

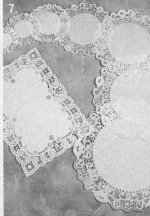

Baking Tools & Accessories

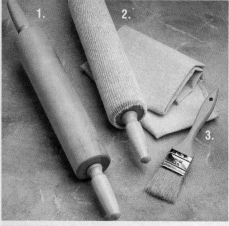

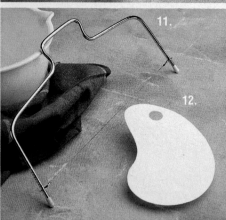

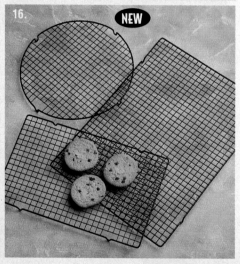

1. ROLLING PIN
Durable, non-absorbent rock maple with easy rolling nylon bearings. 10 x 2 1/2 in.
417-D-36 $12.99 each

2. 2 PC. PASTRY CLOTH/ROLLING PIN COVER SET
Canvas cloths promote even rolling without sticking.
417-D-42 $4.99 set

3. PASTRY BRUSH
Soft, natural bristles leave no marks when brushing liquids and glazes. 1 1/2 in.
417-D-54 $2.99 each

4. 2 1/2 CUP LIQUID MEASURING CUP
Dishwasher and microwave safe, with easy-to-read measurements.
417-D-174 $3.99 each

5-6. STAINLESS STEEL WHISKS
Long, solid handle provides control, 8 flexible wires make whipping easy.
5. 12 in. 417-D-78 $6.99 each
6. 10 in. 417-D-72 $5.99 each

7. 3 CUP STAINLESS STEEL SIFTER
Easy trigger-action and triple-mesh design provide fast, efficient sifting.
417-D-84 $7.99 each

8. STAINLESS STEEL SUGAR/FLOUR SHAKER
Well-perforated cap evenly covers baked goods. Holds 6 oz. or 3/4 cup.
417-D-120 $7.49 each

9. COOKIE SCOOP
Spring-action stainless steel scoop quickly forms and releases perfect portion of cookie dough. Scoop holds 1 oz.
417-D-150 $9.99 each

10. 3 PC. MIXING BOWL SET
1 1/2 qt., 2 qt. and 3 qt. bowls with clearly marked measurements and easy-grip handles. Bottom rubber ring prevents slipping.
417-D-168 $14.99 set

11. CAKE LEVELER
Levels, tortes cakes to 10 in. wide x 2 in. high.
415-D-815 $2.99 each

12. SPATCH-IT SCRAPER
Gets to the bottom of the bowl. 6 1/2 x 4 in.
417-D-90 99¢ each

13. DECORATING TRIANGLE
Each side adds a different contoured effect to icing; easy to hold and use. 5 x 5 in. plastic.
417-D-162 99¢ each

14. DECORATING COMB
Easy-to-use tool forms ridges in icing for an elegantly finished cake. 12 x 1 1/2 in., plastic.
417-D-156 $1.29 each

LARGE CAKES NEED OUR COOLING GRIDS!
Versatile grids handle tiers, character and sheet cakes up to 12 x18 in. Tightly woven grids mean even the smallest cookies won't fall through; prevents cracking of crusts. Heavy-gauge chrome-plated steel protects countertops and tables from heat, while providing even support. Easy-cleaning non-stick also available.

15. CHROME-PLATED STEEL GRIDS
10 x 16 in.	2305-D-128	$4.99 each
14 1/2 x 20 in.	2305-D-129	$7.99 each
13 in. Round	2305-D-130	$6.49 each
3 Pc. Stackable	2305-D-151	$10.99 each

16. NON-STICK STEEL GRIDS
10 x 16 in.	2305-D-228	$7.99 each
14 1/2 x 20 in.	2305-D-229	$11.99 each
NEW 13 in. Round	2305-D-230	$7.99 each

NOTE: Prices and products offered in this Yearbook may not apply in Canada.

Wilton Tier Pan Sets keep your decorating options open! Use them together to create a high-rise masterpiece, or on their own for smaller celebrations. Durable anodized aluminum pans resist chipping and flaking and are dishwasher safe. To beautifully showcase your tiered cakes, see our selection of cake stands on page 154.

1. 4 PC. 2 IN. DEEP ROUND PAN SET
Set includes 6, 8, 10, 12 in. aluminum pans.
2105-D-2101 $24.99 set

2. 4 PC. 3 IN. DEEP ROUND PAN SET
Set includes 8, 10, 12, 14 in. aluminum pans.
2105-D-2932 $34.99 set

3. 4 PC. OVAL PAN SET
Set includes four 2 in. deep aluminum pans. Sizes are 7 3/4 x 5 5/8 in.; 10 3/4 x 7 7/8 in.; 13 x 9 7/8 in.; 16 x 12 3/8 in.
2105-D-2130 $27.99 set

4. 4 PC. HEXAGON PAN SET
Set includes 6, 9, 12, 15 in. aluminum pans, 2 in. deep.
2105-D-3572 $30.99 set

5. 4 PC. PETAL PAN SET
A pretty shape that's popular for showers, weddings and anniversaries. Set includes 6, 9, 12 and 15 in. 2 in. deep aluminum pans.
2105-D-2134 $29.99 set

12 in. only 2105-D-5117 $8.99 each

6. 4 PC. HEART PAN SET
Celebrate showers, weddings and more with the ultimate heart-shaped cake. Set includes 6, 9, 12 and 14 1/2 in. diameter aluminum pans. 2 in. deep.
2105-D-2131 $29.99 set

INDIVIDUAL PANS AVAILABLE
6 in.	2105-D-4781	$4.99 each
9 in.	2105-D-5176	$6.99 each
12 in.	2105-D-5168	$8.99 each

PROFESSIONAL-QUALITY desserts and cakes begin with the finest bakeware. Ovencraft™ Bakeware is the professional's choice—every pan is built to the highest standards for consistent, superior baking results.

— **EXTRA-THICK ALUMINUM** means Ovencraft™ pans provide the best heat distribution and will never warp. Compare these pans to ordinary bakeware and you'll see why Ovencraft™ pans can last for a lifetime.

— **DESIGNED FOR PRECISION**: each pan with special features which enhance its performance. Extra depth versus ordinary bakeware to reduce overflow...perfectly straight sides and 90° corners on squares and sheets for exact results...welded corners for strength.

— **A PROFESSIONAL FINISH.** Quality aluminum will not rust, discolor, chip or peel—it's the best finish for your baked goods. Cleans easily, releases food quickly and evenly.

OVENCRAFT™
Professional Bakeware

2 IN. DEEP ROUND PANS
Ideal for two-layer cakes and tier cakes.
6 in.	2105-D-5601	$5.49 each
8 in.	2105-D-5602	$5.99 each
9 in.	2105-D-5619	$6.99 each
10 in.	2105-D-5603	$7.49 each
12 in.	2105-D-5604	$10.99 each
14 in.	2105-D-5605	$13.99 each
16 in.	2105-D-5606	$16.99 each

3 IN. DEEP ROUND PANS
Bake beautiful, tall cakes.
6 in.	2105-D-5620	$5.99 each
8 in.	2105-D-5607	$6.99 each
10 in.	2105-D-5608	$8.99 each
12 in.	2105-D-5609	$11.99 each
14 in.	2105-D-5610	$14.99 each

3 IN. DEEP HALF-ROUND PAN
Use to bake an 18 in. round cake in conventional size oven.
18 in. 2105-D-5622 $14.99 each

SQUARE PANS
Perfectly square corners and 2 3/16 inch depth produce professional quality cakes.
8 in.	2105-D-5611	$8.99 each
10 in.	2105-D-5612	$12.99 each
12 in.	2105-D-5613	$15.99 each
14 in.	2105-D-5614	$19.99 each

SHEET PANS
Endless options with this multi-use shape. Perfectly square corners. 2 3/16 in. deep.

9 x 13 in.
2105-D-5616 $13.99 each
11 x 15 in.
2105-D-5617 $16.99 each
12 x 18 in.
2105-D-5618 $19.99 each

Non-Stick

Excelle®
PREMIUM NON-STICK BAKEWARE

- **DOUBLE NON-STICK COATING**
- **HEAVY GAUGE STEEL CONSTRUCTION**
- **QUICK, EVEN HEATING**
- **RECIPE ON EVERY LABEL**

Two layers of non-stick coating make Excelle® Bakeware superior. The double coated surface has a slicker feel than other non-stick bakeware – meaning food release is easy and clean-up is a breeze. Excelle® Bakeware also feels heftier – its heavy-gauge steel construction assures more durable performance and a longer life. And Excelle® Bakeware is designed to conduct heat quickly and effectively, without burning your baked goods. You'll love the results from the complete Excelle® line!

NEW MUFFIN CAPS & MUNCHIES (not shown)
Bake the best part – the tops! Muffin Caps Pan has 6 cups, each $3\frac{1}{2}$ x $\frac{1}{2}$ in. Muffin Munchies Pan has 24 cups, each 2 x $\frac{5}{8}$ in.

Muffin Caps®	2105-D-124	$10.99 each
Muffin Munchies®	2105-D-125	$10.99 each

NEW MINI FLUTED MOLD (not shown)
4 cups, each 4 in. diameter x $2\frac{1}{4}$ in.

	2105-D-126	$14.99 each

ROUND CAKE PAN

$8\frac{7}{8}$ x $1\frac{3}{8}$ in.	2105-D-102	$6.99 each
NEW 2 Pc. Set	2105-D-127	$10.99 set

SHEET PAN

9 x 13 x 2 in.	2105-D-103	$10.99 each
NEW 7 x 11 x 2 in.	2105-D-128	$8.49 each

COOKIE PANS

$10\frac{1}{4}$ x $15\frac{1}{4}$ x $\frac{7}{8}$ in.	2105-D-100	$10.99 each
$11\frac{1}{4}$ x $17\frac{1}{4}$ x $\frac{7}{8}$ in.	2105-D-101	$11.99 each

2 PC. SHEET PAN WITH COVER SET
See-thru cover helps desserts arrive fresh and protected! 9 x 13 x 2 in. (3 in. deep with cover.)

	2105-D-118	$13.99 set

BROILER PAN

9 x 13 x 2 in.	2105-D-116	$15.99 each

2 PC. ROASTING PAN WITH NON-STICK RACK SET

9 x 13 x 2 in.	2105-D-117	$15.99 set

MUFFIN PANS

12 Cup Mini	2105-D-113	$7.99 each
12 Cup Standard	2105-D-105	$11.99 each
6 Cup Standard	2105-D-109	$9.99 each

SQUARE CAKE PAN

$8\frac{1}{2}$ x $8\frac{1}{2}$ in.	2105-D-108	$7.99 each

FLUTED MOLD PAN

9 in.	2105-D-111	$11.99 each

2 PC. ANGEL FOOD PAN

10 in.	2105-D-115	$13.99 each

MINI ANGEL FOOD PAN (not shown)
4 cups, each 4 in. diameter x $2\frac{1}{2}$ in.

	2105-D-121	$14.99 each

SPRINGFORM PAN WITH SERVING TRAY
(not shown) Bake and serve elegantly in one pan.

9 x 3 in.	2105-D-123	$19.99 each

2 PC. SPRINGFORM PANS
Waffle-texture bottom supports heavy cakes!

6 x 3 in.	2105-D-106	$8.99 each
9 x 3 in.	2105-D-107	$11.99 each

PIE PAN

9 in.	2105-D-119	$4.99 each

LOAF PAN

9 x 5 x $2\frac{1}{2}$ in.	2105-D-104	$6.99 each

MINI LOAF PAN (not shown)
Great gift breads; pâtés. 4 cups, each $4\frac{1}{2}$ x $2\frac{1}{2}$ in.

	2105-D-120	$14.99 each

2 PC. MEAT LOAF PAN WITH DRIP RACK SET

9 x 5 x $3\frac{7}{8}$ in.	2105-D-114	$14.99 set

PIZZA PAN

12 in. diameter	2105-D-110	$9.99 each

ONE MIX HEART PAN (not shown)

9 in. x 2 in. deep	2105-D-122	$9.99 each

POPOVER MUFFIN PAN (not shown)
6 cups, each 3 in. diameter x $2\frac{1}{2}$ in.

	2105-D-112	$13.99 each

Even-Bake®

INSULATED BAKEWARE BROWNS WITHOUT BURNING!

Quality that can be warranted for life – Even-Bake® Insulated Bakeware promises years of baking excellence and uniform browning. The difference is an insulating layer of air between two sheets of high-quality aluminum. The bottom layer protects the top from the intense heat of your oven.

- **UNIFORM BAKING**
- **IMMERSIBLE AND DISHWASHER SAFE**
- **EASY GRIP LIP**

1. ROUND PAN
9 x 1 7/8 in.
2105-D-2666   **$14.49 each**

2. COOKIE SHEETS
13 x 17 x 1/4 in.
2105-D-2644   **$14.99 each**
10 1/4 x 15 1/2 x 1/4 in.
2105-D-2646   **$12.99 each**

3. 2 PC. SHEET PAN WITH COVER SET
See-thru cover helps desserts arrive fresh!
9 x 13 x 2 in.
2105-D-2667   **$20.99 set**

4. 2 PC. JELLY ROLL PAN WITH COVER SET
See-thru cover helps protect desserts!
10 1/2 x 15 1/2 x 1 1/8 in.
2105-D-2620   **$22.99 set**

Bake loaves of every size and style with the great selection of Wilton loaf pans. Crusty breads, meat loaves, individual fruit breads perfect for giving — Wilton quality aluminum loaf pans let you do it all.

5. PETITE LOAF PAN
Create individual bread loaves for each of your guests. Great for single-size dessert cakes, frozen bread dough. Nine cavities are 2 1/4 x 3 3/8 x 1 1/2 in. each. Aluminum .
2105-D-8466   **$9.99 each**

6. MINI LOAF PAN
Great for individual-sized nut breads, cakes. Six individual loaves are 4 1/2 x 2 1/2 in. x 1 1/2 in. deep. Aluminum.
2105-D-9791   **$9.99 each**

7. 9 x 5 IN. LOAF PAN
Favorite size for homemade breads and cakes. 2 3/4 in. deep. Aluminum.
2105-D-3688   **$5.99 each**

8. LONG LOAF PAN
Bake classic cakes or angel food delights. Legs provide proper support for cooling angel food cakes. 16 x 4 x 4 1/2 in. deep. Aluminum.
2105-D-1588   **$11.99 each**

NOTE: Prices and products offered in this Yearbook may not apply in Canada.

Insulated Pans

Loaf Pans

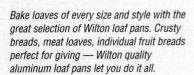

Performance Pans®

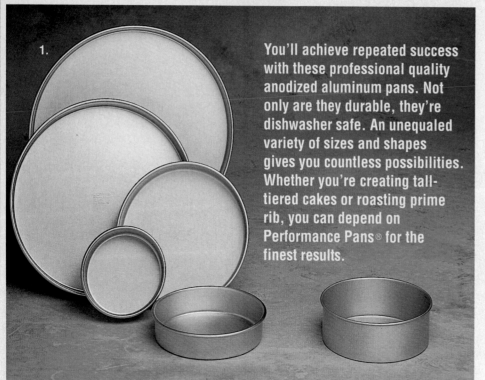

You'll achieve repeated success with these professional quality anodized aluminum pans. Not only are they durable, they're dishwasher safe. An unequaled variety of sizes and shapes gives you countless possibilities. Whether you're creating tall-tiered cakes or roasting prime rib, you can depend on Performance Pans® for the finest results.

1. ROUND PANS 2 IN. DEEP

Bake everything from a cake for two to a wedding cake for hundreds in these quality pans. Aluminum.

6 in.	2105-D-2185	$5.49 each
7 in.	2105-D-2190	$5.99 each
8 in.	2105-D-2193	$6.49 each
10 in.	2105-D-2207	$7.49 each
12 in.	2105-D-2215	$9.99 each
14 in.	2105-D-3947	$12.99 each
16 in.	2105-D-3963	$15.99 each
9 in.		
2-Pan Set	2105-D-7908	$10.99 set

ROUND PANS 3 IN. DEEP

Bake impressive high cakes. Perfect for tortes, fruit and pound cakes and cakes to be covered with fondant icing. Aluminum.

8 in.	2105-D-9104	$6.99 each
10 in.	2105-D-9945	$8.99 each

2. SHEET PANS 2 IN. DEEP

A priceless collection for any baker or cook. These pans will be in constant use for everything from special occasion cakes to holiday dinners. The versatility and high quality of these pans make them invaluable for any kitchen. Aluminum.

7 x 11 in.	2105-D-2304	$6.99 each
9 x 13 in.	2105-D-1308	$8.99 each
11 x 15 in.	2105-D-158	$13.49 each
12 x 18 in.	2105-D-182	$15.49 each

3. SQUARE PANS 2 IN. DEEP

The shape that offers an extensive variety of baking and cooking options. Can be used in cake designs from simple to fancy. A great collection to have close at hand. Aluminum.

6 in.	507-D-2180	$4.99 each
8 in.	2105-D-8191	$6.99 each
10 in.	2105-D-8205	$8.99 each
12 in.	2105-D-8213	$11.99 each
14 in.	2105-D-8220	$15.99 each
16 in.	2105-D-8231	$17.99 each

4. 9 X 13 IN. CAKE COVER

Just the protection you need when transporting decorated cakes and desserts. Plastic raised dome lid keeps cakes and other foods fresh in the pan, even after slicing.
415-D-903 $4.49 each

5. CAKE SAVER - 2 PIECE SET

Designed to carry most elaborately decorated cakes. Generous size accommodates borders and top decorations easily. Use to carry or store all types of cakes, including fancy ring, angel food, cheese cakes, even pies, as well as layer cakes. Maintains freshness. Wide enough for a 10 in. cake with borders or a 12 in. cake without borders. Includes one 14 in. round base and one 6 in. high cover.
415-D-905 $11.99 set

6. BAKE-EVEN STRIPS SETS

An innovative way to bake perfectly level, moist cakes. Avoid high-rise centers, cracked tops or crusty edges. Just dampen strips and wrap around the pan before baking. Each band is 1 1/2 in. wide x 30 in. long, with 1 in. overlap.

2 PC. SMALL SET

Contains 2 bands, enough for two 8 or 9 in. round pans.
415-D-260 $6.99 set

4 PC. LARGE SET

Contains 4 bands, enough for one of each of the following: 10, 12, 14 and 16 in. round pans.
415-D-262 $14.99 set

NOTE: Prices and products offered in this Yearbook may not apply in Canada.

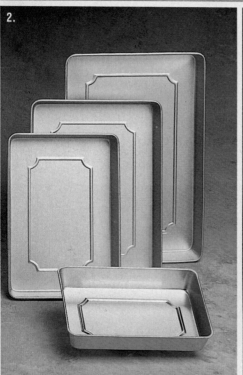

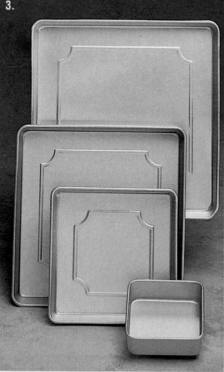

1. MUFFIN CAPS® PAN
Makes only the best part of the muffin – the chewy top! Great for brownies, ice cream sandwiches, too! 6 cups, each $3\frac{1}{2}$ in. x $\frac{1}{2}$ in. Pan is $12\frac{1}{2}$ x $8\frac{1}{4}$ x $\frac{1}{2}$ in. Aluminum.
2105-D-2106 $9.99 each

2. MUFFIN MUNCHIES® PAN
Great muffin-top texture in a small size. Perfect for lunchboxes, afterschool snacks or brunch buffets. 24 cups, each 2 in. x $\frac{5}{8}$ in. Pan is 15 x $9\frac{3}{4}$ x $\frac{5}{8}$ in. Aluminum.
2105-D-2124 $9.99 each

3. MINI MUFFIN PANS
Great size for brunches or large gatherings! Create muffins, cheesecakes, cupcakes and more in these even-baking pans. Convenient 24 cup size makes dozens in minutes. Cups are 2 in. x $\frac{3}{4}$ in. Aluminum.
12 Cup ($7\frac{3}{4}$ x 10 x $\frac{3}{4}$ in.)
2105-D-2125 $7.99 each
24 Cup ($17\frac{1}{2}$ x $11\frac{1}{2}$ x $\frac{3}{4}$ in.)
2105-D-9313 $15.99 each

4. STANDARD MUFFIN PANS
Most popular size for morning muffins, after-school cupcakes and desserts. 12 Cup size can serve an entire brunch or birthday party. Cups are 3 in. diameter x 1 in. Aluminum.
6 Cup ($7\frac{3}{8}$ x $10\frac{3}{4}$ x 1 in.)
2105-D-5338 $7.99 each
12 Cup ($16\frac{1}{2}$ x $12\frac{7}{8}$ x $1\frac{1}{8}$ in.)
2105-D-9310 $14.99 each

5. JUMBO MUFFIN PAN
Bake super-size cupcakes and muffins! Pan is $13\frac{1}{2}$ x $9\frac{1}{4}$ x 2 in. Cups are 4 in. x 2 in. Aluminum.
2105-D-1820 $15.99 each

6. MINI SHELL PAN
Six single-serving shells create graceful filled cakes, molded candies and salads. A wonderful shower shape. One mix bakes 15-20 cakes. Pan is $8\frac{1}{2}$ x 14 x $1\frac{1}{2}$ in., each shell is $3\frac{3}{4}$ x $3\frac{1}{4}$ x $\frac{3}{4}$. Aluminum.
2105-D-4396 $10.99 each

7. SHELL PAN
Simple elegance — for cakes, gelatins or molded salads. A pan you'll reach for occasion after occasion. Pan is $11\frac{1}{2}$ x $12\frac{1}{4}$ x 2 in. Aluminum.
2105-D-8250 $9.99 each

8. 2 PC. 4 IN. DEEP SPRINGFORM PAN
Create extra-tall, professional-looking cheesecakes and molded desserts with this deep-sided pan. Waffle-textured bottom adds support and reduces sticking. Springlock releases sides for easy removal. Aluminum.
8 in. 2105-D-8040 $11.99 each

9. 2 PC. NON-STICK HEART SPRINGFORM
Serve the classic Valentine cheesecake with this lovely heart-shaped pan. Waffle-textured bottom adds support and reduces sticking. Springlock releases sides for easy removal. 3 in. deep.
9 in. Heart 2105-D-2122 $9.99 each

10. 2 PC. NON-STICK SPRINGFORM PANS
Quality non-stick finish on heavy-gauge steel. Waffle-textured bottom adds support and reduces sticking. Even heating. Springlock releases sides for easy removal. 3 in. deep.
6 in. 2105-D-218 $7.99 each
9 in. 2105-D-219 $10.99 each

11. 2 PC. SPRINGFORM PANS
Waffle-textured bottom adds support and reduces sticking. Even heating. Springlock releases sides for easy removal. 3 in. deep. Aluminum.

6 in.	2105-D-4437	$8.99 each
8 in.	2105-D-8464	$9.99 each
9 in.	2105-D-5354	$10.99 each
10 in.	2105-D-8465	$11.99 each

Bakes Just The Top!

Bakes Just The Top!

Basic Pans

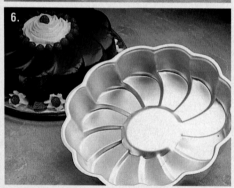

1. FANCY RING MOLD PAN
Beautiful bundt-style pan, ideal for pound cakes, mousse and more! Takes one standard bundt-type mix. 10 x 3 in. Aluminum.
2105-D-5008 $9.99 each

2. PETITE FANCY RING MOLD PAN
Serve impressive desserts in dramatic individual servings. 6 cups, each 4 x 1 1/2 in. One mix makes 12 cakes. Aluminum.
2105-D-2097 $17.99 each

3. RING MOLD PAN
Turn out spectacular cakes, gelatin molds and more. 10 1/2 x 3 in. Aluminum.
2105-D-4013 $8.99 each

4. 2 PC. ANGEL FOOD PAN SET
Banana bread or chiffon cakes also turn out beautifully. Removable inner core sleeve. Cooling legs. 7 in. size pan is 7 in.x 4 1/2 in. and holds 1/2 standard mix. 10 in pan is standard mix size; 10 x 4 in. Aluminum .
7 in.   2105-D-9311 $9.99 set
10 in.   2105-D-2525 $13.99 set

5. MINI ANGEL FOOD PAN
Versatile pan makes four elegant individual dessert cakes at a time. Also excellent for quick breads, chiffon cakes and gelatin molds. Individual cakes are 4 in. x 2 3/4 in. Aluminum.
2105-D-9312 $14.99 each

6. VIENNESE SWIRL PAN
The foundation for elegant continental style desserts. One mix pan is 11 1/2 in. x 1 7/8 in. Aluminum.
2105-D-8252 $9.99 each

7. 2 PC. COVERED SHEET PAN SET
Clear, durable cover makes transporting desserts easy, keeps baked goods fresh. Quality pans provide excellent baking results. Aluminum .
9 x 13 x 2 in.
2105-D-3850 $13.99 set
11 x 15 x 2 in.
2105-D-3849 $16.99 set

8. JELLY ROLL/COOKIE PANS
Two sizes come in handy for bar cookies, jelly rolls and more. Aluminum.
10 1/2 x 15 1/2 x 1 in.
2105-D-1269 $9.99 each
12 x 18 x 1 in.
2105-D-4854 $11.99 each

9. COOKIE SHEETS
Easy-to-handle, even-browning sheets in two convenient sizes. Aluminum.
10 x 15 in.
2105-D-1265 $6.99 each
12 1/2 x 16 1/2 in.
2105-D-2975 $10.99 each

10. PIZZA PAN
Unique perforated waffle surface allows heat to penetrate and moisture to escape, resulting in light and crispy crust. 14 1/2 in. diameter fits pizzas up to 12 inches diameter. Aluminum.
2105-D-3901 $11.99 each

1. JUNGLE LION PAN
This king of beasts tastefully reigns over every celebration! One-mix pan is 13 x 11 1/2 x 2 in. Aluminum.
2105-D-2095 $9.99 each

2. MINI JUNGLE ANIMALS PAN
Make treats kids go wild for! One cake mix will make 20-24 mini lions and giraffes. 6 cup pan is 10 1/2 x 14 in.; cups are 3 3/4 x 4 1/2 x 1 1/4 in. Aluminum.
2105-D-2096 $10.99 each

3. DALMATIAN PAN
Man's best friend celebrates birthdays and parties all-year-long. One-mix pan is 14 x 10 x 2 in. Aluminum.
2105-D-9334 $9.99 each

4. CUTE CLOWN PAN
Create a cake that will bring a circus of smiles to every celebration. One-mix pan is 15 x 10 3/4 x 2 in. Aluminum.
2105-D-6711 $9.99 each

5. ROCKING HORSE PAN
A Wild West carnival or Christmas-time are just a couple of the themes to give this lovable cake. It's a winner for birthdays and baby showers. One-mix aluminum pan is 13 1/2 x 13 1/2 x 2 in.
2105-D-2388 $9.99 each

6. KITTY CAT PAN
Immortalize this most popular house pet in buttercream. Create sleek or long-haired breeds. One-mix pan is 9 x 15 x 2 in. Aluminum.
2105-D-1009 $9.99 each

7. DOUBLE-TIER ROUND PAN
Create two classic tiers – 6 and 10 inch cakes. A year-round party pleaser. One-mix pan is 9 3/4 x 3 in. Aluminum.
2105-D-1400 $9.99 each

8. CAROUSEL HORSE PAN
Center of attention at baby showers, children's birthdays and more. One-mix pan is 14 x 13 x 1 7/8 in. Aluminum.
2105-D-6507 $9.99 each

Novelty Pans

These anodized aluminum pans keep every detail of your cake intact. Aluminum is the best heat conductor, so cakes release easily and brown perfectly. For a foolproof way to remove a cake from the pan, see page 90.

1. MINI DINOSAUR PAN
Earth-shaking fun in individual servings. One cake mix makes 12-15 prehistoric treats. Aluminum pan is 13 3/4 x 10 1/2 x 1 1/8 in. and has six individual cakes approximately 4 x 3 x 1 in. each.
2105-D-9331 $10.99 each

2. PARTYSAURUS PAN
Our prehistoric party animal is a must-have at all sorts of fun fests. One-mix aluminum pan is 16 x 10 x 1 7/8 in.
2105-D-1280 $9.99 each

3. MINI BALLOON PAN
Create a bright bunch of balloons for birthday fun! There are more great decorating ideas on the label. One mix makes about 12-15 balloons. Aluminum pan is 11 1/4 x 8 3/4 x 1 3/8 in. and has six individual cakes 3 x 3 1/2 x 1 3/4 in. each.
2105-D-2024 $10.99 each

4. LITTLE FIRE TRUCK PAN
Make any occasion a five-alarm success – birthdays, school parties, even a retirement party. One-mix aluminum pan is 16 x 9 1/8 x 2 in.
2105-D-9110 $9.99 each

5. BOOK PAN
This open book details every one of life's important chapters- birthdays, baby showers, graduations and much more. Five ways to decorate included. One-mix aluminum pan is 13 x 9 1/2 x 2 in.
2105-D-972 $9.99 each

6. TWO-MIX BOOK PAN
This great volume serves up to 30 guests. The story unfolds as the crowd gathers to celebrate any occasion. Aluminum pan is 11 1/2 x 15 x 2 3/4 in.
2105-D-2521 $12.99 each

7. CUTE BABY PAN
A bundle of joy for showers, birth announcement celebrations, first birthdays and more. One-mix aluminum pan is 16 1/4 x 9 3/4 x 2 in.
2105-D-8461 $9.99 each

8. HORSESHOE PAN
Say "good luck" for graduations, birthdays, bon voyage! One-mix aluminum pan is 12 x 1 3/4 in.
2105-D-3254 $9.99 each

NOTE: Prices and products offered in this Yearbook may not apply in Canada.

1. HOME RUN HITTER PAN
Celebrate opening day, birthdays, special occasions, the World Series! One-mix aluminum pan is 15 x 10$\frac{1}{4}$ x 1$\frac{7}{8}$ in.
2105-D-2020 $9.99 each

2. 4 PC. SPORTS BALL PAN SET
Have a ball with this multi-use pan. Set includes two 6-in. diameter half ball aluminum pans and two metal baking stands. Each pan half takes 2$\frac{1}{2}$ cups batter.
2105-D-6506 $9.99 set

3. MINI BALL PAN
These little treats are perfect in any championship season. Ice mini-balls and push together for a 3-D effect. One cake mix will make 12 to 15 balls. Aluminum pan is 11$\frac{1}{2}$ x 7$\frac{1}{2}$ x 1$\frac{1}{2}$ in.
2105-D-1760 $10.99 each

4. BASEBALL GLOVE PAN
The home team will love this mitt that can be customized with name and team colors. One-mix aluminum pan is 12 x 12$\frac{1}{4}$ x 1$\frac{3}{4}$ in.
2105-D-1234 $9.99 each

5. FIRST AND TEN FOOTBALL PAN
Perfect for Super Bowl parties, homecomings, award dinners and much more. One-mix aluminum pan is 12 x 7$\frac{3}{4}$ x 3 in.
2105-D-6504 $9.99 each

6. LITTLE TRAIN PAN
The little birthday and all-occasion train packs a cargo-load of fun for party guests and the guest of honor. One-mix aluminum pan is 8$\frac{3}{4}$ x 15$\frac{3}{4}$ x 2 in.
2105-D-6500 $9.99 each

7. 2 PC. CHOO CHOO TRAIN PAN SET
Here's the little 3-D engine that could – pulling through with a trainload of uses. Two-part aluminum pan snaps together. Pan is 10 x 6 x 4 in. Takes 6 cups of firm-textured batter.
2105-D-2861 $10.99 set

8. MINI LOCOMOTIVE PAN
All aboard! One cake mix will make 14-16 single-serving mini locomotives. Six cavity aluminum pan is 13$\frac{3}{4}$ x 10$\frac{1}{2}$ x 1$\frac{3}{4}$ in.
2105-D-9332 $10.99 each

Novelty Pans

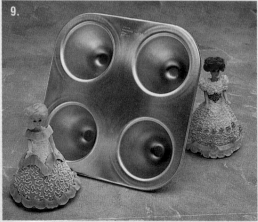

1. OVER THE HILL TOMBSTONE PAN
Optimistically mark the passing of one more year. One-mix aluminum pan is 13 x 9 1/4 x 2 in.
2105-D-1237 $9.99 each

2. WESTERN BOOT PAN
Have a boot-scooting, stomping good time! One-mix aluminum pan is 12 x 10 3/4 x 2 in.
2105-D-1238 $9.99 each

3. GRADUATE PAN
Make the grade with a successful celebration. One mix aluminum pan is 14 1/2 x 8 3/4 x 2 in.
2105-D-1800 $9.99 each

4. MINI EMBOSSED HEART PAN
Profess adoration in so many ways! One cake mix makes 20-24 mini hearts. 6 cavity aluminum pan is 10 x 14 in.; individual cakes are 3 1/2 x 3 1/2 x 1 in. deep.
2105-D-8255 $10.99 each

5. 10 PC. NUMBERS PAN SET
Decorating instructions for nine easy-to-make designs. Set of 10 aluminum pans, each approximately 5 x 3 x 1 3/4 in. deep. Includes: 0, 1, 2, 3, 4, 5, 6 (doubles as 9), 7, 8, and ?. One cake mix makes 8-10 cakes.
2105-D-9336 $19.99 set

6. STAR PAN
What better way to honor the celebrity in your life? Brighten birthdays, opening nights, even law enforcement occasions. One-mix aluminum pan is 12 3/4 in. x 1 7/8 in.
2105-D-2512 $9.99 each

7. MINI STAR PAN
Make your celebrations brighter. One cake mix makes 20-24 mini stars. 6 cavity aluminum pan is 14 1/2 x 11 in.; individual cakes are 4 3/4 in. diameter x 1 1/4 in. deep.
2105-D-1235 $10.99 each

8. WONDER MOLD KIT
Use alone or with another design. Aluminum pan (8 in. diam., 5 in. deep) takes 5-6 cups of firm-textured batter. Heat-conducting rod assures even baking. Kit contains pan, rod, stand, 7 in. doll pick and instructions.
2105-D-565 $12.99 kit

TEEN DOLL PICK
7 in. high.
2815-D-101 $2.99 each

9. MINI WONDER MOLD
Couple with Small Doll Picks for a quartet of party treats. Great with Wonder Mold kit for a color-coordinated bridal party centerpiece. One cake mix makes 4 to 6 cakes. Aluminum pan is 10 x 10 x 3 in. Individual cakes are 3 1/2 x 3 in.
2105-D-3020 $9.99 each

SMALL DOLL PICKS
4 1/2 in. high.
1511-D-1019 $5.99 pk. of 4

Bears are definite kid-pleasers! Our bevy of bears includes unique mini and upright designs — great for boys or girls birthdays.

1. MINI BEAR PAN
Every kid deserves his own little bear! Make six individual servings at once. One cake mix will make 12-16 bears. Aluminum, individual cakes are 4 1/2 x 4 1/2 x 1 1/4 in.
2105-D-4497 $10.99 each

2. PETITE HUGGABLE BEAR PAN
Bite-size bears are just right for muffins, brownies, cookies and gelatin treats! One cake mix will make 12-16 bears. Aluminum, individual cakes are 1 1/2 x 1 3/4 x 1 in.
2105-D-3655 $8.99 each

3. 10 PC. 3-D CUDDLY BEAR PAN SET
Five great decorating ideas on the box! Two-piece aluminum pan takes 6 1/2 cups of firm textured batter. Includes 6 clips, heat conducting core and instructions. Pan is 9 1/2 x 8 5/8 in. tall.
2105-D-603 $16.99 set

4. 2 PC. PANDA MOLD SET
Aluminum 2-pc. mold/pan is perfect for baking cakes and molding candy, ice cream, and sugar. 4 3/4 in. high.
518-D-489 $5.99 set

5. BALLERINA BEAR PAN
Please kids and adults alike with her fancy designs. One-mix aluminum pan is 15 3/4 x 9 1/2 x 1 15/16 in.
2105-D-2021 $9.99 each

6. TEDDY BEAR WITH BLOCK PAN
Use teddy's block to announce ages, names, messages! One-mix aluminum pan is 13 x 9 1/2 x 2 in.
2105-D-8257 $9.99 each

7. HUGGABLE TEDDY BEAR PAN
His happy mood fits so many occasions. Ideas for birthdays and baby showers included. One-mix aluminum pan is 13 1/2 x 12 1/4 x 2 in.
2105-D-4943 $9.99 each

8. HAPPY BIRTHDAY PAN
The message is loud and clear! One-mix aluminum pan is 10 in. x 2 in.
2105-D-1073 $9.99 each

NOTE: Prices and products offered in this Yearbook may not apply in Canada.

Valentine

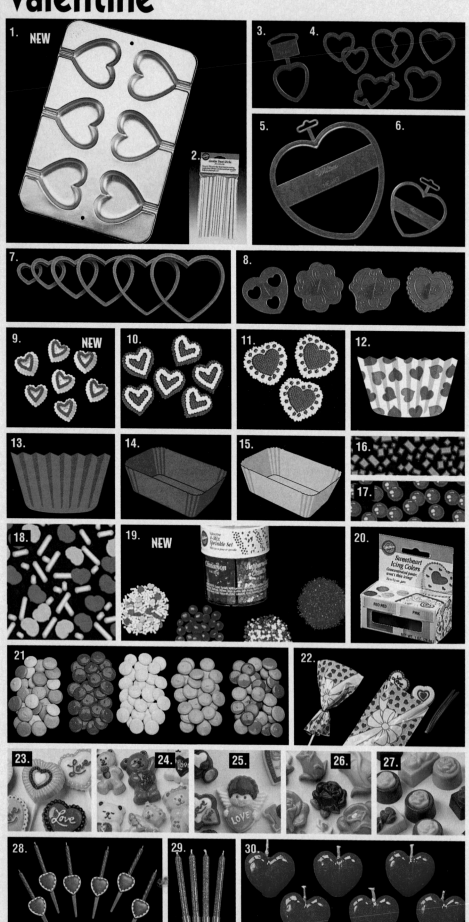

1. NEW **HEART COOKIE TREAT PAN**
Just press in your favorite cookie dough over our Cookie Treat Sticks. Six cups, each 3 x 3 1/2 x 1/4 in.
2105-D-8104 $7.99 each

2. COOKIE TREAT STICKS
6 in. sticks for use with Wilton Cookie Treat Pans.
1912-D-9319 $1.99 pk. of 20

BITE SIZE PERIMETER CUTTERS   1 1/2 x 1 1/2 in.
3. Heart   2303-D-203   49¢ each
4. 5-Pc. Set   2303-D-9318 $2.49 set

5. GIANT HEART   7 1/2 x 7 in.
2303-D-95 $1.49 each

6. HEART PERIMETER CUTTER   3 x 4 in.
2303-D-100   69¢ each

7. 6 PC. HEART SET   Sizes from 1 1/4 to 4 1/8 in.
2304-D-115 $2.99 set

8. 4 PC. HEART FAVORITES SET
Great for treats year-round! Each approx. 3 x 4 in.
2304-D-808 $2.99 set

HEARTS ICING DECORATIONS
Sugar flavored, fit any cupcake. Certified Kosher.
9. NEW Mini   710-D-524 $1.99 pk. of 15
10. Petite   710-D-840 $1.99 pk. of 12
11. Doily   710-D-510 $1.99 pk. of 9

BAKING CUPS
Grease-resistant, microwave-safe paper in holiday theme. Great for baking or to hold candy and nuts.
12. Hearts
NEW Petite Loaf   415-D-410 $1.49 pk. of 24
Standard   415-D-210 $1.49 pk. of 50
Mini   415-D-310 $1.49 pk. of 75
13. Red glassine
Standard   415-D-211 $1.49 pk. of 50
14. NEW Red foil
Petite Loaf   415-D-106 $1.49 pk. of 24
15. NEW Silver foil
Petite Loaf   415-D-407 $1.49 pk. of 24

SPRINKLE DECORATIONS
Large-size box with V-shaped spout for pouring or sprinkling. Certified Kosher. 4 - 5 1/4 oz.
16. Red Crystal   710-D-813 $1.99 pk.
17. Cinnamon   710-D-814 $1.99 pk.
18. Hearts Mix   710-D-806 $1.99 pk.

19. NEW **4 MIX SPRINKLE SHAKER**
Contains 1 oz. Cinnamon, .75 oz. Heart Mix, 1 oz. Peppermint Crunchies, 1.1 oz. Red Sugar.
710-D-730 $4.99 pk.

20. 2 PC. VALENTINE ICING COLORS SET
Red and Pink in 1/2 oz. jars.
601-D-5570 $2.99 set

21. CANDY MELTS®*
14 oz. bag. Certified Kosher. $2.50 each
Pastel Mix (Pink, Lavender, Blue) 1911-D-1637
(Available 12/1-5/31)
Red   (Available 9/4-1/31)   1911-D-499
White   1911-D-498
Pink   1911-D-447
Pastel Mint (White, Pink, Green)   1911-D-1923
Vanilla flavored, unless otherwise noted.*brand confectionery coating

22. HEART TREAT BAGS
Perfect for any treat. Plastic bags are 4 x 6 in.
1912-D-2344 $1.89 pk. of 40 bags with 40 ties

23. HEART LOLLIPOP MOLD   7 molds, 2 designs.
2114-D-2835 $1.99 each

24. LOVING BEARS   8 molds; 8 designs.
2114-D-9322 $1.99 each

25. I LOVE YOU LOLLIPOP   8 molds; 8 designs.
2114-D-91911 $1.99 each

26. ROSES 'N BUDS
10 molds; 2 designs; 2 lollipops.
2114-D-91101 $1.99 each

27. ROSES   10 molds; 3 designs.
2114-D-91511 $1.99 each

28. NEW **10 PC. CANDLE HOLDER SET**
5 holders, 5 spiral candles 4 in. high.
Pink 2811-D-156 $1.99 set

29. GLITTER CANDLES   2 1/2 in. Holders included.
Pink 2811-D-0244   99¢ pk. of 10

30. HEARTS CANDLES   1 1/4 in. high.
2811-D-9328 $2.99 pk. of 6

1. MINI EMBOSSED HEART PAN
Serve lovely individual size desserts, molded salads and appetizers. Beautifully sculpted shape, with raised center that looks great with fruit or whipped cream. One mix makes 12-15 cakes. Aluminum pan is 14 x 10 x 1 1/4 in. deep; cavities, each 3 3/4 x 3 1/4 x 1 1/4 in. deep.
2105-D-8255 $10.99 each

2. EMBOSSED HEART PAN
Raised heart center and scalloped sides display culinary love! Perfect for elegant gelatin and mousse desserts, fondant and glaze-covered cakes. One-mix aluminum pan is 12 x 11 x 2 in.
2105-D-9340 $8.99 each

3. MINI HEART PAN
Each heart of this 8 x 11 1/8 in. aluminum pan is 3 1/2 x 1 1/4 in. One cake mix makes 12 hearts.
2105-D-11044 $8.99 each

4. PETITE HEART PAN
Win hearts with bite-size muffins, brownies, tarts and cookies. Aluminum pan contains 12 molds. Each cavity is 1 7/8 x 1 1/2 x 3/4 in. One cake mix makes 16-24 hearts.
2105-D-2432 $8.99 each

5. HEART ANGEL FOOD PAN
Cooling legs and removable bottom for easy release. Aluminum pan.
10 5/8 x 10 1/8 x 4 in. **2105-D-6509 $13.99 each**
(Takes one angel food or chiffon mix.)
7 1/2 in.   **2105-D-9339 $ 9.99 each**
(Takes 1/2 angel food or chiffon mix.)

6. HEART RING PAN
Fill with fresh fruit, whipped cream, shaved chocolate. A heart's delight. Two-mix aluminum pan is 11 x 2 5/8 in.
2105-D-3219 $12.99 each

7. 4 PC. HEART PAN SET
Celebrate with the ultimate heart-shaped cake. Set includes 6, 9, 12 and 14 1/2 in. diameter aluminum pans. 2 in. deep.
2105-D-2131 $29.99 set

8. HEART PANS
For the most romantic occasions. The 2-in. deep aluminum pans are sold separately.
  6 in. Heart   2105-D-4781 $4.49 each
  9 in. Heart   2105-D-5176 $6.49 each
12 in. Heart   2105-D-5168 $8.99 each

9. 10 IN. HEART DOILIES
A pretty presentation, with the look of embroidered lace. Red foil resists grease from your treats.
2104-D-89995 $2.49 pk. of 6

10. NEW HEART SPRINGFORM PAN
Perfect for a classic Valentine cheesecake, its springlock release makes for easy removal of delicate desserts. Non-stick pan is 9 3/4 x 9 1/2 x 2 7/8 in. deep.
2105-D-2122 $9.99 each

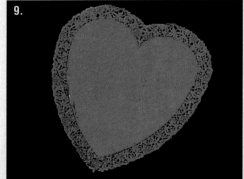

NOTE: Prices and products offered in this Yearbook may not apply in Canada.

Easter

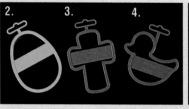

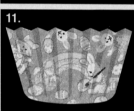

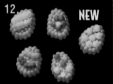

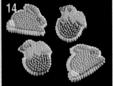

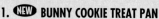

NEW

1. NEW BUNNY COOKIE TREAT PAN
Six cups, each $3 \frac{1}{2}$ x $2 \frac{3}{4}$ x $\frac{1}{4}$ in.
2105-D-8106 $7.99 each
1A. COOKIE TREAT STICKS
1912-D-9319 $1.99 pk. of 20
STANDARD SIZE PERIMETER CUTTERS   3 x 4 in.
2. Egg   2303-D-119   69¢ each
3. Cross   2303-D-141   69¢ each
4. Duck   2303-D-148   69¢ each
BITE SIZE PERIMETER CUTTERS $1 \frac{1}{2}$ x $1 \frac{1}{2}$ in.
5. 5 Pc. Set   2303-D-9319 $2.49 set
6. Bite Size Duck   2303-D-213   49¢ each
7. 5 PC. EASTER FAVORITES SET
Open cutters $3 \frac{1}{4}$ to $4 \frac{3}{8}$ in. high; $2 \frac{1}{2}$ to $4 \frac{1}{2}$ in. wide.
2304-D-1519 $2.99 set
8. 4 PC. NESTING BUNNIES SET $1 \frac{1}{4}$ to $4 \frac{1}{8}$ in.
2303-D-9270 $2.99 set
9. NEW SHAPED EASTER TREAT BAGS!
Shaped like an Easter Bunny! $4 \frac{1}{2}$ in. x 6 $\frac{1}{2}$ in.
1912-D-2219 $1.89 pk. of 25 bags, 25 ties
10. EASTER TREAT BAGS
Plastic bags are 3 x 4 in.
1912-D-2348 $1.69 pk. of 40 bags with 40 ties
11. EASTER BAKING CUPS
Grease-resistant, microwave-safe paper.
NEW Petite Loaf   415-D-419 $1.49 pk. of 24
Standard   415-D-219 $1.49 pk. of 50
Mini   415-D-319 $1.49 pk. of 75
ICING DECORATIONS Ⓤ
Sugar flavored edible shapes. Certified Kosher.
12. **NEW** Mini Eggs   710-D-526 $1.99 pk. of 15
13. Eggs and Baskets   710-D-551 $1.99 pk. of 9
14. Petite Bunnies and Chicks
                        710-D-509 $1.99 pk. of 12
15. Bunnies   710-D-842 $1.99 pk. of 9
SPRINKLE DECORATIONS Ⓤ
V-shaped spout. Certified Kosher. $3 \frac{1}{2}$ oz.
16. Easter Eggs Mix   710-D-816 $1.99 pk.
17. Bunny/Ducks Mix   710-D-809 $1.99 pk.
18. NEW 4 MIX SPRINKLE SHAKER
Includes 1.1 oz. Green Sugar, 1.1 oz. Yellow Sugar,
.75 oz. Easter Eggs Mix, .75 oz. Bunnies & Ducks Mix.
710-D-731 $4.99 each
19. 2 PC. EASTER ICING COLORS SET
Lemon Yellow, Violet in $\frac{1}{2}$ oz. jars.
601-D-5571 $2.99 set
20. NEW HAPPY EASTER BUNNY CANDY MAKING KIT
Includes 12 oz. Candy Melts, 2 pc. bunny mold and
2 oz. colorful jelly bean eggs.
2114-D-4101 $7.99 kit
21. NEW EASTER BASKET TREATS CANDY MAKING KIT
Includes White, Pink, Yellow and Blue Candy Melts®
(10 oz. total), candy/lollipop mold (10 molds, 5 designs),
10 lollipop sticks, 10 lollipop bags with twist ties.
2114-D-4100 $6.99 kit
22. CANDY MELTS® *   14 oz. bag. Certified Kosher.
Pastel Mint (Pink, Green, White)
(Available 12/1-5/31)   1911-D-1923 $2.50 pk.
Chocolate Mint   1911-D-1920 $2.50 pk.
White   1911-D-498 $2.50 pk.
Pink   1911-D-447 $2.50 pk.
Pastel Mix (Pink, Lavender, Blue)
(Available 12/1-5/31)   1911-D-1637 $2.50 pk.
Yellow   1911-D-463 $2.50 pk.
Green   1911-D-404 $2.50 pk.
Vanilla flavored, unless otherwise noted. *brand confectionery coating
CANDY MOLDS
23. NEW 6 PC. EGG MAKING SET
Includes 3 two-piece egg molds; small (3 x $2 \frac{1}{4}$ x $2 \frac{1}{2}$ in.),
medium ($4 \frac{1}{4}$ x 3 x $3 \frac{1}{4}$ in.) and large (5 x 4 x 3 $\frac{3}{4}$ in.).
2114-D-1215 $4.99 set
24. BUNNY FACE   1 design, 7 molds.
2114-D-2839 $1.99 each
25. EASTER TREATS   8 designs, 8 molds.
2114-D-91000 $1.99 each
26. PLAYFUL BUNNIES   8 designs, 8 molds.
2114-D-90999 $1.99 each

1. PETITE EGG PAN
Make individual-size cookies, candies, muffins, brownies and treats; enough to fill dozens of baskets! 12 cup aluminum pan. Each cup is $1\frac{1}{2}$ x 2 x $\frac{7}{8}$ in.
2105-D-4794 $8.99 each

2. MINI EGG PAN
Use them as colorful place markers at the holiday table. One cake mix makes about 12-20 cakes. Eight cup aluminum pan, each oval well is $3\frac{1}{2}$ x $2\frac{3}{8}$ x $1\frac{3}{4}$ in. deep.
2105-D-2118 $8.99 each

3. 3 PC. 3-D EGG PAN SET
Makes a great holiday centerpiece. Two-piece aluminum pan takes just one cake mix. Each half is $8\frac{3}{4}$ x $5\frac{3}{8}$ in. and includes a ring base for level baking.
2105-D-4793 $9.99 set

4. PEEK-A-BOO BUNNY PAN
Celebrate springtime and other hoppy occasions! Four different decorating ideas on label. One-mix aluminum pan is 16 x $8\frac{3}{4}$ x 2 in.
2105-D-4395 $7.99 each

5. MINI BUNNY PAN
Make six bunny-shaped treats in no time flat. One mix makes about 12-16 bunnies. Aluminum pan; each cup is $4\frac{1}{2}$ x $3\frac{1}{2}$ x $1\frac{1}{2}$ in.
2105-D-4426 $8.99 each

6. 2 PC. STAND-UP LAMB PAN SET
A beautiful centerpiece for your Easter table. Two-piece aluminum pan is 10 x 7 in. tall and takes 6 cups of pound cake batter. Instructions included.
2105-D-2010 $10.99 set

7. NEW BITE-SIZE BUNNY PAN
Sized just right for kids – cute Easter bunnies they can have fun decorating. Nine cup aluminum pan is ideal for cookies, brownies, crispy rice snacks and cakes. Each cup $3\frac{1}{2}$ x $2\frac{1}{2}$ x $\frac{3}{4}$ in. One cake mix makes 18 to 24 bunnies.
2105-D-2120 $8.99 each

8. 29 PC. PANORAMIC EGG KIT
"Look-inside" sugar eggs are surprisingly easy to make — just add sugar and icing colors! Includes: egg mold, decorating bags, tips, meringue powder, icing decorations, complete step-by-step instructions.
2104-D-1750 $9.99 kit

9. CROSS PAN
Bake and decorate this cake for holidays, christenings and other religious occasions. Instructions include a birthday and family reunion cake. One-mix aluminum pan is $14\frac{1}{2}$ x $11\frac{1}{8}$ x 2 in.
2105-D-2509 $9.99 each

10. MINI LAMB PAN
A wonderful brunch treat — individual-sized stand-up lamb cakes. Just ice two lambs together, following great designs on the label. One mix makes about 12-16 lambs. Aluminum pan; each cup is $3\frac{1}{2}$ x $4\frac{3}{4}$ x 1 in.
2105-D-1275 $9.99 each

NOTE: Prices and products offered in this Yearbook may not apply in Canada.

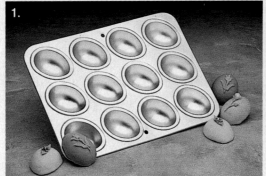

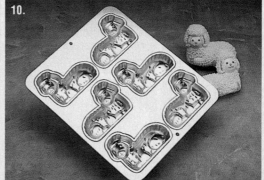

Graduation

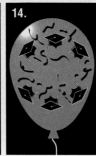

NEW

diploma

Graduation

Stars and Stripes

HAPPY BIRTHDAY

NEW

NEW

1. GRADUATE PAN
Ideal for male or female graduates! One mix aluminum pan is 14 1/2 x 8 3/4 x 2 in.
2105-D-1800 $9.99 each

2. 4 PC. COOKIE CUTTER SET   3 to 4 in.
2304-D-1800 $2.99 set

3. BAKING CUPS
Grease-resistant, microwave-safe paper.
Standard 415-D-248 $1.49 pack of 50

4. ICING DECORATIONS
Sugar flavored, fit any cupcake. Certified Kosher.
710-D-473 $1.99 pk. of 12

5. CANDY MOLD   11 molds, 5 designs.
2114-D-92818 $1.99 each

6. TREAT BAGS
Perfect for any treat. Plastic bags are 4 x 6 in.
1912-D-1800 $1.89 pk. of 40 bags with 40 ties

7. DOILIES
Cap and confetti design. Grease-resistant, with lacy border – great for cakes, desserts, snacks and table decorations.
  8 in.   2202-D-1808 $1.99 pk. of 8
10 in.   2202-D-1810 $1.99 pk. of 6

8. CANDLES   1/2 to 2 in. high.
2811-D-1800 $2.99 set

9. 2 PC. GRADUATION CAPS SET   2 in. high.
Black 2113-D-1801 $1.99 set
White 2113-D-1800 $1.99 set

10. HAPPY GRADUATE TOPPER   5 in. high.
2113-D-1818 $2.09 each

11. GLAD GRADUATE TOPPER   4 1/2 in. high.
2113-D-1817 $2.09 each

12. GLOWING GRAD TOPPER   4 1/2 in. high.
2113-D-1833 $1.69 each

13. SUCCESSFUL GRAD TOPPER   4 1/4 in. high.
2113-D-4549 $1.69 each

14. BALLOONS
Helium quality latex; longer floating, easier inflation.
2203-D-1441 $1.99 pk. of 6

15. STAR PAN
Versatile shape for July 4, Christmas, birthdays.
One-mix aluminum pan is12 3/4 in. x 1 7/8 in.
2105-D-275 $9.99 each

16. MINI STAR PAN
One cake mix makes 20-24 mini stars. 6 cup aluminum pan is14 1/2 x 11 in.; cups are 4 3/4 in. diameter x 1 1/4 in. deep.
2105-D-1235 $10.99 each

17. STAR COOKIE TREAT PAN
6 cup aluminum pan is 13 1/2 x 9 1/2 x 1/2 in.
2105-D-8102 $7.99 each

18. COOKIE TREAT STICKS
1912-D-9319 $1.99 pk. of 20

19. TREAT BAGS
Perfect for any treat. Plastic bags are 4 x 6 in.
1912-D-704 $1.89 pk. of 40 bags with 40 ties

STAR COOKIE CUTTERS
20. 6 Pc. Nesting Set   1 5/8 to 4 5/8 in.
                2304-D-111 $2.99 set
21. Standard 3 x 4 in.   2303-D-135   69¢ ea.
22. Bite-Size 1 1/2 x 1 1/2 in. 2303-D-218   49¢ ea.

23. NEW **BAKING CUPS**
Grease-resistant, microwave-safe paper.
Standard 415-D-704 $1.49 pack of 50

24. NEW **ICING DECORATIONS**
Sugar flavored, fit any cupcake. Certified Kosher.
710-D-726 $1.99 pk. of 9

25. RED & BLUE SPARKLERS
6 1/2 in. high. 2811-D-704   99¢ pk. of 18

6 PC. CANDLE SETS   1 3/4 to 2 in. high.
26. Beer Cans 2811-D-9326 $2.99 set
27. Dynamite 2811-D-9325 $2.99 set

28. SPRINKLE DECORATIONS
Large-size box with V-shaped spout for pouring or sprinkling. Certified Kosher. 4 - 5 1/4 oz.
710-D-7040 $1.99 pk.

1. NEW **12 PC. JACK-O-LANTERN COOKIE CUTTER CANISTER SET**
Ten favorite spooky shapes in a lovable pumpkin storage container! Recipe card included for Goblin Goodies Roll-out Cookies. Canister is 5 1/4 in. diameter x 5 1/4 in. high. Cutters are 2 1/2 to 3 1/2 in.
2304-D-1035 $5.99 set

2. JACK-O-LANTERN COOKIE TREAT PAN
Treat pops create Halloween excitement! 6 cup aluminum pan is 13 1/2 x 9 1/2 x 1/2 in.
2105-D-8100 $7.99 each

3. 6 IN. COOKIE TREAT STICKS
Thicker, sturdier sticks are great for cookie pops, lollipops and crafts.
1912-D-9319 $1.99 pk. of 20

COOKIE CUTTERS
Child-safe, most include a cookie recipe on the label!

4. 3 PC. NESTING GHOSTS SET
3 to 7 in.
2303-D-1031 $2.99 set

5. 4 PC. JACK-O-LANTERN SET
Four graduated sizes, 2 1/4 to 5 1/4 in. tall; 2 3/8 to 5 in. wide.
2303-D-191 $2.99 set

6. 4 PC. HALLOWEEN FAVORITES SET
3 x 4 in.
2304-D-800 $2.99 set

7. 10 PC. SPOOKY HALLOWEEN SET
3 to 4 1/4 in.
2304-D-9210 $3.99 set

8. GIANT JACK-O-LANTERN
Decorate his face funny or frightening!
7 1/2 x 8 in.
2303-D-9320 $1.49 each

9. 5 PC. BITE-SIZE HALLOWEEN SET
1 1/2 x 1 1/2 in.
2303-D-9316 $2.49 set

10. 2 PC. ICING COLORS SET
1/2 oz. jars, Orange and Black.
601-D-3010 $2.69 set

11. NEW **DOILIES**
Glowing pumpkin design makes all your Halloween treats look more fun! Grease-resistant, with lacy border – great for cakes, desserts, snacks and table decorations.
8 in. 2104-D-1213 $1.99 pk. of 8
10 in. 2104-D-1214 $1.99 pk. of 6

12. TRICK OR TREAT BAKING CUPS
Grease-resistant, microwave-safe paper in a Halloween theme. Also great for candy and nuts.
Petite Loaf   415-D-413 $1.49 pk. of 75
Standard   415-D-213 $1.49 pk. of 50
Mini   415-D-340 $1.49 pk. of 75

13. NEW **GLOWING PUMPKIN BAKING CUPS**
Grease-resistant, microwave-safe paper in a pumpkin theme. Also great for candy and nuts.
Standard   415-D-223 $1.49 pk. of 50

14. BALLOONS
Helium quality latex for longer floating, easy inflation.
2203-D-1455 $1.99 pk. of 6

NOTE: Prices and products offered in this Yearbook may not apply in Canada.

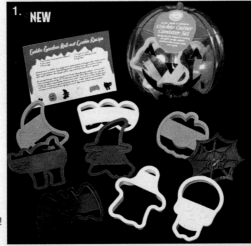

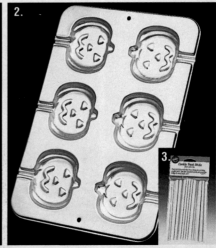

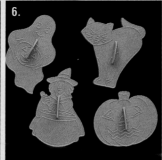

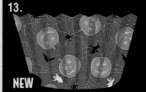

Halloween

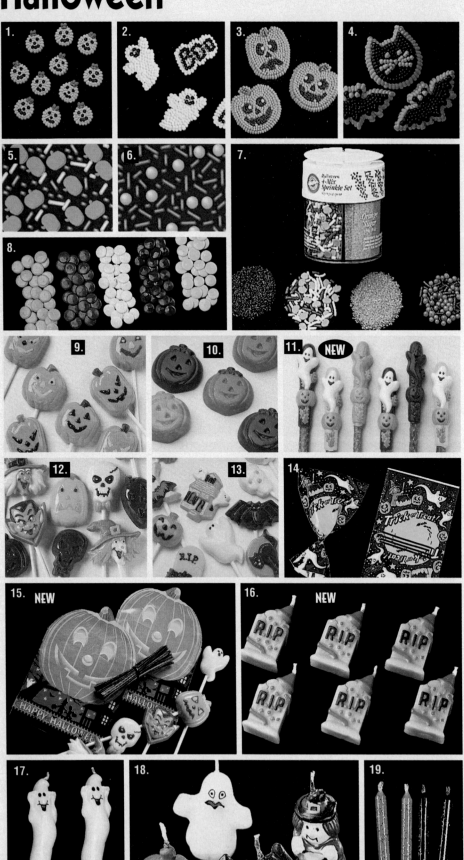

ICING DECORATIONS
Sugar flavored edible shapes. Certified Kosher.
1. **Mini Pumpkins**   710-D-523 $1.99 pk. of 15
2. **Petite Boo and Ghost**
   710-D-512 $1.99 pk. of 12
3. **Pumpkins**   710-D-835 $1.99 pk. of 9
4. **Cats and Bats**   710-D-834 $1.99 pk. of 9

SPRINKLES DECORATIONS
Large-size package with V-shaped spout.
Certified Kosher. 4 - 5 1/4 oz.
5. **Halloween Mix**   710-D-807 $1.99 each
6. **Pumpkin Mix**   710-D-810 $1.99 each

7. 4-MIX SPRINKLE DISPENSER
Includes 1.1 oz. Orange Sugar, 1 oz. Halloween Mix, 1.1 oz. Black Sugar, .7 oz. Pumpkin Mix.
710-D-728 $4.99 each

8. CANDY MELTS® *
Ideal for all your candy making—molding, dipping and coating. 14 oz. bag. Certified Kosher. **$2.50 each**
Orange (Available 7/16-10/31) 1911-D-1631
Light Cocoa (all natural Cocoa flavor) 1911-D-544
White 1911-D-498
Dark Cocoa (all natural Cocoa flavor) 1911-D-358
Yellow 1911-D-463
Vanilla flavored, unless otherwise noted.
*brand confectionery coating

CANDY MOLDS
9. 8 IN. JACK-O-LANTERN LOLLIPOP
Designed for 8 inch pops, sticks line up to fit neatly in the freezer. 7 molds, 2 designs.
2114-D-2836 $1.99 each

10. PUMPKINS
12 identical smiling molds.
2114-D-90740 $1.99 each

11. NEW HALLOWEEN CANDY PRETZEL MOLD
Here's an easy trick for treats – just position pretzel rod in mold, spoon in melted Candy Melts and refrigerate to make apretzel pop kids will love to eat, stick and all. 6 molds, 1 design.
2115-D-1500 $1.99 each

12. SCARY HALLOWEEN
5 designs. 7 molds.
2114-D-1033 $1.99 each

13. HAUNTED HOUSE
8 molds.
2114-D-9320 $1.99 each

14. TREAT BAGS WITH TIES
Plastic bags in spooky pumpkin shape brightly wrap candy or cookie treats. 4 1/2 x 6 in.
1912-D-2346 $1.89 pk. of 40 bags, 40 ties

15. NEW SHAPED TREAT BAGS WITH TIES
Plastic bags with die-cut pumpkins are 4 x 6 in.
For candy or cookie treats.
1912-D-2800 $1.89 pk. of 25 bags, 25 ties

16. NEW 6 PC. TOMBSTONE CANDLE SET
Fast fun, 1 1/2 in. high.
2811-D- 9331 $2.99 set

17. 2 PC. PARTY TAPER CANDLE SET
Hand painted ghost with jack-o-lantern tapers for use in your candle sticks or holders.
Height: 7 in.
2811-D-1032 $4.99 set

18. 4 PC. HALLOWEEN CANDLE SET
Glowing ghouls. Height: 1 1/4 to 2 in.
2811-D-9315 $2.99 set

19. GLITTER CANDLES
Holders included to protect cake from glitter.
2 1/2 in. high.
Black   2811-D-0247   99¢ pk. of 10
Orange 2811-D-0249   99¢ pk. of 10

1. NEW PUMPKIN PIE PAN

Brighten your Halloween and Thanksgiving gatherings with this fun fall shape. You'll use it all year long for apple, peach and cherry pies, too! Use any ready-to-bake pie crust. 9 in. diameter x 1 1/4 in. deep aluminum pan. **Holds one 15 oz. can of pumpkin pie filling.**
2105-D-3970 **$6.99 each**

2. PETITE JACK-O-LANTERN PAN

12 cup aluminum pan. Each cup measures 2 x 2 x 1 1/8 in. One cake mix makes 18-24 pumpkins.
2105-D-8462 **$8.99 each**

3. MINI PUMPKIN PAN

Create kid-pleasing party cakes year 'round. One cake mix makes 12-16 pumpkins. Each cup of this aluminum pan takes 1/2 cup of cake batter and measures 4 x 3 3/4 x 1 1/2 in.
2105-D-1499 **$8.99 each**

4. JACK-O-LANTERN PAN

Carve out his grin for the next Halloween party. One-mix aluminum pan is 12 1/4 x 11 5/8 x 2 in.
2105-D-3068 **$7.99 each**

5. 2 PC. STAND-UP JACK-O-LANTERN PAN SET

3-D Halloween treat comes with complete instructions for all skill levels. One-mix aluminum pan is 7 x 5 1/4 x 6 1/2 in.
2105-D-3150 **$9.99 set**

6. NEW JACK-O-LANTERN GRID

Ideal as a base for craft projects or to cool Halloween goodies! Includes 6 exciting decorating ideas – fun projects like a scarecrow banner, a giant pumpkin cookie, and a floral door decoration – with recipes and instructions. 13 1/2 x 12 1/4 in.; wire steel with food safe powder coating.
2305-D-200 **$9.99 each**

7. OVER THE HILL TOMBSTONE PAN

A memorable monument to Halloween fun or a milestone birthday! One-mix aluminum pan is 13 x 9 1/4 x 2 in.
2105-D-1237 **$9.99 each**

8. MINI GHOST PAN

Create gobs of goblins at a time! One cake mix makes 12-16 ghosts. Aluminum pan; each cup measures 4 x 5 x 1 3/8 in.
2105-D-3845 **$8.99 each**

9. HALLOWEEN CANDY KIT

Includes candy/lollipop mold (10 molds, 5 designs), 10 lollipop sticks, 10 lollipop bags, 3 disposable bags, 10 oz. Dark Cocoa, White and Orange Candy Melts®*
2114-D-1032 **$6.99 kit**

10. HAUNTED PUMPKIN DECORATION KIT

Create spooky "look-inside" sugar decorations great for party tables! Includes 2 pc. mold, premade icing decorations, decorating bags and tips, meringue powder, instructions.
2104-D-1751 **$9.99 kit**

NOTE: Prices and products offered in this Yearbook may not apply in Canada.

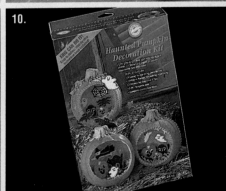

Christmas

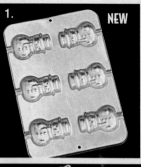
NEW

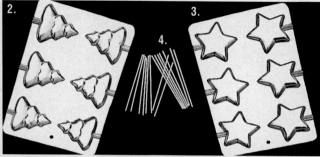

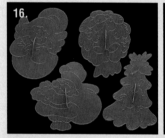

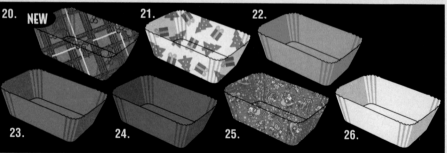

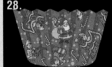
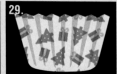

COOKIE TREAT PANS
Just press dough in pan to make treats on a stick! 6 cup aluminum pan is 13 1/2 x 9 1/2 x 1/2 in.
1. **NEW** Snowman 2105-D-8107 $7.99 each
2. Christmas Tree 2105-D-8101 $7.99 each
3. Star 2105-D-8102 $7.99 each

4. COOKIE TREAT STICKS
Thicker, sturdier 6 in. sticks are great for cookie pops, lollipops and crafts.
1912-D-9319 $1.99 pk. of 20

STANDARD SIZE PERIMETER CUTTERS
A shape for every occasion! 3 in. wide x 4 in. long. All are 69¢ each.
5. Christmas Tree 2303-D-132
6. 6 Pt. Star 2303-D-122
7. Bell 2303-D-125
8. 5 Pt. Star 2303-D-135
9. Gingerbread Boy 2303-D-164
10. Turkey 2303-D-163

BITE SIZE PERIMETER CUTTER
Wonderful stocking stuffers or bread dough ornament shapes. 1 1/2 x 1 1/2 in.
11. 5 Pt. Star 2303-D-218 69¢ ea.

12. GIANT TREE CUTTER
Cutter approximately 7 1/2 x 9 in. high.
2303-D-96 $1.49 each

13. 5 PC. BITE SIZE CUTTER SET 1 1/2 x 1 1/2 in.
2303-D-9317 $2.49 set

14. 4 PC. GINGERBREAD FAMILY SET
Set includes two 5 1/2 x 4 in. adults and two 2 1/2 x 1 1/2 in. children.
2304-D-121 $2.99 set

15. 4 PC. CHRISTMAS FAVORITES SET
Cookies make the season jolly! Each is 3 x 4 in.
2304-D-801 $2.99 set

16. 4 PC. CHRISTMAS CUTTER SET
Angel, Santa, Wreath, Tree. 4 1/4 to 5 in.
2304-D-995 $2.99 set

17. 2 PC. ICING COLORS SET
1/2 oz. jars, Green and Christmas Red.
601-D-3011 $2.99 set

18. SANTA'S COOKIE WHEEL
Roll six 2 in. holiday-shaped cookies quick and easy; tree, bell, snowman, bear, gingerbread boy and star.
2304-D-803 $5.99 each

19. 10 PC. CHRISTMAS COOKIE COLLECTION SET
Yuletide cutters make holiday baking a breeze! Each cutter 3 x 4 in.
2304-D-802 $3.99 set
Most cutters include a cookie recipe on the label.

BAKING CUPS
Petite Loaf 3 1/4 x 2 1/8 in.
Fits Petite Loaf Pan shown on p. 163.
20. **NEW** Plaid 415-D-421 $1.49 pk. of 24
21. Christmas Trees 415-D-451 $1.49 pk. of 24
22. Gold Foil 415-D-452 $1.49 pk. of 24
23. Red Foil 415-D-106 $1.49 pk. of 24
24. Green Foil 415-D-107 $1.49 pk. of 24
25. Santa & Elves 415-D-408 $1.49 pk. of 24
26. White 415-D-450 $1.49 pk. of 50
Grease-resistant, microwave-safe paper in holiday theme. Also great for candy and nuts.
27. Plaid
Standard 415-D-217 $1.49 pk. of 50
28. Santa Claus & Elves
Standard 415-D-208 $1.49 pk. of 50
Mini 415-D-308 $1.49 pk. of 75
29. Christmas Trees
Standard 415-D-209 $1.49 pk. of 50
Mini 415-D-309 $1.49 pk. of 75
30. Red (glassine paper)
Standard 415-D-211 $1.49 pk. of 50
Red & Green (mixed; glassine paper)
Bon Bon 1912-D-1247 $1.29 pk. of 75

1. SANTA'S HOLIDAY TREATS!
Sensational recipes and ideas for the season.
Soft cover; 96 color pages; 8 1/2 x 11 in.
902-D-1224 $7.99 each

2. CHRISTMAS!
Create festive main dishes, appetizers, cakes, and more. Soft cover, 96 color pages. 8 1/4 x 10 3/4 in.
902-D-250 $7.99 each

3. 4 MIX SPRINKLE SHAKER
Includes 1 oz. Holly Mix, 1.1 oz. Green Sugar, .75 oz. Christmas Tree Mix, 1 oz. Peppermint Munchies.
710-D-729 $4.99 each

ICING DECORATIONS
Sugar flavored edible shapes. Certified Kosher.
4. **Mini Wreaths** 710-D-522 **$1.99 pk. of 15**
5. **Christmas Trees** 710-D-838 **$1.99 pk. of 9**
6. **Santa Claus** 710-D-837 **$1.99 pk. of 9**
7. **Petite Wreaths and Snowmen**
   710-D-517 **$1.99 pk. of 12**
8. **NEW Poinsettias** (4 Poinsettias, 3 Leaves)
   710-D-220 **$3.99 pk. of 7**

SPRINKLE DECORATIONS
Large-size package with V-shaped spout. Certified Kosher. 4 - 5 1/4 oz. **$1.99 each**
9. **Christmas Tree Mix** 710-D-811
10. **Holly Mix** 710-D-813
11. **Red Crystal** 710-D-812
12. **Green Crystal** 710-D-829
13. **Peppermint Crunchies** 710-D-808

14. CANDY MELTS®*
Ideal for all your candy making – molding, dipping and coating. 14 oz. bag. Certified Kosher. **$2.50 pk.**

Red (Available 9/4-1/31)	1911-D-499
Light Cocoa (all natural Cocoa flavor)	1911-D-544
White	1911-D-498
Green	1911-D-404
Dark Cocoa (all natural Cocoa flavor)	1911-D-358
Christmas Mix (Red, Green)	1911-D-1624

(Available 9/4-12/15)
Vanilla flavored, unless otherwise noted. *brand confectionery coating

CANDY MOLDS
15. 8 IN. SANTA/TREE LOLLIPOP
Designed for longer pops, sticks line up to fit neatly in the freezer. 7 molds, 2 designs per sheet.
2114-D-2838 $1.99 each

16. CHRISTMAS I 8 festive molds, 7 designs.
2114-D-94136 $1.99 each

17. CHRISTMAS TREES 14 molds, 1 classic design.
2114-D-91099 $1.99 each

18. NORTH POLE 8 molds, 7 designs.
2114-D-9321 $1.99 each

19. CHRISTMAS LOLLIPOP 8 molds, 8 designs.
2114-D-97536 $1.99 each

20. THANKSGIVING
3 traditional designs. 9 molds. 2 lollipops.
2114-D-91128 $1.99 each

TREAT BAGS WITH TIES
Bright Christmas designs for candy and cookie treats. Plastic bags are 4 x 6 in.; shaped 4 1/2 x 6 in.

21. **NEW Shaped Santa**
1912-D-2214 $1.89 pk. of 25 bags, 25 ties
22. **Snowman**
1912-D-2496 $1.89 pk. of 40 bags, 40 ties
23. **Christmas**
1912-D-2345 $1.89 pk. of 40 bags, 40 ties

24. NEW CHRISTMAS PRETZEL CANDY MOLD
Just position pretzel rod in mold, spoon in melted Candy Melts and refrigerate. 6 molds, 1 design.
2115-D-1501 $1.99 each

25. 2 PC. CHRISTMAS PARTY TAPER CANDLES SET
Hand painted Santa and Elves. Height: 7 in.
2811-D-1224 $4.99 set

26. BALLOONS
Helium quality latex–longer floating, easy inflation.
2203-D-1454 $1.99 pk. of 6

27. 4 PC. NUTCRACKER CANDLE SET
Holiday favorites in candles! Height: 1 1/4 to 2 in.
2811-D-162 $2.99 set

NOTE: Prices and products offered in this Yearbook may not apply in Canada.

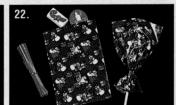

Christmas

1. NEW PRE-BAKED GINGERBREAD HOUSE ORNAMENT KIT
Fun family project, that is quick and easy to do. Exciting holiday houses, ready to assemble, decorate and hang on your tree. Kit includes everything needed to make two decorated ornament houses (2 in. wide x 2 in. high) – Just add your own confectioners'sugar. Instructions and great design ideas included.
2104-D-1515 **$5.99 kit**

2. NEW PRE-BAKED GINGERBREAD KIDS ORNAMENT KIT
Fun family project, that is quick and easy to do. Fun gingerbread kid shapes, ready to decorate and hang on your tree. Kit includes everything needed to make two decorated ornament kids (3½ in. wide x 5 in. high) – Just add your own confectioners'sugar. Instructions and great design ideas included.
2104-D-1514 **$5.99 kit**

3. NEW PRE-BAKED GINGERBREAD TREE ORNAMENT KIT
Fun family project, that is quick and easy to do. Fun, green colored, gingerbread tree shapes, ready to decorate and hang on your tree. Kit includes everything needed to make two decorated ornament trees (4 in. wide x 5 in. high) – Just add your own confectioners' sugar. Instructions and great design ideas included.
2104-D-1513 **$5.99 kit**

4. PRE-BAKED GINGERBREAD COOKIE TREE KIT
Fun Family project, that is quick and easy to do. Build a decorative holiday centerpiece with ready to assemble, green colored, gingerbread cookie tree sections, assorted candies and icing. Kit also includes, decorating bag and tip, meringue powder for making royal icing and complete instructions with great design ideas. – Just add your own confectioners' sugar. Complete tree size (10 in. wide x 10½ in. high x 10 in. deep).
2104-D-1512 **$14.99 kit**

5. PRE-BAKED GINGERBREAD HOUSE KIT
Fun Family project, that is quick and easy to do. Build a decorative holiday centerpiece with ready to assemble, gingerbread house sections, assorted candies and icing. Kit also includes, decorating bags and tips, meringue powder for making royal icing and complete instructions with great design ideas. – Just add your own confectioners' sugar. Completed house size (8 in. wide x 6½ in. high x 7 in. deep).
2104-D-1511 **$14.99 kit**

6. GINGERBREAD HOUSE KIT
Kit includes patterns, 3 plastic gingerbread people cutters, disposable bags, tips, instruction booklet.
2104-D-1525 **$7.49 kit**

7. CHRISTMAS COOKIE TREE KIT
Create a beautiful Yule tree in about 30 minutes — it's easy and fun! Just bake, stack and decorate. Kit includes 10 star cookie cutters in graduated sizes from small to large, 3 disposable decorating bags, decorating tips #3 and #16, cookie and icing recipes, baking and decorating instructions for 5 great designs.
2104-D-1501 **$7.99 kit**

8. SANTA'S TREASURES CANDY MAKING KIT
Includes candy/lollipop mold (10 cavities, 5 designs), 10 lollipop sticks, 10 lollipop bags, 3 disposable bags, 10 oz. Dark Cocoa, White and Red Candy Melts®*
2114-D-1223 **$6.99 kit**

*brand confectionery coating

NOTE: Prices and products offered in this Yearbook may not apply in Canada.

1. NEW SMILING SANTA PAN
He's happy to be part of the holiday fun! 5 great design ideas, including an easy brownie Santa. One-mix pan is 15 x 11 ¼ x 2 in. Aluminum.
2105-D-3310 $7.99 each

2. SANTA CHECKING LIST PAN
Add your name to his list for holiday fun! One-mix pan is 10 ½ x 13 ½ x 2 in. Aluminum.
2105-D-3323 $7.99 each

3. NEW 2 PC. STAND-UP TREE PAN SET
Bake a 3-D tree to decorate in so many ways. Instructions for 6 great ideas – including fruit cake and cinnamon tree recipes! Each pan half is 9 ½ x 9 ½ x 3 ¼ in. Pan takes 6 cups of pound cake batter. Includes heat conducting core and 6 clips. Aluminum.
2105-D-750 $16.99 each

4. PETITE CHRISTMAS TREE PAN
Ideal for bite-size muffins, tarts, brownies or gelatins; ready for easy decorating. One-mix makes approx. 18-24 cakes. Cups are 2 x 2 ¼ x ⅝ in. each. Aluminum.
2105-D-8463 $8.99 each

5. MINI CHRISTMAS TREE PAN
Little trees to decorate each guest's place setting. One-mix makes approximately 15-18 cakes. Six cups, 4 x 4 ½ x 1 ½ in. each. Aluminum.
2105-D-1779 $8.99 each

6. TREELITEFUL PAN
Our most popular holiday pan. Instructions include great year-round ideas. One-mix pan is 15 x 11 x 1 ½ in. Aluminum.
2105-D-425 $7.99 each

7. MINI SNOWMAN PAN
Build a blizzard of snowmen, 6 at a time! One-mix pan makes 15-18 snowmen. Six cups are 3 x 4 ¾ x 1 ⅞ in. Aluminum.
2105-D-472 $8.99 each

8. NEW HOLIDAY TREE GRID
Ideal as a base for craft projects or to cool holiday goodies! Includes 6 exciting decorating ideas – fun projects like a colorful banner, real pine branch and berry tree and a cookie making gift tree – plus recipes and instructions. 14 x 17 ½ in.; wire steel with food safe green powder coating.
2305-D-202 $8.99 each

9. MINI GINGERBREAD BOY PAN
Little ones will love having their own individualized ginger boy at Christmas dinner. One mix makes 12-15 cakes. Six cups are 4 ¾ x 4 ¼ x 1 ¼ in. Aluminum.
2105-D-6503 $8.99 each

10. BITE-SIZE GINGERBREAD BOY PAN
Bake gingerbread boys by the bunch! 9 cup pan is 10 ½ x 14 x ¾ in.; one cake mix yields 18 to 24 bite-size cakes. Aluminum.
2105-D-926 $8.99 each

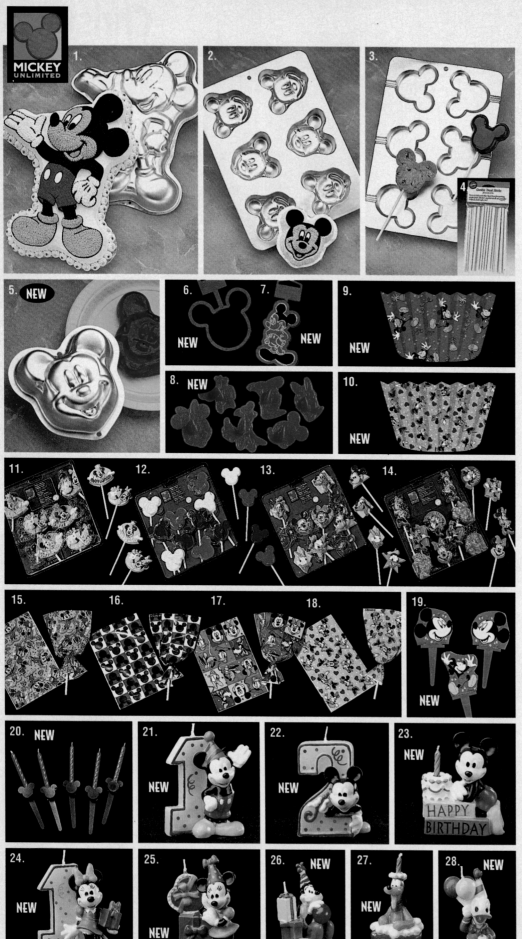

1. CAKE PAN
Beloved around the world! One-mix pan is 16 x 13 x 2 in. Aluminum.
2105-D-3601 **$9.99 each**

2. MINI PAN
One cake mix makes 12-16 cakes. Cakes are 4 x 4 x 1 in. Aluminum.
2105-D-3600 **$10.99 each**

3. COOKIE TREAT PAN*
Exciting Mickey cookie or crisped cereal treats on a stick! Six cavities, each 3½ x 3 x ½ in. deep. Aluminum.
2105-D-8103 **$7.99 each**

4. COOKIE TREAT STICKS
Sturdy 6 in. sticks designed for use with Wilton Cookie Treat Pans.
1912-D-9319 **$1.99 pk. of 20**

5. NEW SINGLES!™
Personal size mold great for cakes, gelatin, ice cream and more. Holds ¾ cup batter, 4 x 4 in.
2105-D-1136 **$1.99 each**

NEW COOKIE CUTTERS *
Perimeter style, 3 x 2½ in.

6. MICKEY FACE SILHOUETTE
2303-D-361 **79¢ each**

7. MICKEY MOUSE FULL BODY
2303-D-360 **79¢ each**

8. NEW 6 PC. MINI COOKIE CUTTER SET *
Child-safe plastic, 1½ x 1½ in.
2304-D-3600 **$2.99 set**

NEW BAKING CUPS
Standard size, grease-resistant, microwave-safe paper. **$1.49 pk. of 50**
9. Mickey Mouse 415-D-226
10. Minnie Mouse 415-D-227

LOLLIPOP MOLDS

11. HAPPY BIRTHDAY
7 molds, 2 designs.
2114-D-3600 **$1.99 each**

12. MICKEY SILHOUETTE
7 molds, 1 design.
2114-D-3601 **$1.99 each**

13. MICKEY & FRIENDS
7 molds, 7 designs.
2114-D-3602 **$1.99 each**

14. MINNIE MOUSE
7 molds, 6 designs.
2114-D-3603 **$1.99 each**

LOLLIPOP BAGS
Great for cookie and candy pops and other treats. 6 in. high, 4 in. wide.
All are $1.89 pk. of 40 bags, 40 ties.

15. HAPPY BIRTHDAY 1912-D-3600
16. MICKEY SILHOUETTE 1912-D-3601
17. MICKEY & FRIENDS 1912-D-3602
18. MINNIE MOUSE 1912-D-3603

19. NEW 12 PC. CAKE PICK SET
2113-D-3600 **$1.69 set**

20. NEW 10 PC. CANDLE HOLDER SET 5 holders, 5 spiral candles. 4 in.
2811-D-3600 **$1.99 set**

NEW CANDLES Great handpainted detail, 3 in. high. **$3.99 each**
21. MICKEY #1 2811-D-3601
22. MICKEY #2 2811-D-3602
23. HAPPY BIRTHDAY 2811-D-3603
24. MINNIE #1 2811-D-3604
25. MINNIE WITH PACKAGES 2811-D-3605
26. GOOFY 2811-D-3606
27. PLUTO 2811-D-3607
28. DONALD DUCK 2811-D-3608

© Disney. *Cookie recipes included.

1. CAKE PAN
This childhood favorite dips into the "hunny" pot for a treat. One-mix pan is 13 x 10 x 1⁷⁄₈ in. Aluminum.
2105-D-3000 $9.99 each

2. 7 PC. COOKIE WHEEL SET *
Just roll along to cut six super Pooh shapes! Cookies are 1¹⁄₂ x 2 in.
2104-D-9775 $7.99 set

3. 4 PC. COOKIE CUTTER SET *
Pooh Corner favorites in 4 child-safe plastic cutters, 2¹⁄₂ to 4 in. high.
2304-D-9775 $2.99 set

4. LOLLIPOP MOLD
Great detail! 7 molds, 6 designs.
2114-D-3000 $1.99 each

5. LOLLIPOP BAGS
Makes pops party-ready. 4 x 6 in.
1912-D-3000 $1.89 pk. of 40 bags, 40 ties

6. BAKING CUPS
Standard size, grease-resistant, microwave-safe paper.
415-D-255 $1.49 pk. of 50

7. TOAST MARKER
Imprint Pooh's face on bread, then watch him appear on toast! 4 x 4 in.
417-D-53356 $1.99 each

8. 2 PC. ICING COLORS SET
Pooh (Gold) and Red ¹⁄₂ oz. jars produce Winnie The Pooh colors.
601-D-3000 $2.69 set

9. NEW 10 PC. CANDLE HOLDER SET
5 holders, 5 spiral candles. 4 in. high.
2811-D-3000 $1.99 set

NEW CANDLES
2 to 3 in. high **$3.99 ea.**
10. Age 1 Pooh 2811-D-3001
11. Age 2 Pooh 2811-D-3002
12. Pooh & Hunny Pot 2811-D-3003
13. Tigger 2811-D-3004
14. Eeyore 2811-D-3005
15. Piglet 2811-D-3006

© Disney. Based on the "Winnie The Pooh" works. Copyright A. A. Milne and E. H. Shepard.

Experience the magic and romance of Disney's The Hunchback of Notre Dame at your next party!

16. NEW 2 PC. ESMERALDA CAKE PAN SET
Beautiful, spirited gypsy dancer. Plastic facemaker included. One-mix pan is 13 x 10 x 1⁷⁄₈ in. Aluminum.
2105-D-3800 $10.99 set

17. NEW 4 PC. COOKIE CUTTER SET*
Child-safe plastic cutters, 2¹⁄₂ to 3 in. high.
2304-D-3800 $2.99 set

18. NEW BAKING CUPS
Standard size, grease-resistant, microwave-safe paper.
415-D-280 $1.49 pk. of 50

19. NEW 12 PC. CAKE PICK SET
2113-D-3800 $1.69 set

20. NEW LOLLIPOP MOLD
Great detail! 9 molds, 7 designs.
2115-D-3800 $1.99 each

21. NEW LOLLIPOP BAGS
Makes pops party-ready. 4 x 6 in.
1912-D-3800 $1.89 pk. of 40 bags, 40 ties

22. NEW 10 PC. CANDLE HOLDER SET
5 holders, 5 spiral candles. 4 in. high.
2811-D-3800 $1.99 set

© Disney.

1.

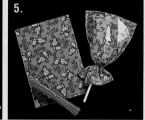

2.

Pooh

3.

4.

5.

6.

7.

8.

9. NEW

10. NEW

11. NEW

12. NEW

13. NEW

14. NEW

15. NEW

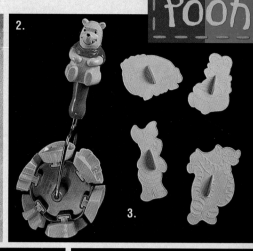

16. NEW

17. NEW

DISNEY'S
THE HUNCHBACK OF NOTRE DAME

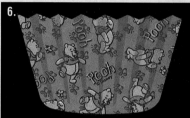

18. NEW

19. NEW

20. NEW

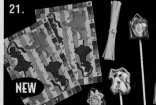

21. NEW

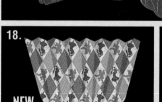

22. NEW

DISNEY'S POCAHONTAS

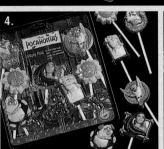

1. 2 PC. CAKE PAN SET
Enchanting design inspired by the fun and adventure of Disney's Pocahontas! Plastic facemaker included. One-mix pan is 15 1/4 x 10 1/4 x 2 in. deep. Aluminum.
2105-D-3700 $9.99 set

2. 4 PC. COOKIE CUTTER SET *
Child-safe cutters, 1 1/2 to 2 in. high, 2 to 3 in. wide.
2304-D-3700 $2.99 set

3. CANDLE
3 1/4 in. high.
2811-D-3700 $2.99 each

4. LOLLIPOP MOLD
7 molds, 6 Pocahontas designs.
2114-D-3700 $1.99 each

5. LOLLIPOP BAGS
Brighten treats. 6 in. high, 4 in. wide.
1912-D-3700 $1.89 pk. of 40 bags, 40 ties.

6. BAKING CUPS
Standard size, grease-resistant, microwave-safe paper in Pocahontas theme.
415-D-272 $1.49 pk. of 50

7. CAKE PICKS   3 1/4 in. high.
Fast fun for cupcakes and ice cream.
2113-D-3700 $1.69 pk. of 20

THE LION KING

8. NEW

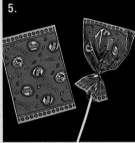
9. NEW

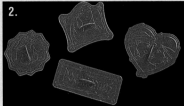
10. NEW

8.-16. NEW DISNEY CANDLES
Start the celebration with the great stars of these Disney favorites! Handpainted, clean burning. Candles and candle holders are 3 in. high.

8. NEW SIMBA STAR
2811-D-3852 $3.99 each

9. NEW SIMBA AND NALA
2811-D-3854 $3.99 each

10. NEW 10 PC. LION KING CANDLE HOLDER SET
5 holders, 5 candles.
2811-D-3850 $1.99 set

DISNEY'S Aladdin

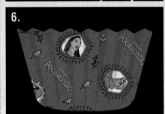
11. NEW

12. NEW

13. NEW

11. NEW JASMINE
"Jewel"-adorned design befitting a princess.
2811-D-3751 $3.99 each

12. NEW ALADDIN
2811-D-3753 $3.99 each

13. NEW 10 PC. ALADDIN CANDLE HOLDER SET
5 holders, 5 candles.
2811-D-3750 $1.99 set

© Disney.

GARGOYLES

14. NEW

15. NEW

16. NEW

14. NEW GOLIATH
2811-D-3652 $3.99 each

15. NEW GARGOYLES LOGO
2811-D-3651 $3.99 each

16. NEW 10 PC. GARGOYLES CANDLE HOLDER SET
5 holders, 5 candles.
2811-D-3650 $1.99 set

© BVTV

BEAUTIFUL DAY BARBIE ®

1. 4 PC. COOKIE CUTTER SET *
Make all-occasion cookies all girls will love! 2½ to 3 in. high, 2½ to 3 in. wide.
2304-D-3505 $2.99 set

2. 3 PC. CAKE PAN SET
Beautiful Day Barbie — decorate Barbie for an evening gala, a walk in the park, or a day at the beach. Includes one facemaker and one full body Barbie figure maker, plus instructions for all three designs. One-mix pan is 15 x 13 x 2 in. deep. Aluminum.
2105-D-3500 $10.99 set

3. BAKING CUPS
Standard size, grease-resistant, microwave-safe paper in Barbie theme.
415-D-252 $1.49 pk. of 50

4. ICING DECORATIONS
Mint flavored edible shapes. Certified Kosher.
710-D-350 $1.99 pk. of 8

5. CAKE PICKS
Instant fun for cupcakes, more. 3½ in. high.
2113-D-3500 $1.69 pk. of 20

6. CANDLE
Beautifully sculpted to brighten a special cake. 3¼ in. high.
2811-D-3500 $2.99 each

7. CANDY MOLD
7 molds, 4 Barbie designs.
2114-D-3500 $1.99 each

8. BAKING CUPS
Standard size, grease-resistant, microwave- safe paper.
415-D-243 $1.49 pk. of 50

9. CAKE PAN
This lovable guy brings smiles to everyone at the party. One-mix pan is 13½ x 9 x 1¾ in. Aluminum.
2105-D-6713 $9.99 each

10. 4 PC. COOKIE CUTTER SET *
Children love to help when the cookies star Barney® and Baby Bop®! Child-safe, 3 to 3¼ in. high.
2304-D-9420 $2.99 set

11. 2 PC. ICING COLORS SET
½ oz. jars of Purple and Green produce realistic Barney® colors.
601-D-3015 $2.99 set

©1993 The Lyons Group, Inc.

*Cookie recipe included.

Barney™

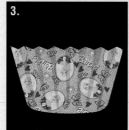 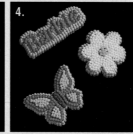       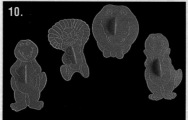  

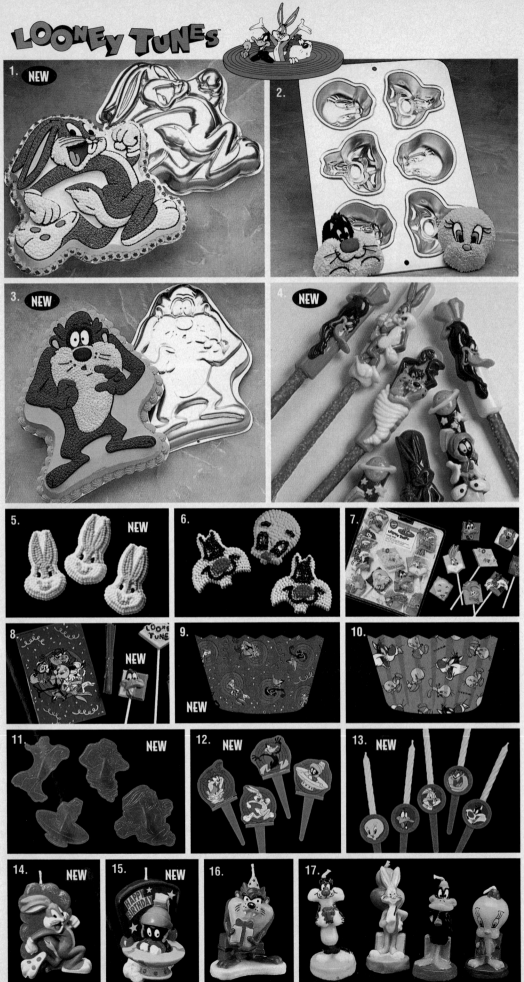

LOONEY TUNES™

1. NEW BUGS BUNNY PAN
Catch that kwazy wabbit in full stride! One-mix pan is 13 x 10¾ x 2 in. Aluminum.
2105-D-3200 **$9.99 each**

2. SYLVESTER AND TWEETY MINI PAN
Favorite foes share a fun pan! One mix makes about 12-16 mini cakes. Sylvester cups are 3½ x 3¾ x 1¼ in.; Tweety cups are 3½ x 3 x 1½ in. Aluminum.
2105-D-8471 **$10.99 each**

3. TASMANIAN DEVIL CAKE PAN
Taz is jazzed to come to the party! One-mix pan is 14¼ x 12 x 2 in. Aluminum.
2105-D-1236 **$9.99 each**

4. NEW PRETZEL CANDY MOLD
Create fun pretzel pops starring everyone's favorite rabbit. 6 molds, 4 designs.
2115-D-3200 **$1.99 each**

ICING DECORATIONS
Mint flavored edible shapes. Certified Kosher.

5. NEW BUGS BUNNY
710-D-320 **$1.99 pk. of 9**

6. SYLVESTER AND TWEETY
710-D-521 **$1.99 pk. of 9**

7. CANDY MOLD
8 molds, 8 Looney Tunes designs.
2114-D-2831 **$1.99 each**

8. NEW LOLLIPOP BAGS
Brighten treats. 6 in. high, 4 in. wide.
1912-D-3200 **$1.89 pk. of 40 bags, 40 ties.**

BAKING CUPS
Standard size, grease-resistant, microwave-safe paper.

9. NEW BUGS & FRIENDS
415-D-220 **$1.49 pk. of 50**

10. SYLVESTER AND TWEETY
415-D-247 **$1.49 pk. of 50**

11. NEW 4 PC. COOKIE CUTTER SET *
Four poses featuring Bugs, Taz, Daffy and Marvin the Martian. Easy to handle, child-safe. 3 to 3½ in. high.
2304-D-3200 **$2.99 set**

12. NEW 12 PC. CAKE PICK SET
Bugs and friends shake up cakes, ice cream, cupcakes and other treats! Safe plastic picks, 2¾ in. high.
2113-D-3200 **$1.69 each**

13. NEW 10 PC. CANDLE HOLDER SET
Five favorite Looney Tunes characters; 5 holders, 5 spiral candles. 4 in. high.
2811-D-3200 **$1.99 each**

CANDLES

14. NEW BUGS BUNNY 3¼ in. high.
2811-D-3201 **$3.99 each**

15. NEW MARVIN THE MARTIAN 3¼ in. high.
2811-D-3202 **$3.99 each**

16. TASMANIAN DEVIL 3¼ in. high.
2811-D-3203 **$3.99 each**

17. 4 PC. CANDLE SET
Candles approximately 2½ in. high.
2811-D-9313 **$3.99 set**

1. NEW ELMO PAN
He's sweet, lovable and more popular with kids every day! One-mix pan is 13 1/2 x 10 1/2 x 2 in. Aluminum.
2105-D-4298 $9.99 each

2. BIG BIRD WITH BANNER PAN
Big Bird announces birthdays, events, thanks!. One-mix pan is 13 1/8 x 12 x 12 1/4 in. Aluminum.
2105-D-3654 $9.99 each

3. NEW 6 PC. COOKIE CUTTER SET *
Up close and personal faces of Sesame Street friends. Child-safe cutters are 1 1/2 to 2 in high.
2304-D-130 $2.99 set

4. 8 PC. "GOING PLACES" COOKIE CUTTER CANISTER SET *
Eight fun ways to get back to Sesame Street. Child-safe cutters are 3 to 5 3/4 in high.
2304-D-118 $5.99 set

5. 4 PC. COOKIE CUTTER SET *
Big Bird, Cookie Monster, Ernie and Bert easy to handle, child-safe cutters. Cutters are 3 to 4 in high.
2304-D-129 $2.99 set

6. 4 PC. BLOCK CANDLES SET
Colorful decals brighten 1 1/4 in. square candles.
2811-D-161 $3.99 set

7. BAKING CUPS
Standard size, grease-resistant, microwave-safe paper in Sesame Street theme.
415-D-251 $1.49 pk. of 50

8. 5 PC. SESAME STREET CAKE TOP SET †
Big Bird 3 in., Oscar the Grouch 2 in., Cookie Monster 2 1/4 in., Bert 2 1/4 in., Ernie 2 in. high.
2113-D-1728 $2.99 set

9. BIG BIRD HAPPY BIRTHDAY CANDLE
3 in. high.
2811-D-910 $2.79 each

10. BIG BIRD WITH #1 AGE CANDLE
3 in. high.
2811-D-911 $2.79 each

Sesame Street Characters © Jim Henson Productions, Inc. All Rights Reserved.

* Cookie recipe included.

† CAUTION: Contains small parts. Not recommended for use by children 3 years and under.

CTW SESAME STREET®

Happy Birthday Jody

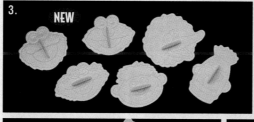

NEW

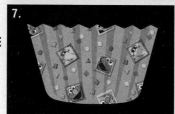

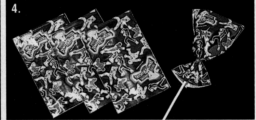

1. CAKE PAN
Create the Red, Blue, Yellow, Black, Pink, or White Ranger cakes! One-mix aluminum pan comes with decorating instructions for all Rangers. 13 x 12 1/2 x 2 in.
2105-D-5975 $9.99 each

2. 4 PC. COOKIE CUTTER SET*
Embossed design imprints on cookie dough. 2 1/2 to 3 1/2 in. high.
2304-D-5975 $2.99 set

3. CANDY MOLD
8 molds in 8 different designs.
2114-D-5975 $1.99 each

4. LOLLIPOP BAGS
Action-packed design for packing treats. Bags are 6 in. high, 4 in. wide.
1912-D-5975 $1.89 pk. of 40 bags, 40 ties

5. BAKING CUPS
Standard size, grease-resistant, microwave safe paper in Mighty Morphin Power Rangers theme.
415-D-275 $1.49 pk. of 50

6. ICING DECORATIONS
5 different edible designs. Mint-flavored, certified Kosher.
710-D-545 $1.99 pk. of 10

7. LOGO CANDLE
Add big thrills to your cake with this 3 x 4 in. handpainted candle.
2811-D-5976 $2.99 each

8. 5 PC. CANDLE SET
Handpainted detail captures the Power Rangers perfectly! 3 in. high.
2811-D-5975 $4.99 set

9. 5 PC. CAKE TOP SET
Plastic toppers sized 1 3/4 to 2 in.
2113-D-5975 $3.99 set

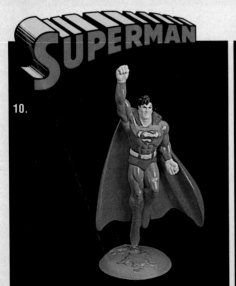

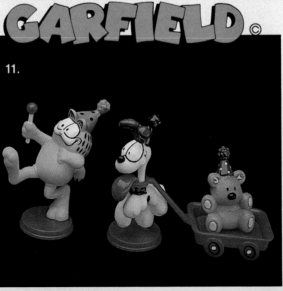

10. CAKE TOP
You can't top the man of steel! 4 in. high plastic.
2113-D-3782 $2.99 each

11. 4 PC. CAKE TOP SET
Fun party parade, with Garfield, Odie, Pookie and wagon! 1 1/2 to 3 in. high.
2113-D-9210 $2.99 set

*Cookie recipes included.

NOTE: Prices and products offered in this Yearbook may not apply in Canada.

1. CANDY MOLD
8 molds, 7 Batman designs.
2114-D-2830 $1.99 each

2. CAKE TOPPER
4 in. high action figure captures the excitement of the series! Washable, reusable plastic.
2113-D-3781 $2.99 each

3. CAKE PAN
It's everyone's favorite crime-fighting caped crusader. One-mix aluminum pan is 13 x 13½ x 2 in.
2105-D-6501 $9.99 each

4. BAKING CUPS
Standard size, grease-resistant, micro-wave-safe paper in Batman theme.
415-D-246 $1.49 pk. of 50

5. CANDLE 3 in. high.
2811-D-9650 $1.99 each

6. ICING DECORATIONS
Mint flavored edible shapes. Certified Kosher.
710-D-520 $1.99 pk. of 9

TM & © 1994 DC Comics.

7. 2 PC. CAKE TOPPERS SET
1½ in. high.
2113-D-349 $3.99 set

8. CAKE PAN
Thomas The Tank Engine arrives to brighten birthdays and school parties. One-mix aluminum pan is 13½ x 9 x 2 in.
2105-D-1349 $9.99 each

9. 4 PC. COOKIE CUTTER SET*
A fun cookie caravan starring Thomas The Tank Engine and his Shining Time Station friends. 2½ to 3½ in. high.
2304-D-349 $2.99 set

Britt Allcroft is a trademark of the Britt Allcroft Group Limited Britt Allcroft's Thomas the Tank Engine & Friends based on The Railway Series by The Rev. W. Awdry, ©Britt Allcroft (Thomas) Limited 1994, Thomas the Tank Engine & Friends is a trademark of Quality Family Entertainment Inc. All publishing and underlying copyright worldwide William Heinemann Limited.

10. CAKE PAN
Charming design for life's celebrated occasions. One-mix aluminum pan is 15¾ x 9 x 2 in.
2105-D-9365 $9.99 each

11. CANDY MOLD
8 molds, 8 Precious Moments designs.
2114-D-9325 $1.99 each

12. 8 PC. COOKIE CUTTER SET*
Charming details make these all-occasion favorites. 3 to 4½ in. high.
2304-D-996 $3.99 set

© 1993 Precious Moments, Inc.

*Cookie recipes included.

NOTE: Prices and products offered in this Yearbook may not apply in Canada.

191

Call now...
join the fun!

One of the joys of cake decorating is the reaction you get when your guests first see your creations. Whether they're aged eight or eighty, it's a great feeling when you watch those faces light up with delight.

Cake decorating.
It's easy to learn.

You can learn to create beautifully decorated cakes at a Wilton Method Cake Decorating Class near you. It's fun and easy. In just four weekly, 2-hour classes, you'll be introduced to all the fundamentals of cake decorating — and you'll have a great time doing it. Wilton Method Classes are informal and casual. And everybody has a good time.

The instructors work closely with you, leading you step-by-step along the way. Their enthusiasm is contagious. They enjoy sharing their craft so classes are as exciting for them as for you.

Before
*Here's your ordinary cake.
Tastes great, but...*

Develop new talents. Make new friends.

You'll be surprised how quickly you learn and how fast your talents develop. With your new skills, you'll be able to decorate sensational cakes — as well as fanciful appetizers, entrees and desserts. And you'll enjoy sharing your learning experience with the people you meet in class. It's a great way to make new friends.